SOCIAL STRUCTURE

SOCIAL STRUCTURE

GEORGE PETER MURDOCK

Copyright © 1949 by The Macmillan Company

Printed in the United States of America

Collier-Macmillan Canada, Ltd., Toronto, Ontario

The Free Press, *New York*
Collier-Macmillan Limited, *London*

Collier-Macmillan Canada, Ltd., Toronto, Ontario

FIRST FREE PRESS PAPERBACK EDITION 1965

Second Printing March 1966

Preface

THIS VOLUME represents a synthesis of five distinct products of social science—one research technique and four systems of theory. It grows out of, depends upon, and reflects all five. It is the result of a conscious effort to focus several disciplines upon a single aspect of the social life of man—his family and kinship organization and their relation to the regulation of sex and marriage. In intent, and hopefully in achievement, the work is not a contribution to anthropology alone, nor to sociology or psychology, but to an integrated science of human behavior.

The research technique upon which the volume depends, and without which it would not have been undertaken, is that of the Cross-Cultural Survey. Initiated in 1937 as part of the integrated program of research in the social sciences conducted by the Institute of Human Relations at Yale University, the Cross-Cultural Survey has built up a complete file of geographical, social, and cultural information, extracted in full from the sources and classified by subject, on some 150 human societies, historical and contemporary as well as primitive. From these files it is possible to secure practically all the existing information on particular topics in any of the societies covered in an insignificant fraction of the time required for comparable library research.

The author began the present study in 1941 by formulating a schedule of the data needed on the family, on kinship, on kin and local groups, and on marriage and sex behavior, and by abstracting such data from the files of the Cross-Cultural Survey on all societies for which sufficient information had been reported. In a very few weeks he was able in this way to assemble the relevant materials for 85 societies, which are indicated by asterisks in the bibliography.

This number, though large, still fell far short of the cases required for reliable statistical treatment, and the author set out to secure further information by the usual methods of library research. Eventually he secured data on 165 additional societies, making a total of 250 in all. The labor required to secure these additional cases was immense, consuming well over a year of research effort or more than ten times that spent in obtaining the original 85 cases. Moreover, the results were both quantitatively and qualitatively inferior, since the author had to content himself in most instances with a single book or article in contrast to the complete source coverage for the cases derived from the Survey files. The informed reader who detects factual gaps or errors in our tabulated data will usually find, by referring to the bibliography, that they are due to the failure to use some recognized source. The author's only excuse for his incomplete coverage in the additional 165 societies is that he simply could not afford the extra years of research labor that would have been required to attain the degree of thoroughness achieved by the Cross-Cultural Survey. If the Survey ever reaches its goal of covering a representative ten per cent sample of all the cultures known to history, sociology, and ethnography, it should be possible to produce several studies like the present one, far more fully and accurately documented, in the time needed to compile and write this volume.

The use of statistics and of the postulational method of scientific inquiry has been contemplated from the beginning [1] as a major objective in the utilization of the accumulated materials of the Cross-Cultural Survey files. The present author has departed from plan mainly in abandoning the sampling technique in favor of using all available cases in areas such as South America and Eurasia for which there are too few sufficiently documented cases to obtain an adequate sample. In other areas, too, he has occasionally chosen a society because a good source was readily accessible rather than

[1] See G. P. Murdock, "The Cross-Cultural Survey," *American Sociological Review*, V (1940), 369-70.

because a sample was demanded. He has, however, sought consciously to avoid any appreciable over-representation of particular
culture areas. In short, departures from strict sampling, where they
occur, reflect availability or non-availability of suitable sources and
no other basis of selection. This explains why the sample includes
70 societies from native North America, 65 from Africa, 60 from
Oceania, 34 from Eurasia, and 21 from South America rather than
an approximately equal number from each of the five.

To avoid any possible tendency to select societies which might
support his hypotheses or to reject those which might contradict
them, the author included all societies with sufficient information
in the Cross-Cultural Survey files and adopted a standard policy
for the additional cases. Having first determined that a particular
society would meet the sampling criteria, he turned to the available
sources and quickly flipped the pages. If there seemed at a glance
to be data on kinship terminology, on sex and marriage, and on
familial, kin, and local groups, he accepted the case before examining any of the information in detail, and resolved not to exclude it
thereafter. This policy resulted in the inclusion of a number of
societies for which the data are scanty and possibly unreliable. In
nine instances—the Arawak, Fulani, Hiw, Huichol, Jivaro, Kamba,
Mohave, Pomo, and Sinhalese—the information proved so wholly
inadequate in early tabulations that the resolution was abandoned
and the cases excluded. In at least nine other instances—the Getmatta;
Hawaiians, Hupa, Mataco, Mikir, Nambikuara, Ruthenians, Twi,
and Vai—similar inadequacies showed up later, but resolve stiffened
and they were retained.

It would have been scientifically desirable to examine every
negative or exceptional case to determine the countervailing factors
apparently responsible for its failure to accord with theoretical expectations, since there can be no genuine exceptions to valid scientific
principles. An attempt has been made to do so in Chapter 8 and
occasionally elsewhere. To have followed this policy throughout,
however, would have been impracticable in view of the fact that the
250 cases have been subjected to hundreds of different tabulations.

Although most sociologists and the functionalists among anthropologists fully recognize that the integrative tendency in the

process of cultural change justifies the treatment of individual cultures as independent units for statistical purposes, many historical anthropologists and a few other social scientists still suspect that the fact of diffusion—the known dependence of most societies upon borrowing from others for a large proportion of their cultural elements—invalidates this statistical assumption. The author could doubtless argue his case at great length without convincing these skeptics. He therefore determined to face the issue squarely in an appendix, recalculating a series of tabulations using as units not individual tribes but culture areas and linguistic stocks, the two most widely recognized groupings of peoples with indisputable historical connections. Several trial calculations yielded results practically identical with those obtained with tribal units. This plan was abandoned, however, when a much more satisfactory method was discovered whereby our hypotheses could be validated by strictly historical means. This is done in Appendix A.

The fact that our historical test corroborates our statistical demonstration, coupled with the sampling method of selecting tribal units, with the confirmation from trial tests with other units, and with the specific disproof in Chapter 8 that historical connections significantly affect the forms of social organization, should shift the burden of proof squarely upon the skeptics. Unless they can specifically demonstrate, upon a scale at least comparable to that of the present work, that diffusion negates the tendency of cultures to undergo modification in the direction of the integration of their component elements, the assumption that historical contacts do not destroy the independent variability of cultural units stands immune to challenge.

As regards statistical operations, we have adopted two indices for each computation—Yule's Coefficient of Association (Q) for purposes of comparison and a Chi Square (χ^2) index for showing the probability of the particular distribution occurring by chance. For advice on statistical methods, the author is greatly indebted to Dr. Irvin L. Child, Dr. Carl I. Hovland, Dr. Douglas H. Lawrence, Dr. Bennet B. Murdock, Dr. Oystein Ore, Dr. Fred D. Sheffield, and Dr. John R. Wittenborn. It is scarcely necessary to state that there has been no rejection of tabulations yielding low or negative coefficients. In the very small number of cases in which a calculation has yielded a coefficient with negative sign, analysis has revealed some defect in the hypothesis, which was then revised. The coefficients which test the corrected hypotheses in this volume are not infrequently too low to be statistically significant, but more important is the fact that out of hundreds of computations not a single one has turned out genuinely negative in sign. The chances of such an outcome, if the theories tested were unsound in any substantial respect, are incredibly infinitesimal.

Without the Cross-Cultural Survey the present study could scarcely have been made, or its methods applied on so large a scale. The author consequently owes a deep debt of personal and professional gratitude to Dr. Mark A. May, Director of the Institute of Human Relations, for his unwavering support of the project. He is also greatly indebted to the Carnegie Corporation, and particularly to Charles Dollard, now its president, for financial aid to the Survey during a war emergency; to the Coordinator of Inter-American Affairs, and particularly to Dr. Willard Z. Park and his staff, for supporting an immense increment of materials from modern Latin American societies under a war project called the Strategic Index of the Americas; to the Navy Department, and particularly to Captain A. E. Hindmarsh, USN, and to Captain Harry L. Pence, USN, for making possible complete coverage during the war of the then Japanese-controlled islands of the Pacific. Appreciation for their assistance must also be acknowledged to Mrs. Aimee Alden, John M. Armstrong, Jr., Dr. Wendell C. Bennett, Ward H. Goodenough, Geoffrey Gorer, Mrs. Frances Campbell Harlow, Dr. Harry Hawthorn, Dr. Allan R. Holmberg, Dr. Donald Horton, Mrs. Lois Howard, Dr. Benjamin Keen, Dr. Raymond Kennedy, Dr. William Ewart Lawrence, Dr. Oscar Lewis, Professor Leonard Mason, Dr. Alfred Métraux, Dr. Alois M. Nagler, Dr. Benjamin Paul, Dr. Gitel Poznanski, Dr. John M. Roberts, Jr., Dr. Mary Rouse, Dr. Bernard Siegel, Dr. Leo W. Simmons, Mrs. Marion Lambert Vanderbilt, and the many others who have been associated with the Cross-Cultural Survey in some of its aspects, but especially to Dr. Clellan S. Ford and Dr. John W. M. Whiting, who have been intimately connected with the project throughout its development.

Of the four systems of social science theory which have influenced this volume and are reflected in its results the first is that of sociology.

Here the author must repeat the acknowledgment [2] of his enormous intellectual indebtedness to Albert G. Keller, under whom he did his graduate work and with whom he was associated for many years as a junior colleague. From Professor Keller he acquired the conviction that the only road to genuine knowledge is the arduous path of science and the realization that social behavior in our own modern society can best be comprehended from a background of the comparative study of earlier and simpler peoples. Through Keller, too, he became aware of the major contributions of William Graham Sumner—the relativity of culture and the still incompletely appreciated fact of its affective basis and its permeation with sanction and moral values.

More important even than the above, however, was the discovery that culture is adaptive or "functional," subserving the basic needs of its carriers and altering through time by a sort of mass trial-and-error in a process which is truly evolutionary, i.e., characterized by orderly adaptive change.[3] This was Keller's own contribution—not inherited from Sumner—and of itself would justify for its author a place among the great social scientists of all time. So valid is this conception, and so vastly more sophisticated than the views of the nature of culture and cultural change held by anthropologists and other sociologists at the time, that it went almost completely unrecognized. Only in the last decade or two has this point of view gained general acceptance, largely through the "functionalism" of Malinowski and the more recent studies of "culture and personality," yet even today Keller's priority is practically unknown. Most of what other anthropologists have subsequently learned from Malinowski had already become familiar to the present author through the influence of Keller. For these reasons he will be eternally thankful that he did his graduate work under Keller in sociology, though he might have received a technically more exacting training under Boas in anthropology.

Unfortunately, marked disadvantages accompanied these values, and made it necessary for the author to deviate from the Sumner-Keller tradition on important issues. A genuine respect for science

[2] See G. P. Murdock, *Studies in the Science of Society* (New Haven, 1937), pp. vii–xx.
[3] See A. G. Keller, *Societal Evolution* (New York, 1915).

seemed inconsistent with the intolerance of other approaches so often manifested by Professor Keller and his disciples, for work of obvious importance was being done by other sociologists and by psychologists and cultural anthropologists of several schools. Moreover, value judgments buttressed with cases too frequently masqueraded as science. Above all, *The Science of Society* (New Haven, 1927) is so permeated with survivals of nineteenth century evolutionism, which historical anthropologists have long since disproved, that a very high degree of selectivity is required in accepting its conclusions, with the result that impatient, insufficiently skilled, or hypercritical scholars often prefer to reject it *in toto*. But however seriously discounted, the Sumner-Keller approach nevertheless remains perhaps the most influential single intellectual stimulus behind the present volume.

Among his other former sociological colleagues at Yale the author has profited particularly from professional and personal associations with E. Wight Bakke, Maurice R. Davie, Raymond Kennedy, James G. Leyburn, Stephen W. Reed, and Leo W. Simmons. Among sociologists in other institutions he has been especially influenced by the contributions to cultural theory of William F. Ogburn, by the rigorous scientific objectivity of George Lundberg, by the methodological versatility of Raymond V. Bowers, and by the contributions to social structure of Kingsley Davis, Robert Merton, and Talcott Parsons.

The second profound influence upon this work stems from the group of American historical anthropologists of whom Franz Boas was the pioneer and intellectual leader. The author must stress particularly his genuine indebtedness to this school and his sincere appreciation of its contributions, since he will find it necessary on occasion to take sharp issue with their conclusions. At the beginning of the twentieth century, thought and theory in anthropology and related social sciences were saturated with evolutionistic assumptions which barred the way to further scientific development. Boas and his disciples assumed as their principal function the riddance of this intellectual debris, and so skillfully and energetically did they pursue this task that by 1920 evolutionism in the social sciences was completely defunct. This feat was accomplished by concentration upon field research and by demonstration of the historical interrelatedness of the cultures in particular areas, such as the Plains and the North-west Coast. In addition to revealing the fallacy of unilinear evolution, this activity established field research as the hallmark of professional anthropology—such early theorists as Bachofen, Durkheim, Frazer, Graebner, Lippert, Lubbock, Marett, McLennan, Schmidt, Sumner, Tylor, and Westermarck were not field workers—and thereby resulted in equipping anthropologists with that first-hand experience with alien cultures which is the best guarantee of realism in theoretical interpretations. The importance of these contributions can scarcely be overemphasized.

The school accomplished distressingly little, however, toward the advancement of cultural theory. Having exorcised the bogey of evolutionism, it could discover no promising new objectives. Boas himself, who has been extravagantly overrated by his disciples,[4] was the most unsystematic of theorists, his numerous kernels of genuine insight being scattered amongst much pedantic chaff. He was not even a good field worker.[5] He nevertheless did convey to his students a genuine respect for ethnographic facts and for methodological rigor. In the hands of some of his followers, however, his approach degenerated into a sterile historicism consisting of rash inferences concerning prehistory from areal distributions. With others it became converted into an unreasoning opposition to all new trends in anthropology.

In Leslie Spier the virtues of the Boas approach find their purest distillation. Despite certain limitations in outlook, he is a sound and systematic ethnographer, he reaches historical conclusions with a caution and a respect for detail that evoke admiration, and he exhibits considerable capacity for theoretical formulations. The author values his years of close association with Spier, and acknowledges a strong indebtedness to him for indoctrination into the tradition of American historical anthropology. Among other students of Boas, Robert H. Lowie has also done outstanding work, particularly in the field of social organization, and A. L. Kroeber appears to the author the leading anthropologist of his own and adjacent genera-

[4] Cf. R. H. Lowie, *History of Ethnological Theory* (New York, 1937), pp. 128-155.

[5] Despite Boas' "five-foot shelf" of monographs on the Kwakiutl, this tribe falls into the quartile of those whose social structure and related practices are least adequately described among the 250 covered in the present study.

tions. Despite his defensiveness respecting the historical approach
and his occasional rash use of its methods, Kroeber kept American
anthropology alive through an ineffectual generation by his origi-
nality, his concern with vital issues, and his analytical insight. If a
tree is to be judged by its fruits, Boas is justified by these three men,
even though the whole weight of his personal influence after 1920
was directed toward stemming the natural development of a scientific
anthropology.

From Clark Wissler, initially through his writings and subsequently through personal contact, the author first acquired an adequate appreciation of the relation of cultures to their geographic
backgrounds and of the regional distribution of cultural elements,
a contribution from American historical anthropology of fundamental importance. To Edward Sapir he is indebted for such linguistic knowledge as he possesses and for his initiation into field
work, and he readily acknowledges that the field of culture and
personality owes its initial stimulus very largely to Sapir's extraordinary intuitive flair and verbal facility. It becomes increasingly
apparent, however, that the permanent contributions of Sapir to
cultural theory are relatively slight in comparison to those which
he achieved in linguistic science. For Ralph Linton the author feels
only the most profound respect. In him, the historical, functional,
and psychological approaches are welded into a harmonious synthesis which typifies modern cultural anthropology at its best. In
fields in which both he and the author possess professional compe-
tence, the latter has seldom been able to discover a significant difference of opinion on theoretical issues.

A decade ago the author might have been inclined to rank functional anthropology among the important influences upon his think-
ing. Not so today. Personal contact with Bronislaw Malinowski
brought intellectual stimulation and some clarification respecting
social institutions but no fundamental point of view not previously
acquired from Keller. The work of Radcliffe-Brown on social organization appears exceedingly impressive upon superficial acquaint-
ance and was, indeed, the factor which first induced the author to
specialize in the field. On closer view, however, its virtues wane, and
they fade into insubstantiality with intensive study. In the controversy between Kroeber and Radcliffe-Brown, for example, the ex-

pressed views of the latter seemed, and still seem, appreciably
sounder, but in the actual analysis and interpretation of data the
former has proved right and the latter wrong in nearly every instance.

The principal impact of functional anthropology appears to have
been the revolution it has wrought in the younger generation of
American anthropologists, who for the most part are no longer
purely historical, or functional, or psychological, but who wield
several instruments at the same time with an often extraordinary
degree of skill. In the hands of these capable and catholic men lies
the future of anthropology, and perhaps even that of social science
in general. Among them the author acknowledges special intellectual
indebtedness to H. G. Barnett, Fred Eggan, Clellan S. Ford, John
P. Gillin, A. I. Hallowell, Allan R. Holmberg, Clyde Kluckhohn, W.
E. Lawrence, Morris E. Opler, Alexander Spoehr, Julian H. Steward,
W. Lloyd Warner, and John W. M. Whiting.

The third system of organized knowledge which has significantly
influenced this volume is behavioristic psychology. Although the
author had become acquainted with the work of Pavlov and Watson
early in his career, and had reacted favorably, it was not until he
met Clark L. Hull a decade ago and became familiar with the latter's
work that he fully appreciated the soundness of the approach and
recognized its extraordinary utility for cultural theory. Of all the
systematic approaches to the study of human behavior known to the
author, that of Hull exceeds all others in scientific rigor and objectivity, and it is the only one against which he can level no serious
criticism. Without it, the main conclusions of the present work
would have been virtually impossible. It appears capable of shedding
more light upon cultural problems than any other product of psychological science. By contrast, the social psychologies, Gestalt, and
even psychoanalysis seem comparatively slender. For making available to him this source of illumination the author is under the
deepest debt to Professor Hull, as well as to John Dollard for introducing him to it. He is also greatly obligated to Carl I. Hovland,
Donald G. Marquis, Mark A. May, Neal E. Miller, O. H. Mowrer,
Robert Sears, and John Whiting for interpreting the principles of
learning and behavior to him.

The fourth and final body of theory which has substantially influenced this volume is psychoanalysis. Recognition is fully and gladly accorded herewith to the genius of Freud, to the keenness of his insight into a previously obscure realm of phenomena, and to the extreme importance and essential soundness of his discoveries. Without disparagement of the above, and without denying the unquestionable value of Freudian therapeutic techniques, the author must nevertheless express his conviction that the theoretical system of psychoanalysis is in the highest degree obscure, that its hypotheses are frequently overlapping and even contradictory, and that it fulfills few of the requisites of a rigorous, testable, and progressive body of scientific knowledge. In his opinion, therefore, it is probably destined to disappear as a separate theoretical discipline as its findings are gradually incorporated into some more rigorous scientific system such as that of behavioristic psychology. Considerable progress has already been made in this direction, but the absorption is still very far from complete. The author has therefore been compelled to use unassimilated Freudian theory in two sections of this book, namely, in the interpretation of avoidance and joking relationships in Chapter 9 and in the analysis of incest prohibitions in Chapter 10.

For introducing him to this exceedingly significant though somewhat unsatisfactory scientific approach the author is deeply indebted to John Dollard. He is equally obligated to Earl F. Zinn for guiding him through fifteen months of analysis and for prior and subsequent exposition of Freudian principles. Neal Miller, Hobart Mowrer, and John Whiting have also participated in his education, and he has derived benefit from Erich Fromm, Karen Horney, and Abram Kardiner in the attempt to apply psychoanalytic principles to cultural materials.

In conclusion, a fitting tribute should be paid to the Institute of Human Relations and to its director, Dr. Mark A. May, for the enlightened policy of bringing these several disciplines and techniques together with the aim of developing a coordinated and interdisciplinary science of human behavior.

New Haven, Connecticut
September, 1948

GEORGE PETER MURDOCK

Contents

Chapter		Page
	Preface	vii
1	The Nuclear Family	1
2	Composite Forms of the Family	23
3	Consanguineal Kin Groups	41
4	The Clan	65
5	The Community	79
6	Analysis of Kinship	91
7	Determinants of Kinship Terminology	113
8	Evolution of Social Organization	184
9	The Regulation of Sex	260
10	Incest Taboos and Their Extensions	284
11	Social Law of Sexual Choice	314
	Appendix A: A Technique of Historical Reconstruction	323
	Bibliography	353
	Index	379

1

THE NUCLEAR FAMILY

THE FAMILY is a social group characterized by common residence, economic cooperation, and reproduction. It includes adults of both sexes, at least two of whom maintain a socially approved sexual relationship, and one or more children, own or adopted, of the sexually cohabiting adults. The family is to be distinguished from marriage, which is a complex of customs centering upon the relationship between a sexually associating pair of adults within the family. Marriage defines the manner of establishing and terminating such a relationship, the normative behavior and reciprocal obligations within it, and the locally accepted restrictions upon its personnel.

Used alone, the term "family" is ambiguous. The layman and even the social scientist often apply it undiscriminatingly to several social groups which, despite functional similarities, exhibit important points of difference. These must be laid bare by analysis before the term can be used in rigorous scientific discourse.

Three distinct types of family organization emerge from our survey of 250 representative human societies. The first and most basic, called herewith the *nuclear family*, consists typically of a married man and woman with their offspring, although in individual cases one or more additional persons may reside with them. The nuclear family will be familiar to the reader as the type of family recognized to the exclusion of all others by our own society. Among the major-

ity of the peoples of the earth, however, nuclear families are combined, like atoms in a molecule, into larger aggregates. These composite forms of the family fall into two types, which differ in the
principles by which the constituent nuclear families are affiliated. A
polygamous [1] *family* consists of two or more nuclear families affiliated by plural marriages, i.e., by having one married parent in common.[2] Under polygyny, for instance, one man plays the role of husband and father in several nuclear families and thereby unites them
into a larger familial group. An *extended family* consists of two or
more nuclear families affiliated through an extension of the parent-
child relationship rather than of the husband-wife relationship, i.e.,
by joining the nuclear family of a married adult to that of his parents. The patrilocal extended family, often called the patriarchal
family, furnishes an excellent example. It embraces, typically, an
older man, his wife or wives, his unmarried children, his married
sons, and the wives and children of the latter. Three generations,
including the nuclear families of father and sons, live under a single
roof or in a cluster of adjacent dwellings.

Of the 192 societies of our sample for which sufficient information
is available, 47 have normally only the nuclear family, 53 have
polygamous but not extended families, and 92 possess some form of
the extended family. The present chapter will concern itself exclusively with the nuclear family. The composite forms of family
organization will receive special attention in Chapter 2.

The nuclear family is a universal human social grouping. Either
as the sole prevailing form of the family or as the basic unit from
which more complex familial forms are compounded, it exists as a
distinct and strongly functional group in every known society. No
exception, at least, has come to light in the 250 representative cultures surveyed for the present study, which thus corroborates the

---

[1] The terms "polygamy" and "polygamous" will be used throughout this work
in their recognized technical sense as referring to any form of plural marriage;
"polygyny" will be employed for the marriage of one man to two or more women,
and "polyandry" for the marriage of one woman to two or more men.

[2] Cf. M. K. Opler, "Woman's Social Status and the Forms of Marriage,"
American Journal of Sociology, XLIX (1943), 144; A. R. Radcliffe-Brown, "The
Study of Kinship Systems," *Journal of the Royal Anthropological Institute*, LXXI
(1941), 2.

conclusion of Lowie: [3] "It does not matter whether marital relations are permanent or temporary; whether there is polygyny or polyandry or sexual license; whether conditions are complicated by the addition of members not included in *our* family circle: the one fact stands out beyond all others that everywhere the husband, wife, and immature children constitute a unit apart from the remainder of the community."

The view of Linton [4] that the nuclear family plays "an insignificant rôle in the lives of many societies" receives no support from our data. In no case have we found a reliable ethnographer denying either the existence or the importance of this elemental social group. Linton mentions the Nayar of India as a society which excludes the husband and father from the family, but he cites no authorities, and the sources consulted by ourselves for this tribe do not substantiate his statement. Whatever larger familial forms may exist, and to whatever extent the greater unit may assume some of the burdens of the lesser, the nuclear family is always recognizable and always has its distinctive and vital functions—sexual, economic, reproductive, and educational—which will shortly be considered in detail. It is usually spatially as well as socially distinct. Even under polygyny a separate apartment or dwelling is commonly reserved for each wife and her children.

The reasons for its universality do not become fully apparent when the nuclear family is viewed merely as a social group. Only when it is analyzed into its constituent relationships, and these are examined individually as well as collectively, does one gain an adequate conception of the family's many-sided utility and thus of its inevitability. A social group arises when a series of interpersonal relationships, which may be defined as sets of reciprocally adjusted habitual responses, binds a number of participant individuals collectively to one another. In the nuclear family, for example, the clustered relationships are eight in number: husband-wife, father-son, father-daughter, mother-son, mother-daughter, brother-brother,

---

[3] R. H. Lowie, *Primitive Society* (New York, 1920), pp. 66–7. Cf. also F. Boas *et al*, *General Anthropology* (Boston, etc., 1938), p. 411; B. Malinowski, "Kinship," *Encyclopaedia Britannica* (14th edit., London, 1929), XIII, 404.

[4] R. Linton, *The Study of Man* (New York, 1936), pp. 153 (quoted), 154–5.

sister-sister, and brother-sister.[5] The members of each interacting pair are linked to one another both directly through reciprocally reinforcing behavior and indirectly through the relationships of each to every other member of the family. Any factor which strengthens the tie between one member and a second, also operates indirectly to bind the former to a third member with whom the second maintains a close relationship. An explanation of the social utility of the nuclear family, and thus of its universality, must consequently be sought not alone in its functions as a collectivity but also in the services and satisfactions of the relationships between its constituent members.

The relationship between father and mother in the nuclear family is solidified by the sexual privilege which all societies accord to married spouses. As a powerful impulse, often pressing individuals to behavior disruptive of the cooperative relationships upon which human social life rests, sex cannot safely be left without restraints. All known societies, consequently, have sought to bring its expression under control by surrounding it with restrictions of various kinds.[6] On the other hand, regulation must not be carried to excess or the society will suffer through resultant personality maladjustments or through insufficient reproduction to maintain its population. All peoples have faced the problem of reconciling the need of control with the opposing need of expression, and all have solved it by culturally defining a series of sexual taboos and permissions. These checks and balances differ widely from culture to culture, but without exception a large measure of sexual liberty is everywhere granted to the married parents in the nuclear family. Husband and wife must adhere to sexual etiquette and must, as a rule, observe certain periodic restrictions such as taboos upon intercourse during menstruation, pregnancy, and lactation, but normal sex gratification is never permanently denied to them.

This sexual privilege should not be taken for granted. On the contrary, in view of the almost limitless diversity of human cultures in so many respects, it should be considered genuinely astonishing that some society somewhere has not forbidden sexual access to

[5] See Chapter 6 for a more detailed consideration of these relationships in connection with kinship structure.

[6] These will be considered in detail in Chapter 9.

married partners, confining them, for example, to economic cooperation and allowing each a sexual outlet in some other relationship.
As a matter of fact, one of the societies of our sample, the Banaro
of New Guinea, shows a remote approach to such an arrangement.
In this tribe a groom is not permitted to approach his young wife
until she has borne him a child by a special sib-friend of his father.
Certain peasant communities in eastern Europe are reported to
follow a somewhat analogous custom. A father arranges a marriage
for his immature son with an adult woman, with whom he lives and
raises children until the son is old enough to assume his marital
rights.[7] These exceptional cases are especially interesting since they
associate sexual rights, not with the husband-wife relationship
established by marriage, but with the father-mother relationship
established by the foundation of a family.

As a means of expressing and reducing a powerful basic drive, as
well as of gratifying various acquired or cultural appetites, sexual
intercourse strongly reinforces the responses which precede it. These
by their very nature are largely social, and include cooperative acts
which must, like courtship, be regarded as instrumental responses.
Sex thus tends to strengthen all the reciprocal habits which characterize the interaction of married parents, and indirectly to bind each
into the mesh of family relationships in which the other is involved.

To regard sex as the sole factor, or even as the most important one,
that brings a man and a woman together in marriage and binds them
into the family structure would, however, be a serious error. If all
cultures, like our own, prohibited and penalized sexual intercourse
except in the marital relationship, such an assumption might seem
reasonable. But this is emphatically not the case. Among those of our
250 societies for which information is available, 65 allow unmarried
and unrelated persons complete freedom in sexual matters, and 20
others give qualified consent, while only 54 forbid or disapprove
premarital liaisons between non-relatives, and many of these allow
sex relations between specified relatives such as cross-cousins.[8]

[7] Cf. R. F. Kaindl, "Aus der Volksüberlieferung der Bojken," Globus, LXXIX
(1901), 155.

[8] A cross-cousin is the child of a father's sister or of a mother's brother. The
children of a father's brother and of a mother's sister are technically known as
"parallel cousins."

Where premarital license prevails, sex certainly cannot be alleged as the primary force driving people into matrimony.

Nor can it be maintained that, even after marriage, sex operates exclusively to reinforce the matrimonial relationship. To be sure, sexual intercourse between a married man and an unrelated woman married to another is forbidden in 126 of our sample societies, and is freely or conditionally allowed in only 24. These figures, however, give an exaggerated impression of the prevalence of cultural restraints against extramarital sexuality, for affairs are often permitted between particular relatives though forbidden with non-relatives. Thus in a majority of the societies in our sample for which information is available a married man may legitimately carry on an affair with one or more of his female relatives, including a sister-in-law in 41 instances.[9] Such evidence demonstrates conclusively that sexual gratification is by no means always confined to the marital relationship, even in theory. If it can reinforce other relationships as well, as it commonly does, it cannot be regarded as peculiarly conducive to marriage or as alone accountable for the stability of the most crucial relationship in the omnipresent family institution.

In the light of facts like the above, the attribution of marriage primarily to the factor of sex must be recognized as reflecting a bias derived from our own very aberrant sexual customs. The authors who have taken this position have frequently fallen into the further error of deriving human marriage from mating phenomena among the lower animals.[10] These fallacies were first exposed by Lippert[11] and have been recognized by a number of subsequent authorities.[12]

In view of the frequency with which sexual relations are permitted outside of marriage, it would seem the part of scientific caution to assume merely that sex is an important but not the exclusive factor in maintaining the marital relationship within the nuclear family,

[9] For detailed information see Chapter 9.
[10] See, for example, E. Westermarck, The History of Human Marriage (5th edit., New York, 1922), I, 72; A. M. Tozzer, Social Origins and Social Continuities (New York, 1925), p. 145.
[11] J. Lippert, Kulturgeschichte der Menschheit in ihrem organischen Aufbau (Stuttgart, 1886–87), I, 70–4; II, 5.
[12] See, for example, R. Briffault, The Mothers (New York, 1927), I, 608; W. G. Sumner and A. G. Keller, The Science of Society (New Haven, 1927), III, 1495–8, 1517; P. Vinogradoff, Outlines of Historical Jurisprudence, I (New York, 1920), 203.

and to look elsewhere for auxiliary support. One such source is found in economic cooperation, based upon a division of labor by sex.[13] Since cooperation, like sexual association, is most readily and satisfactorily achieved by persons who habitually reside together, the two activities, each deriving from a basic biological need, are quite compatible. Indeed, the gratifications from each serve admirably to reinforce the other.

By virtue of their primary sex differences, a man and a woman make an exceptionally efficient cooperating unit.[14] Man, with his superior physical strength, can better undertake the more strenuous tasks, such as lumbering, mining, quarrying, land clearance, and housebuilding. Not handicapped, as is woman, by the physiological burdens of pregnancy and nursing, he can range farther afield to hunt, to fish, to herd, and to trade. Woman is at no disadvantage, however, in lighter tasks which can be performed in or near the home, e.g., the gathering of vegetable products, the fetching of water, the preparation of food, and the manufacture of clothing and utensils. All known human societies have developed specialization and cooperation between the sexes roughly along this biologically determined line of cleavage.[15] It is unnecessary to invoke innate psychological differences to account for the division of labor by sex; the indisputable differences in reproductive functions suffice to lay out the broad lines of cleavage. New tasks, as they arise, are assigned to one sphere of activities or to the other, in accordance with convenience and precedent. Habituation to different occupations in adulthood and early sex typing in childhood may well explain the observable differences in sex temperament, instead of vice versa.[16]

The advantages inherent in a division of labor by sex presumably account for its universality. Through concentration and practice each partner acquires special skill at his particular tasks. Comple-

---

[13] See W. G. Sumner and A. G. Keller, *The Science of Society* (New Haven, 1927), III, 1505–18.

[14] *Ibid.*, I, 111–40.

[15] See G. P. Murdock, "Comparative Data on the Division of Labor by Sex," *Social Forces*, XV (1937), 551–3, for an analysis of the distribution of economic activities by sex in 224 societies.

[16] Cf. M. Mead, *Sex and Temperament in Three Primitive Societies* (New York, 1935).

mentary parts can be learned for an activity requiring joint effort.
If two tasks must be performed at the same time but in different
places, both may be undertaken and the products shared. The labors
of each partner provide insurance to the other. The man, perhaps,
returns from a day of hunting, chilled, unsuccessful, and with his
clothing soiled and torn, to find warmth before a fire which he
could not have maintained, to eat food gathered and cooked by the
woman instead of going hungry, and to receive fresh garments for the
morrow, prepared, mended, or laundered by her hands. Or perhaps
the woman has found no vegetable food, or lacks clay for pottery or
skins for making clothes, obtainable only at a distance from the
dwelling, which she cannot leave because her children require care;
the man in his ramblings after game can readily supply her wants.
Moreover, if either is injured or ill, the other can nurse him back
to health. These and similar rewarding experiences, repeated daily,
would suffice of themselves to cement the union. When the powerful
reinforcement of sex is added, the partnership of man and woman
becomes inevitable.

Sexual unions without economic cooperation are common, and
there are relationships between men and women involving a division
of labor without sexual gratification, e.g., between brother and sister,
master and maidservant, or employer and secretary, but marriage
exists only when the economic and the sexual are united into one
relationship, and this combination occurs only in marriage. Marriage, thus defined, is found in every known human society. In all
of them, moreover, it involves residential cohabitation, and in all of
them it forms the basis of the nuclear family. Genuine cultural
universals are exceedingly rare. It is all the more striking, therefore,
that we here find several of them not only omnipresent but everywhere linked to one another in the same fashion.

Economic cooperation not only binds husband to wife; it also
strengthens the various relationships between parents and children
within the nuclear family. Here, of course, a division of labor according to age, rather than sex, comes into play. What the child receives
in these relationships is obvious; nearly his every gratification depends upon his parents. But the gains are by no means one-sided.
In most societies, children by the age of six or seven are able to
perform chores which afford their parents considerable relief and

help, and long before they attain adulthood and marriageability they become economic assets of definite importance. One need only think here of the utility of boys to their fathers and of girls to their mothers on the typical European or American farm. Moreover, children represent, as it were, a sort of investment or insurance policy; dividends, though deferred for a few years, are eventually paid generously in the form of economic aid, of support in old age, and even, sometimes, of cash returns, as where a bride-price is received for a daughter when she marries.

Siblings [17] are similarly bound to one another through the care and help given by an elder to a younger, through cooperation in childhood games which imitate the activities of adults, and through mutual economic assistance as they grow older. Thus through reciprocal material services sons and daughters are bound to fathers and mothers and to one another, and the entire family group is given firm economic support.

Sexual cohabitation leads inevitably to the birth of offspring. These must be nursed, tended, and reared to physical and social maturity if the parents are to reap the afore-mentioned advantages. Even if the burdens of reproduction and child care outweigh the selfish gains to the parents, the society as a whole has so heavy a stake in the maintenance of its numbers, as a source of strength and security, that it will insist that parents fulfill these obligations. Abortion, infanticide, and neglect, unless confined within safe limits, threaten the entire community and arouse its members to apply severe social sanctions to the recalcitrant parents. Fear is thus added to self-interest as a motive for the rearing of children. Parental love, based on various derivative satisfactions, cannot be ignored as a further motive; it is certainly no more mysterious than the affection lavished by many people on burdensome animal pets, which are able to give far less in return. Individual and social advantages thus operate in a variety of ways to strengthen the reproductive aspects of the parent-child relationships within the nuclear family.

The most basic of these relationships, of course, is that between mother and child, since this is grounded in the physiological facts of pregnancy and lactation and is apparently supported by a special

---

[17] The term "sibling" will be employed throughout this work in its technical sense as designating either a brother or a sister irrespective of sex.

innate reinforcing mechanism, the mother's pleasure or tension release in suckling her infant. The father becomes involved in the care of the child less directly, through the sharing of tasks with the mother. Older children, too, frequently assume partial charge of their younger siblings, as a chore suited to their age. The entire family thus comes to participate in child care, and is further unified through this cooperation.

No less important than the physical care of offspring, and probably more difficult, is their social rearing. The young human animal must acquire an immense amount of traditional knowledge and skill, and must learn to subject his inborn impulses to the many disciplines prescribed by his culture, before he can assume his place as an adult member of his society. The burden of education and socialization everywhere falls primarily upon the nuclear family, and the task is, in general, more equally distributed than is that of physical care. The father must participate as fully as the mother because, owing to the division of labor by sex, he alone is capable of training the sons in the activities and disciplines of adult males.[18] Older siblings, too, play an important role, imparting knowledge and discipline through daily interaction in work and play. Perhaps more than any other single factor, collective responsibility for education and socialization welds the various relationships of the family firmly together.

In the nuclear family or its constituent relationships we thus see assembled four functions fundamental to human social life—the sexual, the economic, the reproductive, and the educational. Without provision for the first and third, society would become extinct; for the second, life itself would cease; for the fourth, culture would come to an end. The immense social utility of the nuclear family and the basic reason for its universality thus begin to emerge in strong relief.

Agencies or relationships outside of the family may, to be sure, share in the fulfillment of any of these functions, but they never supplant the family. There are, as we have seen, societies which permit sexual gratification in other relationships, but none which deny it to married spouses. There may be extraordinary expansion in economic specialization, as in modern industrial civilization, but

---

[18] Cf. R. Linton, *The Study of Man* (New York, 1936), p. 155.

the division of labor between man and wife still persists. There may, in exceptional cases, be little social disapproval of childbirth out of wedlock, and relatives, servants, nurses, or pediatricians may assist in child care, but the primary responsibility for bearing and rearing children ever remains with the family. Finally, grandparents, schools, or secret initiatory societies may assist in the educational process, but parents universally retain the principal role in teaching and discipline. No society, in short, has succeeded in finding an adequate substitute for the nuclear family, to which it might transfer these functions. It is highly doubtful whether any society ever will succeed in such an attempt, utopian proposals for the abolition of the family to the contrary notwithstanding.

The above-mentioned functions are by no means the only ones performed by the nuclear family. As a firm social constellation, it frequently, but not universally, draws to itself various other functions. Thus it is often the center of religious worship, with the father as family priest. It may be the primary unit in land holding, vengeance, or recreation. Social status may depend more upon family position than upon individual achievement. And so on. These additional functions, where they occur, bring increased strength to the family, though they do not explain it.

Like the community, the nuclear family is found in sub-human societies, although here the father is less typically a member and, where he is, is usually less firmly attached. But man's closest animal relatives possess, at best, only a rudimentary division of labor by sex, and they seem to lack culture altogether. The universal participation of the father in the human family would thus seem to depend mainly upon economic specialization and the development of a body of traditional lore to be transmitted from one generation to the next. Since both are products of cultural evolution—indeed, amongst the earliest of such—the human family cannot be explained on an instinctive or hereditary basis.

This universal social structure, produced through cultural evolution in every human society as presumably the only feasible adjustment to a series of basic needs, forms a crucial part of the environment in which every individual grows to maturity. The social conditions of learning during the early formative years of life, as well as the innate psychological mechanism of learning, are thus essentially the same for all mankind. For an understanding of the behavior acquired under such conditions the participation of the social scientist would seem as essential as that of the psychologist. It is highly probable, for instance, that many of the personality manifestations studied by depth psychology are rooted in a combination of psychological and social-cultural constants. Thus the "Œdipus complex" of Freud seems comprehensible only as a set of characteristic behavioral adjustments made during childhood in the face of a situation recurrently presented by the nuclear family.[19]

Perhaps the most striking effect of family structure upon individual behavior is to be observed in the phenomenon of incest taboos. Since Chapter 10 will present *in extenso* a theory of the genesis and extension of incest taboos, we need not concern ourselves here with explanations. The essential facts, however, must be stated at this point, since an understanding of them is absolutely crucial to the further analysis of social structure. Despite an extraordinary variability and seeming arbitrariness in the incidence of incest taboos in different societies, they invariably apply to every cross-sex relationship within the nuclear family save that between married spouses. In no known society is it conventional or even permissible for father and daughter, mother and son, or brother and sister to have sexual intercourse or to marry. Despite the tendency of ethnographers to report marriage rules far more fully than regulations governing premarital and postmarital incest, the evidence from our 250 societies, presented in Table 1, is conclusive.

The few apparent exceptions, in each instance too partial to

TABLE 1

Relative (of man)	Premarital Intercourse		Postmarital Intercourse		Marriage	
	Forbidden	Permitted	Forbidden	Permitted	Forbidden	Permitted
Mother	76	0	74	0	184	0
Sister	109	0	106	0	237	0
Daughter	—	—	81	0	198	0

[19] Unlike other psychological systems, that of Freud thus rests on cultural as well as physiological assumptions. See G. P. Murdock, "The Common Denominator of Cultures," *The Science of Man in the World Crisis*, ed. R. Linton (New York, 1945), p. 141.

appear in the table, are nevertheless illuminating, and all those encountered will therefore be mentioned. Certain high Azande nobles
are permitted to wed their own daughters, and brother-sister marriages were preferred in the old Hawaiian aristocracy and in the
Inca royal family. In none of these instances, however, could the
general population contract incestuous unions, for these were a
symbol and prerogative of exalted status. Among the Dobuans,
intercourse with the mother is not seriously regarded if the father
is dead; it is considered a private sin rather than a public offense.
The Balinese of Indonesia permit twin brothers and sisters to marry
on the ground that they have already been unduly intimate in their
mother's womb. Among the Thonga of Africa an important hunter,
preparatory to a great hunt, may have sex relations with his daughter
—a heinous act under other circumstances. By their special circumstances or exceptional character these cases serve rather to emphasize
than to disprove the universality of intra-family incest taboos.

The first consequence of these taboos is that they make the nuclear
family discontinuous over time and confine it to two generations.
If brother-sister marriages were usual, for example, a family would
normally consist of married grandparents, their sons and daughters
married to one another, the children of the latter, and even the
progeny of incestuous unions among these. The family, like the
community, the clan, and many other social groups, would be
permanent, new births ever filling the gaps caused by deaths. Incest
taboos completely alter this situation. They compel each child to
seek in another family for a spouse with whom to establish a marital
relationship. In consequence thereof, every normal adult in every
human society belongs to at least two nuclear families—a *family
of orientation* in which he was born and reared, and which includes
his father, mother, brothers, and sisters, and a *family of procreation* [20] which he establishes by his marriage and which includes his
husband or wife, his sons, and his daughters.

This situation has important repercussions upon kinship. In a
hypothetical incestuous family, it would be necessary only to differentiate non-members from members and to classify each according to age and sex. An extremely simple kinship system would
suffice for all practical needs. Incest taboos, however, create an

---

[20] For these very useful terms we are indebted to W. L. Warner.

overlapping of families and arrange their members into different degrees of nearness or remoteness of relationship. A person has his *primary relatives* [21]—his parents and siblings in his family of orientation and his spouse and children in his family of procreation. Each of these persons has his own primary relatives, who, if they are not similarly related to Ego, rank as the latter's *secondary relatives*, e.g., his father's father, his mother's sister, his wife's mother, his brother's son, and his daughter's husband. The primary relatives of secondary kinsmen are Ego's *tertiary relatives*, such as his father's sister's husband, his wife's sister's daughter, and any of his first cousins. This stepwise gradation of kinsmen extends indefinitely, creating innumerable distinct categories of genealogical connection. To avoid an impossibly cumbersome system of nomenclature, every society has found it necessary to reduce the total number of kinship terms to manageable proportions by applying some of them to different categories of relatives. The principles governing this reduction, and the types of kinship structure which result under different social conditions, will be analyzed in Chapters 6 and 7.

Some of the intimacy characteristic of relationships within the nuclear family tends to flow outward along the ramifying channels of kinship ties. A man ordinarily feels closer, for example, to the brothers of his father, of his mother, and of his wife than to unrelated men in the tribe or the community. When he needs assistance or services beyond what his family of orientation or his family of procreation can provide, he is more likely to turn to his secondary, tertiary, or remoter relatives than to persons who are not his kinsmen. But to which of these relatives shall he turn? Owing to the ramification of kinship ties which results from incest taboos, a person may have 33 different types of secondary relatives and 151 different types of tertiary relatives, and a single type, such as father's brother, may include a number of individuals. All societies are faced with the problem of establishing priorities, as it were, i.e., of defining for individuals the particular group of kinsmen to whom they are privileged to turn first for material aid, support, or ceremonial services. All cultures meet this problem by adopting a rule of *descent*.

[21] The terms "primary, secondary, and tertiary relatives" are adopted from A. R. Radcliffe-Brown, "The Study of Kinship Systems," *Journal of the Royal Anthropological Institute*, LXXI (1941), 2.

A rule of descent affiliates an individual at birth with a particular group of relatives with whom he is especially intimate and from whom he can expect certain kinds of services that he cannot demand of non-relatives, or even of other kinsmen. The fundamental rules of descent are only three in number: *patrilineal descent,* which affiliates a person with a group of kinsmen who are related to him through males only; *matrilineal descent,* which assigns him to a group consisting exclusively of relatives through females; and *bilateral descent,*[22] which associates him with a group of very close relatives irrespective of their particular genealogical connection to him. A fourth rule, called *double descent,*[23] combines patrilineal and matrilineal descent by assigning the individual to a group of each type.

An earlier generation of anthropologists completely misunderstood rules of descent, assuming that they meant a recognition of certain genealogical ties to the exclusion of others, e.g., that a matrilineal people is either ignorant of, or chooses to ignore, the biological relationship of a child to its father. Science owes a debt to Rivers [24] for pointing out that descent refers only to social allocation and has fundamentally nothing to do with genealogical relationships or the recognition thereof. It is now known that the Hopi and most other societies with matrilineal descent do not deny or ignore the relationship of a child to its father and his patrilineal kinsmen; frequently, indeed, they specifically recognize it by forbidding marriage with paternal as well as maternal relatives. A comparable situation prevails among patrilineal peoples. A number of Australian tribes, indeed, actually follow patrilineal descent while specifically denying the existence of any biological tie between father and child. In Africa and elsewhere, moreover, it is common for the illegitimate children of a married woman by another man to be unquestioningly affiliated by patrilineal descent with her husband, their "sociological father."

---

[22] It has been suggested that this might more accurately be called "multilineal descent." See T. Parsons, "The Kinship System of the Contemporary United States," *American Anthropologist,* n.s., XLV (1943), 26.

[23] See G. P. Murdock, "Double Descent," *American Anthropologist,* n.s., XLII (1940), 555–61.

[24] W. H. R. Rivers, *Social Organization* (New York, 1924), p. 86. See also B. Z. Seligman, "Incest and Descent," *Journal of the Royal Anthropological Institute,* LIX (1929), 248.

Descent, in fine, does not necessarily involve any belief that certain genealogical ties are closer than others, much less a recognition of kinship with óne parent to the exclusion of the other, although such notions have been reported in exceptional cases. It merely refers to a cultural rule which affiliates an individual with a particular selected group of kinsmen for certain social purposes such as mutual assistance or the regulation of marriage. The various types of kin groups which result from the several rules of descent will be analyzed in Chapter 3.

The incest taboos which regularly prevail within the nuclear family exert still another extremely important effect on social organization. In conjunction with the universal requirement of residential cohabitation in marriage, they result inevitably in a dislocation of residence whenever a marriage occurs. Husband and wife cannot both remain with their own families of orientation in founding a new family of procreation. One or the other, or both, must move. The possible alternatives are few in number, and all societies have come to adopt one or another of them, or some combination thereof, as the culturally preferred rule of *residence*. If custom requires the groom to leave his parental home and live with his bride, either in the house of her parents or in a dwelling nearby, the rule of residence is called *matrilocal*. If, on the other hand, the bride regularly removes to or near the parental home of the groom, residence is said to be *patrilocal*. It should be emphasized that this rule implies, not merely that a wife goes to live with her husband, but that they establish a domicile in or near the home of his parents.

Some societies permit a married couple to live with or near the parents of either spouse, in which case such factors as the relative wealth or status of the two families or the personal preferences of the parties to the union are likely to determine whether they will choose to reside matrilocally or patrilocally. The rule of residence in such cases is termed *bilocal*.[25] When a newly wedded couple, as in our own society, establishes a domicile independent of the location of the parental home of either partner, and perhaps even at a considerable distance from both, residence may be called *neolocal*. In

---

[25] See E. A. Hoebel, "Comanche and Hekandika Shoshone Relationship Systems," *American Anthropologist*, n.s., XLI (1939), 446. The term "ambilocal" has also been suggested for this rule.

the ethnographic literature this rule is unfortunately often confused with patrilocal residence. A fifth alternative, which we shall term *avunculocal* [26] residence, prevails in a few societies which prescribe that a married couple shall reside with or near a maternal uncle of the groom rather than with the parents of either spouse or in a separate home of their own.

Though other rules of residence are theoretically possible, the five alternatives described above, either alone or in combination, cover all the cases actually encountered in our 250 sample societies. The Dobuans of Melanesia reveal a special combination of matrilocal and avunculocal residence whereby the two rules alternate with one another, periodically, throughout the married life of a couple. A more frequent compromise consists in requiring matrilocal residence for an initial period, usually for a year or until the birth of the first child, to be followed by permanent patrilocal residence. For this combination, which is really only a special variant of patrilocal residence, we propose the term *matri-patrilocal* as preferable to "intermediate" or "transitional" residence.[27] The distribution of these various rules among our 250 societies is as follows: 146 patrilocal, 38 matrilocal, 22 matri-patrilocal, 19 bilocal, 17 neolocal, and 8 avunculocal. It is probable, however, that some of the tribes reported as patrilocal actually follow the neolocal rule.

Rules of residence reflect general economic, social, and cultural conditions. When underlying conditions change, rules of residence tend to be modified accordingly. The local alignment of kinsmen is thereby altered, with the result that a series of adaptive changes is initiated which may ultimately produce a reorganization of the entire social structure. The fundamental role of residence rules in the evolution of social organization is demonstrated in Chapter 8.

The primary effect of a rule of residence is to assemble in one locality a particular aggregation of kinsmen with their families of procreation. Patrilocal and matri-patrilocal residence bring together

[26] This term is proposed in A. L. Kroeber, "Basic and Secondary Patterns of Social Structure," *Journal of the Royal Anthropological Institute*, LXVII (1938), 301. For several years previously, however, it had been used in classroom lectures by the present author—an interesting instance of parallel invention.

[27] Cf. E. B. Tylor, "On a Method of Investigating the Development of Institutions," *Journal of the Royal Anthropological Institute*, XVIII (1889), 245-69.

a number of patrilineally related males with their wives and children. Matrilocal and avunculocal residence aggregate matrilineal kinsmen and their families. Bilocal residence produces a local alignment of bilateral relatives. Out of such local clusters of kinsmen may arise two major types of social groups—extended families and clans. These will be considered, respectively, in Chapters 2 and 4. Neolocal residence is the only rule that definitely militates against the develop- ment of such larger aggregations of kinsmen.

The spouse who does not have to shift his residence in marriage enjoys certain advantages over the other. He or she remains at home in familiar physical and social surroundings, and his family of pro- creation can maintain a close connection with his family of orienta- tion. The other spouse, however, must break with the past in some measure, and establish new social ties. This break is not serious where marriages are normally contracted within the same local community, for the spouse who has shifted residence still remains close enough to his family of orientation to continue daily face-to- face associations. Where marriages are exogamous [28] with respect to the community, however, spouses of one sex find themselves living among comparative strangers, to whom they must make new personal adjustments and upon whom they must depend for the support, pro- tection, and social satisfactions which they have previously received from relatives and old friends. They thus find themselves at a con- siderable psychological and social disadvantage in comparison with the sex which remains at home.

Although a change in community is theoretically possible under any rule of residence, the data from our sample reveal that it is rarely customary except when residence is patrilocal, matri-patrilocal, or avunculocal, i.e., when it is regularly the woman rather than the man who changes domicile. The evidence is presented in Table 2. While male dominance in consequence of physical superiority may be partially responsible for the vastly greater frequency with which women move to a new community in marriage, the author is inclined, with Linton,[29] to seek the explanation mainly in economic factors.

[28] The term "exogamy" refers to a rule of marriage which forbids an in- dividual to take a spouse from within the local, kin, or status group to which he himself belongs. The complementary term, "endogamy," refers to a rule which requires him to marry within his own group.
[29] R. Linton, The Study of Man (New York, 1936), p. 165.

TABLE 2

Rule of Residence	Community Exogamy or Tendency Thereto	Local Community Neither Exogamous nor Endogamous	Community Endogamy or Tendency Thereto
Patrilocal	54	40	7
Matri-patrilocal	5	6	2
Avunculocal	4	2	0
Bilocal	2	9	3
Neolocal	0	9	4
Matrilocal	5	2	17

particularly those which derive from the division of labor by sex. These will be considered fully in Chapter 8 in connection with the exceedingly important bearing of the facts in question upon the evolution of social organization.

Rules of residence, and especially the extent to which they involve a shift to a new community by the woman, are significantly related to the modes of contracting marriages. If a bride leaves her parental home when she marries, her nuclear family parts with a productive worker. Her parents, in particular, lose a potential source of help and support in their declining years. Moreover, they dispense with the potential assistance of a son-in-law, who would live with them and work for them if residence were matrilocal. Small wonder, then, if parents consent to allow a daughter to leave them in patrilocal or avunculocal marriage only if they receive some substantial compensation.

If a woman, even though she removes to her husband's home when she marries, still remains in the same community, the loss to her parents is less severe. The help and support which she and her husband can still give them may even amount to full compensation. If, however, she removes to another settlement, some form of remuneration becomes almost inevitable.

The modes of contracting marriage fall into two major classes: those with and those without consideration.[30] Where a consideration is required, it may be rendered either in goods, or in kind, or in services, resulting respectively in the payment of a bride-price, in

[30] Cf. E. Westermarck, *The History of Human Marriage* (5th edit., New York, 1922), II, 354–431.

the exchange of a sister or other female relative for a wife, and in bride-service performed for the parents-in-law. Where no consideration is demanded, a marriage may be solemnized by an exchange of gifts of approximately equal value between the families of the contracting parties, or the bride may be released with a dowry of valuable goods, or the wedding may be devoid of any property transactions and be contracted through wife-capture, elopement, or a relatively informal initiation of cohabitation. Wife-capture is exceedingly rare as a normal mode of marriage, not appearing as such in any of the societies of our sample, and elopements are usually later legitimized by the performance of the customary ceremonies and property transactions.

The data from our 250 societies, as compiled in Table 3, reveal that some form of consideration ordinarily accompanies marriage when residence rules remove the bride from her home. The payment of a

TABLE 3

	Marriages with Consideration			Marriages without	
Rule of Residence	Bride-Price	Exchange of Women	Bride-Service	without Consideration	Totals
Patrilocal	103	10	2	25	140
Matri-patrilocal	6	0	13	2	21
Avunculocal	2	0	4	2	8
Bilocal	6	2	1	10	19
Neolocal	0	0	2	15	17
Matrilocal	4	0	8	24	36
TOTALS	121	12	30	78	241

bride-price and the giving of a sister or other female relative in exchange for a wife are almost exclusively associated with patrilocal residence. Bride-service normally accompanies matri-patrilocal residence and is also common under matrilocal residence, from which it is not always clearly differentiated in the literature. Payment of a bride-price or other consideration is particularly common under patrilocal or matri-patrilocal residence when the bride is removed not only from her home but from the local community in which she has grown up. The evidence, excluding other rules of residence, is shown in Table 4.

TABLE 4

Bride Is Removed from Her Local Community	Marriages with Consideration			Marriages without Consideration
	Bride-Price	Exchange of Women	Bride-Service	
Usually or always	44	6	6	4
Sometimes or often	27	2	4	8
Rarely or never	5	0	1	6

Individual cases are often illuminating. Among the Abelam, for example, the usual bride-price is omitted when the married couple come from the same hamlet. Among the Copper Eskimo, if a daughter remains in the community after marriage, she and her husband render assistance to her parents and no bride-price is required, but in the exceptional case of a patrilocal intervillage marriage the groom must compensate his bride's parents for their loss. Among the patrilocal Hupa and Yurok of northwestern California, a man who cannot afford the full bride-price pays half of it and resides with and works for his father-in-law in what is called "half-marriage." Eight of our societies reveal an adjustment which is especially common in Indonesia and is there called *ambil-anak*.[31] In these societies, when a family has daughters but no sons, an exception to the customary patrilocal rule is made in the case of one daughter, who is married without the usual bride-price and whose husband comes to reside matrilocally with her parents and takes the place of a son.

A bride-price is more than a compensation to parents for the loss of a daughter who leaves their home when she marries. It is commonly also a guarantee that the young wife will be well treated in her new home. If she is not, she can ordinarily return to her parents, with the result that her husband forfeits his financial investment in her. That these are the true functions of the bride-price has been pointed out by a generation of anthropologists, and students of ancient civilizations have reached the same conclusion.[32] Seldom if ever is it regarded as a price paid for a chattel, or as comparable to the sum paid for a slave.

[31] For an extended discussion, with cases, see W. G. Sumner and A. G. Keller, *The Science of Society* (New Haven, 1927), III, 1654–8.

[32] See, for example, M. Burrows, "The Basis of Israelite Marriage," *American Oriental Series*, XV (1938), 1–72.

Because the conclusion of marriage is the regular means of establishing a nuclear family, because the marital relationship forms the very warp of the family fabric, and because the regulation of marriage through sex taboos produces far-reaching effects upon family structure itself, it has been necessary to consider these aspects of marriage. Others will be treated in later chapters, to illuminate other features of social structure. For wedding ceremonial, for divorce usages, and for other non-structural aspects of marriage, however, the reader must be referred to the works of Westermarck and other standard authorities.

2

COMPOSITE FORMS OF THE FAMILY

I N A minority of societies, including our own, each nuclear family
stands alone as a sort of independent atom in the community,
as a unit separate from all others of its kind. In the great majority,
however—in 140 out of the 187 in our sample for which data are
available—nuclear families are aggregated, as it were, into molecules.
Clusters of two, three, or more are united into larger familial groups
which commonly reside together and maintain closer ties with one
another than with other families in the community. Physically, such
composite family groups usually form a household, marked by joint
occupancy either of a single large dwelling, or of a cluster of adjacent huts, or of a well-defined compound. Socially, the nuclear
families thus associated are almost invariably linked to one another
not only by the bond of common residence but also through close
kinship ties. Unrelated or distantly related families, to be sure, occasionally form a common household, but this is not the usual
practice in any of the societies studied.

The two principal types of composite families have already been
briefly noted. The *polygamous family,* it will be recalled, consists of
several nuclear families linked through a common spouse. The *extended family* includes two or more nuclear families united by consanguineal kinship bonds such as those between parent and child or
between two siblings. In a hypothetical but typical case, for instance,
such a group might embrace the families of procreation of a father

23

and his two adult sons. Each son would be a member of two nuclear families—his own and his father's—and would have a primary relative, his brother, in the third. The father and mother would each, of course, have a primary relative, a son, in the two nuclear families of which they were not themselves members. While the norm naturally does not prevail in all individual cases, the evidence is nevertheless overwhelming that the characteristic and crucial bond of union in composite families of every type is the existence of close kinship ties linking members of the constituent nuclear families.

The polygamous family can appear, of course, only in societies which permit plural marriages. It cannot coexist with strict monogamy, which prevails in 43 societies in our sample as opposed to 195 which allow at least limited plural marriage. Theoretically, polygamy can assume any one of three possible forms: *polygyny* or the marriage of one man to two or more wives at a time, *polyandry* or the coexistent union of one woman with two or more men, and *group marriage* or a marital union embracing at once several men and several women. Of these, only the first is common.

Group marriage, though figuring prominently in the early theoretical literature of anthropology,[1] appears never to exist as a cultural norm. It occurs in but a handful of the tribes in our sample, and then only in the form of highly exceptional individual instances. Its most frequent occurrence is among the Kaingang of Brazil, a tribe with exceedingly lax and fluid sexual associations. A statistical analysis [2] of Kaingang genealogies for a period of 100 years showed that 8 per cent of all recorded unions were group marriages, as compared with 14 per cent for polyandrous, 18 per cent for polygynous, and 60 per cent for monogamous unions. Even the Chukchee of Siberia and the Dieri of Australia, the societies to which the institution has been most frequently ascribed, cannot truly be said to practice group marriage. These tribes and others, to be sure, often extend sexual privileges to a group of males and females, but never the economic responsibilities upon which genuine marriage must likewise always rest. In fine, there

---

[1] Cf. L. H. Morgan, *Ancient Society* (New York, 1877), p. 416; J. Lubbock, *The Origin of Civilisation and the Primitive Condition of Man* (5th edit., New York, 1892), pp. 86–98; J. G. Frazer, *Totemism and Exogamy* (London, 1910), IV, 151; W. H. R. Rivers, *Social Organization* (New York, 1924), p. 80; R. Briffault, *The Mothers* (New York, 1927), I, 614–781.

[2] J. Henry, *Jungle People* (New York, 1941), p. 45n.

is no evidence that group marriage anywhere exists, or ever has existed, as the prevailing type of marital union.[3]

The polyandrous family occurs so rarely that it may be regarded as an ethnological curiosity. In only two of the tribes in our sample, the Marquesans of Polynesia and the Todas of India, is polyandry the normal and preferred form of marriage, although it appears in sporadic instances in a few other societies. Despite the paucity of cases there seems reason to assume that polyandry may sometimes be due to a scarcity of women resulting from the practice of female infanticide.[4] Whatever its causes, however, polyandry is so infrequent a phenomenon that there is no justification for assigning to it, as was done by McLennan,[5] an important place in the evolution of social organization.

Recent ethnographers[6] have shown an unfortunate tendency to apply the term "polyandry" to sporadic instances of the association of several men with one woman in contravention of cultural norms, or to cases where a woman enjoys sexual privileges with the brothers of her husband although she does not cooperate economically with them. The extension of the sexual rights of either partner in a marital union to his siblings-in-law of opposite sex is by no means a rare phenomenon. It was found by the present writer in all three of the tribes among which he has done personal field work, namely, the Haida, Tenino, and Trukese, and is attested for 41 societies in our sample, or considerably more than half of those for which pertinent information is available. Such sexual privileges, however, by no means constitute marriage. Cooper[7] is thus correct in his insistence that the term "polyandry" be reserved exclusively for a form of marriage which is socially sanctioned and culturally pat-

[3] Cf. R. H. Lowie, *Primitive Society* (New York, 1920), pp. 49–62.

[4] Among the Todas, for example, the numerical disproportion of the sexes is very marked. See W. H. R. Rivers, *The Todas* (London, 1906), pp. 477–80.

[5] J. F. McLennan, *Studies in Ancient History* (London, 1876), p. 132.

[6] See, for example, J. H. Steward, "Shoshoni Polyandry," *American Anthropologist*, n.s., XXXVIII (1936), 561–4; W. Z. Park, "Paviotso Polyandry," *American Anthropologist*, n.s., XXXIX (1937), 366–8; O. C. Stewart, "Northern Paiute Polyandry," *American Anthropologist*, n.s., XXXIX (1937), 368–9; D. G. Mandelbaum, "Polyandry in Kota Society," *American Anthropologist*, n.s., XL (1938), 574–83.

[7] J. M. Cooper, "Temporal Sequence and the Marginal Cultures," *Catholic University of America Anthropological Series*, X (1941), 52–3.

terned and which involves economic cooperation and residential cohabitation as well as sexual rights. More recently the whole problem has been clarified in admirable fashion by Marvin Opler.[8]

The polyandrous family may appear in two different forms, a non-fraternal and a fraternal form. Non-fraternal polyandry is exemplified by the Marquesans, among whom a number of unrelated men join the household of a woman of high status and participate jointly in economic responsibilities and sexual privileges. Fraternal polyandry is the usual form among the Toda, although they occasionally practice non-fraternal polyandry as well. Several brothers establish a common household with one woman. The exact paternity of her children is a matter of indifference and is established legally by a rite during her first pregnancy in which one brother presents her with a toy bow and arrow. In some subsequent pregnancy another brother may perform the ceremony. A child is always ascribed to the last husband to execute the rite, even though he may have been dead for years. It is perhaps significant that co-husbands among the Todas occupy one house when they are brothers, but in the occasional instances of non-fraternal polyandry they maintain separate dwellings where they are visited in rotation by their common wife.[9]

A definition of polygyny is indispensable to an analysis of the polygynous family. Polygyny can be said to exist, of course, only when the plural marriages are contemporaneous, for if they are successive the second spouse is a stepparent or sociological parent to any children of the first who remain at home, and the structure is that of a nuclear family. Secondly, all the unions must be genuine marriages, involving residential cohabitation and economic cooperation as well as sexual association. Hence concubinage, even when culturally permissible, is to be distinguished from polygyny when it does not meet the economic criterion of marriage, and its presence is not necessarily inconsistent with true monogamy. Finally, the

---

[8] M. K. Opler, "Woman's Social Status and the Forms of Marriage," *American Journal of Sociology*, XLIX (1943), 130–46.

[9] New light on polyandry may be expected from Prince Peter of Greece, who is making a life study of the subject. Lecturing in the United States in 1948, he presented an illuminating functional interpretation of polyandry in western Tibet, where it is normally fraternal but becomes non-fraternal in exceptional matrilocal marriages where the family line is carried on by a daughter in default of sons.

unions must have the support of culture and public opinion. The occurrence of occasional plural unions in defiance of law and custom, like bigamy and the maintenance of mistresses and their children in our own society, does not suffice to establish polygyny. Whenever these criteria are not met, a society must be classed as monogamous.

Granted that plural unions are not expressly forbidden by cultural taboos, how much social sanction do they require, and how numerous must they be, in order to justify speaking of the society as polygynous? With respect to the degree of social sanction, it is here suggested that a society be characterized as polygynous if plural unions enjoy superior prestige, as compared with monogamy, so that successful males in the society will seek to acquire secondary wives if they can. We have consequently classified as monogamous a few tribes in which plural unions occur occasionally but without indication that they are preferred. Most of these are instances in which a special exception is made for men whose first wives prove barren. Not only do such cases suggest no preference for polygyny but a secondary marriage under these conditions does not actually create a composite family; the first wife is an appendage to the nuclear family like an aged parent or an unmarried sibling.

A numerical criterion for polygyny is unsatisfactory, since monogamous unions nearly always outnumber polygynous ones at any given period of observation, even in societies where the preference for plural wives is extreme. This is assured by the natural sex ratio; except under extraordinary conditions and for short periods the number of females in a population cannot greatly exceed the number of males. Hence, roughly speaking, for every man who has two wives there must be another who lives in enforced celibacy. To be sure, this situation is rectified in part by the higher mortality of males and by the differential age of marriage, which is usually appreciably lower for females. Nevertheless, even in strongly polygynous societies it is principally the men who have reached a relatively ripe age that are found to have several wives, the majority of males having to content themselves with one wife or none. Polygyny may be the ideal, and it may even be attainable for most men, but they must ordinarily wait for years before they can expect to purchase or inherit a second wife. An impartial observer employing the criterion of numerical preponderance, consequently, would be compelled to characterize nearly every known human society as monogamous, despite the preference for and frequency of polygyny in the overwhelming majority.

Rejecting the numerical criterion, we shall classify a society as polygynous whenever the culture permits, and public opinion encourages, a man to have more than one wife at a time, whether such unions are common or comparatively rare, confined to men of outstanding prestige or allowed to anyone who can afford them. On this basis, 193 societies in our sample are characterized by polygyny, and only 43 by monogamy and 2 by polyandry.

In a number of societies which are polygynous according to the above definition, monogamous unions may actually be considerably commoner for men of all ages because economic conditions strongly favor them. Only a few unusually energetic or capable men, perhaps, can successfully support two families. In other cases, polygyny is confined largely to chiefs or men of wealth and status, or is limited in other ways. So long, however, as it enjoys superior prestige and is not the exclusive prerogative of a very small status group, it is assumed to be the cultural norm.

The numerical problem shifts slightly in reference to the polygynous family. Here the issue is less what is culturally permitted or preferred than what is the normal social structure under which the majority of the population actually live. As will be seen in Chapter 8, monogamous and polygynous families exert a differential influence on kinship terminology and other aspects of social structure. Despite the superior prestige of plural marriages, the polygynous family cannot be expected to exercise a preponderant influence if it actually occurs only infrequently. In the case of polygynous societies where plural marriages are in actuality quite rare, consequently, we have chosen to designate the prevailing form of the family as monogamous rather than as polygynous. The dividing line has been set arbitrarily at 20 per cent. Any society in which plural unions, however strongly favored, actually occur in less than this percentage of all marriages, is considered monogamous with respect to the family though polygynous with respect to marriage. Of the 193 polygynous societies in our sample, 61 appear to fall below the 20 per cent limit.

In connection with polygyny, it becomes important to draw a distinction between primary and secondary marriages. A *primary marriage* is typically the first union which an individual contracts; a *secondary marriage* is any subsequent union. The distinction acquires importance from the fact that many cultures prescribe quite different rules in the two cases. The regulations governing primary marriages ordinarily exclude certain relatives as too closely akin and frequently define other relatives, e.g., cross-cousins, as preferred mates. In secondary marriages, though the choice of a spouse is sometimes wider, it is often much more limited. In particular, the relationship of the second to the first spouse may be a determining factor. This is true both of successive marriages following the death or divorce of previous spouses, and of polygamous unions.

The principal special regulations governing secondary marriages are the levirate and the sororate. The *levirate* is a cultural rule prescribing that a widow marry by preference the brother of her deceased husband, thus often becoming his secondary spouse as he is hers. When applied not to successive but to contemporary marriages, the levirate rule results in *fraternal polyandry* as it has been described above. The *sororate*, conversely, is a rule favoring the marriage of a widower with the sister of his deceased wife. When applied to plural rather than to successive marriages, it yields *sororal polygyny* or the preferred union of one man with two or more sisters.[10] These terms should not be applied to societies where levirate or sororate unions occur only occasionally or incidentally, as they do for instance even amongst ourselves, but only when they are common and genuinely preferential.

Both the levirate and the sororate are exceedingly widespread phenomena. The former is reported to be present in a definitely preferential form in 127 of our sample societies, and to be absent or merely occasional in only 58, with no data on the remaining 65. The preferential sororate is reported present in 100 societies, absent in 59. Frequently levirate marriage is permitted only with a younger brother of the deceased husband, and the sororate only with a deceased wife's younger sister. The "junior levirate" and "junior sororate" are specified for 28 and 9 societies, respectively, among those enumerated above, and these numbers would doubtless be larger if information were complete. Other preferred secondary

---

[10] In the literature, "sororate" is often applied to polygynous as well as to successive marriages with sisters, but this usage is here avoided as confusing.

marriages, resembling the levirate and sororate but much less common than either, are those of a man with the widow of his paternal or maternal uncle, with his father's widow other than his own mother, and with the daughter of his deceased wife's sister or brother.

The polygynous family creates problems of personal adjustments which do not arise under monogamy, notably disputes arising from sexual jealousy and over the distribution of economic tasks in the feminine sphere of activity. A number of cultural solutions are apparent in the data. We have already noted the frequency with which co-wives are assigned separate dwellings. Another common solution is to give one wife, usually the one first married, a superior social status and to delegate to her a general supervisory authority over the feminine tasks of the household. Thirdly, sexual jealousy is commonly allayed by requiring the husband to cohabit with each wife in regular rotation. He may not actually have intercourse with an old or unattractive wife, or with one whom he has come to dislike, but he sleeps in their huts on the nights when their turns come around, and they are spared the mortification of public rejection.

These facts, coupled with information kindly furnished by Kimball Young, suggest some of the reasons for the failure of the Mormon experiment with polygyny in the United States. Wives of disparate origin were kept in one establishment, where nerves were easily frayed by too close contact. Status was insecure, since each successive wife was likely to be for a period the favorite of her husband, and with his support to exercise unwelcome authority over her elder co-wives. Sexually interested in the most recent addition to his menage, a husband tended to cohabit with her to the exclusion of the rest, who were thereby not only physically frustrated but socially humiliated. It was very probably their internal troubles in making the institution operate harmoniously, rather than external pressures, that induced the Mormons ultimately to abandon polygyny. That it can be made to work smoothly is perfectly clear from the evidence of ethnography.

One simple means of reducing the friction among co-wives is to institute sororal polygyny as the preferred form. Sisters, of course, have learned to adapt their behavior to one another in their family of orientation, and they carry their habits of cooperation and mutual tolerance with them when they move from the home of their father to that of their husband. Unlike other co-wives, they do not have to start from scratch, so to speak, in the learning of adaptive behavior. Our data show preferential sororal polygyny to be exceedingly widespread. It is reported for 14 of the 61 societies with permitted but infrequent polygyny. Among the 132 societies with general polygyny, it is the exclusive form in 18 and occurs in 38 others, not exclusively but preferentially, along with non-sororal polygyny. This total of 70 would doubtless be considerably increased if the data were more complete.[11]

Since problems of personal adjustment among co-wives who are not sisters to each other become particularly acute when they must live in the same house, it is not surprising to find this fact either specifically or tacitly recognized in primitive societies. Among the Crow, Sinkaietk, and Soga, for example, the ethnographers report that co-wives regularly reside in the same dwelling if they are sisters but occupy separate habitations if they are unrelated. Gross statistics are even more convincing. In 18 of the 21 societies with exclusive sororal polygyny for which information is available, co-wives live together in the same house. In the majority of societies with non-sororal polygyny (28 out of 55) co-wives occupy separate dwellings, and in many of the cases where they share the same house it is a large dwelling in which they are provided with separate apartments. Tribes with both sororal and non-sororal polygyny, as might be expected, hold an intermediate position—16 with single and 8 with plural dwellings.

Sororal polygyny is peculiarly well adapted to matrilocal residence. Non-sororal polygyny, though possible under any other rule of residence, can occur only in exceptional cases when men regularly remove to the homes of their wives upon marriage. Under these circumstances the only women ordinarily available as secondary wives, without violating the residence rule, are the sisters and other close female relatives of the first wife. Though uniquely suited to matrilocal residence, exclusive sororal polygyny can and does occur under other residence rules. Its distribution in our sample is as

---

[11] Societies for which polygyny is reported without specifying its type have been regularly classed as non-sororal. These include 52 with general polygyny and 18 with infrequent polygyny.

follows: present in 12 out of 38 societies with matrilocal residence, in 14 out of 176 with patrilocal, matri-patrilocal, or avunculocal residence, and in 6 out of 36 with bilocal or neolocal residence.

Extended families may be compounded from polygamous families, from monogamous nuclear families, or from both. The polygamous family, when it is absorbed in a larger familial aggregate, may be called the *dependent polygamous family*. When it stands alone, in the absence of extended families, it may be termed the *independent polygamous family*. The nuclear family, similarly, may be dependent or independent. In the presence of general polygamy or of extended families, which subordinate it in a larger composite family, it may be called the *dependent nuclear family*. In the absence of either, when it stands alone as the only familial cluster in the society, it may be termed the *independent nuclear family*. The distribution of these types of family organization is compiled in Table 5.

TABLE 5

Type of Family Organization	Number of Societies
Independent nuclear families	
With monogamy	24
With infrequent polygyny	23
Dependent nuclear families	
With monogamy	16
With infrequent polygyny	26
(Also the 98 societies with polygamous families tabulated below)	
Independent polygamous families	
With polyandry	2
With polygyny	51
Dependent polygamous families	
With polyandry	0
With polygyny	45
Insufficient data for classification	63

Independent nuclear and polygamous families are alike differentiated from extended families by their transitory character.

Both dissolve and disappear as the parents die and the children establish new families of procreation. Normally, therefore, both consist of members of only two generations. Extended families, on the other hand, consist of three or more generations and are characterized by indefinite continuity over time. In societies with independent nuclear or polygamous families, marriage establishes a new family of procreation and separates both spouses, socially if not physically, from their respective families of orientation. Whenever a typical form of the extended family prevails, however, only one of the spouses breaks the tie with his family of orientation. The other remains at home, where he is joined by his spouse, and through his person his family of procreation is linked with his family of orientation in a composite familial aggregate. Since this process is normally repeated in each generation, the resulting extended family acquires temporal permanence. This continuity over time, which characterizes the extended family alone among the forms of family organization, classes it with unilinear kin groups and the community, which are also relatively permanent social groupings.

One comparatively rare form of the family occupies, in some respects, an intermediate position. This type, which we shall call the *fraternal joint family,* occurs when two or more brothers with their wives establish a common household. Whereas the basis of affiliation of the constituent nuclear families is the husband-wife relationship in the case of the polygamous family, and the parent-child relationship in the usual extended family, it is the brother-brother relationship which unites the fraternal joint family. Like the independent nuclear and polygamous families, the fraternal joint family ordinarily includes only two generations and lacks temporal continuity. Like the extended family, however, the bond of union is a consanguineal rather than a marital tie. The fraternal joint family occurs as a common, but not exclusive, form of family organization among three of the tribes in our sample—the Iatmul of New Guinea, the Manus of Melanesia, and the Tenino of Oregon.

The several types of extended family depend primarily upon the prevailing rule of residence. To be sure—and this should be emphasized—no rule of residence will suffice of itself to create an extended family. Nevertheless, if economic or other factors are present which tend to unite contiguous families of adjacent generations into larger familial aggregates, the rule of residence which produces physical proximity among families of particular kinship connections will determine that these, and not others, will be the ones combined in the larger familial constellations.

Except for neolocal residence, which is inconsistent with extended family organization, any rule of residence tends to align families spatially in approximate accordance with a principle of descent. Oftentimes, however, this principle is not culturally recognized, or quite another rule of descent is followed. The rule of residence, by contrast, is always in harmony with the prevailing type of extended family organization. We shall consequently follow Kirchhoff [12] and name the types of extended families after their several residence rules, to wit, the patrilocal, matrilocal, bilocal, and avunculocal extended families.

Alternative names abound in the literature, e.g., patrilineal, matrilineal, and bilateral extended families; paternal, maternal, and avuncular families; patriarchal and matriarchal families. It is confusing, however, to speak of extended families as patrilineal or matrilineal when the rule of descent is bilateral rather than unilinear. Terms like "paternal" and "maternal" are too indefinite. Finally, "patriarchal" and "matriarchal" carry a misleading connotation of the attribution of domestic authority exclusively to one sex or the other. Residential terms have none of these disadvantages, and they correctly suggest the crucial differentiating factors. Occasionally, to avoid the confusing repetition of lengthy terms, we shall expand upon a useful suggestion by Lawrence [13] and speak of "patri-families," "matri-families," and "avuncu-families" instead of patrilocal, matrilocal, and avunculocal extended families, respectively.

Where residence is patrilocal or matri-patrilocal, and factors favoring the development of an extended family are present, there appears a type of composite organization based upon the father-son relationship as the binding link. This is the *patrilocal extended family*, which includes the families of procreation of a man, his married sons, his sons' sons, etc. Under matrilocal residence, similarly, there results the *matrilocal extended family*, comprising the families of procrea-

[12] P. Kirchhoff, "Kinship Organization," *Africa*, V (1932), 190.
[13] W. E. Lawrence, "Alternating Generations in Australia," *Studies in the Science of Society*, ed. G. P. Murdock (New Haven, 1937), p. 319.

tion of a woman, her daughters, and her daughters' daughters. In our sample of 250 societies, 52 are characterized by patrilocal and 23 by matrilocal extended families.

Under bilocal residence, either the son or the daughter, depending upon the circumstances of the particular case, may remain at home and thereby attach his family of procreation to his family of orientation. This results in a *bilocal extended family*, which unites the nuclear family of a married couple with those of some but not all of their sons, of some but not all of their daughters, and of some but not all of their grandchildren of either sex. Nuclear families of adjacent generations, in short, may be linked by any type of parent-child relationship. Extended families of this type are comparatively rare, numbering only 10 in our sample, since economic conditions usually exert a pressure in the direction either of patrilocal or of matrilocal residence and thus tend in time to upset the delicate balance of residential choice upon which the bilocal extended family rests.

Where avunculocal residence prevails, still another type of composite structure may emerge—the *avunculocal extended family*, of which our sample reveals seven instances. The Haida of British Columbia will serve as an illustration. In this tribe boys at about ten years of age take permanent leave of their parental homes and go to live with one of their maternal uncles in another village. The uncle's dwelling and his position as house chief are ultimately inherited by one of the nephews who reside with him, and this nephew often marries his uncle's daughter. Some of the sons of this nephew's sisters will in their turn come to live with him. Consequently a typical Haida household consists of the householder, his wife or wives, his young sons and unmarried daughters, several of his sisters' adolescent but unmarried sons, a sister's son who is married to his daughter, the young children of the latter couple, possibly other married nephews or daughters with their families, and occasionally even a grand-nephew or two. In this instance the associated nuclear families are linked through two relationships, that between parent and daughter and that between maternal uncle and nephew. In some societies with this type of extended family, however, the nephew does not marry the daughter, so that the uncle-nephew link alone connects the associated nuclear families of adjacent generations.

Since independent nuclear and polygamous families are formed anew in each generation they are little influenced by historical vicissitudes. The temporal continuity of extended families, however, makes them subject to change as the conditions of life are modified. Repeatedly, for example, they have encountered the condition of an increase in population, outstripping the land or other resources available to them for economic exploitation. When this occurs, they commonly split, sending off branches which migrate and settle elsewhere. This fissive tendency has frequently been noted as a characteristic of societies with an extended family organization. Population growth and expansion may also convert an extended family into a clan. Indeed, as will be shown in Chapter 4, this is one of the commonest origins of clan organization.

A special investigation of the factors predisposing a society toward one or another type of family structure would doubtless yield illuminating results. Unfortunately the present study can shed little light directly upon this subject, since evidence was not gathered on exploitative techniques, division of labor, property, and other aspects of basic economy which presumably play a determining role. It may not be amiss, however, to advance a few tentative suggestions supported by a residual impression from the sources read.

The division of labor by sex in a particular economic setting may well determine in considerable measure the preferred form of marriage. Where women make an insignificant contribution to the economic life, as among the Todas,[14] polyandry becomes a satisfactory adjustment. When the productive accomplishment of the two sexes is approximately equal, and a small unit is as efficient as a larger one, monogamy may be economically advantageous. When woman's economic contribution is large, and a man can produce enough in his sphere to satisfy the needs of several women, polygyny fits the circumstances. In suggesting the basic importance of economic factors we do not, of course, disclaim the auxiliary influence

[14] "The men, in addition to their political, religious, and ceremonial functions, do the herding, milking, churning, fuel gathering, building, trading, and cooking. In the absence of agriculture and important domestic arts, the female share in the division of labor by sex is confined to such comparatively minor activities as fetching water, mending and embroidering clothes, pounding and sifting grain, sweeping the floor, and cleaning the household utensils." G. P. Murdock, *Our Primitive Contemporaries* (New York, 1934), p. 124.

of others, e.g., the prestige value of plural wives or the sexual outlet offered by polygyny when continence is demanded during pregnancy and lactation.

The prevailing rule of residence is certainly an important element in the formation of extended families, but a consideration of the influences responsible for residence rules must be deferred until Chapter 8. Certain property factors probably operate to favor the continuity of the family and thus to promote the development of some form of extended family. Where possessions are few, or where they are readily movable or transferable, they offer no obstacle to family discontinuity. Where, however, property in agricultural land, large permanent houses, localized fishing or grazing sites, and other immovables constitutes a major form of wealth, especially if the most efficient unit for economic cooperation is larger than the nuclear family, each new family of procreation will tend to cleave to and assist the family of orientation of the spouse who can expect to share in the inheritance of such property. In this way, probably, the prevailing forms of property and the mode of its inheritance can predispose a society to a particular form of extended family.

The subject of the inheritance of property, having been introduced, deserves some parenthetical consideration. Evidence on inheritance rules was gathered incidentally during the course of the study, and some of the results may be presented here. In the literature,[15] two primary modes of inheritance are commonly distinguished, namely, patrilineal and matrilineal. They are differentiated according to whether the preferred heir traces his relationship to the deceased through males or through females. Thus if a man's property passes to his son, inheritance is patrilineal; if to his sister's son, it is matrilineal; if to his brother, it may be either, with the rule becoming clear only when there are no surviving brothers. Table 6 summarizes our evidence on the mode of inheritance of masculine property in relation to rules of residence and descent.

It will be noted that matrilineal inheritance, though normally associated with matrilocal or avunculocal residence and with matrilineal descent, occurs in conjunction with patrilocal or matri-patrilocal residence in eight societies and with bilateral descent in three.

[15] See, for example, W. H. R. Rivers, *Social Organization* (New York, 1924), pp. 87–8.

TABLE 6

Rules of Residence and Descent	Patrilineal Inheritance	Matrilineal Inheritance	Mixed Inheritance	Totals
Residence				
Patrilocal	87	6	5	98
Matri-patrilocal	10	2	0	12
Avunculocal	0	6	2	8
Matrilocal	5	13	2	20
Bilocal	8	0	3	11
Neolocal	9	0	1	10
Descent				
Patrilineal	61	0	1	62
Double	6	1	3	10
Matrilineal	6	23	7	36
Bilateral	46	3	2	51
TOTAL CASES	119	27	13	159

Moreover, patrilineal inheritance appears in five matrilocal and six matrilineal tribes. These results lend support to the contention of Lowie [16] that matrilineal and matrilocal customs are not inevitably linked in a consistent complex.

In actuality, the complexity of inheritance rules is such as to make the simple dichotomy of patrilineal and matrilineal highly inadequate for satisfactory analysis. In the first place, property may be destroyed, or given away, or disposed of by testament at the death of the owner, instead of descending to definite heirs. Secondly, the respective proprietary rights of the two sexes may exert a significant influence upon inheritance; there are usually articles such as clothing and occupational implements which are owned exclusively by the sex that uses them and inherited only by persons of the same sex, and there are objects such as money and valuables which may often be owned by either sex and transmitted to either sex. For this and other reasons, distinct rules of inheritance may prevail for different types of goods. Again, all the relatives of a given category may share alike, or a preference may be shown for the eldest or the youngest, as in primogeniture and ultimogeniture. Affinal relatives, such as the

[16] R. H. Lowie, "The Matrilineal Complex," *University of California Publications in American Archaeology and Ethnology*, XVI (1919), 29–45.

spouse or the children-in-law, may participate or be excluded; siblings may enjoy a preference over children, or *vice versa;* and so on. A really adequate study of property rights and inheritance in cross-cultural perspective still remains to be made.

Our digression into the field of the inheritance of property leads to the kindred subject of succession to positions of authority, which our study enables us to relate more closely to family structure. Final or supreme authority within the family, whatever the type of the latter, is almost universally vested in one person. In societies characterized by independent nuclear or polygynous families, this person is always, so far as our evidence goes, the husband and father. Where the extended family prevails, however, there are several alternatives. Authority within the household may be vested, for example, in the senior matron, as among the Iroquois, or in the senior maternal uncle, or—most commonly of all—in the paternal grandfather. Succession to this position may be either matrilineal or patrilineal, subject to most of the qualifications already noted in the case of inheritance. Similar rules, of course, prevail with respect to chiefship in the community and in the tribe, but these do not concern us here. Incomplete evidence as to the mode of succession in societies possessing extended families reveals that, with one exception, succession is always matrilineal in matrilocal and avunculocal extended families, and patrilineal in bilocal and patrilocal extended families. The single exception is the Ashanti of West Africa, who have the patrilocal extended family but matrilineal succession. In this society men exercise greater authority over their sororal nephews in other households than over their sons in their own.

Linton [17] distinguishes two fundamentally different types of family structure: the "conjugal family," which capitalizes upon sexual attraction and consists of a nucleus of spouses and offspring surrounded by a fringe of comparatively unimportant relatives, and the "consanguine family," which capitalizes upon the asexual associations formed during childhood and consists of a nucleus of blood relatives surrounded by a fringe of comparatively unimportant spouses. It is clear that the latter category corresponds closely to our extended family, whereas the "conjugal family" includes both the independent nuclear and independent polygamous families of our own classifica-

[17] R. Linton, *The Study of Man* (New York, 1936), pp. 159–63, *et passim.*

tion. Linton regards the conjugal family as primordial, and he attributes the development of the consanguine family to a number of inherent advantages which it possesses. Among these he lists its permanency, the opportunity which this provides for the early development of adjustive habits, its superiority in numbers and hence in cooperative ability, its advantages in care for the aged and in self-protection, and its greater suitability as a property-holding and status-giving body. With this analysis the present author is in substantial accord.

Linton errs, however, in failing to recognize the universality of the nuclear family. He treats the extended (consanguine) family as an indivisible unit instead of viewing it as a cluster of nuclear families held together by interlocking primary relationships. He even goes to the extreme of stating that "spouses are of only incidental importance" in the extended or consanguine family. In composite families of this type, to be sure, certain of the economic and educational functions ordinarily fulfilled by the nuclear family are frequently shared in part by the larger group. Only in part, however, for, as has already been pointed out, the constituent nuclear families always retain at least some distinctiveness as cooperative economic units and regularly bear the primary burden of child care, education, and socialization, in addition to which they maintain intact their unique sexual and reproductive functions. Despite such minor shortcomings, Linton's remains the most thoughtful analysis of composite forms of the family to be found in the existing literature, and is to be recommended as a supplement to the present chapter.

3

CONSANGUINEAL KIN GROUPS

SOCIAL GROUPINGS based upon kinship ties are called *kin groups*. The nuclear family is, of course, a kin group, since each of its members is a primary relative of each of the others. The polygamous family is also a kin group. In addition to primary relatives, however, it regularly includes a number of secondary relatives who are found only occasionally or incidentally in the household of a nuclear family, particularly stepparents, half siblings, and stepchildren. Extended families, whether of the patrilocal, matrilocal, avunculocal, or bilocal types, are likewise kin groups. Unlike nuclear and polygamous families, they regularly include tertiary relatives, such as a brother's son's wife or a father's brother's son in a patri-family, and often embrace remoter relatives as well.

It is important to note, however, that in every type of family organization the kinship bonds which link the members to one another are always in part affinal and never exclusively consanguineal. In the nuclear family, for example, the tie between father and mother, or husband and wife, is one of marriage; incest taboos universally prevent their being primary consanguineal relatives. In composite forms of the family a number of members are linked only by affinal bonds. But whether their ties are consanguineal or affinal, the members of a family, whatever its type, are also united by common residence. These characteristics of mixed consanguineal and affinal ties and of common residence distinguish one of the

41

major types of kin groups, that of the *residential kin group,* which
includes all forms of the family.

A second major type of kin group is the *consanguineal kin group.*
The members of such groups are bound together exclusively by consanguineal kinship ties. If an affinal connection can be traced between any two members, it is always indirect and incidental. Since
persons whose relationship is primarily affinal cannot belong to the
same consanguineal kin group, husband and wife can be co-members
only under very special circumstances. Incest taboos and their extensions in the form of exogamous rules ordinarily require a person
to marry outside of his own consanguineal kin group, with the result
that spouses are normally members of different groups. Brother and
sister, on the other hand, are always consanguineal kinsmen and
members of the same group. Since marriage brings together in
common residence both husband and wife, who cannot belong to
the same consanguineal kin group, and since incest taboos ordinarily
separate married brothers and sisters, who regularly belong to the
same group, a consanguineal kin group cannot be characterized by
common residence.

The basic characteristics of the two types of kin groups may be
summed up as follows. The residential type is always characterized
by common residence; the consanguineal type, never. The consanguineal type includes only consanguineal relatives; the residential
type always excludes some consanguineal relatives and includes
some affinal ones. The residential type regularly includes husband
and wife but not brother and sister. The consanguineal type invariably includes both brother and sister but almost never both
husband and wife. These basic characteristics apply to all kin groups
of the two types, whatever their size or name and whatever the
rule of residence or descent. A further generalization is that the
form of a residential kin group is determined primarily by the prevailing rule of residence, that of a consanguineal kin group primarily
by the rule of descent.

It has already been pointed out that descent is not synonymous
with genealogical relationship. Even unilinear descent does not
imply that the kinship tie with one parent is recognized to the exclusion of, or is closer than, that with the other, for there are instances
of patrilineal descent in societies which do not recognize the biolog-

ical connection of father and child. Descent refers solely to a cultural principle whereby an individual is socially allocated to a specific group of consanguineal kinsmen.

Kin groups represent, so to speak, the individual's second line of defense. When a person is in danger or in trouble, when he needs help in the performance of an economic task or a ceremonial obligation, whenever, in short, he requires a measure of assistance beyond what his own immediate family can provide, he can turn to the members of his larger kin group for aid or succor. Because they are bound to him by extended kinship ties, their obligation to help him is stronger than that of other members of the tribe or the community. He in turn, of course, is under reciprocal obligations toward them. Consanguineal kin groups are of particular importance, for a person ordinarily feels closer to his own "blood relatives" than to those who are related to him only through marriage.

To which of his consanguineal relatives can the individual turn for support, and to which of them does he owe reciprocal obligations? Consanguineal kinship ties ramify endlessly, and if carried far enough embrace all members of the local community or even of the tribe. Some discrimination must be made among them. There must be some selection of those with whom the individual is to be particularly closely affiliated. The decision must be reached at the time of his birth if confusion is to be avoided. The birth of a new child in any society inevitably affects the rights and privileges of other members. Some are compelled to assume new obligations. Others may gain new rights. The prospects of others are altered with respect to such matters as inheritance, succession, and marriage. In short, jural relations are modified in various ways, and everyone must know how his own are affected. Unless uncertainty and controversy are to reign, the social placement of the infant must be settled at the outset.

The date of one's birth may determine the age-grade to which one belongs. The place of birth may determine membership in a particular household, community, or residential kin group. But there are other kinds of social groups in which membership must also be decided at birth but where there are no obvious external guides to a decision among alternatives. Such a problem arises, for example, in the case of the offspring of a marriage between persons of different status groups, such as castes or social classes. To which caste shall a mulatto or Eurasian child belong; to which class the child of a free-man and a slave woman or of a noble father and a common mother? There are two alternatives of affiliation, and the decision, unless it is to become a bone of contention in every instance, must be pre-scribed in advance by a specific cultural provision.

The determination of the particular group of relatives with whom an individual is to be affiliated, and to whom he is to enter into reciprocal obligations, presents a precisely similar situation. In most societies these kinsmen begin to function shortly after his birth—usually at a ceremony in which the newborn infant is given his name and is formally accepted by his relatives. But whether or not they assemble for such an occasion, they must know in advance who they are, and how their jural rights are affected. This knowledge is supplied in all societies by a culturally formulated rule of de-scent.

There is nothing inherently obvious or "natural" about any rule of descent. By virtue of incest taboos, which universally prevent marriage within the nuclear family, the father and mother cannot have the same kinsmen. If a child were affiliated with all the relatives of both parents, his consanguineal kin group would be double the size of theirs, and in a few generations the kin group would become coextensive with the community, or even the tribe, and would lose its significance. It is imperative, therefore, that the kin group of the the child be restricted to approximately the size of that of either parent. To accomplish this, some of the members of the parents' kin groups must be eliminated from that of the child. There are three principal ways in which this can be done, and they constitute the three primary rules of descent.

Patrilineal descent accomplishes the selection by discarding the mother's kin group and affiliating the child exclusively with the con-sanguineal kin group of the father. *Matrilineal descent* similarly dis-cards all the father's relatives and assigns the child to his mother's kin group. *Bilateral descent* accomplishes the same result by exclud-ing some of the members of the father's kin group and some of those of the mother's and affiliating the child with a special group consist-ing of some of the members of both. In most cases these are his own nearest genealogical kinsmen, irrespective of through which parent they are related to him. Each of these rules produces consanguineal kin groups of several characteristic types.

It is also possible for a particular society to combine two rules of descent. Combinations of matrilineal and patrilineal descent are particularly common. Thus in certain Indonesian societies with *ambil-anak* marriage the usual patrilineal rule is suspended for a generation in the case of a family without sons, and matrilineal descent through a matrilocally residing daughter supervenes to continue the family line. Among the Apinaye of Brazil, matrilineal descent prevails for females and patrilineal descent for males. Among the Mundugumor of New Guinea, on the other hand, a daughter is affiliated with her father, and a son with his mother, in a kin group which zigzags between the sexes from generation to generation [1] like sex-linked characteristics in heredity. Among the Buginese and Macassar of Celebes, the first, third, and other odd-numbered off-spring are affiliated with the mother, and even-numbered progeny with their father.[2] In all of these cases, it is important to note, one unilinear rule is applied in particular individual cases, the other in others. Both are not applied at the same time to one individual.

When patrilineal and matrilineal descent are applied together, and not alternatively in combinations like the above, their joint application is known as *double descent*.[3] In this case the society possesses both patrilineal and matrilineal kin groups, and a person is affiliated at the same time with the patrilineal group of his father and the matrilineal group of his mother, the relatives of his father's matrilineal and of his mother's patrilineal group being discarded. Since under certain conditions double descent produces consanguineal kin groups of unique type, it might be ranked as a fourth primary rule of descent rather than as merely a combination of the patrilineal and matrilineal rules.

Our own society is characterized by bilateral descent and by the presence of kin groups of a typically bilateral type, technically

[1] See M. Mead, *Sex and Temperament in Three Primitive Societies* (New York, 1935), pp. 176–7.

[2] See R. Kennedy, "A Survey of Indonesian Civilization," *Studies in the Science of Society,* ed. G. P. Murdock (New Haven, 1937), p. 291.

[3] For a detailed exposition see G. P. Murdock, "Double Descent," *American Anthropologist,* n.s., XLII (1940), 555–61. Cf. also R. F. Fortune, "A Note on Some Forms of Kinship Structure," *Oceania,* IV (1933), 1–9.

called the *kindred* [4] but popularly known under such collective terms as "kinfolk" or "relatives." Since bilateral kin groups represent an especially difficult problem, and one to which anthropologists have devoted relatively little attention, it will be preferable to give first consideration to the kin groups resulting from unilinear descent, i.e., patrilineal and matrilineal. These are reported in the literature under a welter of terms: clan, gens, lineage, moiety, phratry, ramage, sept, sib, etc. Several generations of anthropologists have made notable progress in the analysis of these groups and in the assignment of appropriate terms to those of different type. We shall in general follow the classic work of Lowie,[5] wherein is found the nearest approach to a complete clarification of the subject.

The consanguineal kin groups which result from patrilineal and matrilineal descent parallel one another almost exactly, being differentiated only in their modes of affiliation and in the particular relatives whom they include. Each constitutes a similar graded series, comprising types which reflect the varying degrees to which recognition of unilinear affiliation may be extended. These types bear identical names, the rule of descent being indicated by the adjectives "patrilineal" and "matrilineal" or by the prefixes "patri-" and "matri-".

A consanguineal kin group produced by either rule of unilinear descent is technically known as a *lineage* when it includes only persons who can actually trace their common relationship through a specific series of remembered genealogical links in the prevailing line of descent. Oftentimes, though by no means always, a lineage consists of the unilinearly related persons of one sex who form the core of a patrilocal, matrilocal, or avunculocal extended family, together with their siblings of opposite sex who reside elsewhere and, of course, not including their spouses who live with them. Although our own society is bilateral, the patrilineal inheritance of surnames results in name-groups which resemble lineages. Thus all persons born with the surname Smith who can trace actual descent in the male line from a common ancestor constitute a sort of patri-lineage.

[4] See W. H. R. Rivers, *Social Organization* (New York, 1924), p. 16.
[5] R. H. Lowie, *Primitive Society* (New York, 1920). A second edition of this work (New York, 1947) contains a few significant corrections and addenda.

When the members of a consanguineal kin group acknowledge a traditional bond of common descent in the paternal or maternal line, but are unable always to trace the actual genealogical connections between individuals, the group is called a *sib*.[6] If all persons born with the name Smith in our society regarded themselves as related, they would constitute a patri-sib. Some unilinear societies lack true sibs, possessing only lineages. The great majority, however, possess sibs, which are the most characteristic of all unilinear consanguineal kin groups. A sib normally includes several lineages, though these need not be culturally defined. Groups intermediate between sibs and lineages, which are found in some societies, may be called *sub-sibs*.

Occasionally two or more sibs recognize a purely conventional unilinear bond of kinship, more tenuous than that which unites a sib but nevertheless sufficient to distinguish the constellation of sibs from others of its kind. A consanguineal kin group of this higher order is called a *phratry*. When a society has only two sibs or phratries, so that every person is necessarily a member of one or the other, the dichotomy results in so many distinctive features in social structure that a special term, *moiety*, is applied to them. If our own society included only people named Smith and Jones, and if each group considered themselves patrilineally related, they would constitute patri-moieties.

The most widespread characteristic of unilinear consanguineal kin groups is exogamy, i.e., the rule requiring all members to seek their spouses in some other group. The smaller the kin group, in general, the stronger the tendency toward exogamy. Lineages, for example, are sometimes completely exogamous when sibs are only partially so, and moieties are non-exogamous more often than any of the smaller unilinear groups. Social units that simulate kin groups but are not based upon a rule of descent, e.g., the pseudo-moieties of some tribes that live on opposite sides of a village square or oppose one another in games, and whose membership is determined on some non-kinship basis, must not be confused with genuine unilinear kin groups, even of non-exogamous type.

[6] See R. H. Lowie, *Primitive Society* (New York, 1920), p. 111. This exceedingly useful term has not yet achieved the universal acceptance which it deserves.

For purposes of structural analysis, such as the interpretation of kinship terminology, unilinear societies whose kin groups are completely non-exogamous must usually be treated as though they were bilateral in descent, for endogamous unions prevent the expected spatial and social alignments of kinsmen. Of the 178 unilinear societies in our sample, only 10 reveal a complete absence of exogamy. In half of these instances the kin groups appear to be emergent and not yet fully elaborated. Thus the Balinese, Tongans, and Tswana have patri-lineages, apparently based upon patrilocal residence, without having yet developed a rule of exogamy, and non-exogamous matri-lineages are similarly found among the matrilocal Kallinago. The Ontong-Javanese possess non-exogamous groups of both types, the patri-lineages being land-owning units and the matri-lineages house-owning groups. In five other instances the kin groups appear decadent and on the point of disappearing. Among the Kababish of the Sudan and the Kurds of Iraq the introduction of Islam has destroyed sib exogamy by introducing preferential marriage with the father's brother's daughter. The patrilineal kin groups of the Fox, Pima, and Tewa of North America are likewise clearly decadent.

The above list of societies with unilinear but non-exogamous kin groups might have been expanded slightly by a somewhat broader definition. Thus the Ruthenians and Yankees might have been placed in the same category because of their patrilineally inherited name groups, which are possibly survivals of sibs. The Buin of Melanesia have matrilineally inherited totems, and the Edo of Nigeria have patrilineally inherited food taboos, either of which may represent decadent or incipient sibs. The Washo Indians have patrilineal descent groups whose only function is apparently to oppose one another in games. For various reasons, however, it has seemed preferable not to class these phenomena with kin groups except for such purposes as testing the tendency of exogamy to be associated with any unilinear grouping of kinsmen. On comparable grounds, the following have not been classed as moieties: the two divisions of the Sabei, since they are presumably merely local; the endogamous Tartharol and Teivaliol branches of the Toda, since they show marked affinity with castes; and the two patrilineal divisions of the Longuda, since they are primarily religious and ceremonial in character. With perhaps no better justification, however, the non-exogamous dual divisions of the Pukapukans and the Yuchi have been classed, respectively, as matrilineal and patrilineal moieties. Since borderline cases raise difficulties in any classification, all instances encountered have been enumerated above.

A classification of the 175 unilinear societies of our sample by type of kin group and the prevalence of exogamy is shown in Table 7. The inclusion of tribes with double descent in both columns accounts for the apparent numerical excess.

TABLE 7

Type of Kin Group and Prevalence of Exogamy	Patrilineal Descent	Matrilineal Descent
With exogamous moieties	10	19
With non-exogamous moieties and exogamous sibs	4	5
With moieties and other kin groups, all non-exogamous	3	0
With exogamous phratries	9	5
With exogamous sibs	74	33
With non-exogamous sibs and exogamous lineages	4	0
With non-exogamous sibs and lineages	3	0
With exogamous lineages only	10	5
With non-exogamous lineages only	6	3
TOTALS	123	70

Another common characteristic of lineages, sibs, and moieties is totemism. For an analysis of this controversial phenomenon the reader must be referred to other sources,[7] since its bearing on the formal structuring of social relations is comparatively slight. One of the most widespread features of the so-called totemic complex is the assigning of animal names to kin groups. The explanation may be quite simple. If a people who call their fraternal orders Eagles, Elks, and Moose, who dub their professional baseball teams Cubs, Orioles, and Tigers, who denote the student bodies and teams of their academic institutions Bulldogs, Panthers, Terrapins, and Golden Bears, who use the Gopher and the Wolverine to symbolize states and the Bull Moose, the Donkey, and the Elephant to represent political parties, and who see their American Eagle competing

[7] See especially A. A. Goldenweiser, *History, Psychology, and Culture* (New York, 1933), pp. 213–356; J. G. Frazer, *Totemism and Exogamy* (4 vols., London, 1910); R. H. Lowie, *Primitive Society* (New York, 1920), pp. 137–45.

for world power or struggling for international peace with the British Lion and the Russian Bear—if such a people were to have sibs, would they be likely to arrive at names for them very different from the Bear, Beaver, Hawk, Turtle, Wolf, etc., chosen by the Iroquois Indians?

If social groups are to receive names, animal designations are as obvious as any. The important fact, however, is that consanguineal kin groups have names, not that these are so commonly those of animals. Oftentimes, of course, the names are derived from plants, natural objects, localities, chiefs, or ancestors rather than from birds and mammals. Naming is important because a common name can identify a member of a kin group who resides apart from his relatives, thus helping to keep alive the consciousness of group membership. It is probable, indeed, that the extension of a distinguishing name to all persons born in a locality, and its retention by those who have left their homes in marriage, is one of the principal means by which lineages and sibs have evolved.[8]

Totemic food taboos can serve a similar purpose. Even in our own society, members of certain religious sects are commonly distinguished by their abstention from meat on certain days or from pork at all times. Though the elements of the totemic complex are doubtless diverse in kind and origin, many of them certainly fulfill the same function of supporting the social unity of the consanguineal kin group in the face of the dispersion of its members.

In societies which possess both patrilineal and matrilineal lineages, sibs, or phratries, double descent introduces no novel structural features. Kin groups with both rules of descent exist, and the individual is affiliated with both the patrilineal group of his father and the matrilineal group of his mother. Among the Ashanti, for example, an individual inherits his "blood" through affiliation with his mother's matri-sib and his "spirit" through membership in his father's patri-sib, both of which are exogamous and totemic.[9] The Herero, too, have exogamous, totemic matri-sibs and patri-sibs, the former primarily social in character, the latter religious.[10] In no case do such

---

[8] Cf. R. H. Lowie, *Primitive Society* (New York, 1920), pp. 157–8.

[9] See R. S. Rattray, *Ashanti* (Oxford, 1923), pp. 77–8.

[10] See H. G. Luttig, *The Religious System and Social Organization of the Herero* (Utrecht, 1934), pp. 58–67.

groups differ in any significant respect from those found under a single unilinear rule of descent.

If, however, a society with double descent possesses moieties among its various component kin groups, there tends to emerge with exogamy an entirely new type of structure which may be called the *bilinear kin group*. In contrast to both unilinear and bilateral groups, a bilinear kin group is composed of persons who are affiliated with one another by both patrilineal and matrilineal ties, including those who stand to one another in such relationships as own siblings, parallel cousins, paternal grandfather and son's child, and maternal grandmother and daughter's child. Excluded from one's own group will be all persons who are related only patrilineally or only matrilineally to Ego, as well as those who are not connected in either line.

Bilinear kin groups, technically called *sections,* have long been known in aboriginal Australia, and from the time of Galton [11] their bilinear character has been dimly recognized. Knowledge of the subject was greatly advanced by Deacon,[12] who discovered sections in Melanesia and interpreted them correctly. It remained for Lawrence,[13] however, to clear up the entire matter in what is certainly one of the most original and significant contributions in the entire literature on social organization. Radcliffe-Brown,[14] in other respects the outstanding authority on aboriginal Australian social structure, has seen fit to criticize Lawrence in an article which deals with ethnographic minutiæ and evades the real issue. It therefore becomes necessary to emphasize that on this important matter Lawrence is right whereas Radcliffe-Brown has been consistently wrong.

The crucial issue concerns the determinants of social systems of the Australian type. The interpretation guessed by Galton, confirmed by Deacon, conclusively demonstrated by Lawrence, and accepted here is that such systems result from the interaction of patrilineal

[11] F. Galton, "Note on the Australian Marriage Systems," *Journal of the Royal Anthropological Institute,* XVIII (1889), 70–2.

[12] A. B. Deacon, "The Regulation of Marriage in Ambrym," *Journal of the Royal Anthropological Institute,* LVII (1927), 325–42.

[13] W. E. Lawrence, "Alternating Generations in Australia," *Studies in the Science of Society,* ed. G. P. Murdock (New Haven, 1937), pp. 319–54.

[14] A. R. Radcliffe-Brown, "Australian Social Organization," *American Anthropologist,* XLIV (1947), 151–4.

and matrilineal kin groups in the presence of moieties and rigorous exogamy. Radcliffe-Brown, who has disagreed with Deacon [15] as well as with Lawrence, ascribes them to the influence of kinship terminology.[16] Depending upon the type of kinship system they happen to have, some Australian tribes will allegedly be characterized by preferential cross-cousin marriage, others by preferred marriage with a second cross-cousin, kin groups being entirely secondary and inconsequential.[17] When forced by the facts to recognize that marriage is commonly also permitted with relatives to whom other kinship terms are applied, Radcliffe-Brown attempts to escape the dilemma by statements to the effect that these relatives "stand in an equivalent relation" to the preferred spouse. Analysis of the data shows that those who "stand in an equivalent relation" are regularly members of the same bilinear kin group. In other words, what really regulates marriage is not kinship terminology, as Radcliffe-Brown asserts, but the prevailing kin groups, as Lawrence demonstrates.

One of the most definite conclusions of the present work (see Chapters 7 and 10) is that kin groups are the primary determinants of both kinship terminology and marriage rules. Nowhere else in the world can we find evidence for the primacy of either of the latter, and Australia could hardly be expected to constitute the only exception, even if Lawrence had not adduced the proof. In addition to providing the most satisfactory explanation of the known facts, Lawrence's interpretation accounts for such peculiarities as the dispute between Mathews and Spencer as to whether the Arunta are matrilineal or patrilineal, whereas in reality they are both. Above all, however, it brings Australian social organization for the first time within the same frame of reference as social systems elsewhere in the world, composed of identical elements, accountable to the same influences, and differentiated only by the relative complexity of its configurations. Radcliffe-Brown's interpretation, on the other hand, would leave native Australian institutions in that morass of

[15] See A. R. Radcliffe-Brown, "Regulation of Marriage in Ambrym," *Journal of the Royal Anthropological Institute*, LVII (1927), 347.

[16] See A. R. Radcliffe-Brown, "The Social Organization of Australian Tribes," *Oceania*, I (1930), 43–5 *et passim*.

[17] See A. R. Radcliffe-Brown, "Three Tribes of Western Australia," *Journal of the Royal Anthropological Institute*, XLIII (1913), 190–3.

the seemingly bizarre, unique, and scientifically inexplicable whence Lawrence has rescued them.

When mysticism is swept away, the essential nature of the so-called "two-class," "four-class," and "eight-class" systems of Australian social organization is relatively easy to comprehend. All of them are based on a combination of matrilineal and patrilineal kin groups which always includes both exogamous matri-moieties and the exogamous patri-lineages or patri-sibs which constitute the core of the ubiquitous local groups or "hordes." In the absence of any complicating factors, these two groups in conjunction produce a situation in which the native-born members of each local horde or patri-clan, i.e., the members of the localized patri-lineage or patri-sib, are divided in alternating generations between the two matri-moieties. A male Ego, his father's father, his son's son, and the siblings and parallel cousins of all of them fall into one moiety; Ego's father, his son, and the siblings and parallel cousins of both fall into the other. Since the matri-moieties extend throughout the tribe, alternating generations in all local groups throughout the society are affiliated. Exogamous rules permit a man to marry any woman of the opposite matri-moiety provided she is not a member of his own patri-sib; she must come from another local group and from one of the alternate generations there which are equated with the moiety to which his own father and son belong. This is the so-called "two-class system," and differs from an ordinary system of exogamous matri-moieties only through the addition of patrilineal descent.

In a considerable part of the Australian area of double descent, patrilineal descent has been extended beyond the local group so that all the patri-sibs of the tribe are aggregated into two interspersed sets, which constitute exogamous patri-moieties. These patri-moieties intersect the two matri-moieties to form four sections. In a "four-class system" of this type, each section forms a bilinear kin group, united by double descent. For any given individual, all the members of his own section are both patrilineally and matrilineally related to him, i.e., they all belong both to his patri-moiety and to his matri-moiety. A second section includes all the persons who belong to his patri-moiety but to the opposite matri-moiety. A third section embraces all matrilineal kinsmen who do not belong to his patri-moiety. The fourth section includes everyone who is related to him in neither the male nor the female line, i.e., who belongs both to the opposite patri-moiety and to the opposite matri-moiety. Since both moieties are exogamous, it is from this fourth section, and this one only, that he can take a spouse. Double moiety exogamy explains the otherwise peculiar fact that in Australia marriage is permitted into only one other kin group, whereas in most societies with exogamous moieties and sibs a person may marry into any of the sibs of the opposite moiety.

Cleared of the obscurities which befog the descriptions in much of the literature, Australian "four-class systems" exhibit none of the complexities which readers have been led to expect. They are, on the contrary, exceedingly easy to comprehend. For the guidance of the layman, Table 8 lists the section membership of the more important primary, secondary, and tertiary relatives of a male Ego. Relatives are abbreviated according to a system proposed elsewhere,[18] which will be followed hereinafter.

In a still more limited area in native Australia there occurs the so-called "eight-class system," wherein each section is subdivided into two *subsections*. This results from the imposition of an exogamous taboo upon one's mother's patrilineal kinsmen, which is extended throughout the society to form a third moiety dichotomy. This third exogamous dichotomy divides the members of each section into two groups, those belonging to one of the third pair of moieties and those belonging to the other. In the wife's section, for example, cross-cousins are grouped with MoFa in the prohibited subsection, and Ego is compelled to seek a wife in the other subsection, which includes his FaMo and certain second cross-cousins. It is in consequence of this third moiety dichotomy that a person is allowed to take a spouse from only one of the seven subsections other than his own, and that the nearest eligible mate is normally a second cross-cousin who belongs neither to his own matri-moiety, nor to his patri-moiety, nor to the third moiety which includes his mother's patrilineal kinsmen. For further details the reader must be referred to Lawrence's work and to the descriptive literature.

[18] G. P. Murdock, "Bifurcate Merging," *American Anthropologist*, n.s., XLIX (1947), 56, n. 2.

TABLE 8

| Relative | Members of Ego's Patri-Moiety | | Members of Opposite Patri-Moiety | |
	Ego's Matri-Moiety	Opposite Matri-Moiety	Ego's Matri-Moiety	Opposite Matri-Moiety
FaFa	X	—	—	—
FaMo	—	—	—	X
MoFa	—	—	—	X
MoMo	X	—	—	—
Fa	—	X	—	—
Mo	—	—	X	—
FaBr, FaSi	—	X	—	—
MoBr, MoSi	—	—	X	—
FaBrWi, FaSiHu	—	—	X	—
MoBrWi, MoSiHu	—	X	—	—
WiFa	—	—	X	—
WiMo	—	X	—	—
Br, Si	X	—	—	—
Wi	—	—	—	X
FaBrSo, FaBrDa	X	—	—	—
FaSiSo, FaSiDa	—	—	—	X
MoBrSo, MoBrDa	—	—	—	X
MoSiSo, MoSiDa	X	—	—	—
WiBr, WiSi	—	—	—	X
BrWi, SiHu	—	—	—	X
WiBrWi, WiSiHu	X	—	—	—
So, Da	—	X	—	—
BrSo, BrDa	—	X	—	—
SiSo, SiDa	—	—	X	—
SoWi, DaHu	—	—	X	—
WiBrSo, WiBrDa	—	—	X	—
WiSiSo, WiSiDa	—	X	—	—
SoSo, SoDa	X	—	—	—
DaSo, DaDa	—	—	—	X

The Ranon of the New Hebrides, and apparently also the Pentecost, reveal a "six-class system," a variation apparently not reported for Australia. The six sections are produced by the intersection of three exogamous patri-sibs by two exogamous matri-moieties. A man can take a wife from only one of the three sections of the opposite moiety, namely, the one which belongs neither to his own nor to his mother's patri-sib. True bilinear kin groups or sections have never been reported outside of Australia and a limited area in Melanesia. Despite occasional allegations to the contrary, the complex social systems of eastern Indonesia, of the Naga tribes of Assam, of the Ge tribes of east central Brazil, and of such North American tribes as the Cherokee bear no relationship to those of Australia. Perhaps the most obvious criterion of a genuine bilinear kin group is that no individual can belong to the same group as either his father, his mother, his son, or his daughter. It is also likely to be diagnostic if he is permitted to marry into only one other kin group in the society. The crucial factor, however, is the presence of double descent with moieties and exogamy. The only society in our sample for which bilinear kin groups seem possible, though unreported, is the Wogeo of New Guinea, who have exogamous matri-moieties and local exogamy in connection with a group based on patrilocal residence. That they apparently lack some type of "marriage classes" is presumably due to the considerable measure of deviation from the normal residence rule.

Double descent should not be confused with bilateral descent, which, unlike the former, is not a simple combination of patrilineal and matrilineal rules. The distinction becomes clear in examining Ego's relation to his four grandparents. He is aligned in the same kin group as his father's father under patrilineal descent, in the same group as his mother's mother under matrilineal descent, and in different kin groups with each under double descent. In none of these instances, however, does he find himself in the same kin group with either his father's mother or his mother's father. Under bilateral descent, however, he is affiliated equally with all four grandparents, and all four, being secondary relatives of his, will necessarily be members of any consanguineal kin group of bilateral type to which he himself belongs. Bilateral descent, instead of being a combination of patrilineal and matrilineal, reflects a complete absence of any unilinear emphasis.

The commonest type of bilateral kin group, as previously noted, is the kindred. In our own society, where its members are collectively called "kinfolk" or "relatives," it includes that group of near kinsmen who may be expected to be present and participant on important ceremonial occasions, such as weddings, christenings, funerals, Thanksgiving and Christmas dinners, and "family reunions." Members of a kindred visit and entertain one another freely, and between them marriage and pecuniary transactions for profit are ordinarily taboo. One turns first to them for aid when one finds oneself in difficulties. However much they may disagree or quarrel, they are expected to support one another against criticism or affronts from outsiders. The kindred in other societies has comparable characteristics and functions.

Bilateral kin groups have received little attention from anthropological theorists. Consequently ethnographers rarely notice their presence and almost never report their absence. Specific descriptions or clear inferences attest the presence of kindreds in 33 societies in our sample, though further research would doubtless reveal them in others. Kindreds are occasionally reported for patrilineal societies, such as the Bena, Ojibwa, and Tikopia, and for matrilineal tribes, such as the Hopi, Iroquois, and Nayar, but the overwhelming majority are recorded for bilateral societies or for tribes with non-exogamous sibs or lineages, like the Fox and Tswana. They appear especially common with bilocal residence, though they also occur frequently with neolocal residence. In general, they are clearly associated with an absence of, or a minimal stress upon, unilinear descent. Probably they will ultimately appear to be characteristic of most bilateral societies. However, since kindreds normally exhibit a tendency toward exogamy comparable to that of lineages, the fact that 13 bilateral societies in our sample reveal no bilateral extension of sex prohibitions suggests that kindreds are probably completely lacking in at least some of these cases. If this is true, there are a few societies with no consanguineal kin groups intermediate between the nuclear family and the community.

Since the cultural rule of bilateral descent corresponds exactly with the facts of genealogical relationship, and since most peoples recognize the biological connection between a child and both of its parents, it might be expected that the majority of societies would choose this alternative as the cultural norm. In our sample of 250, however, only 75, representing but 30 per cent of the total, follow the rule of bilateral descent. The comparative rarity of bilateral descent and the widespread prevalence of other rules, all of which appear inconsistent with well-known biological facts, certainly demand explanation.

Suggested explanations have been numerous and diverse. The evolutionist anthropologists [19] of the nineteenth century assumed that social evolution must have begun with the matrilineate because primitive man could not have known the facts of physical paternity. In their opinion, patrilineal institutions evolved later as the male sex gradually achieved dominance, while bilateral descent became established only with the emergence of higher civilization and the accompanying realization of the equal roles of both parents. American anthropologists [20] of the early twentieth century, in criticizing the evolutionists for ignoring the nuclear family, ascribed priority to bilateral descent and regarded the matrilineate as a relatively late development, without, however, accounting for its origin. Historical anthropologists [21] of several persuasions—British, Austrian, and American—have regarded unilinear descent as so anomalous that they attribute it to a limited number of cultural inventions and to worldwide diffusion from its points of origin. All these hypotheses will be analyzed in Chapter 8, where their defects and their inconsistency with distributional facts will be demonstrated.

For enlightenment we must turn to theorists who consider the functional significance of the several types of consanguineal kin groups. Linton [22] advances several suggestions, among them the hypothesis that "an emphasis on unilinear descent is an almost unavoidable accompaniment of the establishment of family units on the consanguine basis." If this theory were correct, unilinear descent should tend to be strongly associated with the presence of extended families, and bilateral descent with their absence. Our data, however, fail strikingly to confirm this expectation. To be sure, patri-

[19] See especially J. J. Bachofen, *Das Mutterrecht* (Stuttgart, 1861); J. F. McLennan, *Studies in Ancient History* (London, 1876); L. H. Morgan, *Ancient Society* (New York, 1877).

[20] See especially J. R. Swanton, "The Social Organization of American Tribes," *American Anthropologist*, n.s., VII (1905), 663–73; R. H. Lowie, "Social Organization," *American Journal of Sociology*, XX (1914), 68–97.

[21] See especially W. J. Perry, *The Children of the Sun* (New York, 1923); W. Schmidt and W. Koppers, *Völker und Kulturen* (Regensburg, 1924); R. L. Olson, "Clan and Moiety in Native America," *University of California Publications in American Archaeology and Ethnology*, XXX (1933), 351–422.

[22] R. Linton, *The Study of Man* (New York, 1936), p. 166.

lineal descent occurs in 69 per cent (36 out of 52) of the societies in our sample with patrilocal extended families, and matrilineal descent in 73 per cent (22 out of 30) of those with matrilocal or avunculocal extended families, but the same unilinear rules also occur in 60 per cent (68 out of 113) of the societies which completely lack any kind of extended family.

Lowie [23] believes that "the transmission of property rights and the mode of residence after marriage have been the most effective means of establishing the principle of unilateral descent." The alleged influence of the inheritance of property cannot be tested, since Lowie does not indicate what particular inheritance rules should coexist with bilateral descent. The hypothesis that residence rules can be instrumental in establishing unilinear descent is also advanced by Linton,[24] who states: "Matrilineal descent is normally linked with matrilocal residence, patrilineal with patrilocal." This theory is supported by the data compiled in Table 9, and will be fully validated in Chapter 8.

TABLE 9

Rules of Residence	Matrilineal Descent	Patrilineal Descent	Double Descent	Bilateral Descent	Totals
Matrilocal and avunculocal	33	0	0	13	46
Patrilocal and matri-patrilocal	15	97	17	39	168
Neolocal and bilocal	4	8	1	23	36
TOTALS	52	105	18	75	250

With such support from the evidence, we must agree with Lowie and Linton that a fixed rule of residence, whereby spouses of a particular sex regularly continue to reside with or near their linear relatives of the same sex after marriage, is conducive to unilinear rather than bilateral descent. The question still remains, however, of whence residence rules acquire the power to override the common knowledge of the genealogical bond between a child and both parents, and to produce rules of descent which affiliate a child

[23] R. H. Lowie, *Primitive Society* (New York, 1920), p. 157.
[24] R. Linton, *The Study of Man* (New York, 1936), p. 169.

with the relatives of only one parent. The fact that certain of the latter are congregated in the same locality by any unilocal rule of residence, thereby rendering their affiliation the more obvious, unquestionably provides an important part of the answer. It is clear, however, that unilocal residence alone does not produce unilinear descent, as is attested by the 52 societies in our sample which are bilateral in descent though characterized by matrilocal or patrilocal residence.

A supplementary hypothesis states that unilinear kin groups possess certain advantages not shared by the bilateral kindred, and that these add their weight to the factor of proximity in many cases and help to tip the scales in favor of matrilineal or patrilineal descent. Radcliffe-Brown,[25] for example, attributes unilinear forms of organization to "certain fundamental social necessities," namely, a need for the precise formulation of jural rights so as to avoid conflicts, and a need for continuity in the social structure which defines such rights. Linton [26] mentions the same factors. These suggestions would seem to warrant a reexamination of the kindred.

The most distinctive structural fact about the kindred is that, save through accident, it can never be the same for any two individuals with the exception of own siblings. For any given person, its membership ramifies out through diverse kinship connections until it is terminated at some degree of relationship—frequently with second cousins, although the limits are often drawn somewhat closer or farther away than this and may be rather indefinite. The kindreds of different persons overlap or intersect rather than coincide. Those, for example, of first cousins, the sons of two brothers, have part of their membership in common—the near relatives through their respective fathers—and the rest distinct; the kinsmen of either cousin through his mother do not belong to the kindred of the other.

Since kindreds interlace and overlap, they do not and cannot form discrete or separate segments of the entire society. Neither a tribe nor a community can be subdivided into constituent kindreds. This intersecting or non-exclusive characteristic is found only with bilateral descent. Every other rule of descent produces only clearly

[25] A. R. Radcliffe-Brown, "Patrilineal and Matrilineal Succession," *Iowa Law Review*, XX (1935), 301-3.
[26] R. Linton, *The Study of Man* (New York, 1936), pp. 160-2, 166-7.

differentiated, isolable, discrete kin groups, which never overlap with others of their kind.

One result of this peculiarity is that the kindred, though it serves adequately to define the jural rights of an individual, can rarely act as a collectivity. One kindred cannot, for example, take blood vengeance against another if the two happen to have members in common. Moreover, a kindred cannot hold land or other property, not only because it is not a group except from the point of view of a particular individual, but also because it has no continuity over time. Hence under circumstances favorable either to the communal ownership of property or to the collective responsibility of kinsmen, the kindred labors under decided handicaps in comparison to the lineage or sib.

A particular disadvantage of the kindred appears in the instances in which an individual belongs to the kindreds of two other persons and thereby becomes involved in conflicting or incompatible obligations. If they get into serious difficulties with one another, for example, he may be required to avenge the one and yet to defend the other. If they become estranged, both are likely to turn to him for support and to subject him to emotional conflict and strain. The reader can supply numerous examples from the rankling family quarrels in our own society. In a tribe segmented into lineages, sibs, or moieties, however, the individual knows exactly where he stands in such instances. If both disputants are members of his own kin group, he is expected to remain neutral and to use his good offices to compose their differences. If neither is a member, the affair is none of his business. If one is a member but the other is not, he is expected to support his sibmate, regardless of the rights in the matter. In short, most conflict situations are simply and automatically resolved.

The Tenino of Oregon illustrate how conflicts in ceremonial obligations can arise in a sibless society. In this tribe weddings are solemnized by an elaborate series of property exchanges between the kindreds of the bride and the groom. The relatives of the bride, of both sexes, bring clothing, baskets, bags, vegetal foods, and other articles produced in the feminine sphere of economic activity. Those of the groom bring horses, skins, meat, and other masculine products. Each participant then exchanges his gifts with a particular member of the other kindred. It nearly always happens, of course, that a number of people are related to both the bride and the groom, and are forced to decide on which side they shall participate; they cannot play two contradictory roles at once. Moreover, the numbers in either party must be the same. These problems are settled only after protracted discussions among the parties concerned and persons in authority, and they not infrequently generate jealousy, friction, and injured feelings.

Under unilinear descent such conflicts could never arise. All kin groups produced by patrilineal, matrilineal, or double descent are discrete social units. The role of every participant in a ceremonial activity, of every bystander in a dispute of any sort, is automatically defined for him by his kin group membership. This advantage may well account in considerable measure for the marked preponderance of unilinear descent throughout the world.

The kindred is roughly comparable to the lineage, not only in approximate size but also in the fact that the genealogical connections of all of its members to Ego are known and traceable. Are there larger bilateral kin groups which are comparable to the sib both in size and in the traditional rather than demonstrable bonds of kinship which unite their members? No such groups have received extensive theoretical consideration in the literature. Nevertheless, the results of the present study indicate that there is one type of larger bilateral kin group which is fairly common, and which exerts an influence upon kinship terminology and sex behavior comparable to that exerted by sibs and other recognized consanguineal kin groups.

This group is most clearly observable in the endogamous local community which is not segmented by unilinear consanguineal groupings of kinsmen. By virtue of the rule or strong preference for local endogamy, the inhabitants are necessarily related to one another through intermarriage, although they cannot always trace their exact kinship connections. They are consequently bound to one another not only by common residence but also by consanguinity, as is, in fact, usually specifically recognized. Within such a group the only social structuring is commonly into families, which may be of either nuclear, polygamous, or extended type. Except for family ties, the strongest sense of identification is usually with the community as a whole, which is viewed as a consanguineal unit in relation to other communities in a manner quite comparable to the attitude towards one's own sib in a unilinear society. In our sample, endogamous localized kin groups of this type are attested with reasonable certainty for the Aymara, Chiricahua, Comanche, Cuna, Inca, Kiowa Apache, Mentaweians, Nuba, Pawnee, Ruthenians, Shoshone, Sinkaietk, Siriono, Taos, and Wichita, and they are probably present in at least some of the following: Carib, Cayapa, Copper Eskimo, Kaingang, Mataco, Nambikuara, Tupinamba, and Washo.

In view of the fact that this type of kin group will later be found to be substantially associated with other social phenomena, such as kinship terminology, it seems desirable to give it specific recognition and a distinctive name. So far as the author's knowledge goes, it has not been christened, and none of the terms that are standard in social organization appears applicable. He has therefore sought for a new name which would be as short and distinctive as "sib" and which already has both a local and a genealogical connotation.

Search led eventually to the social organization of ancient Attica, where a local group called the *deme* (pronounced like "deem"), roughly comparable to an English parish, was substituted for a unilinear descent group in the political reforms of Cleisthenes, who made membership in it hereditary.[27] While our source does not reveal whether the original deme was endogamous, it was certainly a local group and, at least in later times, was also consanguineal. It therefore seems to suit our purposes adequately, and, in addition to being short and easily pronounceable, has the advantage of being already established in English dictionaries. That the term has appeared briefly in the anthropological literature,[28] only to be quickly forgotten, does not prevent our reintroducing it with our own definition. Henceforth, therefore, we shall regularly employ "deme" for an endogamous local group in the absence of unilinear descent, especially when we are regarding it as a kin group rather than as a community.

[27] See E. M. Walker, "Athens: the Reform of Cleisthenes," *Cambridge Ancient History*, IV (New York, 1926), 142–8.

[28] Cf. A. W. Howitt and L. Fison, "On the Deme and the Horde," *Journal of the Royal Anthropological Institute*, XIV (1885), 142.

The widespread tendency to extend incest taboos throughout any kin group, which will be considered in Chapter 10, naturally does not leave the deme unaffected. On the basis of the tradition of common descent among its members, exogamy can and does extend, in many instances, from the kindred to the deme, as from the lineage to the sib. When this occurs, local exogamy replaces local endogamy, and the constitution of the deme is fundamentally changed. Members are required to marry outside of the community, and in doing so naturally conform to the prevailing rule of residence. Exogamous demes, where unilinear descent has not become established, may be distinguished according to residence rules as *patri-demes* and *matri-demes*. If necessary to differentiate the original endogamous deme from them, it may be called the *endo-deme*. As will be seen in the next chapter, exogamous demes constitute one of the two principal origins of clans.

4

THE CLAN

TWO MAJOR types of kin groups have previously been distinguished. One, the residential kin group, is based primarily upon a rule of residence. It necessarily includes both husband and wife, since they always reside together. Almost as inevitably it cannot include married brothers and sisters, since they are separated by incest taboos and residence rules, and can consequently rarely live together. Hence the relatives aggregated in a residential kin group always include some whose kinship ties are primarily affinal, as in the case of husband and wife or of stepparent and stepchild, and others whose ties are purely consanguineal, as in the case of parent and child or of two brothers or parallel cousins. The most characteristic of residential kin groups are the several varieties of families described in Chapters 1 and 2.

The second major type is the consanguineal kin group, which is regularly based on a rule of descent rather than of residence. In consequence, it almost never includes both husband and wife, or any other pair of affinal relatives, but always includes brothers and sisters, after as well as before their marriage. It also embraces all other consanguineal relatives under the prevailing rule of descent as far as connections are traced for the purposes of group membership. In view of these characteristics it can practically never be a residential unit. Its principal forms—the lineage, sib, phratry, moiety, section, kindred, and deme—have been analyzed in Chapter 3.

We now come to a third major type of kin group, which is based upon both a rule of residence and a rule of descent, insofar as the two can be reconciled, and which may therefore be called a *compromise kin group*. The problem of reconciliation arises only with unilocal residence and unilinear descent. Of the two principal varieties of bilateral consanguineal kin groups, the kindred is not a group at all, except from the point of view of a particular individual, and hence cannot be localized, whereas the deme is in the fullest sense both a residential and a consanguineal group without any necessity for compromise. We have already seen, however, that incest taboos and the residential cohabitation of husband and wife prevent the localization of a unilinear consanguineal kin group in its entirety under any rule of residence. This can be approximated only by combining a unilocal rule of residence with a consistent unilinear rule of descent and effecting a compromise whereby some affinal relatives are included and some consanguineal kinsmen excluded. Of the several possibilities, as we shall see, all involve the exclusion of the adult consanguineal kinsmen of one sex and the inclusion of the spouses of those of the opposite sex.

A compromise kin group is commonly larger than an extended family, but the alignment of kinsmen is identical. The principal distinction is the addition of a unilinear rule of descent as an integral factor in the structure of the group. The core of a unilocal extended family always consists of persons of one sex who are in fact unilinearly related, but this relationship is purely incidental, need not be formulated, and is frequently not even recognized. The bond of union is primarily and often exclusively residential. In a compromise kin group, on the other hand, the unilinear relationship of the core of the group is at least as crucial an integrating fact as the residential alignment.

The existence and essential nature of compromise kin groups has been dimly recognized for some time, but they have commonly been confused with the extended family on the one hand or with the sib on the other, depending upon whether the particular author has chosen to stress the residential or the consanguineal bond. Even Lowie,[1] who has cleared up satisfactorily so much of the confusion

---

[1] R. H. Lowie, *Primitive Society* (New York, 1920), pp. 111–85.

about unilinear kin groups inherited from the past, has failed to make explicit the crucial distinction here involved, although he appears to understand it. The clarification of this issue, which is fundamental to an adequate comprehension of unilinear institutions, is the primary objective of the present chapter.

The selection of an appropriate term for compromise kin groups presents the most serious problem of nomenclature encountered in the present work. In the literature they are rarely distinguished from sibs, and the same term is usually applied indiscriminately to both groups. The term most widely used is *clan*, and it is this which we have chosen to adopt after considerable hesitation rather than clutter an already overburdened nomenclature with a new term. There are, it must be admitted, significant disadvantages in this choice. Foremost among them is that fact that "clan" has been used in two other distinct senses in the technical literature on social organization. From the time of Powell until very recently most American anthropologists have used it to designate a matrilineal sib in contradistinction to a patri-sib, for which the term "gens" has been employed. This usage is now obsolescent, since increasing recognition of the essential similarity of sibs under the two rules of descent renders their terminological distinction no longer necessary. Far more serious is the use of "clan" by British anthropologists for any unilinear consanguineal kin group of the type which we, following Lowie, have termed the "sib." Among recent American anthropologists, "clan" and "sib" have run a close race for acceptance in this sense. We have given preference to "sib" over "clan" primarily because the former has never been applied to kin groups other than consanguineal ones with unilinear descent, so that its use by us in this sense could lead to no confusion.

Despite the disadvantages of employing "clan" for compromise kin groups, and particularly the initial confusion which it may create in the minds of some readers, our choice has been dictated by a number of positive advantages. In the first place, the term itself is too apt and too widely known to be discarded completely, as we should have to do if we chose another term after having preferred "sib" as a designation for the most typical of unilinear consanguineal kin groups. In the second place, "clan" has in fact been frequently used by anthropologists for compromise kin groups, and is indeed almost the only term that has ever been applied to them. Even when specifically differentiated from sibs in the literature, they are most commonly called "localized clans." Finally, our use and proposed redefinition of the word accord very closely with its popular connotations. Webster,[2] for example, gives the following as the primary definition of clan: "A social group comprising a number of households the heads of which claim descent from a common ancestor. . . ." Any group which comprises households related through their heads necessarily includes wives with their husbands but not married sisters with their brothers, and is consequently not a consanguineal kin group or sib but a kin group of the compromise type. Our proposal thus returns the word to its original non-technical meaning.

For a group to constitute a genuine clan it must conform to three major specifications. If any one of the three is lacking, the group is not a clan, however greatly it may resemble one in composition and external appearance. In the first place, it must be based explicitly on a unilinear rule of descent which unites its central core of members. Unilocal extended families and exogamous demes reveal a composition identical with that of clans, from which they differ only in lacking the unifying principle of descent; unilinear descent is absent in the case of demes, absent or incidental in the case of extended families. In the second place, to constitute a clan a group must have residential unity. This cannot exist if the residence rule is inconsistent with that of descent, e.g., patrilocal or neolocal when the latter is matrilineal. Nor can it exist if any appreciable degree of individual deviation is permitted from the normal rule of residence. In the third place, the group must exhibit actual social integration. It cannot be a mere unorganized aggregation of independent families like those residing in a block in an American residential suburb. There must be a positive group sentiment, and in particular the in-marrying spouses must be recognized as an integral part of the membership.

Above all, it should be emphasized that a clan does not result automatically from the coexistence of compatible rules of residence and descent. Even if residence is strictly patrilocal and descent patri-

[2] *Webster's New International Dictionary of the English Language* (rev. edit., Springfield, 1923), p. 409.

lineal, for example, and the households of the patrilineally related males are actually aggregated in a specific part of the community, the group does not necessarily constitute a clan. The residents may be merely related neighbors. The ethnographer must observe evidences of organization, collective activities, or group functions before he can characterize them as a clan.

The Dobuans of Melanesia provide an example of groups with the membership but not the organization of clans. In consequence of alternating residence and matrilineal descent, the members of a local community consist of unilinearly related males and females with the spouses who are residing temporarily with them. The noteworthy lack of any social integration between these in-marrying spouses and the native-born members of the community, however, prevents recognition of the local group as a genuine clan.

It has already been noted that the normal method of effecting a compromise between a rule of residence and a rule of descent in order to form a clan is by including one sex among the adult members of the consanguineal kin group, by excluding their siblings of opposite sex, and by including the spouses of the former. Logically, there are four ways in which this can be accomplished, since there are two unilinear rules of descent—patrilineal and matrilineal —and two sexes, either of which might theoretically be selected for inclusion as the core of the clan. Actually, only three of the four possibilities occur in the societies of our sample.

The first possibility in clan formation is to localize a patri-lineage or patri-sib around its male members through a rule of patrilocal residence. The group which results includes all the males and the unmarried females of the lineage or sib, together with the wives of the married males. The married females of the lineage or sib, the sisters of the males, are excluded because they have gone to live with their husbands in patrilocal residence in other clans. It is appropriate to designate such a group either as a patrilocal clan or as a patrilineal clan, since it depends equally upon rules of residence and descent. Following a useful suggestion by Lawrence,[3] we shall ordinarily call it a *patri-clan*.

The distinction between the sib or lineage which is localized and

[3] W. E. Lawrence, "Alternating Generations in Australia," *Studies in the Science of Society*, ed. G. P. Murdock (New Haven, 1937), p. 319.

the clan which results from its localization can perhaps be clarified by reference to our own society. Though we lack both sibs and clans, the reader can readily visualize their existence, assuming that our rule of residence were patrilocal rather than neolocal and that our rule of descent were patrilineal rather than bilateral. In such a case our surnames, which are patrilineally inherited, would correspond to both clans and sibs. All males with the surname Wolf, for example, would be members of the Wolf sib, and they would reside together in one or more localized groups, which could be called Wolf clans. All women, however, would change both their local groups and their surnames upon marriage. They would belong to the sibs of their brothers, to the clans of their husbands. In the case of males, the surname Wolf would indicate both sib and clan membership. In the case of women, however, sib membership would be indicated by the maiden name, clan membership by the married name. Miss Mary Wolf would be a member of the Wolf sib, even after she married John Heron and joined the Heron clan. Mrs. James Wolf, *née* Fox, would belong to a Wolf clan but to the Fox sib.

The second possibility in clan formation is to localize a matri-lineage or matri-sib around its female members through a rule of matrilocal residence. The resulting *matri-clan* (matrilocal or matri-lineal clan) embraces all the females and the unmarried males of the sib, together with the husbands of the married females. It does not include the adult males of the sib, since these have married and taken up residence with their wives in other matri-clans.

The third possibility consists in localizing a matri-sib around its male rather than its female members. This is accomplished through avunculocal residence, whereby an unmarried male leaves his paternal home to live with his maternal uncle and brings his wife there when he marries. The resulting group, which may be called an avunculocal clan or *avuncu-clan,* includes a group of matrilineally related males who stand to one another in the relation of uncle and nephew or of real or classificatory brothers, together with their wives and unmarried children, who of course belong to different sibs. The adult women of the clan are the wives and sisters-in-law of the men of their own generation. The adult and married women of the sib reside in other clans with their husbands.

Occasionally in an avuncu-clan the nephews may marry the daughters of their maternal uncles, with the result that at least some of the married women of the clan are the daughters of the older men. To the extent that this is true, the group represents a combination of matri-clan and avuncu-clan, with its females belonging to one sib and its males to another and with matrilocal residence characterizing the former and avunculocal residence the latter. An avuncu-clan, in fine, resembles a patri-clan in the fact that its core consists of a group of unilinearly related males, but it resembles a matri-clan in its acceptance of matrilineal rather than patrilineal descent as the basis of affiliation.

The fourth possibility in clan formation is as yet purely hypothetical. It would consist in localizing a patri-sib around its adult females. This could be accomplished by a cultural provision that unmarried females take up their residence with a paternal aunt and bring their husbands to the aunt's home when they marry. Such a rule of residence, it if should be discovered in future field research, might be called *amitalocal* on the basis of a suggestion by Lowie [4] that the term "amitate" be adopted for a special relationship with the father's sister paralleling "avunculate," which is generally used for the comparable relationship with the mother's brother. The type of clan resulting from such a residence rule in conjunction with patrilineal descent would then be called an amitalocal clan or *amita-clan*.

Among the 250 societies of our sample, the available information, which is often fragmentary, indicates the presence of patri-clans in 72, matri-clans in 11, and avuncu-clans in 4. Clans are definitely absent in 131 tribes, while for 32 unilinear societies the data are too scanty to determine whether clans exist or not. Amita-clans are not reported in our sample, nor has the author ever encountered a description in his general ethnographic reading. That avuncu-clans are not simply a local peculiarity, dependent upon a unique concatenation of circumstances, is shown by the distribution of the four cases in our sample. Two instances (the Haida and Tlingit) are reported from the Northwest Coast of North America, one (the Longuda) from Northern Nigeria in Africa, and one (the Trobrianders) from Melanesia in Oceania.

[4] R. H. Lowie, in *American Anthropologist*, n.s., XXXIV (1932), 534.

The distinction between compromise and consanguineal kin groups, or specifically between clan and sib, is no idle exercise in classificatory ingenuity. On the contrary, it is a matter of profound functional importance. The two kin groups not only differ in constitution, but they appear to be characteristically associated with different functions. These can be illustrated from a tribe known to the author through personal field work.

The Haida of British Columbia, in addition to the nuclear family, are characterized by one type of residential kin group, the avunculocal extended family; by two types of consanguineal kin groups, the matri-sib and the matri-moiety; and by one type of compromise kin group, the avuncu-clan. Each extended family occupies a large plank dwelling. Each avuncu-clan comprises the inhabitants of a particular village—a group of matrilineally related adult males together with their wives, their unmarried or recently married daughters, and their young sons who have not yet left to join the household of a maternal uncle. The wives and children of the adult males of the clan belong, of course, to the opposite matri-moiety. A sib consists of the adult males of an avuncu-clan, and of their sisters and the daughters and young sons of the latter who all reside in other villages. A clan and the corresponding sib thus coincide in somewhat less than half of their membership—their male members over ten years of age, the approximate time at which the shift to avunculocal residence occurs.

The functions of the several Haida kin groups are quite distinctive. The moiety regulates marriage, which is strictly exogamous. It also channelizes rivalries and regulates ceremonial property exchanges. Potlatches, for example, are invariably given to members of the opposite moiety. The extended family is the unit of ordinary domestic life, of primary economic cooperation, of trade, and of property accumulation. The nuclear family, in addition to its usual functions, is the group which gives a potlatch; the wife is technically the donor in major potlatches, but she is assisted by her husband, and their children are the beneficiaries of the resulting enhancement in status. The clan is the community, i.e., the face-to-face group of daily social intercourse. It is also the basic political unit, each clan being independent of all others. All property rights in land are held by the clan, under the trusteeship of its chief.

Movable goods are owned by the extended family or by individuals. Intangible property rights, on the other hand, are vested in the sib. This group owns a fund of personal names, of ceremonial titles for houses and canoes, of totemic crests, and of exclusive rights to songs and ceremonies. Mythology, too, is largely associated with the sib, and it is this group which regulates inheritance and sucession. The sib, moreover, is the ceremonial unit; its members are invited collectively to feasts and potlatches, and they assist one another in preparing for and conducting these ceremonies when any one of them is the host. Finally, the duty of blood vengeance for the murder or injury of one of its members falls upon the sib. Warfare, however, is the function of the clan, whether motivated by vengeance, self-defense, or the desire for booty and slaves.

The role of Haida women in disputes between the men of two villages is especially illuminating. Those who have married from one community into the other find themselves torn by divided loyalties; they are wives and clansmen of one group of disputant men, sisters and sibmates of the other. So long as relations are merely strained, these women act as mediators and strive to settle the differences; they can, of course, move from one village to the other unmolested. If, however, matters reach the breaking point, and war ensues, the women cleave to their husbands rather than to their brothers.[5] In the ultimate crisis, in short, clan ties override the bonds of sib membership. This is particularly enlightening because it contradicts the statement by Linton[6] that in societies organized on a consanguine basis, of which the Haida are certainly an outstanding example, "spouses are of only incidental importance."

The ethnographic literature, despite the prevalent confusion, contains numerous intimations of a similar distribution of functions between clan and sib. In general, the clan seems to function primarily in the economic, recreational, political, and military spheres, while the sib is associated with totemism and ceremonial, acts as a unit in life crisis situations, and regulates marriage and inheritance.

[5] The common confusion between sib and clan led Swanton to make one of his rare misstatements of fact in regard to this point, for he states that in such cases women support their sibmates against their husbands. See J. R. Swanton, "Contributions to the Ethnology of the Haida," *Memoirs of the American Museum of Natural History*, VIII (1909), 62.

[6] R. Linton, *The Study of Man* (New York, 1936), p. 159.

Future field research and a critical reexamination of the existing literature will doubtless clarify the entire situation.

With respect to relative size, clans fall into two major categories. The larger is coextensive with the local community, as in the case of the Haida, and may therefore be designated as a *clan-community*. The smaller type of clan forms merely a segment of the community, such as a ward in a village, or a hamlet when the community consists of a cluster of segregated clans. Since the Spanish word *barrio* can connote divisions of either type, the group will be called a *clan-barrio*. Of the societies in our sample with patri-clans, 45 are characterized by clan-communities and 27 by clan-barrios. Only clan-communities are found in the four avunculocal tribes. The preponderance of clan-communities disappears in matrilocal societies for reasons which will be made clear in Chapter 8. Nine of those in our sample possess clan-barrios exclusively, whereas only two are organized into clan-communities, and both of these, the Vedda of Ceylon and the Yaruro of Venezuela, live in migratory bands rather than settled villages.

For purposes of exposition, the chapter has been written up to this point as though clans originated in societies already possessing unilinear consanguineal kin groups, through a process of localization resulting from the application of a unilocal rule of residence consistent with the preexisting rule of descent. To have complicated the synchronic analysis with diachronic considerations would have resulted only in confusing the lay reader. Now that the analysis is complete, however, the problem of origins may be faced. As this is done, the reader should be specifically warned to disregard the implicit assumption of the temporal priority of the sib to the clan. In actuality, the clan is almost universally the first to make its appearance, and gives rise to the lineage or sib, rather than *vice versa*. While much of the proof must be deferred until Chapter 8, the essential facts regarding sequences must be summarized here, in order to forestall misunderstanding.

It may be stated categorically, disregarding only the most exceptional circumstances, that lineages and sibs invariably arise out of clans by the extension of the recognition of unilinear affiliation from the sex which forms the core of the clan to their siblings of opposite sex who have moved away in marriage. Until this is done, by some mechanism such as sib names, totemism, or inherited taboos, the society possesses clans but not sibs. There are presumably such cases in our sample, but so widespread is the confusion between clan and sib in the literature that wherever we have found indisputable evidence of the former we have felt compelled to assume the existence of the latter. Once sibs or lineages have come into existence, provided they have acquired the characteristic of exogamy, they lead an independent life and are capable of surviving long after the clans from which they sprang have disappeared. No fewer than 56 of the societies in our sample, for instance, lack clans though they possess unilinear consanguineal kin groups—matrilineal in 30 cases, patrilineal in 23, and groups of both types in 3. In 32 other tribes with sibs or lineages, clans are not reported and may very possibly be absent. In other words, on statistical grounds a unilinear society is approximately as likely to lack clans as to possess them.

Clans doubtless originate in some instances merely from a unilocal rule of residence, the incidental result of which is to assemble in one locality a number of unilinearly related adults of one sex together with their spouses and children. In such instances, however, both a principle of organization and a rule of descent must be developed. It is probable, therefore, that clans arise more often from kin groups which, in addition to a similar aggregation of relatives, already possess a principle of organization and consequently require only the development of a rule of descent to be converted into clans. There are two types of kin groups which meet these specifications—unilocal extended families and exogamous demes. All that is necessary to convert an extended family into a clan-barrio, or an exogamous deme into a clan-community, is to give cultural recognition to the unilinear affiliation of the core of the group. When this is extended to their out-marrying siblings, lineages are produced in the one case, sibs in the other. Both theoretical considerations and the evidence of ethnography, therefore, make it probable that clans, and ultimately lineages and sibs as well, arise in most instances either from extended families or from demes which have become exogamous.

The initial phase in the evolution from extended family to clan-barrio is exemplified by the Havasupai of Arizona. On the basis of a rule of matri-patrilocal residence this tribe has developed groups called "camps," which are actually patrilocal extended families. Spier [7] has shown very convincingly how a relatively slight accentuation of factors already in existence, such as an increased emphasis upon patrilineal inheritance and an extension of kinship recognition in the paternal line, would give rise to genuine patri-clans. The Tongans of Polynesia are one of several tribes in our sample which have achieved this step without, however, having yet developed a rule of exogamy.

The Mentaweians of Indonesia illustrate the initial stages of a parallel development from matrilocal extended families to clan-barrios. In this society the village, which has the characteristics of an endogamous deme, is divided into sections, each consisting of a communal house, a number of surrounding dwellings, and out-lying field-houses. These local divisions, which are the primary social, economic, and religious units of Mentaweian society, bear many of the earmarks of extended families comprising a number of nuclear families occupying separate houses. They have not yet become exogamous, however, nor has recognition been accorded to matrilineal descent, which alone is needed to convert them into matri-clans.

A clan-community may arise from a clan-barrio through a process of population growth and fission, which ultimately leaves only a single clan in a community which previously had several. At least as commonly, however, it can develop directly out of an exogamous deme. As incest taboos spread throughout a deme, an inherent tendency in all consanguineal kin groups (see Chapter 10), the rule of endogamy becomes gradually converted into a preference for local exogamy. This produces matri-demes where the rule of residence is matrilocal, patri-demes under patrilocal residence. For reasons to be explained in Chapter 8, matri-demes are rare and are confined almost exclusively to societies with a migratory band organization. In our sample only the Arapaho and Cheyenne reveal matri-demes, incipient in both cases. If either tribe were to adopt strict local exogamy with matrilocal residence, the band would consist of matrilineally related women with their husbands and

[7] L. Spier, "A Suggested Origin for Gentile Organization," *American Anthropologist*, n.s., XXIV (1922), 489.

children. If then this unilinear connection were culturally recognized through a rule of matrilineal descent, and if the out-marrying men retained their kin affiliations with the band members, the tribe would be characterized by matrilineal clan-communities and matri-sibs like the Vedda and Yaruro.

Far more common, however, is the transition from patri-demes to patri-clans and patri-sibs. Our sample includes 13 societies with bilateral descent and a marked tendency toward local exogamy, i.e., with patri-demes. These are the Blackfoot, Eromangans, Hupa, Ona, Quinault, Semang, Shasta, Takelma, Teton, Walapai, Wapisiana, Yaghan, and Yurok. The normal process by which patri-demes may be converted into patrilocal clan-communities, with the eventual emergence of patri-sibs, may be illustrated by reference to the Hupa of northwestern California.

In consequence of the rules of patrilocal residence and local exogamy, the inhabitants of a Hupa village or settlement consist mainly of patrilineally related males and their children with wives whom they have secured from other communities. There is, however, one important exception to the patrilocal rule. Certain poor men, who constitute a not insignificant minority, pay only half of the ordinary bride-price and reside matrilocally with their parents-in-law, working off the balance through bride-service. The children of these "half-married" men continue to live in their mothers' village and are recognized as members thereof. Since a household may include daughters of the owner with their half-married husbands, as well as sons with their wives and children, it is as much a bilocal as a patrilocal extended family. Lowie [8] has clearly pointed out two of the three modifications which would be necessary to produce patri-clans, then patri-sibs. First, the patrilocal rule of residence would have to be made invariable; this would clarify the patri-deme structure. Second, patrilineal descent would have to be recognized as a bond of union among the resident males; this would produce genuine patrilocal clan-communities. Third, "there must be a means of fixing the affiliation of the female no less than of the male members," e.g., by giving a common name to all persons born in the village whereby the original affiliation of out-marrying

[8] R. H. Lowie. *Primitive Society* (New York, 1920), pp. 157–8.

women could be permanently indicated. Once this were accomplished, full-fledged patri-sibs would have come into existence.

The nearly universal derivation of lineages and sibs from clans, and of clans from unilocal extended families and exogamous demes accords with the views of all American anthropologists who have given thoughtful consideration to the problem. More recently than Spier and Lowie, Titiev [9] has come to the same conclusion. The evidence in favor of this hypothesis is overwhelming, as will be seen in Chapter 8. The facts of diachronic sequence render misleading the common designation of clans as "localized" consanguineal kin groups, and demand the acceptance of a distinctive term. If "clan" strikes the reader as unsatisfactory, he is invited to suggest a more appropriate name.

[9] M. Titiev, "The Influence of Common Residence on the Unilateral Classification of Kindred," *American Anthropologist*, n.s., XLV (1943), 511–30.

5

THE COMMUNITY

ANTHROPOLOGISTS from Morgan to Lowie have shown far more interest in the forms of the family, the sib, and the clan than in the organization of social groups upon a strictly local basis. Sociologists, on the other hand, have for some time manifested a strong interest in community organization, and a parallel concern has recently been developing in anthropology, with especially noteworthy contributions from Steward [1] and Linton. [2]

The sociological term *community* is here chosen in preference to less definite or less descriptive alternatives, such as "local group" and "band," as the generic designation for groups organized on a predominantly local basis. It has been defined as "the maximal group of persons who normally reside together in face-to-face association." [3] The community and the nuclear family are the only social groups that are genuinely universal. They occur in every known human society, and both are also found in germinal form on a sub-human level.

Nowhere on earth do people live regularly in isolated families. Everywhere territorial propinquity, supported by divers other bonds,

[1] J. H. Steward, "The Economic and Social Basis of Primitive Bands," *Essays in Anthropology Presented to A. L. Kroeber* (Berkeley, 1936), pp. 331–50.

[2] R. Linton, *The Study of Man* (New York, 1936), pp. 209–30.

[3] G. P. Murdock, C. S. Ford, A. E. Hudson, R. Kennedy, L. W. Simmons, and J. W. M. Whiting, "Outline of Cultural Materials," *Yale Anthropological Studies,* II (1945), 29.

unites at least a few neighboring families into a larger social group all of whose members maintain face-to-face relationships with one another. Weyer,[4] in demonstrating this fact for the Eskimo, has pointed out that community organization provides individuals with increased opportunities for gratification through social intercourse, with more abundant sustenance through cooperative food-getting techniques, and with insurance against temporary incapacity or adversity through mutual aid and sharing. To these advantages may be added protection through numbers and the economies possible with specialization and a division of labor. The chances of survival thus seem to be materially enhanced through community organization, and this, together with the directly perceived gains, doubtless accounts for its universality.

Communities differ in type with their mode of life. Where subsistence depends largely upon gathering, hunting, or herding, which usually require migration from place to place at different seasons of the year, the local group consists typically of a number of families who habitually camp together. This type of community is called a *band*. Agriculture, on the other hand, favors more permanent residence in a single settlement, though exhaustion of the land may compel the community to move to a new site every few years. Fixed residence is also consistent with a fishing economy and even with a hunting economy under exceptional conditions where game is plentiful and non-migratory. With more or less settled residence, the community may assume the form either of a *village*, occupying a concentrated cluster of dwellings near the center of the exploited territory, or of a *neighborhood*, with its families scattered in semi-isolated homesteads, or of some compromise between the two, like the rural American town with its dispersed farm homesteads and its local center with church, school, post office and general store. It is also possible for people to live in settled villages at one season of the year and in migratory bands at another. Of the 241 societies in our sample for which information is available, 39 are organized in bands, 13 in neighborhoods lacking prominent nuclei, and 189 in villages or towns.

[4] E. M. Weyer, *The Eskimos* (New Haven, 1932), pp. 141–4. Cf. also, J. H. Steward, "The Economic and Social Basis of Primitive Bands," *Essays in Anthropology Presented to A. L. Kroeber* (Berkeley, 1936), pp. 332–3.

In size, the community at its lower limit, approached for example by the Reindeer Chukchee, consists of two or three families. The upper limit is seemingly set by "the practical impossibility of establishing close contacts with developing habitual attitudes toward any great number of people." [5] For this reason, presumably, large urban aggregations of population tend to become segmented, when geographical mobility is not excessive, into local districts or wards which possess the outstanding characteristics of communities. A study by Goodenough [6] reveals a maximum range of from 13 to 1,000 in average community population, with 50 as the mean for tribes with migratory bands,[7] 250 for those with neighborhood organization, and 300 for those with settled villages. The normal size of the community was shown by the same study to depend largely upon the prevalent type of food quest. Under a primarily hunting, gathering, or fishing economy, for example, the community averages somewhat fewer than 50 persons, whereas under an agricultural economy with animal husbandry it attains a mean population of about 450.

The community appears always to be associated with a definite territory, whose natural resources its members exploit in accordance with the technological attainments of the culture. Under a hunting or gathering economy, the lands of the community are ordinarily owned and exploited collectively,[8] although in some instances, as Speck [9] has shown for many of the Algonquian tribes of northeastern

[5] R. Linton, The Study of Man (New York, 1936), p. 218.

[6] W. H. Goodenough, "Basic Economy and the Community" (unpublished article, 1941). This study, undertaken in the files of the Cross-Cultural Survey at the suggestion of Professor W. F. Ogburn, covered 40 tribes for which reliable population data were available.

[7] An independent estimate by Steward also arrives at 50 persons as the average population of a band and finds, in addition, that the area exploited by a band averages approximately 100 square miles. See J. H. Steward, "The Economic and Social Basis of Primitive Bands," Essays in Anthropology Presented to A. L. Kroeber (Berkeley, 1936), p. 333.

[8] Cf. J. H. Steward, "The Economic and Social Basis of Primitive Bands," Essays in Anthropology Presented to A. L. Kroeber (Berkeley, 1936), pp. 332-3.

[9] F. G. Speck, "The Family Hunting Band as the Basis of Algonkian Social Organization," American Anthropologist, n.s., XVII (1914), 289-305; "Family Hunting Territories and Social Life of Various Algonkian Bands of the Ottawa Valley," Memoirs of the Canada Department of Mines Geological Survey, LXX (1915), 1-10; "Kinship Terms and the Family Band among the Northeastern Algonkian," American Anthropologist, n.s., XX (1918), 143-61; "Mistassini

North America, they are divided into individual family tracts. The situation tends to be similar in herding societies. Under agriculture, the tillable land is sometimes collectively owned and periodically redistributed among families. Much more frequently, however, it becomes allocated as feudal or private property, although the non-agricultural portions of the community's territory may continue to be collectively owned and utilized. The territorial basis of the community survives even under a mercantile or industrial economy, despite the decline in the relative importance of land as a source of livelihood.

In consequence of its common territory and of the interdependence of its constituent families, the community becomes the principal focus of associative life. Every member is ordinarily acquainted more or less intimately with every other member, and has learned through association to adapt his behavior to that of each of his fellows, so that the group is bound together by a complex network of interpersonal relationships. Many of these become culturally patterned, yielding standardized relationships like those of kinship and those based on age and sex status, which facilitate social intercourse, and many are aggregated into clusters around common interests, forming groups such as clans and associations which help to bind the families of the community to one another.

Since it is mainly through face-to-face relations that a person's behavior is influenced by his fellows—motivated, cued, rewarded, and punished—the community is the primary seat of social control. Here it is that deviation is penalized and conformity rewarded. It is noteworthy that ostracism from the community is widely regarded as the direst of punishments and that its threat serves as the ultimate inducement to cultural conformity. Through the operation of social sanctions, ideas and behavior tend to become relatively stereotyped within a community, and a local culture develops. Indeed, the community seems to be the most typical social group to support a total culture. This, incidentally, provides the theoretical justification for

Hunting Territories in the Labrador Peninsula," *American Anthropologist*, n.s., XXV (1923), 452–71; "Family Hunting Territories of the Lake St. John Montagnais," *Anthropos*, XXII (1927), 387–403; *Penobscot Man* (Philadelphia, 1940), pp. 203–12.

"community studies," a field in which anthropologists, sociologists, and social psychologists alike have shown a marked interest in recent decades.

Under conditions of relative isolation, each community has a culture of its own. The degree to which this is shared by neighboring local groups depends largely upon the means and extent of intercommunication. Ease of communication and geographical mobility may produce considerable cultural similarity over wide areas, as, for example, in the United States today, and may even generate important social cleavages which cut across local groupings, as in the case of social classes. For most of the peoples of the earth, however, the community has been both the primary unit of social participation and the distinctive culture-bearing group.

United by reciprocal relationships and bound by a common culture, the members of a community form an "in-group," [10] characterized by internal peace, law, order, and cooperative effort. Since they assist one another in the activities which gratify basic drives, and provide one another with certain derivative satisfactions obtainable only in social life, there develops among them a collective sentiment of group solidarity and loyalty, which has been variously termed syngenism, we-feeling, *esprit de corps*, and consciousness of kind.

Social life, despite the manifold advantages and rewards which reinforce it, also involves incidental frustrations. The individual must curb certain of his impulses if he is to secure the cooperation of his fellows, and when he fails to do so he experiences the application of painful social sanctions. These frustrations, as always, generate aggressive tendencies.[11] The latter cannot, however, be fully expressed within the in-group, lest mutual aid be withdrawn and further sanctions imposed. Consequently they are displaced toward the outside and drained off in the form of antagonistic sentiments and hostile behavior toward other groups. Intergroup antagonism is thus the inevitable concomitant and counterpart of in-group solidarity.

The tendency to exalt the in-group and to depreciate other

[10] Cf. W. G. Sumner, *Folkways* (Boston, 1906), p. 12.

[11] Cf. J. Dollard, L. W. Doob, N. E. Miller, O. H. Mowrer, and R. R. Sears, *Frustration and Aggression* (New Haven, 1939).

groups, a phenomenon technically known as "ethnocentrism,"[12] though perhaps originally associated primarily with the community, has, with broadening social horizons, become characteristic of all human social groups. Today, for example, it runs the gamut from "local pride," "college spirit," and the *esprit de corps* of a business organization to religious intolerance, race prejudice, the "class struggle," and international conflict. However deplorable from an ethical point of view, it is as inevitable as social life itself; at best it is capable only of being directed into channels that are socially less seriously disruptive.

Since its members are experienced in face-to-face cooperation, a community is ordinarily able to achieve concerted action, at least in emergencies, whether it does so under informal leaders or under chiefs and deliberative bodies with culturally defined authority and functions. Moreover, as the fundamental locus of social control, it maintains internal order and conformity to traditional norms of behavior, if not through formal judicial organs and procedures, at least through the collective application of sanctions when public opinion is aroused by serious deviations. Basically, then, the community is a political group, as well as a localized, face-to-face, culture-bearing in-group. In it is to be sought the germ of government, however simple and informal the organs and procedures.

It should be pointed out incidentally that government, as seen in cross-cultural perspective, has a second primary function. Besides serving as a means of channelizing collective action and social control, which justifies it to the governed, it offers to those in authority an opportunity to use their power for selfish aggrandizement. To the barbaric chieftain, the feudal lord, and the municipal boss, alike, accrue special privilege and pelf. So long as rulers preserve law and order, and their exploitative activities are not disproportionate to the social services they render, people do not ordinarily begrudge them their personal emoluments. Excesses in exploitation, however, tend to precipitate changes in the governing personnel.

Social relationships, even face-to-face ones, are probably never confined exclusively to the community, unless it is completely isolated, like the Polar Eskimos who, when first visited by Ross,[13]

---

[12] See W. G. Sumner, *Folkways* (Boston, 1906), p. 13; G. P. Murdock, "Ethnocentrism," *Encyclopaedia of the Social Sciences*, V (1931), 613–14.

[13] J. Ross, *A Voyage of Discovery* (London, 1819), p. 110.

were surprised to discover that they were not the only human inhabitants of the earth. Trade, intermarriage, and other forces create personal ties between members of different communities, on the basis of which peace and order may be widely extended. The warlikeness and atomism of simple societies have been grossly exaggerated. Primitive man is as capable as ourselves of perceiving the advantages to be obtained through peaceful intercourse with his neighbors, and of controlling his ethnocentric prejudices in order to reap these advantages. Even in regions where war is endemic, it is not waged all of the time nor with all surrounding groups; at the worst, armed truces or temporary alliances occur. Far more commonly, however, peaceful intercommunication prevails as the norm over wide areas.

The extension of personal relationships beyond the community may be facilitated by various cultural devices, e.g., local exogamy, blood brotherhood, safe-conduct, and market peace. It may be regularized by the development of social groups which cut across community lines, e.g., sibs, religious sects, and social classes. Finally, it may be consolidated by political unification, by the organization of a number of local groups under a single district, tribal, or state government. While many societies have followed this last course, an approximately equal number have developed no genuine political integration transcending the community. Evidence on pre-European governmental organization is available for 212 of our sample societies. In 108, each community is politically independent; in 104, definite governmental institutions unite several or many communities into larger organized groups of varying magnitude.

Among the factors favoring wider political organization, settled life appears to be peculiarly important. Table 10 shows that the bands of migratory tribes are usually politically independent, whereas the villages and settlements of sedentary populations are more commonly organized into larger aggregates.

TABLE 10

Community Organization	Bands	Neighborhoods	Villages	Totals
Politically independent	28	8	68	104
Politically dependent	5	4	93	102
TOTALS	33	12	161	206

The problem of achieving concerted action and maintaining law and order becomes far more complex in a larger political society than in a single community. Informal modes of consensus, reciprocity, and social control do not operate where face-to-face association is lacking, and must be supplemented by formal mechanisms and procedures. The interpersonal relationships which bind the members of the larger society together are, of necessity, relatively abstract or conventional rather than concrete or face-to-face. To be sure, they are ordinarily patterned after the intimate relationships developed within the community, but these become formalized and stereotyped as they are extended. The habits of personal interaction which largely govern the relationship of a villager and his local headman, for example, are conventionalized in terms of formal etiquette and of explicitly defined rights and duties when they are extended to apply to the impersonal relationship of a subject to his tribal chief or king. Similarly, rules of judicial procedure tend to supplant informal discussion, systems of taxation and tribute to replace gift-giving, and specialized officials to take over the several functions of the unspecialized local headman.

Even with complex governmental organization, the community normally survives as a political unit, albeit a subordinate one, and a relative simplicity and face-to-face quality still characterize, as a rule, its regulative forms.[14] For this reason, comparative studies of community organization are not vitiated by differences in political complexity. One may, however, seriously question the validity of those comparative studies of government which deal with the largest political aggregates in diverse societies, whether they be communities, organized tribes, or complex states. The Arunta band and the Inca empire, for example, are not comparable units, although it might well be profitable to compare the former with the local Peruvian *ayllu*, or the governmental institutions of the Incas with the Dahomean monarchy.

No special analysis of political structures was made for the present study, and none will be attempted here. The community, however, is one of the social groupings which we shall find to operate significantly in the channeling of kinship nomenclature and sexual behavior, and for this reason it has been necessary to analyze

[14] Cf. the New England "town meeting" in our own society.

it in its relations to the larger political society as well as to its constituent kin groups.

One type of social structure which often transcends the community is the organization into social classes. Information on class stratification was assembled in the hope that the material might prove significant in the interpretation of sexual and kinship behavior. Although this hope has not on the whole been realized, the data are summarized in Table 11 as possibly of general interest.

TABLE 11

Social Class Stratification	Slavery Present	Slavery Absent	No Data on Slavery	Totals
Complex structure of social classes	16	14	2	32
Hereditary aristocracy and commoners	15	18	6	39
Social classes based directly on wealth	10	5	0	15
Wealth distinctions without formal classes	7	16	3	26
Social classes absent	0	72	2	74
No data on class stratification	14	8	42	64
TOTALS	62	133	55	250

Slavery is distinguished in the table from other types of class structure, and the societies possessing and lacking slaves as a definite status group are enumerated in separate columns according to the class typing of the rest of the population. When war captives receive little differential treatment and are speedily adopted into the tribe, a society is considered as lacking a true slave class. A class structure is ranked as complex if it includes three or more definitely stratified groups other than slaves, or if it is complicated by the presence of hereditary and endogamous castes. A distinction is made between types of class structure based predominantly upon wealth and those in which privileged status is reported as primarily hereditary. For a number of societies, differences in wealth are reported to exist but to be associated with no important differences in behavior, thus resembling individual distinctions in skill, valor, and piety rather than status gradations in the stricter sense. These have been distinguished in the tabulation from other classless societies on the one hand and from wealth-stratified societies on the other.

As might be expected, social stratification is especially characteristic of sedentary populations. Slavery, for example, is reported present in 55 societies with settled villages or neighborhoods and absent in 94, whereas it occurs in only 3 of the tribes organized in migratory bands and is specified to be absent in 33. Genuine social classes appear in none of the societies of our sample that are organized in bands, but occur in a majority of those with settled communities, as Table 12 reveals.

TABLE 12

Class Stratification	Bands	Settled Communities	Totals
Complex structure of social classes	0	31	31
Hereditary aristocracy and commoners	0	38	38
Social classes based directly on wealth	0	14	14
Wealth distinctions without formal classes	7	19	26
Social classes absent	27	44	71
TOTALS	34	146	180

Social classes operate not only to unite members of different local groups but also to segment the community itself and to complicate its social structure. Thus a village may be divided into nobles and commoners or into a number of castes. Participation tends to be greater within such groups than between them, and significant cultural differences may emerge. It has been shown by Warner,[15] for example, that a typical New England city is segmented horizontally into six social classes, each with its distinctive cultural characteristics, that intimate social participation is confined primarily to members of the same "clique" within a social class and secondarily to persons belonging to cliques in the same stratum, and that intercourse between classes takes place largely through more formal associations which override class boundaries.

Probably the most significant differences in the internal organization of the community result from the varying ways in which its structure is integrated with that of the varying types of kin groups. In many instances, as has been seen in Chapters 3 and 4, the community itself may be a kin group. Local groups of this type may be collectively designated as *kin-communities*. Among the 222 societies in our sample for which sufficient information is available

[15] W. L. Warner and P. S. Lunt, *The Social Life of a Modern Community* (New Haven, 1941).

on community organization, there are 81 with kin-communities. They include 15 with endogamous bilateral demes, 13 with exogamous patri-demes, 2 with matri-demes, 45 with patrilocal clan-communities, 2 with matrilocal clan-communities, and 4 with avunculocal clan-communities. In some other societies the community is normally divided into a number of clan-barrios. Local groups of this type may be called *segmented communities*. In our sample, 36 societies are characterized by segmented communities— 27 with patrilocal clan-barrios, and 9 with matrilocal clan-barrios. Local groups which are neither segmented into clans, nor themselves organized as clans or demes, may be called *unsegmented communities*. In our sample, 105 societies possess unsegmented communities. In 48 of them neither clans nor extended families are present, and in 17 others clans are absent and extended families unreported. If clans are absent but extended families are present, the community can be regarded as only partially rather than completely unsegmented. This is the case in 40 of our societies—7 with bilocal extended families, 19 with patri-families, 10 with matri-families, and 4 with avuncu-families.

Communities of any of the above types may be further classified, on the basis of the presence or absence of social classes, as *stratified communities* or *unstratified communities*. In our own society, for example, communities are normally stratified but unsegmented.

The classification proposed by Steward [16] for band organization may be compared with that presented above. Steward's "patrilineal band," which is said to be characterized by "land ownership, political autonomy, patrilocal residence, band or local exogamy, and patrilineal land inheritance," [17] includes both our patri-deme and our patrilocal clan-community. His "matrilineal band" embraces our matri-deme and our matrilocal clan-community. His "composite band," which is stated to differ from the "patrilineal band" in not having "band exogamy, patrilocal residence, or land inheritance by patrilineal relatives," [18] would include both the endogamous deme and the unsegmented community in our classification, and probably the segmented community as well.

[16] J. H. Steward, "The Economic and Social Basis of Primitive Bands," *Essays in Anthropology Presented to A. L. Kroeber* (Berkeley, 1936), p. 331.
[17] *Ibid.*, p. 334.
[18] *Ibid.*, p. 338.

A recurrent feature of community organization, noted by Linton,[19] is an internal division into factions, usually two in number. We need instance here only the famous Tartharol and Teivaliol divisions of the Todas, the rivalrous districts of Faea and Ravenga on the tiny isle of Tikopia, the "hostile" and "friendly" factions among the Hopi, and the moiety cleavages of the Apinaye and many other tribes. Miner [20] has described a striking dual alignment in a rural French-Canadian parish, based ostensibly on affiliation with different political parties.

So widespread are such factional divisions, so frequently is their number precisely two, so commonly do they oppose one another in games and other activities, and so often are their reciprocal relations marked by rivalry, boasting, and covert forms of aggression that the phenomenon seems scarcely accidental. Ethnocentrism suggests a possible common function. A dual organization of a community, or of a larger social group, may provide a sort of safety valve whereby aggression generated by in-group disciplines may be drained off internally in socially regulated and harmless ways instead of being translated into out-group hostility and warfare. If this highly tentative hypothesis is valid, opposing factions should be more characteristic of peaceful than of warlike communities. Perhaps herein lies the fundamental social justification of a two-party political system in a modern democratic state.

The analysis of familial, kin, and local groups in the foregoing chapters by no means represents a complete survey of human social organization. Economic, recreational, religious, and ceremonial associations, for example, have been mentioned but not discussed, and the same is true of age, sex, and status groupings. Only a fraction, indeed, of the interpersonal and group relationships which constitute the social situations within which man's behavior is learned and enacted have been presented, and the environmental and technological factors, which are likewise of great importance in influencing behavior, have been omitted altogether. The nature of our primary scientific task has limited us to a consideration of the social groups which appear peculiarly effective in channeling kinship and sexual behavior.

---

[19] R. Linton, *The Study of Man* (New York, 1936), p. 229.
[20] H. M. Miner, *St. Denis* (Chicago, 1939), pp. 58–60, 68–9.

6

ANALYSIS OF KINSHIP

THE SCIENTIFIC significance of kinship systems was first appreciated by Morgan[1] in what is perhaps the most original and brilliant single achievement in the history of anthropology. That many of Morgan's particular interpretations are no longer acceptable does not diminish the luster of his work. Since his day, major contributions to the theory and analysis of kinship have been made by Rivers, Kroeber, Lowie, and Radcliffe-Brown, and important additional light has been shed on the subject by Aginsky, Eggan, Evans-Pritchard, Gifford, Kirchhoff, Lawrence, Lesser, Levi-Strauss, Malinowski, Opler, Sapir, Brenda Seligman, Spier, Spoehr, Tax, Thurnwald, Warner, White, and others. No other anthropological topic, in all probability, has been the beneficiary of so much creative effort. Hence the present author, in sketching the background for his own contribution, must perforce draw heavily on the work of his predecessors.

A kinship system differs in one important respect from the types of social organization previously considered. In the various forms of the family, sib, clan, and community, interpersonal relationships are structured in such a manner as to aggregate individuals into social groups. A kinship system, however, is not a social group, nor does it ever correspond to an organized aggregation of individuals.

[1] L. H. Morgan, "Systems of Consanguinity and Affinity of the Human Family," *Smithsonian Contributions to Knowledge*, XVII (1870), 1–590.

It is merely, as the name implies, a structured system of relationships, in which individuals are bound one to another by complex interlocking and ramifying ties. Particular kinship bonds, isolated from others, may and often do serve to unite individuals into social groups, such as a nuclear family or a lineage, but kinship systems as wholes are not, and do not produce, social aggregates.

The point of departure for the analysis of kinship is the nuclear family.[2] Universally it is in this social group that the developing child establishes his first habits of reciprocal behavior, his first interpersonal relationships. He learns to respond in particular ways toward his father, his mother, his brothers, and his sisters, and to expect certain kinds of behavior in return. His responses, however individualized at first, are gradually modified, as learning and socialization progress, to conform in general to the prevailing cultural norms. Once learned, his behavior in these primary intra-family relationships tends to be extended or "generalized" to persons outside of the family as his circle of personal contacts broadens.[3] Such generalized behavior is rewarded and reinforced when consistent with cultural norms. Otherwise it is not rewarded, or is even punished, and thus becomes extinguished. Discrimination arises, and a situation is created in which distinctive modes of behavior toward other persons can occur and become established, either by trial and error or through imitative learning. In either case, it is the parents, elder siblings, other relatives, and neighbors who set the standards and exert the pressures which ultimately produce conformity with social expectations.

Intra-family relationships are not only the first to be learned in infancy and childhood; they continue to be an individual's most intimate relationships in adulthood. The child, now grown up and married, tends to recreate with his own children and spouse the behavior which his parents exhibited toward him, his siblings, and one another. Family relationships are of necessity highly functional, since they are universally involved in many of life's most important activities—economic cooperation, household routines, sex, reproduction, child care, and education. It is scarcely surprising, therefore,

---

[2] Cf. B. Malinowski, "Kinship," *Man*, XXX (1930), 23-5.

[3] Cf. E. E. Evans-Pritchard, "The Nature of Kinship Extensions," *Man*, XXXII (1932), 13.

that they set the standard for all other kin relationships—standards to which the latter must conform or from which they must be differentiated.

Within the nuclear family are found eight characteristic relationships. Though functionally differentiated, all tend to be characterized, as compared with extra-family relationships, by a high degree of reciprocal cooperation, loyalty, solidarity, and affection. Despite cultural differences, each of the eight primary relationships reveals a markedly similar fundamental character in all societies, in consequence of the universality of the family's basic functions. These relationships, with their most typical features, are as follows:

Husband and wife: economic specialization and cooperation; sexual cohabitation; joint responsibility for support, care, and upbringing of children; well defined reciprocal rights with respect to property, divorce, spheres of authority, etc.

Father and son: economic cooperation in masculine activities under leadership of the father; obligation of material support, vested in father during childhood of son, in son during old age of father; responsibility of father for instruction and discipline of son; duty of obedience and respect on part of son, tempered by some measure of comradeship.

Mother and daughter: relationship parallel to that between father and son, but with more emphasis on child care and economic cooperation and less on authority and material support.

Mother and son: dependence of son during infancy; imposition of early disciplines by the mother; moderate economic cooperation during childhood of son; early development of a lifelong incest taboo; material support by son during old age of mother.

Father and daughter: responsibility of father for protection and material support prior to marriage of daughter; economic cooperation, instruction, and discipline appreciably less prominent than in father-son relationship; playfulness common in infancy of daughter, but normally yields to a measure of reserve with the development of a strong incest taboo.

Elder and younger brother: relationship of playmates, developing into that of comrades; economic cooperation under leadership of elder; moderate responsibility of elder for instruction and discipline of younger.

Elder and younger sister: relationship parallel to that between elder and younger brother but with more emphasis upon physical care of the younger sister.

Brother and sister: early relationship of playmates, varying with relative age; gradual development of an incest taboo, commonly coupled with some measure of reserve; moderate economic cooperation; partial assumption of parental role, especially by the elder.

All of the above relationships, naturally with local elaborations, are found in any complete family with at least two children of each sex. A typical male in every society, at some time in his life, plays the roles of husband, father, son, and brother in some nuclear family, and a female, those of wife, mother, daughter, and sister. Incest taboos, however, prevent a man from being husband and father in the same family in which he is son and brother, and a woman from being wife and mother in the family where she is daughter and sister. Both, on marrying, become members of a nuclear family other than that into which they were born. Hence, as we have seen, every normal adult individual in any society belongs to two nuclear families, the family of orientation in which he was born and reared and the family of procreation which he establishes by marriage. He is a son or daughter and a brother or sister in the former, a husband or wife and a father or mother in the latter.

It is this universal fact of individual membership in two nuclear families that gives rise to kinship systems. If marriages normally took place within the nuclear family, there would be only family organization; kinship would be confined to the limits of the family. But by virtue of the fact that individuals regularly belong to two families, every person forms a link between the members of his family of orientation and those of his family of procreation, and ramifying series of such links bind numbers of individuals to one another through kinship ties.

The term *primary relatives* is applied to those who belong to the same nuclear family as a particular person—his father, mother, sisters, and brothers in his family of orientation, and his husband or wife, his sons, and his daughters in his family of procreation. Each of these relatives will have his own primary relatives, most of whom will not be included among the primary relatives of Ego. From the point of view of the latter these may be called *secondary relatives*. Potentially, a person can have 33 distinct kinds of secondary relatives, namely: FaFa (paternal grandfather), FaMo (paternal grandmother), FaBr (paternal uncle), FaSi (paternal aunt), FaWi (stepmother), FaSo (half brother), FaDa (half sister), MoFa, MoMo, MoBr, MoSi, MoHu, MoSo, MoDa, BrWi, BrSo, BrDa, SiHu, SiSo, SiDa, WiFa (or HuFa), WiMo (or HuMo), WiBr (or HuBr), WiSi (or HuSi), WiHu (or HuWi, i.e., co-spouse), WiSo (or HuSo), WiDa (or HuDa), SoWi, SoSo, SoDa, DaHu, DaSo, and DaDa. Each secondary relative, in turn, has primary relatives who are neither primary nor secondary relatives of Ego, and who may thus be termed *tertiary relatives.* Among these there are 151 possibilities, including eight great-grandparents, eight first cousins, the spouses of all uncles, aunts, nephews, and nieces, and many others. It would be possible in similar fashion to distinguish quaternary relatives (like first cousins once removed), quinary relatives (like second cousins), etc., but for our purposes it will be sufficient to class all who are more remote than tertiary relatives as *distant relatives.*

Primary relatives are linked by bonds of blood or biological kinship, with one exception, namely, husband and wife, who, because of incest taboos, are linked only by a marital bond. This gives rise to a fundamental dichotomy in relatives at all levels. Whenever the connection between two relatives, whether primary, secondary, tertiary, or distant, includes one or more marital links, the two have no necessary biological relationship and are classed as *affinal relatives.* WiMo, DaHu, and MoBrWi are examples. Relatives between whom every connecting link is one of blood or common ancestry, on the other hand, are known as *consanguineal relatives.*

The science of genetics tells us the exact probabilities of common heredity between consanguineal relatives of each degree. A person can be expected to share, on the average, exactly half of the hereditary factors or genes of any primary consanguineal relative. He inherits half of those possessed by his father and half of those carried by his mother. He transmits approximately half of his own to each son and daughter. With each brother and sister (except identical twins) he is likely to share 50 per cent of the half inherited from the father plus 50 per cent of the half inherited from the mother, or half of the total heredity of the sibling. The common heredity of secondary consanguineal relatives approximates one quarter, and of tertiary relatives one eighth. If a pair of kinsmen can trace consanguineal relationship in two lines, the common heredity is the sum of those in both lines. For example, a man and his FaSiDa, being tertiary relatives, ordinarily have one eighth of their heredity in common, but where cross-cousin marriage prevails and the FaSiDa is at the same time a MoBrDa, the couple will share one quarter of the same biological potentialities. In homogeneous and closely inbred populations, of course, the actual biological similarity between related individuals can considerably exceed the proportions indicated above, but even in the most heterogeneous society it cannot be less.[4]

Kinship systems constitute one of the universals of human culture. The author is not aware of any society, however primitive or decadent, that does not recognize a system of culturally patterned relationships between kinsmen. Remembrance of kinship ties naturally tends to disappear with time and with remoteness of actual relationship, but social groupings, like those based on common residence or descent, often help to preserve the memory or tradition of certain kinship bonds for surprising periods. Indeed, the author knows of no society which does not reckon kinship well beyond tertiary relatives, at least in some directions. In many small tribes every member acknowledges some specific kinship tie with every other member. In aboriginal Australia, where preoccupation with kinship was carried to unusual lengths, it is said that a native could, at least theoretically, traverse the entire continent, stopping at each tribal boundary to compare notes on relatives, and at the end of his journey know precisely whom in the local group he should address as grandmother, father-in-law, sister, etc., whom he might associate freely with, whom he must avoid, whom he might or might not have sex relations with, and so on.

Even if we ignore for the moment some of the finer distinctions between relatives made by some societies, any individual in any society has potentially seven different kinds of primary relatives, 33 of secondary relatives, 151 of tertiary relatives, and geometrically increasing numbers of distant relatives of various degrees. To associate a distinctive pattern of behavior with each potentially

---

[4] The geneticist will realize, of course, that this discussion deals with probabilities and ignores chance permutations of genes as well as certain sex-chromosome phenomena, mutations, identical twinning, etc.

distinguishable category of relationship would be impracticable and intolerably burdensome, and no society attempts to do so. The problem is solved in all societies by reducing the number of culturally distinguished categories to a manageable number through grouping or coalescence. The varying methods by which such coalescence is accomplished give rise to many of the principal differences in kinship structure. Before they are considered, however, it is necessary to introduce the subject of kinship terminology.

Part of the reciprocal behavior characterizing every relationship between kinsmen consists of a verbal element, the terms by which each addresses the other. Although some peoples commonly employ personal names even among relatives, all societies make at least some use of special kinship terms, and the great majority use them predominantly or exclusively in intercourse between relatives. An interesting and fairly common usage intermediate between personal names and kinship terms is called *teknonymy*.[5] In its most typical form it consists in calling a person who has had a child "father (or mother) of So-and-so," combining the parental term with the child's name, instead of using a personal name or a kinship term.

Kinship terms are technically classified in three different ways—by their mode of use, by their linguistic structure, and by their range of application.[6] As regards their use, kinship terms may be employed either in direct address or in indirect reference. A *term of address* is one used in speaking to a relative; it is part of the linguistic behavior characteristic of the particular interpersonal relationship. A *term of reference* is one used to designate a relative in speaking about him to a third person; it is thus not part of the relationship itself but a word denoting a person who occupies a particular kinship status. In English, most terms for consanguineal relatives are employed in both ways, though "nephew" and "niece" are seldom used in direct address. Terms for affinal relatives are rarely used in address by English speakers, consanguineal terms or personal names being substituted. Thus a man normally addresses his mother-in-law as "mother," his stepfather as "father," and his brother-in-law by the

[5] See E. B. Tylor, "On a Method of Investigating the Development of Institutions," *Journal of the Royal Anthropological Institute*, XVIII (1889), 248.
[6] Cf. R. H. Lowie, "A Note on Relationship Terminologies," *American Anthropologist*, n.s., XXX (1928), 264.

latter's given name or a nickname. The special terms of address in English are mainly diminutive or colloquial, e.g., "grandpa," "granny," "auntie," "dad," "papa," "ma," "mummy," "hubby," "sis," and "sonny." Some peoples have completely distinct sets of terms for address and reference, others make only grammatical distinctions or none at all, and still others have varying combinations.

Terms of reference are normally more specific in their application than terms of address. Thus, in English, "mother" as a term of reference ordinarily denotes only the actual mother, but as a term of address it is commonly applied also to a stepmother, a mother-in-law, or even an unrelated elderly woman. Moreover, terms of reference are usually more complete than terms of address. It may be customary to use only personal names in addressing certain relatives, or a taboo may prevent all conversation with them, with the result that terms of address for such kinsmen may be completely lacking. Furthermore, terms of address tend to reveal more duplication and overlapping than do terms of reference. For these reasons, terms of reference are much more useful in kinship analysis, and are consequently used exclusively in the present work.

When classified according to linguistic structure, kinship terms are distinguished as elementary, derivative, and descriptive.[7] An *elementary term* is an irreducible word, like English "father" or "nephew," which cannot be analyzed into component lexical elements with kinship meanings. A *derivative term* is one which, like English "grandfather," "sister-in-law," or "stepson," is compounded from an elementary term and some other lexical element which does not have primarily a kinship meaning. A *descriptive term* is one which, like Swedish *farbror* (father's brother), combines two or more elementary terms to denote a specific relative. In actual use, the qualifying lexical element in derivative terms is quite commonly dropped unless there is need to be precise. Thus, in English, a man is as likely to say "my son" as "my stepson" in referring to his wife's son by a previous marriage, and in many societies a mother's sister is optionally referred to as "mother" or designated by a derivative term translatable as "little mother." In all languages it is apparently

[7] Cf. R. H. Lowie, "Kinship," *Encyclopaedia of the Social Sciences,* VIII (1932), 568; K. Davis and W. L. Warner, "Structural Analysis of Kinship," *American Anthropologist,* n.s., XXXIX (1937), 303.

possible to resort to a descriptive term if the reference of any other term is ambiguous. Thus in English, if I mention "my sister-in-law" and am asked to specify which one, I can refer to either "my brother's wife" or "my wife's sister," or even to "my elder brother's second wife," etc. Except for such supplementary clarifying use, descriptive terms appear only sporadically in kinship terminologies, except, as our data show,[8] in a band extending across central Africa from west to east, where a number of Sudanese, Nilotic, and Bantu tribes use descriptive terminology very freely.

As regards range of application, kinship terms are differentiated as denotative and classificatory. A *denotative term* is one which applies only to relatives in a single kinship category as defined by generation, sex, and genealogical connection. Sometimes such a term, for a particular speaker, can denote only one person, as in the case of English "father," "mother," "husband," "wife," "father-in-law," and "mother-in-law."[9] Often, however, a denotative term applies to several persons of identical kinship connection, as do the English words "brother," "sister," "son," "daughter," "son-in-law," and "daughter-in-law." A *classificatory term* is one that applies to persons of two or more kinship categories, as these are defined by generation, sex, and genealogical connection. Thus, in English, "grandfather" includes both the father's father and the mother's father; "aunt" denotes a sister of either parent or a wife of either a maternal or a paternal uncle; "brother-in-law" applies equally to a wife's or a husband's brother or a sister's husband; and "cousin" embraces all collateral relatives of one's own generation, and some of adjacent generations, irrespective of their sex, their line of genealogical connection, or even their degree of remoteness. It is primarily through the liberal use of classificatory terms that all societies reduce the number of kinship categories from the thousands that are theoretically distinguishable to the very modest number, perhaps 25 as an approximate average,[10] which it has everywhere been found practicable to recognize in actual usage.

[8] Cf. also R. H. Lowie, *Culture and Ethnology* (New York, 1917), pp. 105–7.

[9] These have been called "isolating terms." See K. Davis and W. L. Warner, "Structural Analysis of Kinship," *American Anthropologist*, n.s., XXXIX (1937), 300–1.

[10] Cf. A. L. Kroeber, "Classificatory Systems of Relationship," *Journal of the Royal Anthropological Institute*, XXXIX (1909), 79.

From Morgan's day until quite recently it was customary to speak of "classificatory" and "descriptive" kinship systems, the former being regarded as characteristic of primitive tribes and the latter of civilized mankind. These distinctions are now known to be wholly erroneous. The words "classificatory" and "descriptive" refer to particular terms, not to whole systems of terminology. As a matter of fact, with the exception of a few African societies which resort to descriptive terminology on a wholesale scale, every known kinship system is classificatory in the sense of making extensive use of classificatory terms. The systems of western Europe, including our own, employ classificatory terms at least as freely as do those of the average primitive tribe. Indeed, the English system is identical in type to the systems of the Andamanese pygmies, the Ona of Tierra del Fuego, and the Eskimos, and is even technically classified as an "Eskimo system." [11]

The several categories of primary relatives (Fa, Mo, Br, Si, Hu, Wi, So, Da) are denoted by as many different terms in the great majority of societies. These terms are nearly always elementary, though in seven societies in our sample siblings are called by descriptive terms, e.g., "father's daughter" or "mother's daughter" instead of a special term for sister. Terms for primary relatives may be either denotative or classificatory, but if they are the latter they usually include one primary and one or more secondary relatives rather than two categories of primary relatives. Exceptions occur, though they are rare. Occasionally, for example, a term meaning "spouse" is employed for both husband and wife, or a term meaning "child" for both son and daughter, or a sibling term is used by both sexes but denotes "brother" to one and "sister" to the other. In general, however, all primary relatives are terminologically differentiated from each other. In addition, the majority of societies distinguish elder from younger brothers and sisters by separate terms, thus fully reflecting all functional differences in relationships within the nuclear family.

In the designation of secondary, tertiary, and distant relatives, though new elementary terms are applied to distinctive relatives, derivative and descriptive terms appear with increasing frequency.

---

[11] Cf. L. Spier, "The Distribution of Kinship Systems in North America," *University of Washington Publications in Anthropology,* I (1925), 79.

Denotative terms become rare with secondary relatives and practically disappear with tertiary kinsmen, giving way to classificatory terminology. This results in large measure, of course, from the increasing number of potentially distinguishable categories—33 for secondary and 151 for tertiary relatives—and from the correspondingly increased practical necessity of reducing the recognized number by grouping or coalescence. This can be achieved either by extending a term originally denoting some primary relative to one or more categories of secondary or remoter kinsmen, or by applying a distinctive term to several categories of secondary, tertiary, or distant relatives. Our own kinship system follows the latter method exclusively, reflecting the isolated character of our nuclear family, but in cross-cultural perspective the former method is rather more common.

A classificatory term can arise only by ignoring one or more fundamental distinctions between relatives which, if given full linguistic recognition, would result in designating them by different denotative terms. The pioneer researches of Kroeber and Lowie [12] have led to the recognition of six major criteria which, when linguistically recognized as a basis of terminological differentiation, yield denotative terms but the ignoring of any one of which produces classificatory terms. These criteria are generation, sex, affinity, collaterality, bifurcation, and polarity. They are the criteria employed above in calculating the number of potential categories of primary, secondary, and tertiary relatives. In addition, the same authors have isolated three subsidiary criteria—relative age, speaker's sex, and decedence—the linguistic recognition of which makes a classificatory term less inclusive or a denotative term more specific. These nine criteria have an empirical as well as a logical basis; severally and in combination they appear to include all the principles actually employed by human societies in the linguistic classification and differentiation of kinsmen. Each will now be considered individually.

[12] See, in particular, A. L. Kroeber, "Classificatory Systems of Relationship," Journal of the Royal Anthropological Institute, XXXIX (1909), 77–85; R. H. Lowie, "Relationship Terms," Encyclopaedia Britannica (14th edit., London, 1929), XIX, 84–9. Cf. also K. Davis and W. L. Warner, "Structural Analysis of Kinship," American Anthropologist, n.s., XXXIX (1937), 291–313.

The *criterion of generation* rests on a biological foundation. The facts of reproduction automatically align people in different generations: Ego's own generation, which includes brothers, sisters, and cousins; a first ascending generation, which embraces parents and their siblings and cousins; a first descending generation, which includes sons, daughters, nephews, and nieces; a second ascending or grandparental generation; a second descending or grandchildren's generation; and so on. Since marriages in most societies normally occur between persons of the same generation, affinal relatives tend to be aligned by generation in the same manner as consanguineal relatives. Most kinship systems give extensive recognition to generation differences. Our own, for example, ignores them in only a single unimportant instance, namely, when the term "cousin" is applied to a "cousin once (or twice) removed," i.e., one or two generations above or below Ego. Perhaps the most striking examples of classificatory terms resulting from the ignoring of generation differences are found in the so-called "Crow" and "Omaha" types of cross-cousin terminology. In the former, the children of the father's sister are called by the same terms as paternal uncle and aunt, while the mother's brothers' children are classed with fraternal nephews and nieces. In an Omaha system, the situation is roughly reversed; the father's sisters' children are classed with sororal nephews and nieces, and the mother's brothers' children with maternal uncles and aunts.[13]

The *criterion of sex* derives from another biological difference, that between males and females, and is also widely taken into account in kinship terminology. Our own system, for example, ignores sex in respect to only one basic term, namely, "cousin." Some societies employ a single classificatory term for both a son and a daughter, or for a parent-in-law of either sex. The commonest instances of the ignoring of sex in kinship terminology are found, however, in the second descending and second ascending generations, where many societies have terms approximately equivalent

[13] In consequence of merging (see below) it often happens that the term for FaSiSo is "father," that for MoBrSo is "son," and that for MoBrDa is "daughter" in a Crow system, and that the term for MoBrDa is "mother" in an Omaha system. It has often been overlooked that this is only an incidental and not a fundamental feature of Crow and Omaha terminology.

to "grandchild" or "grandparent." It is, of course, in precisely these generations that an individual is most likely to find relatives who are mainly too young to be significantly differentiated sexually or too old to be sexually active.

The *criterion of affinity* arises from the universal social phenomena of marriage and incest taboos. In consequence of the latter, marital partners cannot normally be close consanguineal relatives. Among relatives of like degree, therefore, whether they be primary, secondary, tertiary, or distant, there will always be one group of consanguineal kinsmen, all equally related biologically to Ego, and a second group of affinal relatives whose connection to Ego is traced through at least one marital link and who are biologically unrelated or only remotely related to him. This difference is widely recognized in kinship terminology. In our own system, for example, it is completely ignored only in the term "uncle," which includes the husbands of aunts as well as the brothers of parents, and in the word "aunt," which similarly includes the wives of uncles as well as the sisters of parents. Elsewhere we recognize affinity only partially, through the use of derivative terms with the prefix "step-" or the suffix "-in-law," in which respect we differ from most societies, who ordinarily apply elementary terms to affinal relatives. Classificatory terms resulting from the ignoring of this criterion are particularly common in societies with preferential rules of marriage. For example, under a rule of preferential cross-cousin marriage with the FaSiDa, the latter may be called by the same term as wife, and a single term may suffice for FaSi and WiMo.

The *criterion of collaterality* rests on the biological fact that among consanguineal relatives of the same generation and sex, some will be more closely akin to Ego than others. A direct ancestor, for example, will be more nearly related than his sibling or cousin, and a lineal descendant than the descendant of a sibling or cousin. Our own kinship system consistently recognizes the criterion of collaterality and, with the sole exception of "cousin," never employs the same term for consanguineal kinsmen related to Ego in different degrees. The majority of societies, however, ignore collaterality with greater frequency, and in this way arrive at various classificatory terms. The phenomenon of grouping lineal and collateral kinsmen, or relatives of different degrees, under a single classificatory term is technically known as *merging*.[14] Among the relatives most commonly merged are a parent and his sibling of the same sex, a sibling and a parallel cousin (child of a FaBr or MoSi), a wife and her sister, and a son or daughter and a nephew or niece.

The *criterion of bifurcation* (forking) applies only to secondary and more remote relatives, and rests on the biological fact that they may be linked to Ego through either a male or a female connecting relative. Recognition of this criterion involves applying one term to a kinsman if the relative linking him to Ego is male and quite another term if the connecting relative is female. Our own kinship system ignores the criterion of bifurcation throughout, and derives many of its classificatory terms from this fact. Thus we call a person "grandfather" or "grandmother" irrespective of whether he is the father's or the mother's parent; "uncle" or "aunt" regardless of the sex of the parent through whom the relationship is traced; "brother-in-law" or "sister-in-law," "nephew" or "niece," "grandson" or "granddaughter," without considering the sex of the connecting relative. The majority of societies, however, make terminological distinctions between some or most of these relatives.

The *criterion of polarity*,[15] the last of the six major criteria for differentiating kinship terminology, arises from the sociological fact that it requires two persons to constitute a social relationship. Linguistic recognition of this criterion produces two terms for each kin relationship, one by which each participant can denote the other. When polarity is ignored, the relationship is treated as a unit and both participants apply the same classificatory term to each other. In our own kinship system polarity is recognized throughout, with the sole exception of the term "cousin." The fact that two brothers, two sisters, two brothers-in-law, or two sisters-in-law also apply the same term to one another is really an incidental result of the

[14] See R. H. Lowie, *Culture and Ethnology* (New York, 1917), p. 109.

[15] In the literature this criterion is commonly called "reciprocity." See, for example, A. L. Kroeber, "Classificatory Systems of Relationship," *Journal of the Royal Anthropological Institute*, XXXIX (1909), 80–1; R. H. Lowie, *Culture and Ethnology* (New York, 1917), pp. 165–6. Since the names for all the other criteria suggest a basis of differentiation, whereas "reciprocity" suggests equivalence, the name "polarity" is adopted for the sake of consistency. Moreover, "reciprocity" has another recognized technical meaning in anthropology; see B. Malinowski, *Crime and Custom in Savage Society* (London, 1926), pp. 24–7.

recognition of other criteria, as becomes clear when we observe that the same term can be used for the same relative by a relative of opposite sex, in which case the reciprocal term is different. Polarity is occasionally ignored in sibling relationships, as where a brother calls his sister by the same term that she uses for him, and in avuncular relationships, as where a maternal uncle and his sisters' children refer to one another by the same term. It is most commonly ignored, however, in the terms used by relatives two generations removed; grandparents and grandchildren in many societies refer to one another by identical terms.

The *criterion of relative age* reflects the biological fact that relatives of the same generation are rarely identical in age. Of any pair, one must almost inevitably be older than the other. While ignored completely in our own kinship system, and not treated as one of the six basic criteria in our theoretical analysis, relative age is widely taken into account in kinship terminologies. A significant majority of all systems differentiate terminologically between elder and younger siblings of the same sex, and 100 out of 245 in our sample do likewise for siblings of opposite sex. Some societies, e.g., the Yuman tribes of the American Southwest,[16] make extensive age distinctions in terminology, differentiating, for example, the elder and younger siblings of a parent and the spouses and children of an elder and a younger sibling.

The *criterion of speaker's sex* rests on the biological fact that the user of a kinship term, as well as the relative denoted by it, is necessarily either a male or a female. Kinship systems which recognize this criterion will have two terms for the same relative, one used by a male speaker and the other by a female. Among the Haida,[17] for example, there are two denotative terms for father, one employed by sons and one by daughters. To the Haida, the English word "father" would appear classificatory. The criterion of speaker's sex often operates in conjunction with the criterion of sex, with the result that the sameness or oppositeness of sex of the speaker and relative may appear more important than the actual sex of

[16] See L. Spier, "The Distribution of Kinship Systems in North America," *University of Washington Publications in Anthropology,* I (1925), 75–6.

[17] See G. P. Murdock, "Kinship and Social Behavior among the Haida," *American Anthropologist,* n.s., XXXVI (1934), 360–2.

either. This is especially common in sibling terminology, where one term (or a pair distinguishing relative age) may be used by a man for his brother and by a woman for her sister, while a different term is employed by a man for his sister and by a woman for her brother.

The *criterion of decedence,* the last and least important of the nine, is based on the biological fact of death. Like the criterion of bifurcation, it applies particularly to secondary relatives and depends upon the person through whom kinship is traced. But whereas the crucial fact in bifurcation is whether the connecting relative is male or female, in the criterion of decedence it is whether that relative is dead or alive. A very few societies, especially in California and adjacent areas,[18] have two kinship terms for certain relatives, one used during the lifetime of the connecting relative, the other after his death. The distinction occurs almost exclusively in terms for relatives who are potential spouses under preferential levirate or sororate marriage. With the death of an elder brother, for example, the status of his wife relative to his younger brother may undergo a sharp change; under the levirate she is now destined to marry the younger brother, whereas previously she had not been available to him as a wife. While not itself of great consequence, decedence completes the roster of criteria which, through linguistic recognition or non-recognition, yield most if not all of the known variations in kinship nomenclature.

Though of fundamental importance for analysis, the foregoing criteria do not of themselves explain differences in kinship terminology. The crucial scientific problem is that of discovering the factors which have led different peoples to select or reject particular criteria as a basis for differentiating kinsmen of some categories, and equating others, in arriving at a practicable number of culturally recognized categories out of the hundreds or thousands of potentially distinguishable ones. Before a solution to this problem is sought, consideration must be given to the question of the interrelations between kinship terminology and kinship behavior.

As has already been indicated, terms of address form an integral part of the culturally patterned relationships between kinsmen,

[18] See A. L. Kroeber, "Classificatory Systems of Relationship," *Journal of the Royal Anthropological Institute,* XXXIX (1909), 79. The term "decedence" is proposed by the present author.

even though they are an aspect of habitual verbal rather than gross muscular behavior. Terms of reference, on the other hand, are linguistic symbols denoting one of the two statuses involved in each such relationship (or both statuses where their polarity is ignored). However, since any status is defined in terms of the culturally expected behavior in the relationship in which it is embedded, there are *a priori* reasons for assuming a close functional congruity between terms of reference and the relationships in which the denoted kinsmen interact. The data analyzed for the present study provide abundant empirical support for this assumption, and most students of kinship have arrived at the same conclusion. Radcliffe-Brown [19] sums up existing knowledge on the subject very adequately in the statement: "we can expect to find, in the majority of human societies, a fairly close correlation between the terminological classification of kindred or relatives and the social classification. The former is revealed in kinship terminology, the latter . . . specifically in the attitudes and behavior of relatives to one another." Tax [20] states that as a general rule, subject to some exceptions, "Persons toward whom ego behaves in the same manner he will call by the same term; . . . persons to whom ego behaves in a different manner he will call by different terms."

The congruity between kinship terms and behavior patterns, though firmly established as an empirical generalization, is nevertheless not absolute. Thus as Opler [21] points out, among the Apache tribes of the Southwest differences in behavior between kinsmen sometimes exist without any corresponding differentiation in nomenclature, and terminological distinctions occur in the absence of important differences in social function. Such exceptions are specifically recognized by both Radcliffe-Brown and Tax, and they account for the more cautious statement by Lowie [22] of the same

[19] A. R. Radcliffe-Brown, "Kinship Terminologies in California," *American Anthropologist*, n.s., XXXVII (1935), 531. Cf. also W. H. R. Rivers, *Kinship and Social Organisation* (London, 1914), pp. 11–12.

[20] S. Tax, "Some Problems of Social Organization," *Social Anthropology of North American Tribes*, ed. F. Eggan (Chicago, 1937), pp. 20–1.

[21] M. E. Opler, "Apache Data concerning the Relation of Kinship Terminology to Social Classification," *American Anthropologist*, n.s., XXXIX (1937), 202–5.

[22] R. H. Lowie, *Culture and Ethnology* (New York, 1917), p. 100.

conclusion: "Where relatives whom other people distinguish are grouped together there is some likelihood that the natives regard them as representing the same relationship because they actually enjoy the same privileges or exercise the same functions in tribal life. When relatives whom other peoples group together are distinguished, there is some probability that the distinction goes hand in hand with a difference in social function."

The fact that a people applies a single classificatory term to a variety of different relatives embraced in one conventional kinship category does not imply, of course, that even the standardized behavior exhibited toward all of them is identical. In a society, for example, which extends the kinship term for mother to the father's other polygynous wives, to maternal aunts, and to the wives of the father's brothers, people do not confuse these women with one another. Everyone knows his own mother, reacts toward her in an especially intimate manner, and when necessary can readily distinguish his "classificatory mothers" from her by the use of descriptive terms. Toward these other "mothers" he acts in a generically similar manner, e.g., with respect, helpfulness, and tokens of fondness, but with an attenuation in warmth and responsiveness proportionate to their social remoteness.[23] This point is so obvious that it would require no notice if it had not been ignored by some earlier anthropologists and overemphasized by some later ones.[24]

The use of a single term for several categories of relatives usually means that the behavior toward the functionally less significant ones (the stepmothers and aunts in the above instance), though not identical with that toward the closest or most important relative (the mother), is in general more like the latter than like that exhibited toward other comparable relatives (e.g., a grandmother, paternal aunt, or mother-in-law) who are denoted by different terms. This follows a normal process of linguistic classification. A strictly parallel illustration may be cited from the field of economic relationships. The word "tenant" is applied to a person who holds tenure in landed property either for life, or from year to year, or at will, or at sufferance. In each case his relationship to his landlord

---

[23] Cf. B. Z. Seligman, "Incest and Descent," *Journal of the Royal Anthropological Institute*, LIX (1929), 271.

[24] See, for example, B. Malinowski, "Kinship," *Man*, XXX (1930), 29.

is different, but all have more in common with one another than with other subordinate economic statuses, such as those of a bailee, a debtor, an employee, or a servant. This relative generic similarity suffices to account for the common term.

Although there are substantial grounds for assuming an essential congruity between kinship terms and the culturally patterned behavior toward the relatives they denote, this by no means implies either (1) that the behavior patterns in particular societies are as sharply differentiated from one another as the associated terms, or (2) that the associated behavior patterns in different societies show an approximately equal degree of differentiation. With the exception of derivative and descriptive terms, which constitute a distinct minority, all kinship terms are independent words, and as such are completely and thus equally differentiated from one another. Patterns of kinship behavior, on the other hand, run the gamut between practical identity and extreme dissimilarity, with countless intermediate gradations. The application of completely differentiated terms to incompletely and variably differentiated phenomena results inevitably in a lack of strict comparability.

In different societies the conditions leading to the differentiation of behavior patterns in kin relationships may vary widely. In societies with complex forms of unilinear social organization, for example, the presence of such groupings as moieties, sibs, clans, sections, and extended families may, when added to the universal differentials of behavior within the nuclear family and between persons of different sex and age, readily complicate social interaction to such a degree that every linguistically recognized kinship category may be associated with a highly distinctive set of culturally patterned responses. On the other hand, bilateral societies with simple or amorphous forms of social organization, though known empirically to recognize on the average an approximately equal number of elementary kinship terms, may have a very much smaller number of distinctive behavior patterns to differentiate. Even with special terms assigned to each primary relative, and with terminological distinctions made between other relatives on the basis of such universal differences as those between the sexes, between different generations, and between affinal and consanguineal kinsmen, there may still be leeway for other terminological distinctions before the

maximum practicable number of terms is reached. In this twilight
zone, so to speak, distinctions in terminology may arise or be per-
petuated which have little relation to patterned kinship behavior.

If this interpretation is correct, distinctions in kinship terminology
should appear in association with relatively insignificant functional
differences between kinsmen more often in bilateral than in unilinear
societies. This can be statistically tested. From the point of view of
a male Ego, the relative age of a non-marriageable female relative
is inherently of little functional significance—much less, for example,
than the differences between primary and other relatives, between
persons of different generations, between males and females, between consanguineal and affinal relatives, or between marriageable
and non-marriageable females. Age-differentiating terms used by a
brother for his sisters constitute an example. The extent to which
they are associated with bilateral descent, taken as a rough indication of relative simplicity of social organization, is shown in Table
13. The results show an appreciable tendency toward the anticipated

TABLE 13

Male-speaking Kinship Terms for Elder and Younger Sister	Bilateral Descent	Unilinear Descent
Separate terms	41	59
The same term	39	106

association, which can be expressed statistically by a coefficient
of association of $+.33$. A parallel test of male-speaking terms for
paternal aunts yields a coefficient of association of $+.31$ for the
adhesion between bilateral descent and the occurrence of separate
terms for FaElSi and FaYoSi.

While societies with relatively few and simple forms of social
structure tend to show less differentiation in the kinship behavior
associated with different kinship terms, it is dangerous to assume
the absence of such differentiation. It may merely be difficult to
discover, eluding all but the most meticulous field investigation. The
author can cite an illuminating instance from his own field experience.

When he first went into the field in 1932, among the Haida of
the Northwest Coast, the author was much impressed with the

rich material on kinship behavior that had been gathered in many places by students of Radcliffe-Brown and Malinowski, and he was inclined to be somewhat critical of his American colleagues for the comparative paucity of like material reported in their monographs. This attitude was confirmed when he returned from the Haida with a wealth of data on patterned kinship behavior [25] that even exceeded his own anticipations. Some of his colleagues nevertheless continued to assure him that they had not overlooked the possibility of unearthing such material in their own field work, but that in certain areas, particularly among the bilateral tribes of the Plateau, Great Basin, and California, the most exhaustive research had failed to reveal any significant patterning of kinship behavior beyond the most obvious family relationships. The author kept his peace, but resolved to take advantage of the first opportunity to put the issue to the test.

The opportunity came in 1934, when a month was spent among the Tenino, a typical Plateau tribe in central Oregon. Persistent inquiries about kinship revealed the inevitable differentiation of relationships within the nuclear family and a few behavioral norms obviously correlated with age and sex, but beyond this no significant patterning of behavior. The evidence concerning such matters as mother-in-law avoidance and the avunculate was completely negative, and the field notes bulged with specific denials of relationships characterized by respect, joking, special privileges, and the like. The negative evidence seemed convincing, and on his return the author, both in conversation with his university colleagues and in classroom lectures, retreated from his previous position and admitted the likelihood of the absence of all but an irreducible minimum of patterned kinship behavior in simple sibless tribes.

A second field trip to the Tenino in the summer of 1935 brought out new material. Working not directly with kinship but with other aspects of culture, such as property, house-building, sex, and childhood training, the author found bits of kinship material unexpectedly coming to light in a variety of other connections. When this material was analyzed, it was found to reveal a surprising quantity of kinship patterning, e.g., an obligation on the part of the paternal

[25] See G. P. Murdock, "Kinship and Social Behavior among the Haida," *American Anthropologist*, n.s., XXXVI (1934), 355-85.

grandfather to instil hardihood in his grandson by the imposition of physical ordeals, a fairly typical joking relationship between a father's sister's husband and his wife's brother's child, a patterned privilege of property appropriation between brothers-in-law, and permitted sexual license between siblings-in-law of opposite sex. With such material in hand the author had no alternative save to retract his retraction.

That kinship nomenclature is closely correlated with culturally patterned norms of behavior toward relatives must be assumed. This assumption accords with *a priori* reasoning, with the overwhelming testimony of the data surveyed for the present study, and with the experience and the declared or admitted views of nearly all competent anthropological authorities. Further exploration of the subject would become primarily an exercise in semantics, a study of the relation between words and the things they denote. Moreover, it would be irrelevant, for the real scientific problem is not to derive terminology from patterned behavior, or *vice versa,* but to explain both phenomena on the basis of causal factors lying outside of the kinship complex. The next chapter will seek such an explanation for variations in kinship terminology, and Chapters 9 and 10 will analyze the causes of those aspects of kinship behavior which relate to the regulation of sex.

In both cases the determinants must be independent variables, i.e., causal factors arising outside the realm of kinship phenomena. Such factors can be expected to exert an influence on both behavior patterns and nomenclature. In some cases they may affect both at the same time and in like degree. In others they may change initially only the patterns of kinship behavior, setting in motion an adaptive process which with the passage of time produces congruent modifications in terminology. Sometimes, perhaps, they may even alter first the kinship terms, with behavior undergoing subsequent adjustment, but this is probably relatively rare since new words and new meanings of old words do not ordinarily precede the things they designate. In any event, the ultimate effect of an outside causative factor is to alter both relationships and terminology, which always maintain their essential integration.

7

DETERMINANTS OF KINSHIP TERMINOLOGY

A NALYSIS of the theoretical literature reveals that six groups of external factors have been proposed as determinants of kinship terminology. These are: (1) multiple historical influences, (2) morphological differences in language, (3) elementary psychological processes, (4) universal sociological principles, (5) customs of preferential marriage, and (6) the constitution of kin and local groups. The theories of particular authors, of course, frequently take several factors into account. A discussion of each of the six types of theories will serve to highlight the views of the present writer and to relate them to those of his predecessors.

The attribution of kinship terminology to multiple historical influences has Kroeber as its leading exponent. The kinship publications of this author, in addition to valuable descriptive and invaluable analytical contributions, include a series of controversial papers. He began with sharp attacks on the use of kinship terms for evolutionistic reconstruction,[1] and continued with criticism of later functional and scientific interpretations.[2] Yet he has never denied

[1] A. L. Kroeber, "Classificatory Systems of Relationship," *Journal of the Royal Anthropological Institute*, XXXIX (1909), 82–4; "California Kinship Systems," *University of California Publications in American Archaeology and Ethnology*, XII (1917), 389–90.

[2] A. L. Kroeber, "Yurok and Neighboring Kin Term Systems," *University of California Publications in American Archaeology and Ethnology*, XXXV (1934), 15–22; "Kinship and History," *American Anthropologist*, n.s., XXXVIII (1936), 338–41.

that social institutions can exert an influence on social structure,[3] he has himself proposed at least one significant correlation between kinship terminology and social structure,[4] and he concludes his latest controversial article [5] with the suggestion that all students of kinship can "meet on the common ground that the determinants are multiple and variable." The present author finds no difficulty in agreeing with Kroeber as to the multiplicity of determining influences. Indeed, he finds himself in substantial agreement with practically all of Kroeber's theoretical statements, save for a few *obiter dicta*.

An example of such *obiter dicta* occurs in the following statement by Kroeber [6] of his historical position: "Kin-term systems . . . are subject to modification from within and without. There is always a sufficient number of such 'accidents' to disguise the basic patterns more or less. . . . the essential features of the pattern are . . . likely to be the ones which have the greatest historical depth. The search for them therefore implies a willingness and ability to view data historically. Without such willingness, it is as good as impossible to separate the significant from the trivial . . . and the work becomes merely sociological, an affair of schemes." The wholly acceptable statement to the effect that kinship terminology can change only in consequence of historical events, including internal modifications and borrowings from without, is followed by incidental assumptions leading to the unwarranted characterization of all except historical interpretations as "schemes." Lowie,[7] after making his bow to historical interpretations with the statement that "features of kinship

---

[3] Cf. A. L. Kroeber, "California Kinship Systems," *University of California Publications in American Archaeology and Ethnology*, XII (1917), 389; "Yurok and Neighboring Kin Term Systems," *University of California Publications in American Archaeology and Ethnology*, XXXV (1934), 22.

[4] See A. L. Kroeber, "Zuñi Kin and Clan," *Anthropological Papers of the American Museum of Natural History*, XVIII (1917), 86–7, in which the author takes issue with Lowie on the interpretation of bifurcate merging terminology, which he ascribes to the influence of unilinear descent rather than exogamy.

[5] A. L. Kroeber, "Kinship and History," *American Anthropologist*, n.s., XXXVIII (1936), 340.

[6] A. L. Kroeber, "Yurok and Neighboring Kin Term Systems," *University of California Publications in American Archaeology and Ethnology*, XXXV (1934), 21–2.

[7] R. H. Lowie, "Historical and Sociological Interpretations of Kinship Terminologies," *Holmes Anniversary Volume* (Washington, 1916), pp. 298–300.

terminology are distributed like other ethnographical phenomena and must be approached in the same spirit," exposes the fallacy in Kroeber's remarks when he points out that sociological and historical interpretations are reconcilable when similar causal factors are operative in historically unrelated areas.

The crucial criterion as to the relative appropriateness of comparative or "sociological," as contrasted with purely historical, methods in anthropology is the limitation of possibilities.[8] Where there are no practical limits to the variety of responses which people can make in particular situations, cultural forms can vary endlessly with little comparability between those of unrelated societies, with the result that satisfactory interpretation must depend very heavily upon historical investigation of local and regional influences. Examples include language, since the possibilities of phonetic and morphological variation are immense; ceremonial, since there are no limits to the variety of rites which can be devised and assembled; folktales, since themes and subjects are endless; and much of art, technology, and other aspects of culture. In all such cases, the overwhelming majority of cross-cultural similarities must necessarily be attributed to diffusion. Moreover, since such phenomena are in large measure unique and regionally distributed, problems arising from their influence on other aspects of culture must be attacked locally and by historical methods. The situation is quite different where there are practical limitations to the variety of responses which people can make. Under such conditions cultural similarities will appear in many different places, irrespective of historical contacts, and the influences they exert on other aspects of culture can be treated as comparable. As a result, comparative analysis becomes a highly useful supplement to historical research, and may lead to valid generalizations which are not only valuable in themselves but often capable of being applied with profit by historians.

Does the criterion of limited possibilities apply to kinship terms and their alleged social determinants? The answer to this question is an unambiguous affirmative. While kinship terms themselves show unlimited variability, the methods of classifying them do not. With regard to each of the nine criteria of classification, for example,

---

[8] See G. P. Murdock, "The Common Denominator of Cultures," *The Science of Man in the World Crisis,* ed. R. Linton (New York, 1945), pp. 138–41.

there are only two alternatives; a people can choose only to recognize or to ignore generation, sex, affinity, etc., in assigning a kinship term to a particular relative. There are also limited numbers of possible or practicable marriage forms (monogamy, polyandry, polygyny), preferential marriages (levirate, sororate, cross-cousin marriage, and a few others), rules of descent (bilateral, matrilineal, patrilineal), rules of residence (patrilocal, matrilocal, avunculocal, neolocal, bilocal), family forms (nuclear, polygamous, extended), unilinear kin groups (moieties, phratries, sibs, lineages), and so on. All of these alternatives are widely distributed in historically independent regions, and insofar as they interact with one another or with other aspects of culture it is reasonable to assume that they exert a parallel influence and to seek the character and degree of such influence by comparative studies.

The data in Chapter 8 will demonstrate the extraordinary extent of parallelism, both in kinship terminology and in types of kin and local groups. There are few forms which are not represented in all five of the world's main continental and insular areas. Even more striking, if possible, are the wide divergences in the forms found within each linguistic stock of which our sample includes several tribal representatives. Since language relationships are the most incontrovertible of all evidences of historical contact, we arrive at the curious paradox that kinship terminology and the forms of social organization often differ precisely where historical connections are indisputable and show resemblances where historical relationships are inconceivable. The distributions, in short, are quite unlike those which anthropologists regularly encounter with respect to such phenomena as languages, folktales, cultivated plants, or types of traps. They not only suggest but demand the intervention of determinants that are not historically limited. In seeking these, of course, the author by no means denies that in each individual case the phenomenon has developed through a specific historical process.[9]

When historical causes are exclusively unique or local, the weigh-

[9] The only cultural processes are historical. The author cannot accept the contention of White that evolution is a separate cultural process. See L. A. White, "Kroeber's 'Configurations of Culture Growth,'" *American Anthropologist*, n.s., LXVII (1946), 82.

ing of their respective influence depends wholly upon the judgment of the historian; there is no independent basis of comparison. Historians notoriously differ widely in their judgments, as witness the varied theories of the causation of the American Revolution or the Civil War. When, however, some of the causes of an historical phenomenon are also known to have operated in other situations, comparison of these situations provides some independent basis for estimating the influence to be ascribed to them in particular cases. The wider the comparisons, and the larger the proportion of the causative factors that are susceptible to comparative analysis, the more reliable will be the conclusions as to the weights to be assigned to particular causes. Under favorable circumstances, therefore, the inductions from comparative studies become appreciably more dependable than inferences from historical analysis. Kinship data, in the opinion of the author, provide a nearly ideal case, for not some but many or most of their determinants, including those of the greatest apparent significance, are found in historically diverse societies, and the number of independent cases is sufficient to give statistical reliability to the inductions drawn from their comparison.

A second group of theories attributes variations in kinship terminology to morphological differences in language. According to Gifford,[10] for example, "kinship systems are first of all linguistic phenomena . . . and only secondarily social phenomena. As such they . . . constitute an archaic and highly refractory nucleus, which yields unevenly and only here and there to influences from . . . social structure." Kinship terms as words must of course conform to the morphological principles of the particular language,[11] but the way in which relatives are terminologically classified bears no necessary relation to the nature of the language. As Tax [12] points out, methods of classification often differ considerably, not only in tribes of the same linguistic stock but even in those which are so closely related

[10] E. W. Gifford, "A Problem in Kinship Terminology," *American Anthropologist*, n.s., XLII (1940), 193–4. See also A. L. Kroeber, "Classificatory Systems of Relationship," *Journal of the Royal Anthropological Institute*, XXXIX (1909), 83.

[11] See R. H. Lowie, "Kinship," *Encyclopaedia of the Social Sciences*, VIII (1932), 569.

[12] S. Tax, "Some Problems of Social Organization," *Social Anthropology of North American Tribes*, ed. F. Eggan (Chicago, 1937), p. 6.

that the actual terms are practically identical. Moreover, as Lowie [13] rightly states, "language represents reality and . . . in so far as it is related to social phenomena it is likely to mirror them."

Kirchhoff [14] attributes the bifurcate merging and generation types of kinship terminology to differential principles of word formation. Since all features of linguistic morphology are regionally distributed in consequence of historical contacts and migrations, linguistic interpretations of kinship terminology constitute only a special class of historical interpretations and are answerable in the same way. The only significant example of the influence of language on nomenclature which has come to light during the present study is the previously mentioned tendency to use descriptive terms very freely among tribes within a band across central Africa. This phenomenon undoubtedly has an historical origin, and is very possibly due to some morphological feature common to the languages of the area.

A discussion of linguistic factors seems a logical place into which to inject the observation that kinship terms frequently exemplify the phenomenon of "cultural lag." [15] "One factor that must always be considered," as Lowie [16] correctly states, "is the time element. A recently acquired custom may not yet have developed an appropriate nomenclature, while . . . the nomenclature may survive after the custom has become obsolete." A large proportion of the discrepancies between the kinship terms reported in our sources and the forms theoretically anticipated under the prevailing social conditions are precisely those adapted to conditions which actual or inferential historical evidence indicates existed somewhat prior to the period of observation. It should be emphasized, however, that such "survivals" appear far more frequently in association with functionally insignificant relationships than with functionally important ones. Thus, though they indicate a tendency for kinship terminology to adjust somewhat tardily to changes in social determinants, they do not provide a basis for reconstructing the forms of social institutions in the distant past, as Morgan and other early

[13] R. H. Lowie, "Relationship Terms," *Encyclopaedia Britannica* (14th edit., London, 1929), XIX, 89.
[14] P. Kirchhoff, "Verwandtschaftsbezeichnungen und Verwandtenheirat," *Zeitschrift für Ethnologie*, LXIV (1932), 51.
[15] Cf. W. F. Ogburn, *Social Change* (New York, 1922), pp. 200–80.
[16] R. H. Lowie, *Culture and Ethnology* (New York, 1917), p. 173.

theorists attempted to do.[17] Authorities ranging from Kroeber [18] to Radcliffe-Brown [19] now agree that long-range historical inferences cannot legitimately be drawn from kinship terminologies. It will be shown in Appendix A, however, that short-range historical reconstruction is possible with the aid of survivals in kinship terminology which have not been integrated with the rest of the social structure.

A third group of theories attributes kinship terminology to certain elementary psychological or logical processes. "Terms of relationship," maintains Kroeber,[20] "reflect psychology, not sociology," and subsequently explains that by psychological factors he means those that are "directly expressive of a manner of thought." These seem to include the underlying logic in linguistic morphology. Radcliffe-Brown and his students make extensive use of logical assumptions. For example, the "rules" of "uniform descent," "uniform siblings," "uniform mates," and "uniform ascent," as defined by Tax [21]—meaning, in combination, that if a kinsman whom Ego denotes by term A has any primary relative whom Ego denotes by term B, then Ego will also tend to apply the term B to a comparable relative of any other kinsman whom he also calls A—really rest on certain assumptions about the nature of the fundamental psychological processes underlying reasoning and association. As a matter of fact, they are in substantial accord with the important psychological mechanism known as "generalization." [22]

Properly used, elementary psychological processes can be of great assistance in the interpretation of kinship phenomena, and

[17] Even as late as 1914 Rivers could allege that "it is possible to infer with certainty the ancient existence of forms of marriage from the survival of their results in the terminology of relationship." W. H. R. Rivers, *Kinship and Social Organisation* (London, 1914), pp. 58–9.

[18] A. L. Kroeber, "Classificatory Systems of Relationship," *Journal of the Royal Anthropological Institute*, XXXIX (1909), 82.

[19] A. R. Radcliffe-Brown, "The Social Organization of Australian Tribes," *Oceania*, I (1931), 427.

[20] A. L. Kroeber, "Classificatory Systems of Relationship," *Journal of the Royal Anthropological Institute*, XXXIX (1909), 84; "California Kinship Systems," *University of California Publications in American Archaeology and Ethnology*, XII (1917), 389.

[21] S. Tax, "Some Problems of Social Organization," *Social Anthropology of North American Tribes*, ed. F. Eggan (Chicago, 1937), pp. 19–20.

[22] Cf. C. L. Hull, *Principles of Behavior* (New York, 1943), pp. 183–203.

the present author will draw freely upon them. One fundamental caution, however, must always be observed. Psychology can never be used alone to explain any phenomenon of culture. It merely provides a mechanism by which historical and other influences are translated into patterns of behavior under particular social conditions. Without a knowledge of the conditions of behavior, which cultural anthropology alone can furnish, no comprehension of psychological principles can yield an explanation of cultural forms. But when the conditions and circumstances affecting a change in culture are known, psychology can greatly assist us in comprehending the kind and range of cultural modifications that are likely to ensue. The above-mentioned "rules" propounded by Tax, for example, provide a substantial basis for predicting the future terminological classification of the primary relatives of a person to whom the kinship term A has recently been extended (see Theorem 1 below). Incidentally, they also furnish the first satisfactory explanation of a phenomenon which has long puzzled theorists, namely, why in a society which applies sibling terms to all members of Ego's sib and generation, the parallel cousins who are not sib members, as well as those who are, nearly always are likewise called by sibling terms.[23]

The derivation of kinship terminology from assumed universal sociological principles finds its principal exponent in Radcliffe-Brown. For example, in discussing the hypothesis advanced by Sapir [24] that bifurcate merging terminology may result from the operation of the levirate, Radcliffe-Brown,[25] though accepting the asserted correlation between the two phenomena, refuses to regard one as the effect and the other as the cause but maintains that both "are the result of a single sociological principle, . . . the social equivalence of brothers." According to his student, Tax,[26] Radcliffe-

[23] Lowie, for example, can think of no alternative to the obviously defective hypothesis of Tylor and Rivers that the practice originated under some assumed prior moiety organization. See R. H. Lowie, "Family and Sib," *American Anthropologist*, n.s., XXI (1919), 33.

[24] E. Sapir, "Terms of Relationship and the Levirate," *American Anthropologist*, n.s., XVIII (1916), 327–37.

[25] A. R. Radcliffe-Brown, "Social Organization of Australian Tribes," *Oceania*, I (1931), 429.

[26] S. Tax, "Some Problems of Social Organization," *Social Anthropology of North American Tribes*, ed. F. Eggan (Chicago, 1937), p. 16.

Brown "believes that the necessity for social integration is the fundamental cause of all social institutions—that they have the function of keeping the society integrated."

With hypotheses of the above type the present writer has neither sympathy nor patience. In the first place, the alleged principles are mere verbalizations reified into causal forces. In the second, such concepts as "equivalence of brothers" and "necessity for social integration" contain no statements of the relationships between phenomena under varying conditions, and thus lie at the opposite extreme from genuine scientific laws. Thirdly, being unitary in their nature, they provide no basis for interpreting cultural differences; they should produce the same effects everywhere. To be sure, numerous "principles" are alleged, and it is tacitly assumed that when the anticipated effects of one do not occur some other countervailing principle is operative, but nowhere are the conditions set forth under which particular principles give way to others.[27] Fortunately, Radcliffe-Brown's claim to eminence as a student of kinship rests on other and more substantial grounds.

The term "sociological" as applied to determinants of kinship ordinarily refers, not to the invoking of universal principles, but to the attribution of classificatory terminology to the influence of particular social institutions.[28] These fall into two groups—customs of preferential marriage and the constitution of kin and local groups such as family, clan, sib, and moiety. Rivers [29] expresses one extreme of opinion on their influence when he asserts that "the details which distinguish different forms of the classificatory system from one another have been directly determined by the social institutions of those who use the systems." Sapir [30] expresses the opposite extreme in alleging "that the factors governing kinship nomenclature are very complex and only in part capable of explanation on purely sociological grounds." No authority on the subject denies any influence to sociological factors. The position of the present author

[27] For a parallel criticism of Radcliffe-Brown's universal "laws," see R. H. Lowie, *The History of Ethnological Theory* (New York, 1937), pp. 224–5.

[28] Cf. S. Tax, "Some Problems of Social Organization," *Social Anthropology of North American Tribes*, ed. F. Eggan (Chicago, 1937), p. 10.

[29] W. H. R. Rivers, *Kinship and Social Organisation* (London, 1914), p. 19.

[30] E. Sapir, "Terms of Relationship and the Levirate," *American Anthropologist*, n.s., XVIII (1916), 327n.

lies between those expressed by Rivers and Sapir—closer to the latter in admitting that kinship determinants are complex and multiple, to the former in assigning great weight to sociological determinants.

Rules of marriage may affect kinship terminology when they produce a situation in which Ego can trace a kinship connection to some relative in two different ways. When this happens, the criterion which might otherwise be recognized in distinguishing the two types of bonds tends to be ignored, with the result that relatives of both types tend to be called by the same term. Thus Lowie [31] maintains that wherever, as in native Australia, the preferred mate is always a consanguineal relative, special affinal terms tend to be absent. The criterion of affinity is ignored because the spouse and his or her relatives are also consanguineal kinsmen and can continue to be designated by consanguineal terms. A regular rule of marriage by sister exchange, i.e., when two men obtain wives by exchanging their sisters, leads, says Rivers,[32] to the ignoring of affinity and to the terminological equating of several pairs of relatives, namely, FaSiHu and MoBr, MoBrWi and FaSi, SoWiBr and DaHu, DaHuSi and SoWi. A rule of preferential marriage with a cross-cousin (a child of either FaSi or MoBr) will allegedly lead, in similar fashion, to the use of the same terms for WiFa, MoBr, and FaSiHu, for WiMo, FaSi, and MoBrWi, and for cross-cousins, spouses, and siblings-in-law.[33]

Sapir [34] has suggested and others [35] have agreed that preferential levirate and sororate marriages (and the same holds true for fraternal polyandry and sororal polygyny respectively) may operate to minimize the criterion of collaterality and thus produce kinship

---

[31] R. H. Lowie, "Kinship," *Encyclopaedia of the Social Sciences*, VIII (1932), 570.

[32] W. H. R. Rivers, *Kinship and Social Organisation* (London, 1914), pp. 44-5.

[33] *Ibid.*, pp. 21-5.

[34] E. Sapir, "Terms of Relationship and the Levirate," *American Anthropologist*, n.s., XVIII (1916), 327-37.

[35] See P. Kirchhoff, "Verwandtschaftsbezeichnungen und Verwandtenheirat," *Zeitschrift für Ethnologie*, LXIV (1932), 53; B. W. Aginsky, "The Mechanics of Kinship," *American Anthropologist*, XXXVII (1935), 450-1. For a criticism see R. H. Lowie, *Culture and Ethnology* (New York, 1917), pp. 144-50.

terminology of the so-called "bifurcate merging" [36] type. The argument runs thus: if Ego's mother normally marries the father's brother when the father dies, there will be a tendency to employ the same terms for Fa and FaBr, for Br and FaBrSo, for Si and FaBrDa, for So and BrSo, and for Da and BrDa since to Ego such persons are likely to play similar family or kinship roles. In the same way the sororate would equate MoSi with Mo, MoSiSo with Br, MoSiDa with Si, and a woman's sisters' children with her own.

Preferential secondary marriages with a kinsman of an older or younger generation are similarly alleged to result in ignoring the criterion of generation and thus in classifying relatives of different generations under a single term. Thus Aginsky,[37] Gifford,[38] Lesser,[39] Lowie,[40] and Rivers [41] have accepted a suggestion originally made by Kohler [42] that rules of preferential marriage with a wife's brother's daughter or a mother's brother's widow will produce, or help to produce, respectively, the Omaha and Crow types of terminology for cross-cousins.

Customs of preferential marriage, in the opinion of the present writer, are likely to influence kinship terminology when they apply to all or most marriages within a society, but not when they apply only to occasional unions or to a distinct minority of all that take place. For this reason he professes skepticism concerning the suggested determination of kinship terminology by secondary marriages. Every

[36] In bifurcate merging the father's brother is called "father" and the mother's sister "mother," while separate terms are used for the mother's brother and the father's sister. See R. H. Lowie, "A Note on Relationship Terminologies," *American Anthropologist*, n.s., XXX (1928), 265–6.

[37] B. W. Aginsky, "The Mechanics of Kinship," *American Anthropologist*, n.s., XXXVII (1935), 450–1; "Kinship Systems and the Forms of Marriage," *Memoirs of the American Anthropological Association*, XLV (1935), 34–5.

[38] E. W. Gifford, "Miwok Moieties," *University of California Publications in American Archaeology and Ethnology*, XII (1916), 186–8.

[39] A. Lesser, "Some Aspects of Siouan Kinship," *Proceedings of the International Congress of Americanists*, XXIII (1928), 571; "Kinship in the Light of Some Distributions," *American Anthropologist*, n.s., XXXI (1929), 722–5.

[40] R. H. Lowie, "The Omaha and Crow Kinship Terminologies," *Proceedings of the International Congress of Americanists*, XXIV (1930), 102–8; "Kinship," *Encyclopaedia of the Social Sciences*, VIII (1932), 571.

[41] W. H. R. Rivers, *Kinship and Social Organisation* (London, 1914), pp. 29–42.

[42] See S. Tax, "Some Problems of Social Organization," *Social Anthropology of North American Tribes*, ed. F. Eggan (Chicago, 1937), pp. 12–13.

marriage with a BrWi or MoBrWi is necessarily a second marriage for the woman; every one with a WiSi or WiBrDa, a second (or subsequent) marriage for the man. By the very nature of things such marriages can constitute only a minority of all unions. There must always be a first marriage before there can be any secondary marriage at all. Moreover, if a brother or a maternal uncle dies, his widow is available as a wife to only one of the surviving brothers or nephews, and where there are none she must marry someone else. Hence levirate marriages, even where they are possible and preferred, can actually occur in only a fraction of all cases. Similarly, when a man's wife dies she may have no unmarried sister or brother's daughter whom he can marry in her stead.[43] Even when polygyny prevails, as many observant ethnographers have noted, the majority of men at any given time, or of all men during their lifetimes, normally have only a single wife; only those who survive well into middle age tend to have additional wives. The assumption that the kinship usages of an entire society are determined by the secondary marriages of a relatively small minority of the total population seems clearly deficient in realism.

This criticism is supported by the ethnographic evidence. In a quantitative test of various theories of the causation of bifurcate merging, made by the present writer,[44] the levirate-sororate hypothesis of Sapir failed to receive reliable statistical confirmation, while alternative explanations propounded by Rivers, Lowie, and Kroeber were substantially corroborated. Further factual disproof will be advanced later in the present chapter under Propositions 28, 29, and 30.

The sixth and last of the factors which have been proposed as determinants of kinship terminology is the constitution of kin and local groups. Moieties, as pointed out by Tylor[45] and Rivers,[46] by aligning all members of a society in two unilinear groups, tend to

---

[43] Cf. L. H. Morgan, "Systems of Consanguinity and Affinity of the Human Family," *Smithsonian Contributions to Knowledge*, XVII (1870), 478–9.

[44] G. P. Murdock, "Bifurcate Merging," *American Anthropologist*, n.s., XLIX (1947), 60–2.

[45] E. B. Tylor, "On a Method of Investigating the Development of Institutions," *Journal of the Royal Anthropological Institute*, XVIII (1889), 264.

[46] W. H. R. Rivers, *Kinship and Social Organisation* (London, 1914), pp. 72–3.

group together various relatives who are ordinarily distinguished and thus to result in assigning them a common kinship designation. Thus moieties are very widely associated with bifurcate merging.[47] Some of the same results can be brought about by smaller exogamous kin groups or sibs, as Lowie [48] and Kroeber [49] have pointed out. A rule of patrilocal or matrilocal residence can bring about a similar alignment of kinsmen.[50]

It has been observed [51] that cross-cousin terms of the Crow type tend to be found in tribes with matrilineal sibs, and terms of the Omaha type in those with patrilineal sibs. Iroquois terminology [52] is also common in tribes with both types of descent, and White [53] has suggested a possible basis of differentiation: "When the clan system is young and weak the kinship system will be of the Dakota-Iroquois type, regardless of the sex in which descent is reckoned. As the clan system develops, however, and comes to exert its influence more and more upon the social life of the tribe, the Dakota-Iroquois terminology will be transferred into the Crow type in a matrilineal society and into the Omaha type in a patrilineal society."

Determinants of this last general type seem to the present author perhaps the most significant of all. On *a priori* grounds, the alignment of relatives in extended families, clans, sibs, and moieties, as these are created by rules of residence and descent, would seem to provide precisely the kinds of social situations in which classificatory groupings of kinsmen would be most likely to arise. Abundant evidence for this assumption will be presented below. The contrary hy-

---

[47] Cf. R. H. Lowie, *Culture and Ethnology* (New York, 1917), pp. 136-8; G. P. Murdock, "Bifurcate Merging," *American Anthropologist*, n.s., XLIX (1947), 57-8.

[48] R. H. Lowie, "Exogamy and the Classificatory System of Relationship," *American Anthropologist*, n.s., XVII (1915), 223-39; *Culture and Ethnology* (New York, 1917), pp. 140-60. But cf. "Family and Sib," *American Anthropologist*, n.s., XXI (1919), 33, where Lowie shifts his position.

[49] A. L. Kroeber, "Zuñi Kin and Clan," *Anthropological Papers of the American Museum of Natural History*, XVIII (1917), 86-7.

[50] Cf. A. Lesser, "Kinship Origins in the Light of Some Distributions," *American Anthropologist*, n.s., XXXI (1929), 722-5.

[51] R. H. Lowie, *Culture and Ethnology* (New York, 1917), pp. 151-4.

[52] Characterized by identical terms for cross-cousins of both types.

[53] L. A. White, "A Problem in Kinship Terminology," *American Anthropologist*, n.s., XLI (1939), 569-70. Cf. Theorems 20 and 21 below.

pothesis, namely, that kinship classifications arise first and then give rise to sibs and other comparable groups,[54] does not appear well founded.

The foregoing critical survey of the various theories of the determination of kinship nomenclature should reinforce an important conclusion, to wit, that the causal factors actually operating in any particular situation are always multiple. No single factor or simple hypothesis can account for all observable effects. From this it follows that different determinants must often exert their pressure in opposite directions. What operates is therefore a sort of parallelogram of forces, and the phenomena which ensue represent, not the effects of particular forces but the resultant of them all. Often, indeed, the influences exerted by opposing factors may be so evenly balanced that a relatively insignificant supplementary factor may suffice to tip the scales. Opler [55] records a particularly apt illustration. Speaking of the fact that some Apache tribes classify the maternal aunt with the mother, while others with similar social institutions call her by a distinct term, he notes that either practice may represent a functional adaptation to the situation. Such factors as matrilocal residence are consistent with the former usage, such factors as separate nuclear family dwellings with the latter. Since the Apache are thus faced with a choice between alternatives of approximately equivalent functional utility, minor or even irrelevant factors might decide the issue, here in one way, there in another.

Since multiple factors are nearly always operative, perfect statistical correlations between any particular kinship determinant and the terminological features that it tends to produce should never be expected, even if the hypothesis is entirely sound. The factor of the time lag which commonly intervenes between the appearance of a causal influence and the resulting change in nomenclature also operates to reduce the magnitude of statistical coefficients. Bearing these facts in mind, the reader will realize that positive coefficients

[54] See, for example, E. W. Gifford, "A Problem in Kinship Terminology," *American Anthropologist*, n.s., XLII (1940), 193; A. Lesser, "Kinship Origins in the Light of Some Distributions," *American Anthropologist*, n.s., XXXI (1929), 728.

[55] M. E. Opler, "Apache Data concerning the Relation of Kinship Terminology to Social Classification," *American Anthropologist*, n.s., XXXIX (1937), 208.

of only moderate magnitude may often reflect genuine causal relations of considerable significance.

The presentation and testing of the present writer's theory of the determination of kinship terminology will take as its model the so-called postulational method of scientific inquiry.[56] In this procedure, the most rigorous of scientific methods, all logical or rational operations are performed prior to the final empirical test, so that no fallible mental processes can intervene between the survey of the evidence and the formulation of explanatory hypotheses, to bias or distort the latter—a basic defect in much of social science theory.

In its essence, the postulational method requires the formulation of a set of hypotheses of a general character, called "postulates," and of a series of derivative propositions of a more specific character, called "theorems." Postulates are commonly too broad or general to be capable of direct validation. They are verified through the theorems deduced from them, the latter being formulated in such a manner that they can be projected against a body of facts and tested by merely enumerating agreements and disagreements or by making some other equally simple operation. Each theorem must be subjected to careful logical analysis in order to bring to light any further postulates or axioms which may be necessary to derive it. The theorems for testing any postulate should be as numerous, as diverse, and as representative as possible. Only after the whole framework of postulates and theorems has been systematically worked out, with all terms carefully defined and all implicit assumptions made explicit, is it put to the test by projecting the theorems against the facts. If even a single theorem fails to check with the facts, the postulate from which it is derived must be considered invalid, and the logical structure must be revised and tested again.

We shall fall somewhat short of this scientific ideal. Unfortunately the postulational method, however economical and precise as a tool of research, does not lend itself to simplicity of exposition. In order not to repel the reader, therefore, we shall dispense with as much

[56] Cf. E. V. Huntington, "The Method of Postulates," *Philosophy of Science*, IV (1937), 482–95; G. P. Murdock, "The Cross-Cultural Survey," *American Sociological Review*, V (1940), 369–70.

of the usual elaborate apparatus as we can, and will strive for simplicity. Moreover, a completely rigorous use of the method would require us to reduce much of anthropological, sociological, and psychological theory—we draw heavily upon all three—to a series of logically precise and explicitly defined propositions. While this is a consummation devoutly to be wished, it is a task for the general social scientist and not for the author of a specialized contribution. To attempt it here would be presumptuous and probably premature. We shall therefore attempt a compromise and confine ourselves to our limited field. As a consequence, the propositions which we shall call "postulates" will really have the character of what are technically known as "first-order theorems," and what we call "theorems" will actually be "theorems of the second order." Our real postulates lie, only partially formulated, in our fundamental assumptions, which will shortly be made explicit.

In conjunction with the theorems derived from our own postulates, we shall occasionally test hypotheses advanced by other authors and also some which are not derivable from our postulates but are tentatively proposed as meriting consideration. These will be labeled as "propositions" in order to distinguish them from genuine theorems, although they will be numbered consecutively with the latter.

The testing of theorems and propositions will be accomplished by a simple enumeration of the societies in our sample of 250 which agree and disagree with each. Agreement will mean in some instances that the same kinship term, in others that different terms, are applied to two relatives, disagreement being the opposite in either case. When one of a pair of relatives may be called by either of two terms, one the same as and the other different from that applied to the other, the case is counted as half in agreement and half in disagreement. Cases of derivative terms are similarly split. Thus if MoSi is being compared with Mo, and the term for the former is a derivative one such as "little mother," the terms for the two relatives are considered half the same and half different. The same device is followed when two equally competent authorities differ, the one reporting agreement and the other a disagreement. Genuinely doubtful or inferential cases, moreover, are given only half weight. In all totals, however, fractions are carried to the next whole number.

The results of each enumeration are summarized by a statistical coefficient, accompanied by an index of reliability. The coefficient used is Q, the coefficient of association proposed by Yule.[57] Since the sampling distribution of Q has not been established, the reliability of the associations has been determined by using the chi square (χ^2) test of independence, corrected for continuity, based on the formula given by Snedecor.[58] The statistical tables include, along with the numerical data and the Q values, not the χ^2 values but an indication of the probability of obtaining a χ^2 value as large as or larger than that actually obtained, on the basis of random sampling alone. Thus 1000 indicates a probability of less than 1 in 1,000; 100, of less than 1 in 100; 20, of less than 1 in 20; 10, of less than 1 in 10; 5, of less than 1 in 5; 2, of less than 1 in 2—or, phrased in another way, reliability at or better than the one-tenth-of-one-per-cent level, the one per cent level, the five per cent level, the ten per cent level, the twenty per cent level, and the fifty per cent level of confidence, respectively. The χ^2 column is left blank when the reliability is very low, i.e., at less than the fifty per cent level or below 2. When Q is $+1.00$ or -1.00, the χ^2 value becomes inaccurate or inappropriate because of small cell frequencies, and an asterisk is shown in its place.

Coefficients of association range from $+1.00$, indicating perfect positive association, to -1.00, indicating perfect negative association. A coefficient of .00, or close enough thereto in either direction to be presumed to diverge only through the chance of the particular sample, indicates complete independence, or an absence of association. In the testing of a theorem, such a coefficient constitutes lack of substantiation, unless other samples consistently show positive coefficients with good reliability. Any negative coefficient, of course, constitutes definite invalidation of a theorem, unless the index of reliability is very low. Positive coefficients provide confirmation, though this must be considered merely tentative if the indices of reliability are consistently low. In general, a theorem may be considered validated only when every enumerative test yields a positive coefficient of association, the decisiveness of the validation depend-

[57] G. U. Yule and M. G. Kendall, An Introduction to the Theory of Statistics (11th edit., London, 1937), pp. 44–5.
[58] G. W. Snedecor, Statistical Methods (Ames, 1946), p. 199.

ing upon the consistency of the coefficients and the level of reliability.

When the data were gathered, the author did not intend to undertake an analysis of the determinants of kinship, but expected to use kinship terminology only as one of the aspects of social structure which may operate to channelize sexual behavior. Consequently he recorded only such kinship data as promised to be useful for the purpose in mind. Thus material was gathered on kin relationships between males and females, but not on patterned behavior between pairs of male relatives or pairs of female kinsmen. Similarly, kinship terms were noted only when employed by males for female relatives; no terms for male relatives were collected, and no female-speaking terms for females. Only male-speaking terms for female relatives, therefore, are available for the testing of theorems. While they are probably sufficiently conclusive, a complete demonstration must await comparable analysis of other kinship terms.

The hypothesis to be advanced for the determination of kinship terminology will be formulated in a single very general postulate, from which 26 distinct theorems will be derived and individually tested. The postulate is not designed to cover the entire field of kinship nomenclature but only the area within which the great majority of recognized kinship problems lie, namely, the classification and differentiation of terms for secondary and tertiary relatives of Ego's generation and of the first ascending and first descending generations. Here uniform treatment is possible because the pertinent criteria are the same—generation, sex, affinity, collaterality, bifurcation, and polarity. For primary relatives the subsidiary criteria of relative age [59] and speaker's sex assume equal importance, and provision should be made for them in the formulation of a postulate. On the other hand, in regard to the second and higher ascending and descending generations, and to distant relatives, extension and classification become so general that most and sometimes all of the major criteria are ignored.

The postulational method requires that all assumptions upon

[59] In an analysis of 221 of our sample societies, 43 per cent were found to apply different terms to ElSi and YoSi (male speaking), whereas, if extended sibling terms were excluded, the percentage of age differentiation was only 19 for BrWi, 15 for WiSi, 13 for MoSi, 9 for FaBrWi and MoSiDa, 8 for FaBrDa, 7 for BrDa, 5 for FaSiDa, 4 for FaSi and MoBrDa, 2 for SiDa, and less than 1 for all other categories of secondary and tertiary relatives.

which a postulate is based be made explicit. Although this is almost never done in the theoretical writings of social science, we shall make a serious effort to conform to the scientific ideal. The terms to be employed in the postulate will be precisely defined—another requirement of the method—during the exposition of the underlying assumptions.

Our first assumption is that all human behavior, including that which is called cultural, conforms to the fundamental principles of behavior as these are being laid bare by psychologists. Culture change is the product of individual behavior in the mass, operating over time and adapting to the changing conditions of existence through such mechanisms as trial-and-error learning and imitation.[60] All cultural responses in particular situations are similarly understandable in terms of the established habits of the reacting individuals, their motivations, and the environmental and social conditions under which they must behave. We assume, in short, that there is no conflict whatsoever between valid psychological and cultural interpretations of behavior.

It is assumed, secondly, that all cultural phenomena are historical. We specifically disclaim any evolutionary, cyclical, or other process of change according to which cultural forms are interpreted otherwise than as products of the prior events and existing conditions in the particular local context. Since behavior, whether individual or collective, depends upon the reciprocal interaction of the same factors—external stimuli and conditions, the habitual response tendencies and motivations of the behaving organisms, and an innate mechanism of behavior—we recognize no conflict between history and psychology. We must insist, however, that the psychological mechanism operates only with the materials which history provides, including under history the life histories of individuals. In default of such materials, psychology can offer no valid interpretation of any cultural phenomenon. The social scientist may—indeed, he must—resort to the psychologist for answers to the question "how?" But for a solution of problems concerned with "what?" "when?" "where?" or even "why?" he must look to history for the independent variables.

It is assumed, in the third place, that the terminological classifica-

[60] Cf. N. E. Miller and J. Dollard, *Social Learning and Imitation* (New Haven, 1941).

tion of kinsmen is but a special case of linguistic classification, and that its function is to designate types of relatives in accordance with their socially relevant common characteristics, such as the patterned behavior expected from them. Whenever there is occasion to individualize a relative, personal names provide a universal means of so doing.

It is assumed, fourthly, that the classification of two or more relatives under a single term can occur only on the basis of regular and perceptible similarities, or the absence of regular and significant dissimilarities, between them. This assumption is derived from the psychological process of "stimulus generalization," as identified and described by Hull.[61] Generalization is the mechanism by which any response, learned in connection with a particular stimulus or pattern of stimuli, tends also to be evoked by other stimulus situations in proportion to their similarity to the original one. It follows from our first assumption that any cultural phenomenon in which responses (such as kinship terms) associated with particular stimulus objects (such as relatives) are transferred to other stimulus contexts will reflect in the behavior of numbers of people the same mechanism that is observable in any single individual. Since, however, the cultural phenomenon in question involves symbolic mental processes, i.e., those of language, as well as pluralistic behavior on the part of many individuals in a society, it seems advisable not to speak of the "generalization" of kinship terms but to use the word *extension* (and the verb "extend") to denote the social counterpart and derivative of the psychological process.

A fifth assumption is that different kinship terms will be applied to two or more relatives to the extent that they exhibit regular and significant dissimilarities or the absence of regular and perceptible similarities. This assumption is derived from the psychological process of "discrimination" as defined by Hull [62] by a procedure paralleling that for "generalization." Discrimination is the fundamental mechanism by which the generalization of responses along a continuum of decreasing similarity in the stimuli evoking them

---

[61] C. L. Hull, *Principles of Behavior* (New York, 1943), pp. 183–203. Cf. also E. R. Hilgard and D. G. Marquis, *Conditioning and Learning* (New York, 1940), pp. 176–85.
[62] C. L. Hull, *Principles of Behavior* (New York, 1943), p. 266.

is checked at the point where the behavior ceases to be adaptive and a situation is created favorable to the appearance of other responses. In reference to kinship terminology we shall employ the term *differentiation* (and the verb "differentiate") to denote the symbolic and social counterpart of the psychological process of discrimination.

Our sixth assumption is that the extension or differentiation of kinship terms depends in every individual case upon the total net effect of all similarities and dissimilarities exhibited by the relatives in question. Similarities and dissimilarities can be classified into three groups: (1) the absence or presence of differences inherent in the very nature of kinship structure in consequence of the biology of heredity and of the universal cultural fact of family exogamy; (2) the absence or presence of recurrent but not universal features of social organization and of associated cultural rules of residence, descent, and marriage which have the effect of increasing or decreasing the degree of similarity or dissimilarity prevailing between relatives of particular kinship categories; (3) the absence or presence of other cultural or environmental factors which can affect the degree of similarity between categories of relatives, including in the main local and non-repetitive historical influences.

It is assumed, in the seventh place, that the only inherent differences which are of fundamental significance in the classification of secondary and tertiary relatives are the six major criteria of generation, sex, affinity, collaterality, bifurcation, and polarity. In the postulate and theorems these six criteria will be designated as *inherent distinctions.* The subsidiary criteria of relative age, speaker's sex, and decedence are either rare in themselves or are recognized only infrequently and sporadically in the terminology for secondary and tertiary relatives, and will consequently not be classed for present purposes as inherent distinctions. This seventh assumption is derived from the classic analysis by Kroeber [63] of the factors underlying terminological differentiation.

The term *kin-type,* which will appear in the postulate and theorems, may now be defined. A kin-type is a class of relatives defined by all six major criteria, i.e., consisting exclusively of relatives between

[63] A. L. Kroeber, "Classificatory Systems of Relationship," *Journal of the Royal Anthropological Institute,* XXXIX (1909), 78–81.

whom no inherent distinction exists. A kin-type can include only siblings of the same sex, but not all groups of brothers or of sisters constitute kin-types, since the criterion of collaterality often divides such a group into two kin-types, e.g., Mo and MoSi or SoWi and SoWiSi. The "equivalence of brothers" or of siblings, as used by Radcliffe-Brown,[64] refers to the classificatory similarity of the relatives of a kin-type.

Our eighth assumption is that the six inherent distinctions vary in their relative efficacy in producing differentiation in kinship terminology. By *relative efficacy* we mean the magnitude of the influence of any one, relative to that of the others, in causing terminological differentiation. Relative efficacy can be determined only inductively. Our data do not cover the criteria of sex and polarity, but they make possible an estimate of the relative efficacy of the other four inherent distinctions. This is assumed to be approximately of the order of 25 for generation, 5 for affinity, 1 for bifurcation, and 1 for collaterality on the basis of a wholesale tabulation of data from 221 of our sample societies. For comparability with bifurcation and collaterality, affinal and consanguineal kin-types in Table 14 were tabulated only within the same generation.[65]

TABLE 14

Inherent Distinctions	Pairs of Kin-types Compared	Different Terms		Same Terms	
		Number	Percentage	Number	Percentage
Generation	276	33,071	97.7	796	2.3
Affinity	33	4,518	87.2	662	12.8
Bifurcation	16	1,179	51.6	1,125	48.4
Collaterality	11	678	40.3	1,004	59.7

It is assumed, in the ninth place, that practical considerations everywhere exert pressure in the direction of reducing the total number of kinship terms from the number necessary if all six inherent distinctions were fully and simultaneously recognized (33 secondary plus 151 tertiary kin-types, in addition to the several categories of primary relatives) to a relatively modest optimal number. This

[64] Cf. A. R. Radcliffe-Brown, "The Social Organization of Australian Tribes," *Oceania*, I (1931), 429.

[65] When comparisons were made between all generations, the percentage of identical terms dropped from 12.8 to slightly more than 4.

assumption is derived from observations by Kroeber [66] and others to the effect that the total number of distinct kinship terms in different societies varies within a rather limited range around a mean of about 25. It follows from this assumption that in every kinship system at least some of the six inherent distinctions must be inoperative in at least some secondary and tertiary kin-types, and it follows from the eighth assumption that this will be most likely to happen in the case of those distinctions with the lowest relative efficacy, namely, collaterality and bifurcation. Gross statistics indicate that both of these are ignored or "overridden" approximately as often as they are observed.

It is assumed, in the tenth place, that inherent distinctions are wholly incapable of accounting by themselves for cross-cultural differences in kinship terminology, and are effective only in conjunction with other types of similarities and dissimilarities, which are therefore the real determining factors. This assumption is self-evident; factors which are universally the same can never account for differences.[67]

An eleventh assumption is that certain recurrent but non-universal features of social structure can significantly increase or decrease the similarities or dissimilarities between particular categories of relatives in the societies where they prevail, thus accentuating or minimizing the effect of particular inherent distinctions and thereby operating as determinants of kinship terminology. This assumption is derived principally from the kinship theories of Rivers and Radcliffe-Brown. The number and variety of such features—forms and preferential rules of marriage, types of family and clan organization, rules of residence and descent, and varieties of unilinear and bilateral kin groups—provide a wide range of causal factors. That these are of greater significance as determinants of kinship terminology than local and non-repetitive historical influences is not an assumption of this study, though it is an overwhelming and not wholly expected conclusion from it.

[66] A. L. Kroeber, "Classificatory Systems of Relationship," *Journal of the Royal Anthropological Institute*, XXXIX (1909), 79.

[67] Nevertheless, failure to recognize this logical axiom has been responsible for innumerable fallacies in social theory, including instinctivism and most other psychological explanations of cultural phenomena, as well as the invocation of alleged universal sociological principles as causal factors.

An aspect of social structure or of associated cultural behavior which significantly increases the perceptible dissimilarities between relatives of different kin-types in particular societies will be called a *social differential*. An aspect of social structure or of associated cultural behavior which creates significant similarities between relatives of different kin-types will be called a *social equalizer*. Like inherent distinctions, social differentials and equalizers differ in relative efficacy, which can be determined only inductively. A rough estimate will be attempted at the end of the present chapter.

Social equalizers and differentials appear to exert their minimizing and accentuating effects through the creation of several different kinds of similarity and dissimilarity, of which the following may be distinguished:

Coincidence—a similarity between two kin-types owing to the probability that the members of both are the same persons, as can happen as a result of certain social equalizers. Sororal polygyny, for example, tends to equate WiSi with Wi.

Proximity—a similarity or dissimilarity in spatial relations. For example, matrilocal residence, by bringing Mo and MoSi together as close neighbors or even actual housemates, operates as a social equalizer to make more likely their designation by a single classificatory term, and by separating FaSi spatially from both of them operates as a social differential to favor the application of a special kinship term to her.

Participation—a similarity or dissimilarity in group membership. Thus patrilineal descent places BrDa and Da in the same lineage, sib, or moiety and SiDa in a separate group, thereby promoting extension of the term for Da to BrDa and differentiation of the term for SiDa.

Analogy—a similarity relative to a parallel relationship. Extension of the term "mother" to MoSi, for example, acts as a social equalizer in the case of MoSiDa, increasing her likelihood of being called "sister" even under patrilineal descent when Si and MoSiDa are usually neither sibmates nor neighbors.

Immateriality—a negative similarity resulting from the functional unimportance of the relatives of two kin-types, whereby a sufficient basis for differentiating them is lacking. Immateriality appears chiefly with respect to distant relatives. In the English kinship system, for example, it operates as an equalizer to favor the extension of the term "cousin" to various distant relatives of little importance, without reference to distinctions of sex, generation, or collaterality.

Our twelfth assumption is that the forms of social structure are not determined by kinship patterns or terminology, or influenced in any major degree by them, but are created by forces external to social organization, especially by economic factors. It is assumed herewith, for example, that the available sources of food and the techniques of procuring it affect the sex division of labor and the relative statuses of the sexes, predisposing peoples to particular rules of residence, which can eventuate in the formation of extended families, clans, and sibs. It is further assumed that the prevailing types and distribution of property favor particular rules of inheritance, that wealth or its lack affects marriage (e.g., encouraging or inhibiting polygyny), and that these and other factors external to social structure can strongly influence rules of residence and marriage and through them the forms of social organization and kinship structure. This assumption is derived from the analysis by Lowie [68] of the origin of sibs, from our own supportive evidence as presented in Chapter 8, and from the various theorists from Marx to Keller who have stressed the importance of economic factors in cultural change.[69]

Our thirteenth and final assumption is that a change in social structure which significantly alters the social equalizers and differentials affecting particular kin-types will be followed by adaptive changes in the pertinent kinship terms only after a lapse of time. This assumption is derived from the suggestion by Lowie [70] of the importance of "the time element" and especially from the sociological hypotheses of a "strain toward consistency" and a "cultural lag" between the constituent elements of a culture, as propounded re-

---

[68] R. H. Lowie, *Primitive Society* (New York, 1920), pp. 157–62.

[69] It is not assumed, however, that all determinants of social structure are economic. Both Islam and Christianity, for instance, have demonstrably produced changes in marriage institutions in many places, with resulting modifications in social alignments and kinship terminology.

[70] R. H. Lowie, *Culture and Ethnology* (New York, 1917), p. 173.

spectively by Sumner [71] and Ogburn.[72] Herein lies a probable explanation of many of the instances in which the data from particular societies do not correspond with the theoretical expectations expressed in our postulate.

The underlying assumptions having been made explicit, and all relevant terms having been defined, the basic postulate may now be formulated.

Postulate 1: The relatives of any two kin-types tend to be called by the same kinship terms, rather than by different terms, in inverse proportion to the number and relative efficacy of (a) the inherent distinctions between them and (b) the social differentials affecting them, and in direct proportion to the number and relative efficacy of the social equalizers affecting them.

Rephrased in looser language, the postulate states that the extension and differentiation of kinship terminology is the product of the joint interplay of all inherent and cultural factors which significantly affect the degree of similarity or dissimilarity between particular categories of relatives.

The serious reader who feels that there is something peculiarly incomprehensible or baffling about kinship terminology—an illusion shared even by some anthropologists—is nevertheless urged to make an attempt to understand the theorems and their validation, since they are basic to a comprehension of the general theory of the evolution of social organization in Chapter 8 and of the principles governing the extension of sexual privileges and taboos as presented in Chapters 9 and 10. To paraphrase Lawrence,[73] if any primitive tribe can invent a kinship system, any civilized reader should be capable of comprehending it.

The first theorem to be tested is of a rather special nature, and is given priority in order to provide a basis for the inclusion of certain relatives in the testing of subsequent theorems. It deals with the structural similarity between nuclear families in any society as a social equalizer facilitating the extension of kinship terms by analogy. Whenever, for the various reasons to be disclosed in subsequent

---

[71] W. G. Sumner, *Folkways* (Boston, 1906), pp. 5–6.

[72] W. F. Ogburn, *Social Change* (New York, 1922), pp. 200–80.

[73] W. E. Lawrence, "Alternating Generations in Australia," *Studies in the Science of Society,* ed. G. P. Murdock (New Haven, 1937), p. 327.

theorems, the term for "mother" is extended to MoSi, FaSi, FaBrWi, or MoBrWi, the daughters of such "classificatory mothers" tend to be called by the same term as sister, on the analogy of the relation between own mother and her daughter. Similarly when WiSi or BrWi is called by the term for "wife," WiSiDa or BrDa, respectively, will tend to be called "daughter." In all instances the social equalizer overrides the inherent distinction of collaterality, and in the case of WiSiDa that of affinity as well. While sample tabulations have shown that the same principle operates elsewhere, it is not necessary for our purposes to establish it for other relatives, and the theorem and its validation will consequently be concerned only with the relatives mentioned above.

Theorem 1: When secondary or tertiary relatives of any kin-type are called by a kinship term used to denote a primary relative, the daughters of such secondary or tertiary relatives tend to be called by the same kinship term as the daughter of the primary relative.

In this and all subsequent theorems it is naturally assumed that all factors other than the social equalizers and differentials under consideration are held constant.

Theorem 1 is subjected to test by the data compiled in Table 15. It is decisively validated by high and consistent positive coefficients of association and, in all but one instance, by very high indices of reliability.

TABLE 15

| | Parent Called "Mother" | | Parent Called Otherwise | | | |
Pairs of Relatives	Child Called "Sister"	Child Called Otherwise	Child Called "Sister"	Child Called Otherwise	Statistical Indices Q	χ^2
FaSi-FaSiDa	18	22	42	156	+ .50	1000
MoSi-MoSiDa	110	16	62	34	+ .58	1000
FaBrWi-FaBrDa	85	9	50	24	+ .64	1000
MoBrWi-MoBrDa	17	10	29	113	+ .74	1000

| | Parent Called "Wife" | | Parent Called Otherwise | | | |
	Child Called "Daughter"	Child Called Otherwise	Child Called "Daughter"	Child Called Otherwise		
BrWi-BrDa	25	4	96	68	+ .67	100
WiSi-WiSiDa	10	4	44	33	+ .30	2

The "rule of uniform descent" as defined by Tax [74] corresponds closely to Theorem 1, and is confirmed by the validation of the latter. It should be expressly pointed out that neither the rule nor the theorem invokes a psychological constant as the prime determinant of a cultural variable. On the contrary, they assume only that when a term has been extended to one relative (FaSi, MoSi, FaBrWi, MoBrWi, BrWi, or WiSi) for whatsoever reasons, family structure provides the necessary similarity to facilitate another extension with respect to the daughter of that relative.

Forms of marriage constitute a second principal group of social equalizers and differentials. The major forms are polygyny, polyandry, and monogamy. Polyandry is the general and preferred form in only two of the sample societies, the Marquesans and the Todas, and is consequently too rare for statistically reliable testing. Polygyny may be either common or infrequent. If it is exceptional in actual practice, even though permitted, it cannot be expected to exert any considerable influence upon the alignment or terminological classification of relatives, which should be essentially the same as under monogamy. We have consequently classed as monogamous for present purposes all societies in which less than 20 per cent of all marriages are plural unions, considering as polygynous only those with a higher percentage. Polygyny, moreover, may be either sororal or non-sororal. The polygynous societies have therefore been divided into two groups—one in which secondary wives are exclusively the sisters of the first wife and one in which non-sororal polygyny is common, even though sororal polygyny also occurs or is actually somewhat preferred. For purposes of computation, all polygynous societies for which exclusive sororal polygyny is not specifically reported have been classed as non-sororal.

Sororal polygyny operates as a social equalizer through both coincidence and participation. By making it probable that such relatives as MoSi and Mo, WiSi and Wi, MoSiDa and Si, and WiSiDa and Da will actually be the same persons or at least members of the same family as Ego and one another, it should facilitate the extension of kinship terms, within each pair, from the latter to the former.

[74] S. Tax, "Some Problems of Social Organization," *Social Anthropology of North American Tribes,* ed. F. Eggan (Chicago, 1937), pp. 19–20.

Theorem 2: In the presence of sororal polygyny, terms for primary relatives tend to be extended, within the same sex and generation, to their collateral relatives through females.

The data compiled in Table 16 provide only tentative confirmation of the theorem since, though the coefficients of association are exclusively positive, the indices of reliability are very low throughout. There are indications that the results might be improved by a somewhat less rigorous definition of sororal polygyny.

TABLE 16

Pairs of Relatives	Sororal Polygyny		Other Forms of Marriage		Statistical Indices	
	Same Term	Different Terms	Same Term	Different Terms	Q	χ^2
MoSi-Mo	11	7	117	94	+ .12	—
WiSi-Wi	4	17	20	171	+ .34	2
MoSiDa-Si	16	2	147	54	+ .49	2
WiSiDa Da	6	2	45	35	+ .40	—

In the testing of many of the theorems which follow, it will be useful to employ a fourfold classification of relatives proposed independently by Lowie [75] and Kirchhoff.[76] This classification is based upon the four possible permutations in the application of the inherent distinctions of collaterality and bifurcation. Either or both may be recognized, or both may be ignored, in the terminological designation of kinsmen. The four possibilities can be illustrated by the terms for parents and their siblings. Recognition of both bifurcation and collaterality produces so-called *bifurcate collateral* terminology, in which paternal and maternal uncles and aunts are terminologically differentiated both from parents and from one another. This yields separate terms for Fa, FaBr, MoBr, Mo, MoSi, and FaSi. The recognition of bifurcation combined with the ignoring of collaterality produces *bifurcate merging* terminology, in which the Fa and FaBr are called by one classificatory term, and the Mo and MoSi by a second, while the MoBr and FaSi are denoted by distinct terms.

[75] R. H. Lowie, "A Note on Relationship Terminologies," *American Anthropologist*, n.s., XXX (1928), 265–6; "Relationship Terms," *Encyclopaedia Britannica* (14th edit., London, 1929), XIX, 84–6.

[76] P. Kirchhoff, "Verwandtschaftsbezeichnungen und Verwandtenheirat," *Zeitschrift für Ethnologie*, LXIV (1932), 46–9.

The recognition of collaterality but not of bifurcation yields so-called *lineal* terminology; as in our own system, FaBr and MoBr are grouped under one classificatory term, and FaSi and MoSi under a second, with separate denotative terms for each parent. Finally, the ignoring of both inherent distinctions leads to so-called *generation* terminology, in which the term for father is extended to both uncles, and often to remoter relatives as well, while a second classificatory term serves alike for mother and both aunts.

One or another of the above four types can be applied to any trio of kinsmen in the same generation and of the same sex, provided the second is a collateral relative of the first in the same line of descent and the third is related to Ego in the same manner as the second except for a difference in the sex of the connecting relative. The demonstrations of our theorems will, whenever appropriate, use six such trios, in two of which, the second and sixth in the list below, an additional inherent distinction, that of affinity, is involved. These trios, with the four alternative methods of distributing kinship terms among them, are tabulated below.

Bifurcate Collateral

Mo, MoSi, FaSi
Mo, FaBrWi, MoBrWi
Si, FaBrDa, FaSiDa
Si, MoSiDa, MoBrDa
Da, BrDa, SiDa
Da, WiSiDa, WiBrDa

Lineal Terminology

Mo, MoSi = FaSi
Mo, FaBrWi = MoBrWi
Si, FaBrDa = FaSiDa
Si, MoSiDa = MoBrDa
Da, BrDa = SiDa
Da, WiSiDa = WiBrDa

Bifurcate Merging

Mo = MoSi, FaSi
Mo = FaBrWi, MoBrWi
Si = FaBrDa, FaSiDa
Si = MoSiDa, MoBrDa
Da = BrDa, SiDa
Da = WiSiDa, WiBrDa

Generation Terminology

Mo = MoSi = FaSi
Mo = FaBrWi = MoBrWi
Si = FaBrDa = FaSiDa
Si = MoSiDa = MoBrDa
Da = BrDa = SiDa
Da = WiSiDa = WiBrDa

The fifth theoretically possible combination, that of equating FaSi with Mo and differentiating MoSi from both, or an equivalent grouping in other trios, almost never occurs in actual fact; there are only four sporadic instances for the six trios in our entire sample.

Sororal polygyny, by bringing collateral relatives through females into proximity with lineal relatives and thus separating them spatially from collateral relatives through males, tends to emphasize the inherent distinction of bifurcation as well as to minimize that of collaterality. It should thus operate to produce bifurcate merging terminology. A theorem is formulated to cover the two trios of relatives for which its influence is most directly relevant.

Theorem 3: Sororal polygyny tends to be associated with kinship terminology of the bifurcate merging type for aunts and for nieces by marriage.

This theorem is subjected to test in Table 17. Despite the fact that one computation yields a perfect positive coefficient of association, Table 17 can be regarded as providing only tentative validation of Theorem 3 since the χ^2 index of reliability is low in the only instance where it can appropriately be applied.

TABLE 17

Trios of Relatives	Sororal Polygyny		Other Marriage Forms		Statistical Indices	
	Bifurcate Merging	Other Terms	Bifurcate Merging	Other Terms	Q	χ^2
FaSi-MoSi-Mo	9	9	81	129	+ .23	2
WiBrDa-WiSiDa-Da	5	0	27	42	+ 1.00	*

Polygyny of the non-sororal type operates as a social differential rather than as a social equalizer. Whereas under sororal polygyny MoSi lives in close proximity to Mo, MoSiDa to Si, and WiSiDa to Da, these and all other collateral relatives are spatially separated from lineal relatives under non-sororal polygyny. The mother is now immediately surrounded by her co-wives, not her sisters; the sister and daughter by their half sisters, not their parallel cousins. In other words, the members of the polygynous family intervene to separate the members of the nuclear family from aunts, nieces, and first cousins who might otherwise live in their immediate vicinity. This happens irrespective of rules of residence and descent, and the resulting spatial separation of collateral relatives outside of the polygynous family serves to inhibit the extension to them of the kinship terms for primary relatives. In short, non-sororal polygyny tends to prevent the occurrence of merging.

Theorem 4: In the presence of non-sororal polygyny, collateral relatives outside of the polygynous family tend to be terminologically differentiated from primary relatives of the same sex and generation.

Table 18, which assembles the data to test Theorem 4, yields five low positive coefficients and the only negative coefficient that we shall encounter in testing any of our theorems. This, coupled with the fact that all indices of reliability are low, suggests that the

TABLE 18

Pairs of Relatives	Non-sororal Polygyny		Other Forms of Marriage		Statistical Indices	
	Different Terms	Same Term	Different Terms	Same Term	Q	χ^2
MoSi-Mo	53	58	48	70	+ .14	2
FaBrWi-Mo	36	46	37	45	− .02	—
FaBrDa-Si	28	84	23	95	+ .16	2
MoSiDa-Si	30	78	23	90	+ .21	2
BrDa-Da	38	61	39	73	+ .08	—
WiSiDa-Da	22	28	16	24	+ .08	—

validation of the theorem is inconclusive. Careful analysis, however, counteracts this impression. Non-sororal polygyny, as it happens, is very highly associated with patrilocal residence, patrilineal descent, and the types of kin groups which depend upon these rules, all of which factors, as will presently be seen, exert an influence directly counter to that of polygyny, i.e., in favor of merging. The evidence from our 250 societies shows that non-sororal polygyny tends to occur in the presence of patrilocal residence and patrilineal descent by coefficients of association of +.66 and +.58, respectively, with a χ^2 index of reliability of 1000 in each case. Hence the tendency toward positive association in Table 18 and the appearance of five positive signs out of six, which could occur only about once in ten times by random sampling if the true relationship were zero, are attained in the teeth of the strongest of countervailing factors. Under these circumstances, the results must be regarded as very much more significant than they appear on the surface.

The influence of non-sororal polygyny is shown more clearly when Table 18 is corrected for one of the major groups of countervailing factors. This is done in Table 19 for the factor of patrilineal descent by eliminating from the compilation all societies with exogamous patrilineal lineages, sibs, and moieties. In the new tabulation all the coefficients are positive in sign, their average magnitude is appreciably raised, and in one instance reliability at the five per cent level of confidence is attained, despite the fact that the opposing

TABLE 19

Pairs of Relatives	Non-sororal Polygyny		Other Forms of Marriage		Statistical Indices	
	Different Terms	Same Term	Different Terms	Same Term	Q	χ^2
MoSi-Mo	25	19	34	51	+ .33	2
FaBrWi-Mo	16	11	23	29	+ .30	—
FaBrDa-Si	12	33	18	69	+ .16	—
MoSiDa-Si	11	22	20	68	+ .06	—
BrDa-Da	23	17	28	50	+ .41	20
WiSiDa-Da	7	9	12	16	+ .02	—

factor of patrilocal residence is still not eliminated. Random sampling could produce six positive signs only once in 64 times. Theorem 4 can therefore be regarded as substantially validated.

It is already apparent, and will become increasingly clear below, that kinship terminology in patrilocal and patrilineal societies, in contrast to societies with other rules of residence and descent, regularly reflects two sets of opposing influences. The rules of residence and descent promote merging, whereas the associated phenomenon of general polygyny inhibits the tendency to extend terms from lineal to collateral relatives. Whether merging does or does not occur is therefore likely to depend upon such facts as which of the opposing influences has been longer established or possesses the greater relative efficacy.

By operating as a social differential to oppose merging, non-sororal polygyny militates against kinship terminology of either the generation or the bifurcate merging types. By virtue of its association with patrilocal residence and patrilineal descent, which favor bifurcation, it is more conducive to bifurcate collateral than to lineal terminology. In the usual polygynous society, collateral relatives on the maternal side are ordinarily differentiated from those on the paternal side by the fact that they reside in another clan or community and belong to different consanguineal kin groups. Both types of collateral relatives, moreover, are differentiated from lineal relatives; the half siblings, stepparents and stepchildren of the polygynous family intervene between them. Bifurcate collateral terms accord with these conditions. Non-sororal polygyny is, in fact, the only social determinant we have discovered that favors bifurcate collateral terminology. With it are commonly associated distinct terms for Fa, FaBr, and MoBr, for Mo, MoSi, and FaSi, and for the several members of all comparable trios of relatives.

Theorem 5: Non-sororal polygyny tends to be associated with kinship terminology of the bifureate collateral type.

The theorem is validated by the data assembled in Table 20, wherein the coefficients of association are exclusively positive in sign and reliability attains the five per cent level or better for three of the six trios, despite the fact that patrilocal residence and patrilineal descent again exert their countervailing influence.

TABLE 20

	Non-sororal Polygyny		Other Forms of Marriage			
Trios of Relatives	Bifurcate Collateral Terms	Other Terms	Bifurcate Collateral Terms	Other Terms	Statistical Indices Q	χ^2
FaSi-MoSi-Mo	45	65	32	86	$+$.30	20
MoBrWi-FaBrWi-Mo	23	49	19	54	$+$.14	—
FaSiDa-FaBrDa-Si	17	90	7	110	$+$.50	20
MoBrDa-MoSiDa-Si	20	83	6	100	$+$.60	100
SiDa-BrDa-Da	23	64	27	83	$+$.05	—
WiBrDa-WiSiDa-Da	12	32	7	28	$+$.20	—

Theorem 5 is further validated in Table 21, which corrects Table 20 by eliminating all societies with exogamous unilinear kin groups. These, as will be demonstrated under Theorem 19, tend to produce bifurcate merging terminology, thereby counteracting the influence of non-sororal polygyny in promoting bifurcate collateral nomenclature. Table 21 reveals a consistent increase in the magnitude of coefficients of association, and the indices of reliability, though lowered in two instances by the reduction in the total number of

TABLE 21

	Non-sororal Polygyny		Other Forms of Marriage			
Trios of Relatives	Bifurcate Collateral Terms	Other Terms	Bifurcate Collateral Terms	Other Terms	Statistical Indices Q	χ^2
FaSi-MoSi-Mo	21	9	15	39	+ .54	1000
MoBrWi-FaBrWi-Mo	9	6	7	21	+ .55	10
FaSiDa-FaBrDa-Si	4	27	2	54	+ .60	2
MoBrDa-MoSiDa-Si	5	27	2	54	+ .68	5
SiDa-BrDa-Da	11	16	12	38	+ .35	2
WiBrDa-WiSiDa-Da	4	9	3	14	+ .22	—

cases, in one instance attain the maximum level of confidence at one tenth of one per cent.

Monogamy should not of itself exert any special influence upon kinship terminology, and analysis of the data shows that it tends to be associated with terms consistent with the prevailing rule of residence (see Theorems 6 to 12). The isolated monogamous family, however, is definitely associated with nomenclature of the lineal type (see Theorem 14). Tests of the four theorems concerned with marriage forms have indicated that these exercise an appreciable influence on kinship terminology, although the demonstration has in several cases fallen short of being conclusive.

The various cultural rules prescribing the place of residence of a married couple constitute a third and extremely important group of social equalizers and differentials. To recapitulate, a rule of residence is called "matrilocal" when a married couple normally live with or near the wife's parents, "patrilocal" when they reside with or near the husband's parents, "matri-patrilocal" when the prevailing rule is matrilocal for a year or two and thereafter shifts to patrilocal, "bilocal" when residence is optionally matrilocal or patrilocal depending upon circumstances or personal preferences, "avunculocal" when the couple live with or near the husband's maternal uncle, and "neolocal" when they establish a new household without reference to the location of the families of either. Any rule of residence affects the proximity of particular categories of relatives, operating sometimes as a social differential by regularly separating spatially the members of two kin-types, sometimes as a social equalizer by regularly bringing them into proximity with one another or by separating them from Ego in like degree.

Patrilocal, matri-patrilocal, matrilocal, and avunculocal residence, classed collectively as unilocal rules, tend to bring into physical proximity a group of relatives linked to one another by a single line of descent, i.e., those related either through males or through females, and to segregate them from relatives through the opposite sex. Hence these residence rules, in contrast to bilocal and neolocal residence, operate as a social differential to support the inherent distinction of bifurcation.

Theorem 6: In the presence of patrilocal, matri-patrilocal, matrilocal, or avunculocal residence, separate terms tend to be applied to relatives of the same generation who are linked to Ego through connecting relatives of different sex.

The data assembled in Table 22 decisively validate this theorem. Coefficients of association are uniformly high and positive, and the probabilities of the results occurring by chance are minimal.

TABLE 22

Pairs of Relatives	Unilocal Residence		Neolocal or Bilocal Residence		Statistical Indices	
	Different Terms	Same Term	Different Terms	Same Term	Q	χ^2
FaSi-MoSi	157	49	20	15	+.41	20
FaBrWi-MoBrWi	96	33	14	11	+.39	5
FaBrDa-FaSiDa	136	60	13	24	+.61	1000
MoBrDa-MoSiDa	129	59	11	24	+.65	1000
BrDa-SiDa	143	33	16	13	+.56	100
WiBrDa-WiSiDa	48	17	8	7	+.42	2

Matrilocal residence brings together a group of women who are related to one another through women, and thus tends to minimize the inherent distinction of collaterality and to favor the extension of kinship terms from lineal relatives to the collateral relatives who reside with them. In some instances, as in the case of WiSiDa and Da, it also tends to override the inherent distinction of affinity. These anticipated effects are expressed in Theorem 7. Avunculocal residence creates alignments of relatives which tend to be intermediate between those resulting from patrilocal and from matrilocal residence. Since the cases are too few in number (eight in our total sample) to justify separate statistical treatment, they are grouped with those of matrilocal residence in the following theorems and tabulations.

Theorem 7: In the presence of matrilocal or avunculocal residence, terms for primary relatives tend to be extended, within the same generation, to their collateral relatives through females.

The data in Table 23 confirm Theorem 7 by positive coefficients of association of fair consistency and considerable magnitude and by moderate indices of reliability.

TABLE 23

Pairs of Relatives	Matrilocal or Avunculocal Residence		Other Rules of Residence		Statistical Indices	
	Same Term	Different Terms	Same Term	Different Terms	Q	χ^2
MoSi-Mo	34	12	103	92	+ .46	20
WiSi-Wi	6	33	21	158	+ .16	—
MoSiDa-Si	40	5	139	48	+ .47	10
WiSiDa-Da	13	4	40	35	+ .47	5

As a corollary of Theorems 6 and 7, which show that matrilocal and avunculocal residence promote bifurcation and merging respectively, the same factors should produce bifurate merging terminology.

Theorem 8: Matrilocal and avunculocal residence tend to be associated with kinship terminology of the bifurcate merging type.

The data compiled in Table 24 validate Theorem 8 rather decisively. The coefficients of association are uniformly positive, relatively high, and quite consistent with one another, and the degree of reliability is generally good.

Patrilocal residence with its matri-patrilocal variant should logically produce bifurcate merging terminology precisely as do matrilocal and avunculocal residence. Theorem 6 has shown that it supports the inherent distinction of bifurcation. Since it brings into proximity such relatives as FaBrWi and Mo, FaBrDa and Si, and BrDa and Da, it should also serve to override the inherent distinction of col-

TABLE 24

Trios of Relatives	Matrilocal or Avunculocal Residence		Other Rules of Residence		Statistical Indices	
	Bifurcate Merging	Other Terms	Bifurcate Merging	Other Terms	Q	χ^2
FaSi-MoSi-Mo	23	23	71	121	+ .26	5
MoBrWi-FaBrWi-Mo	15	13	48	77	+ .30	—
FaSiDa-FaBrDa-Si	30	13	95	95	+ .40	20
MoBrDa-MoSiDa-Si	31	12	83	98	+ .51	100
SiDa-BrDa-Da	27	12	84	87	+ .40	20
WiBrDa-WiSiDa-Da	8	4	25	42	+ .54	5

laterality between these relatives, and thus produce merging. That patrilocal residence has these effects is unquestionable, but they tend to be obscured by the strongly associated factor of non-sororal polygyny, which exerts a contrary influence. While patrilocal residence of itself favors bifurcate merging terminology, the polygyny which commonly accompanies it inhibits merging (see Theorem 4) and favors bifurcate collateral nomenclature (see Theorem 5). In formulating a theorem, however, this countervailing influence must be ignored.

Theorem 9: Patrilocal and matri-patrilocal residence tend to be associated with kinship terminology of the bifurcate merging type. The testing of Theorem 9 presents certain difficulties. Matrilocal and avunculocal residence have already been found to exert an identical influence (see Theorem 8), and one which is not appreciably counteracted by non-sororal polygyny. If, consequently, societies with these rules of residence were included in the computations of data, they would tend to hide the influence of patrilocal residence. Table 25 therefore omits all cases of matrilocal and avunculocal residence, comparing patrilocal only with neolocal and bilocal societies. Only three trios of relatives are included—those in which the second member is brought into proximity with the third by patrilocal residence. Aunts and maternal cousins reflect the same influence, but only in derivative fashion, and the wife's nieces are commonly too remote to be significantly affected. Table 25 supports the theorem decisively with positive coefficients of association that are high, consistent, and extremely reliable.

TABLE 25

Trios of Relatives	Patrilocal or Matri-patrilocal Residence		Neolocal or Bilocal Residence		Statistical Indices	
	Bifurcate Merging	Other Terms	Bifurcate Merging	Other Terms	Q	χ^2
MoBrWi-FaBrWi-Mo	42	56	5	19	+ .48	10
FaSiDa-FaBrDa-Si	87	67	9	30	+ .62	1000
SiDa-BrDa-Da	73	64	8	36	+ .67	1000

Theorem 5 has shown that non-sororal polygyny tends to promote bifurcate collateral terminology. We have also noted that a high degree of association exists between this type of polygyny and patrilocal residence. Hence it follows as a corollary that patrilocal residence should tend to be associated with bifurcate collateral terminology, even though it is not to be regarded as a cause of the latter. This anticipated relation may be formulated as a theorem.

Theorem 10: Patrilocal and matri-patrilocal residence, because of their association with non-sororal polygyny, tend to be accompanied by kinship terminology of the bifurcate collateral type.

The data compiled in Table 26 validate this theorem with positive coefficients of association which are consistently positive in sign,

TABLE 26

Trios of Relatives	Patrilocal and Matri-patrilocal Residence		Other Residence Rules		Statistical Indices	
	Bifurcate Collateral Terms	Other Terms	Bifurcate Collateral Terms	Other Terms	Q	χ^2
FaSi-MoSi-Mo	58	100	20	63	+ .29	10
MoBrWi-FaBrWi-Mo	30	68	13	31	+ .03	—
FaSiDa-FaBrDa-Si	19	135	6	75	+ .36	2
MoBrDa-MoSiDa-Si	23	119	5	75	+ .49	2
SiDa-BrDa-Da	37	100	14	60	+ .23	2
WiBrDa-WiSiDa-Da	16	33	4	25	+ .50	5

though the indices of reliability are relatively low. In judging the significance of these results, the reader should not forget that they are attained in the face of the strong countervailing influence demonstrated in Theorem 9.

Bilocal residence produces an alignment of kinsmen very different from that resulting from any rule of unilocal residence. It brings some collateral relatives through males and some through females into proximity with lineal relatives, and thus tends to counteract the inherent distinctions among all three. The overriding of both collaterality and bifurcation produces terminology of the generation type, including the extension of sibling terms to all cousins.

Theorem 11: Bilocal residence tends to be associated with kinship terminology of the generation type.

This theorem is conclusively validated in Table 27. The coefficients of association are high in value, positive in sign, extremely consistent, and almost maximally reliable.

TABLE 27

Trios of Relatives	Bilocal Residence		Other Residence Rules		Statistical Indices	
	Generation Terms	Other Terms	Generation Terms	Other Terms	Q	χ^2
FaSi-MoSi-Mo	9	11	33	187	+ .65	100
MoBrWi-FaBrWi-Mo	6	10	16	121	+ .64	20
FaSiDa-FaBrDa-Si	13	7	46	168	+ .75	1000
MoBrDa-MoSiDa-Si	13	7	46	158	+ .73	1000
SiDa-BrDa-Da	7	12	16	176	+ .73	1000
WiBrDa-WiSiDa-Da	4	8	6	62	+ .68	10

Neolocal residence, such as characterizes our own society, results in the spatial separation of lineal relatives from all collateral relatives irrespective of the sex of the connecting relative. It consequently emphasizes the inherent distinction of collaterality. It minimizes the inherent distinction of bifurcation, since it creates no residential distinctions between collateral relatives through males and those through females. In combination, these two effects produce terminology of the lineal type.

Theorem 12: Neolocal residence tends to be associated with kinship terminology of the lineal type.

Table 28, which tests this theorem, omits the data for a wife's nieces. These relatives are marginal under neolocal residence and, as in our own society, elementary kinship terms are commonly lacking for them. The theorem is conclusively validated by high, positive, consistent, and reliable coefficients.

TABLE 28

	Neolocal Residence		Other Residence Rules		Statistical Indices	
Trios of Relatives	Lineal Terms	Other Terms	Lineal Terms	Other Terms	Q	χ^2
FaSi-MoSi-Mo	5	11	18	206	+ .68	100
MoBrWi-FaBrWi-Mo	3	6	18	125	+ .55	2
FaSiDa-FaBrDa-Si	7	11	19	197	+ .74	1000
MoBrDa-MoSiDa-Si	7	9	19	188	+ .84	1000
SiDa-BrDa-Da	6	10	19	177	+ .70	100

Forms of the family constitute a fourth group of social equalizers and differentials. They differ somewhat from the forms of marriage, since monogamous, polyandrous, and polygynous families may either stand alone or be aggregated into larger extended families. The polyandrous family is too rare for statistical treatment. The influence of the polygynous family has already been shown in Theorems 2 to 5, and the isolated monogamous family will be separately considered in Theorem 14. The several types of extended families—patrilocal, matrilocal, avunculocal, and bilocal—depend upon the prevailing rule of residence and exert the influences upon kinship nomenclature already set forth in Theorems 6 to 11. Over and above the effect of spatial proximity or segregation produced by residence rules, however, extended families introduce the new factor of social participation, since their members not only live nearby but also belong to the same familial group. This should tend to enhance their similarity and to augment the effect of common residence.

However, when societies are classed according to the presence or absence of particular types of extended families, others with the same rules of residence exerting similar influences must be treated as negative cases. This necessarily results in the lowering of coefficients despite the effect of participation. To exclude all cases with similar rules of residence would not so much test the influence of extended family organization as show the contrast between its effects and those of neolocal and bilocal residence, for which after Theorems 11 and 12 no further demonstration is required. We have discovered no way of formulating and testing theorems to cope with this problem, and must therefore be content with summarizing the results of various computations. Matrilocal and avunculocal extended families have been found to be strongly associated with bifurcate merging terminology, and bilocal extended families with generation terminology, but in both cases by coefficients slightly lower in average magnitude than in the tests of the comparable residence rules (see Theorems 8 and 11). With patrilocal extended families bifurcate collateral and bifurcate merging terminology predominates, as anticipated from Theorems 9 and 10. In short, the results conform precisely to theoretical expectations, even though technical difficulties prevent the formulation and testing of the latter in the form of theorems.

Clans constitute a fifth group of social equalizers and differentials. Like the rules of residence that determine their form, they influence kinship terminology through the factor of proximity. Like extended families, they also exert an influence through participation. Furthermore, since clans involve a recognition of unilinear descent as well as of unilocal residence, they exert an effect upon terminology comparable to that which will be demonstrated below for unilinear consanguineal kin groups. All of these influences supplement and reinforce each other. Clan membership increases the similarities between lineal and collateral relatives in the same line of descent, and thus promotes merging. The inherent distinction of bifurcation is supported, since persons related to Ego through intervening relatives of opposite sex are spatially and socially segregated. Hence clans tend to produce kinship nomenclature of the bifurcate merging type.

Theorem 13: Clans, whether patrilocal, matrilocal, or avunculocal in type, tend to be associated with bifurcate merging kinship terminology.

Since patri-clans involve the complicating factor of polygyny, this theorem is first tested with respect to the influence of matrilocal and avunculocal clans. Table 29, from which wife's nieces are omitted because of paucity of data, provides substantial validation in this partial test.

TABLE 29

Trios of Relatives	Matrilocal or Avunculocal Clans		Patrilocal Clans or No Clans		Statistical Indices	
	Bifurcate Merging	Other Terms	Bifurcate Merging	Other Terms	Q	χ^2
FaSi-MoSi-Mo	7	9	75	118	+ .10	2
MoBrWi-FaBrWi-Mo	6	6	48	67	+ .16	—
FaSiDa-FaBrDa-Si	15	2	90	99	+ .74	100
MoBrDa-MoSiDa-Si	15	0	77	99	+ 1.00	*
SiDa-BrDa-Da	9	4	84	89	+ .41	2

With respect to the influence of patri-clans we encounter once more the countervailing factor of non-sororal polygyny, which has been found to favor bifurcate collateral rather than bifurcate merging terminology (see Theorem 5). When only patrilocal residence is involved, polygyny is sufficient, in conjunction with the inherent distinctions of collaterality and bifurcation, to override its influence statistically (see Theorem 10). When, however, participation in the same compromise kin group is added to proximity through patrilocal residence, the effect of polygyny is submerged, and patri-clans are found to be definitely associated with bifurcate merging terminology. Table 30, wherein Theorem 13 is subjected to a second partial test, again provides substantial confirmation.

TABLE 30

Trios of Relatives	Patrilocal Clans		Other or No Clans		Statistical Indices	
	Bifurcate Merging	Other Terms	Bifurcate Merging	Other Terms	Q	χ^2
FaSi-MoSi-Mo	31	38	49	88	+ .18	2
MoBrWi-FaBrWi-Mo	24	23	30	50	+ .27	5
FaSiDa-FaBrDa-Si	41	23	62	78	+ .38	20
MoBrDa-MoSiDa-Si	33	24	59	76	+ .27	5
SiDa-BrDa-Da	36	23	58	68	+ .30	10
WiBrDa-WiSiDa-Da	12	11	18	27	+ .16	2

Neither Table 29 nor Table 30, of course, adequately reflects the influence of clans, for when types of clans are tabulated separately, societies possessing other types exerting an identical influence are necessarily counted as negative cases. This defect is corrected in Table 31, which compares clanless tribes with those possessing clans of any type. Here the confirmation of Theorem 13 is not merely substantial but conclusive.

TABLE 31

Trios of Relatives	Clans Present		Clans Absent		Statistical Indices	
	Bifurcate Merging	Other Terms	Bifurcate Merging	Other Terms	Q	χ^2
FaSi-MoSi-Mo	38	47	44	80	+.33	2
MoBrWi-FaBrWi-Mo	30	29	24	44	+.31	5
FaSiDa-FaBrDa-Si	56	24	49	77	+.57	1000
MoBrDa-MoSiDa-Si	48	24	44	76	+.55	1000
SiDa-BrDa-Da	45	27	49	66	+.39	20
WiBrDa-WiSiDa-Da	13	14	18	24	+.08	—

Now that the influence of extended families and clans has been disposed of, it becomes possible to examine the bearing of the uncomplicated nuclear family upon kinship terminology. This is obscured when families are aggregated into larger kin groups of either the residential or the compromise type. Bifurcate collateral terminology tends to result when nuclear families are combined through plural marriages into non-sororal polygynous families (see Theorem 5) or are grouped by common residence into patrilocal extended families. Bifurcate merging tends to appear when nuclear families are linked together by sororal polygyny (see Theorem 3), or are united by common residence into matrilocal or avunculocal extended families or into clans of any type (see Theorem 13). Generation terminology tends to occur when they are aggregated into bilocal extended families. Is there any form of nomenclature which is typical of instances where the nuclear family stands in majestic isolation, as it does in our own society, uncompounded into larger kin groups?

A partial answer to the above question is provided by the prevailing rules of residence (see Theorems 6 to 12). Nevertheless, one type of kinship terminology appears to be especially characteristic of the *isolated nuclear family*, as we may designate an independent nuclear family in the absence of clans. This is the lineal type of nomenclature. The very isolation of the nuclear family operates as a social differential to favor separate terms for lineal and collateral relatives, and at the same time operates as a social equalizer, either through immateriality or through equivalent lack of proximity, to minimize the inherent distinction between collateral relatives through different sexes.

Theorem 14: In the absence of clans and of polygamous and extended families, the isolated nuclear family tends to be associated with kinship terminology of the lineal type.

In Table 32, which tests this theorem, terms for wife's nieces are omitted because of the infrequency with which they exist or are reported in societies with isolated nuclear families. The theorem is validated by coefficients of association that are positive in sign, high in value, mutually consistent, and reliable in the majority of instances at the five or the one per cent level of confidence.

TABLE 32

Trios of Relatives	Isolated Nuclear Family		Compounded Family Forms		Statistical Indices	
	Lineal Terms	Other Terms	Lineal Terms	Other Terms	Q	χ^2
FaSi-MoSi-Mo	7	23	15	177	+ .56	20
MoBrWi-FaBrWi-Mo	4	11	14	110	+ .41	2
FaSiDa-FaBrDa-Si	9	23	15	170	+ .62	100
MoBrDa-MoSiDa-Si	9	20	15	162	+ .70	100
SiDa-BrDa-Da	6	22	21	148	+ .30	2

A sixth and extremely important group of social determinants includes the various types of consanguineal kin groups—bilateral groups such as the kindred and the deme, unilinear groups such as the lineage, the sib, and the moiety, and bilinear kin groups such as the section. Among these, anthropologists have paid least attention to bilateral kin groups. They have, for example, rarely made a special effort to discover kindreds, and they practically never report their absence. In testing theorems concerning the kindred, therefore, it becomes necessary to compare societies in which it is reported with those in which it is not reported instead of the preferable comparison between those in which it is present and those in which it is absent. This doubtless reduces the magnitude and reliability of coefficients, since presumably a number of tribes in which the kindred is present but unreported are included among the negative cases.

The kindred unites in a social group all of Ego's near relatives regardless of collaterality or bifurcation. It should therefore be expected to operate as a social equalizer to override these inherent distinctions and produce kinship terminology of the generation type.

Theorem 15: Bilateral kindreds tend to be associated with kinship terminology of the generation type.

This theorem is validated in Table 33 by uniformly high and consistent positive coefficients of association with a degree of reliability that is quite satisfactory under the circumstances.

TABLE 33

Trios of Relatives	Kindreds Present		Kindreds Unreported		Statistical Indices	
	Generation Terms	Other Terms	Generation Terms	Other Terms	Q	χ^2
FaSi-MoSi-Mo	10	20	32	166	+ .47	20
MoBrWi-FaBrWi-Mo	4	13	19	114	+ .30	—
FaSiDa-FaBrDa-Si	13	17	46	157	+ .44	20
MoBrDa-MoSiDa-Si	13	17	45	146	+ .42	20
SiDa-BrDa-Da	5	26	16	164	+ .49	2
WiBrDa-WiSiDa-Da	3	8	7	58	+ .57	2

The influence of demes upon kinship terminology presents a special problem, for it appears to be significant only within Ego's own generation. When societies with endogamous demes are compared with other bilateral societies they reveal a practically identical distribution of generation, lineal, bifurcate merging, and bifurcate collateral terms for all relatives of the first ascending and first descending generations. With respect to cousins, however, they show a markedly stronger preponderance of generation terminology, despite the parallel influence of kindreds in many of the bilateral societies with which they are compared. This tendency shows up even more strikingly when they are compared with all other societies, as is done in Table 34. But here, too, no effect is observable on either the first ascending or the first descending generation; tests for the relevant kinsmen reveal low coefficients with either plus or minus signs, indicating that association is purely random.

Why should endogamous demes exert such a marked influence on kinship terminology within Ego's own generation but none whatsoever on other generations, especially since every other type of consanguineal kin group can be statistically shown to affect kinship terms on all generations in similar manner and to approximately the same degree? While we cannot answer this question definitely, we offer a tentative suggestion in the hope that others may be able either to verify it or to propose an acceptable alternative theory.

With the exception of the deme all consanguineal kin groups, whether unilinear or bilateral, divide the local community into members and non-members. Participation and non-participation provide a basis for terminological distinctions on all generations. The deme, however, is coextensive with the community, and hence cannot produce any differentation in kinship terms among its members. Under these conditions family structure becomes peculiarly important. Between generations, the strongly functional parent-child relationships stand out in especially strong relief, with the result that avuncular and nepotic relatives tend to be denoted by distinctive kinship terms. In the societies of our sample which possess endogamous demes, as a matter of fact, the kinship terms for aunts, nieces, uncles' wives, and wife's nieces accord with theoretical expectations on the basis of other factors.

Within the same generation, however, the absence of segmentation in the community removes one of the commonest grounds for differentiating siblings from cousins, and deme organization itself acts as a definite social equalizer to favor the extension of kinship terms from the former to the latter. Moreover, persons of the same generation tend nearly everywhere to be more closely associated in economic and social activities than are persons of different generations, so that family distinctions are more readily overridden than in the first ascending or first descending generation.

The only factual support for this highly tentative hypothesis that we have been able to discover comes from the kinship terminology for parallel cousins in societies with unilinear descent.

In patrilineal societies FaBrDa but not MoSiDa is necessarily a member of Ego's kin group, and in matrilineal societies MoSiDa but not FaBrDa. Yet the overwhelming majority of unilinear societies also extend sibling terms to MoSiDa in the former and to FaBrDa in the latter. Theorem 1 has offered a partial explanation, but an examination of Table 15 will show that it accounts for by no means all of the cases. Omitting instances of double descent, which necessarily affiliates both parallel cousins with Ego, our sample reveals that MoSiDa in societies with exogamous patrilineal kin groups, or FaBrDa in matrilineal tribes, is called by the same term as sister in 100 societies and by another term in 29. Of the latter, 24 have general non-sororal polygyny, which accounts for the differentiation (see Theorem 4). These facts suggest a widespread tendency, not completely explained by the principle of analogy, for sibling terms to be extended to cousins in the absence of specific social differentials. Since, in the presence of demes, this tendency is reinforced by a definite social equalizer, the preponderance of generation terms for all cousins in deme societies may conceivably be accounted for.

Inasmuch as this hypothesis involves assumptions not specified in the formulation of Postulate 1, it must be phrased as a proposition rather than as a theorem.

Proposition 16: In societies with endogamous demes, sibling terms tend to be extended to both cross and parallel cousins.

Table 34, which tests this proposition, omits nine societies for which deme organization seems fairly likely, though not definitely

TABLE 34

Trios of Relatives	Endo-demes Present		Endo-demes Absent		Statistical Indices	
	Generation Terms	Other Terms	Generation Terms	Other Terms	Q	χ^2
FaSiDa-FaBrDa-Si	9	4	47	164	+.77	1000
MoBrDa-MoSiDa-Si	9	5	48	151	+.71	100

established. Since the coefficients of association are not only positive and consistent but unusually high and reliable, the proposition must be regarded as decisively validated.

Patri-demes and matri-demes, even though the societies for which they are reported are too few for reliable statistical analysis, raise no special problems. In distribution of types of kinship terminology, societies with patri-demes are almost exactly intermediate between those with endogamous demes and those with patrilocal clan-communities, as is consistent with the hypothesis that the three types of organization constitute a normal sequence of development. From deme through patri-deme to patri-clan, lineal terminology decreases steadily for all relatives and generation terms for cousins, whereas bifurcate merging terms increase markedly for all relatives, bifurcate collateral terminology remaining relatively constant.

Unilinear kin groups of the consanguineal type affect the terminological classification of kinsmen through similarities and dissimilarities produced by social participation. Proximity is not a factor since their members do not live together except for those who may be aggregated by a rule of residence. The alignment of relatives varies somewhat with the rule of descent but not with the size of the kin group. Lineages, sibs, and phratries with the same rule of descent bring into association the same categories of relatives, and can therefore be treated together. Moieties have a like effect, but create certain additional similarities which will require special theorems to demonstrate. The influences of patrilineal and matrilineal descent are strictly parallel. They sometimes coincide, as when both distinguish FaSi from MoSi. Sometimes they are independent; thus only patrilineal descent directly associates BrDa and Da, and only matrilineal descent WiSiDa and Da. Never, however, do they run counter to each other. Even where they appear independent, they commonly produce similar results, through analogy or otherwise, as in the case of parallel cousins. In this indirect fashion nearly every influence exerted on kinship terminology by one unilinear rule of descent tends also to be exerted by the opposite rule. For this reason it becomes possible in most instances to treat matrilineal and patrilineal kin groups together and to differentiate them only from cases of bilateral descent.

If unilinear kin groups are present in a society, but do not regulate marriage or are endogamous, they fail to produce regular alignments of kinsmen, and their effects upon kinship terminology are minimized. For example, it is customary among many Islamic peoples,[77] including the Kababish and Kurds of our sample, for a man to marry his FaBrDa, who is a member of his own patri-sib. To the children of such a marriage the relatives through both parents belong to the same sib, and indeed are often the same persons. Inherent distinctions such as bifurcation lose their meaning in such a case, and social equalizers and differentials do not produce the expected alignments of relatives. Similar confusion results when violations of exogamy are common. For this reason, in the formulation and testing of theorems on unilinear descent, a society will be classed as unilinear only if its kin groups are exogamous, or reveal a definite tendency toward exogamy. Unilinear societies all of whose kin groups are endogamous or non-exogamous will be classed with bilateral societies. It should perhaps be pointed out, however, that this rarely makes a difference of more than a few points in the magnitude of coefficients.

Membership in the same exogamous unilinear kin group operates as a social equalizer to override the inherent distinction of collaterality and produce the phenomenon of merging. Since the principle of analogy normally extends the merging tendency to parallel relatives outside as well as within the prevailing line of descent, it is possible to formulate a theorem which applies to both unilinear rules of descent at the same time.

Theorem 17: In the presence of exogamous matrilineal or patrilineal
   lineages, sibs, phratries, or moieties, terms for lineal relatives tend
   to be extended, within the same sex and generation, to collateral
   kinsmen who would be affiliated with them under either unilinear
   rule of descent.

In Table 35, which tests this theorem, the usual comparison between FaBrWi and Mo is omitted since these two kinsmen are not necessarily affiliated under either matrilineal or patrilineal descent except in the presence of moieties. The low values and reliability of the coefficients for parallel cousins and siblings are due mainly to the fact that bilateral kin groups normally affect them in much the same way as do unilinear kin groups (see Theorem 15 and Proposi-

[77] See B. Z. Seligman, "Studies in Semitic Kinship," *Bulletins of the School of Oriental Studies,* III (1923), i, 51–68, 263–79.

tion 16). What provides conclusive confirmation of Theorem 17 is the occurrence of high, positive, consistent, and maximally reliable coefficients of association for the comparisons of MoSi with Mo and of BrDa with Da.

TABLE 35

Pairs of Relatives	Exogamous Unilinear Kin Groups Present		Exogamous Unilinear Kin Groups Absent		Statistical Indices	
	Same Term	Different Terms	Same Term	Different Terms	Q	χ^2
MoSi-Mo	106	53	31	51	+ .51	1000
FaBrDa-Si	125	29	64	22	+ .19	2
MoSiDa-Si	114	31	62	23	+ .15	2
BrDa-Da	107	37	34	43	+ .57	1000
WiSiDa-Da	38	25	15	15	+ .21	2

Membership in different unilinear kin groups operates as a social differential to support the inherent distinction of bifurcation and to favor differentiation of kinship nomenclature between kin-types in different lines of descent.

Theorem 18: In the presence of exogamous matrilineal or patrilineal lineages, sibs, phratries, or moieties, separate kinship terms tend to be applied to comparable relatives of the same generation who are linked to Ego by connecting relatives of different sex.

This theorem is decisively validated in Table 36 by positive and consistent coefficients of association that are unusually high both in numerical value and in reliability.

TABLE 36

Pairs of Relatives	Exogamous Unilinear Kin Groups Present		Exogamous Unilinear Kin Groups Absent		Statistical Indices	
	Different Terms	Same Term	Different Terms	Same Term	Q	χ^2
FaSi-MoSi	122	35	52	29	+ .35	20
MoBrWi-FaBrWi	83	26	25	19	+ .48	20
FaSiDa-FaBrDa	124	24	25	60	+ .85	1000
MoBrDa-MoSiDa	117	22	24	61	+ .86	1000
SiDa-BrDa	116	18	49	28	+ .57	1000
WiBrDa-WiSiDa	42	10	14	13	+ .59	20

As a corollary of Theorems 17 and 18, bifurcate merging terminology is to be expected in the presence of exogamous consanguineal kin groups of either unilinear type.

Theorem 19: Exogamous matrilineal or patrilineal lineages, sibs, phratries, and/or moieties tend to be associated with kinship terminology of the bifurcate merging type.

This theorem is tested for matrilineal kin groups in Table 37, for patrilineal kin groups in Table 38, and for both combined in Table 39. It is strongly confirmed in the first partial test and rather less strongly in the second, owing to the contrary influence of non-sororal polygyny which, as previously noted, is highly associated with patrilineal descent. In both partial tests, of course, cases of the opposite unilinear rule are treated as negative cases, with a consequent probable reduction in the magnitude and reliability of coefficients. Table 39, which corrects this defect, is validated by positive, high, and consistent coefficients of association which in four of the six cases are found reliable at the maximum level of confidence (one tenth of one per cent).

TABLE 37

Trios of Relatives	Exogamous Matrilineal Kin Groups Present		Exogamous Matrilineal Kin Groups Absent		Statistical Indices	
	Bifurcate Merging	Other Terms	Bifurcate Merging	Other Terms	Q	χ^2
FaSi-MoSi-Mo	37	28	58	115	+.46	100
MoBrWi-FaBrWi-Mo	24	15	39	74	+.51	100
FaSiDa-FaBrDa-Si	49	12	76	97	+.68	1000
MoBrDa-MoSiDa-Si	49	10	64	98	+.76	1000
SiDa-BrDa-Da	37	15	76	82	+.45	100
WiBrDa-WiSiDa-Da	12	6	22	37	+.54	10

The hypothesis incorporated in Theorem 19 has previously been offered in slightly variant forms by both Lowie [78] and Kroeber.[79] Lowie ascribes bifurcate merging to exogamy, Kroeber to unilinear

---

[78] R. H. Lowie, "Exogamy and the Classificatory System of Relationship," *American Anthropologist*, n.s., XVII (1915), 223–39.

[79] A. L. Kroeber, "Zuñi Kin and Clan," *Anthropological Papers of the American Museum of Natural History*, XVIII (1917), 86–7.

TABLE 38

Trios of Relatives	Exogamous Patrilineal Kin Groups Present		Exogamous Patrilineal Kin Groups Absent		Statistical Indices	
	Bifurcate Merging	Other Terms	Bifurcate Merging	Other Terms	Q	χ^2
FaSi-MoSi-Mo	47	55	48	88	+ .22	5
MoBrWi-FaBrWi-Mo	38	39	24	49	+ .33	10
FaSiDa-FaBrDa-Si	66	33	59	76	+ .44	100
MoBrDa-MoSiDa-Si	54	35	59	73	+ .31	20
SiDa-BrDa-Da	56	34	57	64	+ .30	20
WiBrDa-WiSiDa-Da	20	19	13	24	+ .32	2

TABLE 39

Trios of Relatives	Exogamous Unilinear Kin Groups Present		Exogamous Unilinear Kin Groups Absent		Statistical Indices	
	Bifurcate Merging	Other Terms	Bifurcate Merging	Other Terms	Q	χ^2
FaSi-MoSi-Mo	74	79	21	64	+ .48	1000
MoBrWi-FaBrWi-Mo	53	53	10	35	+ .56	100
FaSiDa-FaBrDa-Si	104	43	21	66	+ .77	1000
MoBrDa-MoSiDa-Si	93	44	21	64	+ .73	1000
SiDa-BrDa-Da	86	45	27	52	+ .57	1000
WiBrDa-WiSiDa-Da	25	24	9	19	+ .37	5

descent *per se*. Lowie's hypothesis differs from that of the present author only by the inclusion, along with exogamous unilinear kin groups, of patri-demes and matri-demes, which are also characterized by exogamy. Kroeber's version, on the other hand, differs by the inclusion of non-exogamous unilinear kin groups. In a previous article,[80] based upon a preliminary analysis of 221 of the 250 societies covered in this work, the present author reached the conclusion that Kroeber's version of the hypothesis enjoyed a slight statistical advantage over Lowie's. With the additional coverage of the present volume and the correction of a few errors, this modest advantage has evaporated. As Table 40 indicates, the three forms of expression of the hypothesis emerge from a new statistical analysis with almost identical support. The figures given are the totals for the six trios of relatives covered in Tables 37, 38, and 39.

[80] G. P. Murdock, "Bifurcate Merging," *American Anthropologist*, n.s., XLIX (1947), 59–60.

TABLE 40

	Unilinear Descent		Bilateral Descent		Statistical Indices	
Theorist	Bifurcate Merging	Other Terms	Bifurcate Merging	Other Terms	Q	χ^2
Kroeber	447	314	94	277	+.615	1000
Lowie	458	332	84	257	+.617	1000
Murdock	435	288	108	301	+.616	1000

Cross-cousin terminology of the Crow type, in which generation levels are overridden by calling FaSiSo by the same term as FaBr (or Fa) and FaSiDa by the same term as FaSi, while MoBrSo is terminologically classed with BrSo (or So) and MoBrDa with BrDa (or Da), has frequently been noted to be particularly characteristic of matrilineal societies.[81] This is accounted for by Postulate 1 since, under matrilineal descent, FaSi and her children are members of the same consanguineal kin group; the fact of such participation presumably operates as a social equalizer to overcome the inherent distinction of generation and produce an extension of kinship terminology from the first ascending generation to lower generations within the same kin group. Once this happens the reciprocal terms for BrSo and BrDa are extended to the other cross-cousins, the children of MoBr, both through analogy and by virtue of the fact that such relatives are all children of the men of Ego's own matri-lineage or matri-sib. Under double descent, the tendency to produce Crow terminology for cross-cousins is neutralized by the opposite influence of patrilineal descent (see Theorem 21). The tendency is also minimized if the matrilineal kin groups are not characterized by exogamy.

Theorem 20: In the presence of exogamous matri-lineages, matri-sibs, or matri-moieties, unless exogamous patrilineal kin groups are also present, kinship terms for FaSi tend to be extended to FaSiDa, and those for BrDa to MoBrDa.

This theorem is conclusively validated in Table 41 by similar high positive coefficients of association with maximal reliability.

Parallel reasoning accounts for cross-cousin terminology of the Omaha type, in which the children of FaSi are classed with SiSo

[81] Cf. R. H. Lowie, *Culture and Ethnology* (New York, 1917), pp. 151–2.

TABLE 41

Pairs of Relatives	Exclusive Matrilineal Descent with Exogamy		Patrilineal, Double, or Bilateral Descent		Statistical Indices	
	Same Term	Different Terms	Same Term	Different Terms	Q	χ^2
FaSiDa-FaSi	21	29	8	181	+.88	1000
MoBrDa-BrDa	15	33	7	181	+.84	1000

and SiDa, and the children of MoBr with the siblings of one's mother. Omaha nomenclature is normally found in societies with patrilineal descent. Under this rule, MoBr and MoBrSo are members of the same kin group, as are MoSi and MoBrDa, and the similarity resulting from their social participation favors the extension of kinship terms across generation lines. The reciprocal terms for SiSo and SiDa tend to be extended to the opposite cross-cousins, the children of FaSi, partly by analogy and partly because paternal cross-cousins and sororal nieces and nephews are all children of the women of Ego's own patri-sib or patri-lineage.

Theorem 21: In the presence of exogamous patri-lineages, patri-sibs, or patri-moieties, unless exogamous matrilineal kin groups are also present, kinship terms for MoSi tend to be extended to MoBrDa, and those for SiDa to FaSiDa.

This theorem is decisively substantiated by the data in Table 42.

TABLE 42

Pairs of Relatives	Exclusive Patrilineal Descent with Exogamy		Matrilineal, Double, or Bilateral Descent		Statistical Indices	
	Same Term	Different Terms	Same Term	Different Terms	Q	χ^2
MoBrDa-MoSi	21	68	3	144	+.87	1000
FaSiDa-SiDa	24	66	6	143	+.79	1000

Most of the cases in Tables 41 and 42 of the occurrence of Crow or Omaha terminology with other than the expected type of social organization are accountable on other grounds. Thus the Pawnee and Siriono have Crow terms with matrilocal residence; the Manus and Pentecost have Crow terms with double descent; the Fox have Omaha terms with non-exogamous patri-sibs, and the

Takelma with patrilocal residence. The only genuinely negative cases are the Bachama, Koranko, and Seniang, who have Crow terms with patrilineal descent and patrilocal residence.

Only about one third of the exclusively matrilineal societies in our sample are characterized by Crow terminology for cross-cousins, and only about one fourth of the patrilineal societies have Omaha terminology. This reflects the fact, already noted, that the inherent distinction of generation, which must be overridden to produce them, is the most resistant, or has the strongest relative efficacy, of all such differentials. To overcome it presumably requires both time and the full elaboration of unilinear institutions. This accords with the hypothesis advanced by White [82] that Crow or Omaha terms tend to appear only when a system of unilinear kin groups is fully developed "and comes to exert its influence more and more upon the social life of the tribe." Evidence to be presented in Chapter 8 will lend strong confirmation to this theory.

The present author suspects that the amitate and the avunculate, the special relationships with a paternal aunt and a maternal uncle respectively, may prove to be important contributory factors in the development of Crow terminology in the one case and of Omaha terminology in the other. He has done personal field work in two matrilineal societies with Crow terminology, the Haida and the Trukese, and in both of them the relation with a paternal aunt is exceedingly important. Among the Haida,[83] for example, the father's sister has special and highly important functions to perform at every crisis in an individual's life—at birth, at puberty, at marriage, at potlatches, in sickness, and at the funeral ceremony. If she is not alive to perform them, her daughter acts in her stead; if no FaSiDa is still living, a FaSiDaDa plays the vital roles. In other words, the functions are inherited in the female line, as is natural under the prevailing social conditions. The functional equivalence of these several relatives, irrespective of generation, presumably reinforces the similarities that flow from participation in the same

[82] L. A. White, "A Problem in Kinship Terminology," *American Anthropologist*, n.s., XLI (1939), 569–70.
[83] See G. P. Murdock, "Kinship and Social Behavior among the Haida," *American Anthropologist*, n.s., XXXVI (1934), 363–5.

kin group and thus accentuates the tendency to apply the same kinship term to all of them.

The role of exogamous moieties as determinants of kinship nomenclature has been stressed by a number of authorities, particularly by Rivers.[84] Theoretical analysis and careful scrutiny of the data, however, indicate that this emphasis is largely unwarranted. Moieties appear to produce precisely the same effects upon terminological classification as do other unilinear consanguineal kin groups. Most of their allegedly unique consequences, such as the application of identical terms to FaBrDa and MoSiDa, can be and are produced in the absence of moieties by unilinear descent coupled with extension by analogy (see Theorem 1). Moieties merely exert the same influences more directly and more sharply. Their presence enhances the tendency to merge lineal and collateral relatives, strongly accentuates the inherent distinction of bifurcation, and increases the incidence of bifurcate merging terminology, all of which have been found characteristic of unilinear groups in general (see Theorems 17, 18, and 19). These influences can be summed up in a single theorem.

Theorem 22: Exogamous moieties tend to be associated with kinship terminology of the bifurcate merging type.

This theorem is conclusively validated in Table 43.

TABLE 43

	Exogamous Moieties Present		Exogamous Moieties Absent		Statistical Indices	
Trios of Relatives	Bifurcate Merging	Other Terms	Bifurcate Merging	Other Terms	Q	χ^2
FaSi-MoSi-Mo	15	8	79	136	+.53	20
MoBrWi-FaBrWi-Mo	14	5	50	83	+.63	100
FaSiDa-FaBrDa-Si	20	3	105	105	+.74	100
MoBrDa-MoSiDa-Si	21	2	92	109	+.85	1000
SiDa-BrDa-Da	16	5	97	92	+.50	10
WiBrDa-WiSiDa-Da	8	4	26	43	+.54	5

[84] W. H. R. Rivers, *Kinship and Social Organisation* (London, 1914), pp. 72–3.

Exogamous moieties also have the effect of aggregating in the same kin group certain affinal and consanguineal relatives who are not ordinarily brought together by sibs or lineages. Among these are MoBrWi, WiMo, and FaSi; FaBrWi, FaWi, and MoSi; WiBrDa, SoWi, and SiDa; WiSiDa, WiDa, and BrDa. In all of these cases, cross-cousin marriage exerts a parallel influence, and does so more strongly (see Theorems 26 and 27), so that the effect of moieties is revealed by statistical coefficients of only modest magnitude and reliability. Among tertiary relatives, only the terminological equating of parallel cousins and WiBrWi appears to reflect primarily the influence of moieties.

Theorem 23: In the presence of exogamous moieties, kinship terms for WiBrWi tend to be the same as those for female parallel cousins.

This theorem is substantially validated in Table 44.

TABLE 44

Pairs of Relatives	Exogamous Moieties Present		Exogamous Moieties Absent		Statistical Indices	
	Same Term	Different Terms	Same Term	Different Terms	Q	χ^2
FaBrDa-WiBrWi	7	4	10	44	+ .77	100
MoSiDa-WiBrWi	7	5	10	41	+ .70	20

The only really peculiar effects of moieties upon kinship structure appear in connection with double descent. The concurrence of matrilineal moieties and patrilineal kin groups gives rise, as was seen in Chapter 3, to so-called "marriage classes," including such bilinear kin groups as sections and subsections. These groups operate as social equalizers favoring the extension and differentiation of kinship terms, in a manner analogous to lineages, sibs, and moieties.

Theorem 24: In the presence of bilinear kin groups, kinship terms tend to be extended to all relatives who belong to the same section or subsection.

Full validation of this theorem would carry us far afield into a discussion of social organization in aboriginal Australia, to which continent, except for a limited region in Melanesia, the conditions in question appear to be confined. Interested readers may turn to the summary of the Australian data by Radcliffe-Brown [85] for the evidence to substantiate the theorem. They will find that within a section, or subsection, the extension of kinship terms is carried to such an extreme that even such highly resistant inherent distinctions as sex and generation are frequently overridden.

For present purposes the demonstration will have to rest on a single tabulation, that of terms for Mo and SoWi in Table 45. Different as these two relatives are, not only in generation but in nearly every aspect of Ego's functional relationships with them, they are nevertheless called by the same kinship term in three of the five societies in our sample which meet the conditions of the theorem and for which information is available, namely, the Arunta and Murngin of Australia and the Ranon of the New Hebrides. The explanation lies in the single common similarity that the two relatives belong to the same section; they are matrilineally but not patrilineally akin to Ego. The Kariera and Pentecost have sections —though dubious in the latter case—and yet differentiate SoWi from Mo, while the Iatmul of New Guinea and the Tallensi of West Africa equate these relatives in terminology but are not reported to have double descent or bilinear kin groups. The data in Table 45 support Theorem 24 by a coefficient of association of extraordinary magnitude and reliability.

TABLE 45

Pairs of Relatives	Sections Present		Sections Absent		Statistical Indices	
	Same Term	Different Terms	Same Term	Different Terms	Q	χ^2
SoWi-Mo	3	2	2	196	+ .99	1000

A seventh group of social equalizers consists of a variety of special rules governing marriage. Consideration has already been given to the influences exerted on kinship structure by monogamy (see Theorem 14), sororal polygyny (see Theorems 2 and 3), non-sororal polygyny (see Theorems 4 and 5), and exogamy (see Theorem

[85] A. R. Radcliffe-Brown, "The Social Organization of Australian Tribes," *Oceania*, I (1930–31), 34–63, 206–46, 322–41, 426–56.

19). There remain to be considered the customs of sister exchange and preferential mating.

Where the regular method of obtaining a wife is for two men to exchange women, each taking a sister of the other as his spouse, coincidence occurs in certain kin-types. As Rivers [86] has pointed out, such relatives as MoBrWi and FaSi, WiBrWi and Si, and WiBrDa and SiDa become the same persons under a rule of sister exchange, and are consequently likely to be designated by identical terms.

Theorem 25: When the normal mode of marriage is by the exchange of sisters, the same kinship terms tend to be applied to MoBrWi and FaSi, to WiBrWi and Si, and to WiBrDa and SiDa.

This theorem is substantially validated by the data in Table 46.

T A B L E   4 6

Pairs of Relatives	Marriage by Sister Exchange		Other Modes of Marriage		Statistical Indices	
	Same Term	Different Terms	Same Term	Different Terms	Q	χ^2
MoBrWi-FaSi	8	2	57	99	+.75	20
WiBrWi-Si	6	1	13	45	+.91	100
WiBrDa-SiDa	8	2	29	56	+.77	20

Rules of preferential mating fall into two groups—those governing primary or first marriages and those governing secondary or subsequent marriages. Of the former type, by far the most common is cross-cousin marriage, i.e., preferential mating with a FaSiDa or a MoBrDa. Cross-cousin marriage is called symmetrical when either of these relatives is a preferred spouse, asymmetrical when only one is eligible or preferred. When a large proportion of marriages within a society are between cross-cousins, coincidence becomes frequent with respect to certain kin-types, with consequent extension of kinship terms.[87] When marriage with a FaSiDa is preferred, a man's paternal aunt becomes his mother-in-law, her

[86] W. H. R. Rivers, *Kinship and Social Organisation* (London, 1914), pp. 44-5.

[87] See W. H. R. Rivers, *Kinship and Social Organisation* (London, 1914), pp. 21-5.

daughter is either his wife, his wife's sister, or his brother's wife, and his sororal niece is his daughter-in-law, and kinship terminology is likely to conform to these equivalences.

Theorem 26: Under a rule of preferential marriage with a FaSiDa, the same kinship terms tend to be applied to FaSi and WiMo, to FaSiDa and Wi and/or WiSi and/or BrWi, and to SiDa and SoWi.

The data in Table 47 confirm this theorem by high and consistent positive coefficients of association which attain an exceptional level of reliability.

TABLE 47

Pairs of Relatives	FaSiDa a Preferred Spouse		FaSiDa Not Preferred		Statistical Indices	
	Same Term	Different Terms	Same Term	Different Terms	Q	χ^2
FaSi-WiMo	14	20	13	139	+ .76	1000
FaSiDa-Wi	6	28	3	159	+ .84	1000
FaSiDa-WiSi	10	18	5	137	+ .88	1000
FaSiDa-BrWi	9	17	5	138	+ .81	1000
SiDa-SoWi	8	18	9	124	+ .72	100

Parallel extensions occur when the preferred union is with a MoBrDa. Under this rule a man's maternal uncle's wife becomes his mother-in-law, her daughter becomes his wife or his sister-in-law, and his wife's brother's daughter becomes his daughter-in-law.

Theorem 27: Under a rule of preferential marriage with a MoBrDa, the same kinship terms tend to be applied to MoBrWi and WiMo, to MoBrDa and Wi and/or WiSi and/or BrWi, and to WiBrDa and SoWi.

This theorem is conclusively validated in Table 48.

Other preferential primary marriages have comparable effects upon kinship nomenclature. Thus the term for WiMo is extended to FaSiDa and MoBrDa among the Lesu, where the preferred union is with the daughter of a female cross-cousin, and to

TABLE 48

Pairs of Relatives	MoBrDa a Preferred Spouse		MoBrDa Not Preferred		Statistical Indices	
	Same Term	Different Terms	Same Term	Different Terms	Q	χ^2
MoBrWi-WiMo	21	17	10	88	+.83	1000
MoBrDa-Wi	7	39	3	145	+.79	100
MoBrDa-WiSi	14	23	7	127	+.83	1000
MoBrDa-BrWi	12	22	5	130	+.87	1000
WiBrDa-SoWi	8	12	5	50	+.74	100

MoMoBrDa and MoFaSiDa among the Arunta, where the favored mates are second cousins who are the daughters of these women. Such cases, however, are too sporadic for reliable statistical testing.

Preferential rules governing secondary marriages, such as the levirate and sororate, have been advanced by many authorities as determinants of kinship terminology. Certain grounds for skepticism regarding such theories were presented earlier in the present chapter. Moreover, it will be shown in Chapter 9 that secondary marriages are largely determined by the forms of social organization, including kinship structure, instead of the causal relationship being the reverse.[88] Since theories asserting the influence of preferential secondary marriages are subject to these objections, and are not derivable from Postulate 1, they cannot be presented as theorems. They may, however, be formulated as propositions in order to subject them to test.

The levirate, it is argued, by bringing about the substitution of BrWi for Wi, creates an equivalence between such relatives as FaBrWi and Mo, FaBrDa and Si, BrWi and Wi, and BrDa and Da, and thus favors the use of the same classificatory terms for the relatives of each such pair of kin-types. While the argument is logical enough, the necessary infrequency of secondary as compared with primary marriages greatly reduces the probability that they can operate as an effective social equalizer in other than exceptional instances. This is borne out by the tests of Proposition 28.

[88] A parallel conclusion is reached in B. Z. Seligman, "Asymmetry in Descent," *Journal of the Royal Anthropological Institute,* LVIII (1928), 534-5.

Proposition 28: In the presence of the levirate, kinship terms tend to be extended from Mo to FaBrWi, from Si to FaBrDa, from Wi to BrWi, and from Da to BrDa.

In Table 49, which tests this proposition, the six societies with bilinear kin groups are omitted, since sections or subsections make the levirate practically inevitable.

TABLE 49

Pairs of Relatives	Levirate Present		Levirate Absent		Statistical Indices	
	Same Term	Different Terms	Same Term	Different Terms	Q	χ^2
FaBrWi-Mo	46	32	20	26	+ .30	5
FaBrDa-Si	84	23	49	16	+ .09	—
BrWi-Wi	20	79	6	51	+ .37	5
BrDa-Da	58	38	42	18	− .21	2

The sororate, similarly, is alleged to effect a terminological equivalence between MoSi and Mo, MoSiDa and Si, WiSi and Wi, and WiSiDa and Da.

Proposition 29: In the presence of the sororate, kinship terms tend to be extended from Mo to MoSi, from Si to MoSiDa, from Wi to WiSi, and from Da to WiSiDa.

Table 50, which tests this proposition, omits two groups of tribes—those with bilinear kin groups, since these make the sororate almost automatic, and those with preferential sororal polygyny. Theorem 2 has already indicated that sororal polygyny has the effects upon kinship terminology here attributed to the sororate, so that the inclusion of cases of the former would give a fictitious impression of the influence of the latter.

TABLE 50

Pairs of Relatives	Sororate Present		Sororate Absent		Statistical Indices	
	Same Term	Different Terms	Same Term	Different Terms	Q	χ^2
MoSi-Mo	38	35	35	29	− .04	—
MoSiDa-Si	53	14	48	16	+ .12	—
WiSi-Wi	9	59	5	54	+ .24	—
WiSiDa-Da	18	16	13	10	− .07	—

Analysis of Tables 49 and 50 indicates that Propositions 28 and 29 lack statistical support. Coefficients of association are low, are inconsistent with each other, and in three of the eight computations are negative in sign. This is, incidentally, the first time that negative coefficients have been encountered, except for one instance in an uncorrected test. Even more significant is the low level of reliability. In no instances does the χ^2 index of reliability attain the ten per cent level of confidence, and of the only three coefficients that attain even the fifty per cent level one is negative in sign. Both propositions, therefore, must be considered invalidated. If either the levirate or the sororate has any genuine influence on kinship terminology, it is comparatively slight and is probably confined to very special circumstances.

The assumption that the levirate and sororate produce merging, invalidated above, led Sapir [89] to the further hypothesis that these rules of preferential secondary marriage may be responsible for the phenomenon of bifurcate merging terminology. Though its basis is now undermined, the theory may be formulated as a proposition and tested.

Proposition 30: The levirate and sororate tend to be associated with kinship terminology of the bifurcate merging type.

This proposition is subjected to test in Tables 51 and 52.

TABLE 51

Trios of Relatives	Levirate Present		Levirate Absent		Statistical Indices	
	Bifurcate Merging	Other Terms	Bifurcate Merging	Other Terms	Q	χ^2
FaSi-MoSi-Mo	39	64	23	40	+ .03	—
MoBrWi-FaBrWi-Mo	38	36	8	34	+ .64	100
FaSiDa-FaBrDa-Si	52	51	30	32	+ .04	—
MoBrDa-MoSiDa-Si	49	49	25	34	+ .15	2
SiDa-BrDa-Da	50	39	31	28	+ .05	—
WiBrDa-WiSiDa-Da	16	26	8	12	− .04	—

The preponderance of low values among the coefficients of association in Tables 51 and 52, the occurrence of one zero coeffi-

[89] E. Sapir, "Terms of Relationship and the Levirate," *American Anthropologist*, n.s., XVIII (1916), 327–37.

TABLE 52

Trios of Relatives	Sororate Present		Sororate Absent		Statistical Indices	
	Bifurcate Merging	Other Terms	Bifurcate Merging	Other Terms	Q	χ^2
FaSi-MoSi-Mo	31	48	22	42	+.16	2
MoBrWi-FaBrWi-Mo	22	31	10	32	+.39	5
FaSiDa-FaBrDa-Si	38	36	31	31	+.03	—
MoBrDa-MoSiDa-Si	36	36	28	33	+.08	—
SiDa-BrDa-Da	35	35	28	28	.00	—
WiBrDa-WiSiDa-Da	13	18	4	13	+.40	2

cient and one with negative sign, and the very low indices of reliability concur in indicating that Proposition 30 is invalid. A possible individual exception may be noted in the case of the wives of uncles, for whom bifurcate merging terminology is fairly strongly associated with the levirate. On the whole, however, it appears clearly unsafe to invoke the levirate or the sororate in explanation of kinship phenomena.

Theories which ascribe kinship terminology to other preferential secondary marriages deserve only passing notice, for they are of even more dubious validity. Although Crow terminology for cross-cousins, for example, has been attributed to the influence of preferential mating with MoBrWi, our data show that such preferred marriages occur with every major type of cross-cousin terminology, and are no more common with Crow than with Iroquois nomenclature. Preferential secondary unions with WiBrDa, which have similarly been regarded as the source of Omaha terminology, are actually found in only a minority of the Omaha societies of our sample, and in a substantial number such marriages are expressly forbidden. The conclusion is therefore inescapable that preferred secondary marriages of whatsoever type are not to be included among the significant determinants of kinship terminology.

The demonstration of Postulate 1 is now complete. From it have been derived 26 separate theorems, which have been tested in 155 different computations. Of these, 35 are preliminary or uncorrected. Analysis of the coefficients of association and the indices of reliability for the 120 final computations indicates that the postulate is decisively validated.

The fact that all 120 coefficients are positive in sign is of the utmost significance. It fulfills to the maximum the rigorous requirement of the postulational method that all theorems, without exception, be found to accord with the facts. It indicates consistency among the several tests of the same theorem, an important criterion of reliability. Even when the specific indices of reliability are low for each separate test of a theorem, the fact that they all yield coefficients of positive sign enormously decreases the probability that the numerical distributions can be due to chance alone.

The magnitude of the coefficients of association themselves is likewise significant. Five sixths of the total of 120 have numerical values higher than + .30. The mean is + .54; the median coefficient, + .55. The distribution, which approximates a normal frequency curve, is as follows:

3 coefficients in the range from + .91 to +1.00
13 coefficients in the range from + .81 to + .90
16 coefficients in the range from + .71 to + .80
16 coefficients in the range from + .61 to + .70
20 coefficients in the range from + .51 to + .60
19 coefficients in the range from + .41 to + .50
13 coefficients in the range from + .31 to + .40
11 coefficients in the range from + .21 to + .30
5 coefficients in the range from + .11 to + .20
4 coefficients in the range from + .01 to + .10
0 coefficients in the range from −1.00 to　.00

Most significant of all, probably, is the very high level of reliabilty revealed by the χ^2 indices. Only for Theorems 2, 3, and 4 do these fall short of providing, by themselves, genuinely substantial confirmation. Since the χ^2 index of reliability is a function of the size of the sample, as well as of its distribution, low indices are not to be regarded as significant when the number of cases is small. The distribution of the 119 indices of reliability—omitting the one inappropriate case where Q is + 1.00—according to their values in relation to the number of cases is shown in Table 53.

Although the above results are perhaps unprecedented in social science, they by no means do justice to the actual possibilities. It must be remembered that multiple factors are operative in every

TABLE 53

Level of Reliability	More than 200 Cases	100 to 200 Cases	Less than 100 Cases	Total
1000 (.001)	25	12	1	38
100 (.01)	8	5	3	16
20 (.05)	10	5	3	18
10 (.10)	3	1	2	6
5 (.20)	1	2	6	9
2 (.50)	10	4	6	20
Less than 2	2	5	5	12

instance, but that in most of our theorems we have isolated only a single factor for analysis. If several factors are taken into consideration at the same time, the magnitude of the coefficients rises appreciably, and usually also their reliability. This can be demonstrated for the social system in our own society. Two of its elements have been individually tested—neolocal residence under Theorem 12 and the isolated nuclear family under Theorem 14. If we combine these two factors and add two other characteristic features of our own social structure—strict monogamy and the absence of exogamous unilinear kin groups—we arrive at the results shown in Table 54. Comparison with Tables 28 and 32 will reveal how the combination of several factors has raised both the values and the reliability of the coefficients. Similar results are obtainable from an exceedingly large number of similar combinations which it would be tedious to detail here.

TABLE 54

Trios of Relatives	Societies Having Monogamy, Isolated Nuclear Families, Neolocal Residence, and No Exogamous Lineages or Sibs		Societies Having Other Combinations of Elements of Social Structure		Statistical Indices	
	Lineal Terms	Other Terms	Lineal Terms	Other Terms	Q	χ^2
FaSi-MoSi-Mo	5	3	16	196	+ .91	1000
MoBrWi-FaBrWi-Mo	3	1	22	167	+ .90	100
FaSiDa-FaBrDa-Si	5	3	19	188	+ .89	1000
MoBrDa-MoSiDa-Si	5	2	19	178	+ .92	1000
SiDa-BrDa-Da	5	3	20	165	+ .86	1000

Postulate 1 having been validated, it will be appropriate to consider briefly the relative influence of the various social factors with which types of kinship terms have been found to be significantly associated. The relative efficacy of the several groups of social equalizers and differentials cannot be deduced from the postulate nor inferred directly from the validation of the theorems, but must be independently determined. Neither the values nor the reliability of the coefficients in the tables can be taken as a direct measure of the efficacy of the factor tested unless its independence of other factors is established. Very few of the factors operate as independent variables. Patri-clans, for example, are always associated with both patrilocal residence and patrilineal descent, which exert an identical influence. When they are found to coexist with particular kinship phenomena, this demonstration of itself gives no indication of how much of the indicated effect is to be attributed to the residence rule, to the rule of descent, or to the factor of clan participation itself. Moreover, patri-clans are strongly associated with non-sororal polygyny, which exerts an opposite influence, yet tests of individual theorems cannot indicate the extent to which this counteracts specifically either the residence, descent, or participational factors. Only when one factor can be demonstrated to be associated with all others in a purely random manner—a condition even remotely approached only in the case of sororal polygyny—can the magnitude and reliability of coefficients be taken as a rough indication of its efficacy.

A complete analysis of the relative efficacy of social equalizers and differentials would require more space than is available, and is probably not necessary. We shall therefore confine ourselves to a consideration of the relative weight to be assigned to three groups of factors which have been found particularly influential—forms of marriage, rules of residence, and descent or participation in consanguineal kin groups.

That the relative efficacy of marriage forms is lower than that of descent or kin group affiliation is suggested by the markedly higher values of coefficients of association and indices of reliability in tests of the theorems concerned with the latter (Theorems 15 to 24) than in those dealing with the former (Theorems 2 to 5). Since patrilineal descent and non-sororal polygyny tend to produce different types of kinship terminology, i.e., bifurcate merging and bifurcate collateral respectively, the distribution of these types when both factors are present should shed light on their relative efficacy. A special tabulation of the incidence of such terms for aunts and nieces, omitting cases of double descent, reveals that bifurcate merging occurs approximately 50 per cent more often, and this is confirmed by the results in Table 38 under Theorem 19. Since sororal polygyny exerts an influence on kinship terms identical with that of unilinear descent, the cases in which only one of the two factors is present provide another opportunity for comparison. They are analyzed in Table 55. Here bifurcate merging terminology is found associated with sororal polygyny in slightly less than half of all instances of bilateral descent, whereas it is associated with unilinear descent in slightly more than half of all instances where sororal polygyny is absent. Only in the case of cousins, to be sure, are the results statistically reliable, but here unilinear descent is shown to be definitely more effective than sororal polygyny. All of the above facts point in the same direction, i.e., toward the superior relative efficacy of rules of descent when compared with forms of marriage.

TABLE 55

Trios of Relatives	Unilinear Descent and Non-Sororal Polygyny		Bilateral Descent and Sororal Polygyny		Statistical Indices	
	Bifurcate Merging	Other Terms	Bifurcate Merging	Other Terms	Q	χ^2
FaSi-MoSi-Mo	67	73	5	7	+ .12	—
MoBrWi-FaBrWi-Mo	48	52	5	3	— .29	—
FaSiDa-FaBrDa-Si	93	42	2	9	+ .82	100
MoBrDa-MoSiDa-Si	82	43	2	9	+ .79	100
SiDa-BrDa-Da	77	43	7	4	+ .01	—
WiBrDa-WiSiDa-Da	23	27	4	0	— 1.00	*

The higher values of coefficients and of indices of reliability in the tests of Theorems 6 to 12, as compared with those under Theorems 2 to 5, suggest that the relative efficacy of marriage forms is also lower than that of rules of residence. This is probably due, however, to the supporting influence of descent, since parallel rules of residence and descent are very strongly associated. A test case is provided by kinship terminology in bilateral societies with both patrilocal residence and general polygyny. With respect to aunts and nieces, at least, bifurcate collateral terms outnumber those of the bifurcate merging type by a ratio of nearly 5 to 1. Since the former are expected with non-sororal polygyny and the latter with patrilocal residence, the preponderance of the former when the opposing factor of unilinear residence is excluded indicates an appreciably higher relative efficacy for the marriage form than for the residence rule. The same interpretation is suggested by Tables 20 and 21 under Theorem 5. Unfortunately a comparison of the influences of sororal polygyny and unilocal residence cannot be made with statistical reliability. From such evidence as is available, nevertheless, we are left with the residual impression, admittedly highly tentative, that the relative efficacy of marriage forms is greater than that of residence rules.

The comparison of descent and residence is relatively easy. Since unilinear descent and unilocal residence have been demonstrated to exert parallel influences on kinship terminology, an analysis of the cases where only one of them is operative, excluding those where neither or both are present, should yield an indication of their relative efficacy. This is done in Table 56. The data here compiled show that unilinear descent is associated with bifurcate merging terminology in approximately two thirds of the instances where unilocal residence is absent, whereas unilocal residence is associated with bifurcate merging in less than one third of the societies that lack unilinear descent. This indicates that the relative efficacy of unilinear descent, i.e., of exogamous unilinear kin groups, is appreciably greater than that of unilocal residence. It also suggests that descent is, in general, a more effective factor than residence, and this is confirmed by the somewhat higher coefficients and indices of reliability that ordinarily support the theorems concerned with descent (Theorems 15 to 24) as compared with those concerned with residence (Theorems 6 to 12).

Despite our tentative conclusion that rules of descent and the kin groups resulting from them rank highest in relative efficacy among the major groups of kinship determinants, followed by forms of marriage and the consequent family types, the influence of residence rules should not be too heavily discounted. It is partially

TABLE 56

Trios of Relatives	Unilinear Descent with Neolocal or Bilocal Residence		Bilateral Descent with Unilocal Residence		Statistical Indices	
	Bifurcate Merging	Other Terms	Bifurcate Merging	Other Terms	Q	χ^2
FaSi-MoSi-Mo	5	5	17	42	+.42	2
MoBrWi-FaBrWi-Mo	4	4	8	20	+.43	2
FaSiDa-FaBrDa-Si	8	3	16	45	+.76	100
MoBrDa-MoSiDa-Si	6	3	15	46	+.72	20
SiDa-BrDa-Da	7	2	20	34	+.71	10
WiBrDa-WiSiDa-Da	3	0	7	10	+1.00	*

obscured, for example, by the fact that non-sororal polygyny is rather more generally associated with unilocal residence than with unilinear descent. Moreover, the time factor (see Assumption 13) probably operates to the disadvantage of residence. As will be shown in Chapter 8, the rule of residence is normally the first aspect of a social system to undergo modification in the process of change from one relatively stable equilibrium to another, the last aspect to change being kinship terminology. Hence in systems undergoing transition, of which any large and random sample of human societies will necessarily include a considerable number, kinship terms will more often be consistent with the conservative rule of descent than with the progressive rule of residence.

In intrinsic interest, kinship terminology cannot compete with sex, marriage, the family, or community organization. Hence the reader who has had the interest and persistence to follow the necessarily dry and monotonous presentation of statistical facts about kinship in the present chapter, as the demonstration of the postulational method has proceeded, deserves some satisfying reward. Perhaps he will find it, as has the author, in the realization that the data of culture and social life are as susceptible to exact scientific treatment as are the facts of the physical and biological sciences. It seems clear that the elements of social organization, in their permutations and combinations, conform to natural laws of their own with an exactitude scarcely less striking than that which characterizes the permutations and combinations of atoms in chemistry or of genes in biology.

8

EVOLUTION OF SOCIAL ORGANIZATION

THE ANALYSIS of the forms of familial, kin, and local groups and of kinship structure in the first six chapters and the demonstration of their interdependence in Chapter 7 have laid a foundation for a consideration of the manner in which social organization changes over time. Since here, as elsewhere in culture, change is an adaptive process, we feel no hesitation in employing the term "evolution" which is used for processes of orderly adaptive change in other sciences. In so doing, we specifically disclaim any identity with the processes of organic evolution in biology as with the processes of cosmic evolution in astronomy. Nor do we use the term in the sense of the evolutionist anthropologists of the nineteenth century. In speaking of the evolution of social organization we refer merely to the normal processes of cultural change as these find special application in the area of social structure.

It was the early evolutionists who first gave serious attention to the problem of the evolution of social organization. During the latter half of the nineteenth century these anthropologists developed the theory that the matrilineal sib is the original form of human social organization, that this form of society gave way to patrilineal and patriarchal institutions as the male sex gradually achieved a position of dominance, and that the emergence of bilateral descent and the independent nuclear family marks a relatively late phase of social evolution. The hypothesis of the priority of the matrilineate

184

was buttressed with a number of extremely plausible arguments—
the presumed ignorance of physical paternity in primitive times, the
biological inevitability of the association of mother and child, the
alleged non-inclusion of the father in the family under early
nomadic conditions, the large number of apparent survivals of
matrilineal customs in patrilineal societies and the rarity of comparable patrilineal traits among matrilineal peoples, the relative
cultural backwardness of matrilineal as compared with patrilineal
societies, and the complete lack of historically attested cases of a
transition from patrilineal to matrilineal institutions.

So logical, so closely reasoned, and so apparently in accord with
all known facts was this hypothesis that from its pioneer formulation
by Bachofen [1] in 1861 to nearly the end of the nineteenth century
it was accepted by social scientists practically without exception.[2]
A really admirable intellectual achievement of early anthropology,
it did not encounter its first serious criticism [3] until several decades
had elapsed, and it still found vigorous supporters [4] sixty and
seventy years after its initial formulation.

The foundations of the evolutionist theory have crumbled exceedingly slowly. That ignorance of paternity, even if it existed, is
irrelevant to the issue had to await the demonstration by Rivers [5]

[1] J. J. Bachofen, *Das Mutterrecht* (Stuttgart, 1861).

[2] See especially A. Bastian, *Rechtsverhältnisse der verschiedenen Völker der
Erde* (Berlin, 1872); A. Giraud-Teulon, *Les origines du mariage et de la
famille* (Genève, Paris, 1884); L. Gumplowicz, *Grundriss der Sociologie* (Wien,
1885); J. Kohler, "Zur Urgeschichte der Ehe," *Zeitschrift für vergleichende
Rechtswissenschaft*, XII (1897), 62; J. Lippert, *Kulturgeschichte der Mensch-
heit in ihrem organischen Aufbau* (2 vols., Stuttgart, 1886–87); J. Lubbock,
The Origin of Civilisation and the Primitive Condition of Man (London, 1873);
J. F. McLennan, *Studies in Ancient History* (London, 1876); L. H. Morgan,
Ancient Society (New York, 1877); II. Spencer, *Principles of Sociology* (3rd
edit., 3 vols., New York, 1899); E. B. Tylor, "On a Method of Investigating
the Development of Institutions, applied to Laws of Marriage and Descent,"
Journal of the Royal Anthropological Institute, XVIII (1889), 245–69.

[3] See E. Westermarck, *The History of Human Marriage* (London, New
York, 1891); G. E. Howard, *A History of Matrimonial Institutions* (3 vols.,
Chicago, 1904).

[4] See, for example, R. Briffault, *The Mothers* (3 vols., New York, 1927);
W. G. Sumner and A. G. Keller, *The Science of Society* (4 vols., New Haven,
1927); P. Vinogradoff, *Outlines of Historical Jurisprudence*, Vol. I (New York,
1920).

[5] W. H. R. Rivers, *Social Organization* (New York, 1924), pp. 85–90.

that descent refers to group membership, not to recognition of kinship. The fact that certain Australian tribes who are quite ignorant of physical paternity [6] nevertheless recognize patrilineal descent is conclusive. The universality of the father's membership in the human family, demonstrated in Chapter 1 of the present volume, has only recently become firmly established. Many of the alleged survivals of the matrilineate in patrilineal societies have been reasonably explained on other grounds.[7]

The evolutionist allegation of the relative cultural backwardness of matrilineal societies is readily checked against the facts of world ethnography. Our own sample of 250 societies is sufficient to establish that the several modes of descent are found at various levels of culture. Among the most primitive or culturally undeveloped tribes in our sample, the Andamanese pygmies, the Paiute of the Great Basin, and the Yaghan of Tierra del Fuego are bilateral in descent, the Vedda of Ceylon, the Ramkokamekra of east central Brazil, and the Kutchin of northern Canada are matrilineal, and the Witoto of Amazonia, the Gilyak of Siberia, and the Miwok of California are patrilineal, while several native Australian tribes are characterized by double descent. All rules of descent are likewise well represented on the intermediate levels of culture, among agricultural and developed pastoral peoples. Even among literate peoples with relatively complex civilizations, our sample includes the bilateral Yankees and Syrian Christians, the patrilineal Chinese and Manchus, and the matrilineal Minangkabau Malays of Sumatra and Nayars of India. While matrilineal societies appear, on the average, to be somewhat more archaic in culture than patrilineal societies,[8] the difference is relatively slight, the overlap is very great, and the disparity may well reflect principally the preponderant influence exerted throughout the world in recent centuries by the bilateral and patrilineal peoples of the Eurasiatic continent. On the whole, the ethnographic evidence fails signally to support the

[6] Cf. B. Spencer, *Native Tribes of the Northern Territory of Australia* (London, 1914), p. 25.

[7] See E. Westermarck, *The History of Human Marriage* (5th edit., 3 vols., New York, 1922), for numerous instances.

[8] See G. P. Murdock, "Correlations of Matrilineal and Patrilineal Institutions," *Studies in the Science of Society*, ed. G. P. Murdock (New Haven, 1937), pp. 463-9, for a statistical demonstration.

evolutionist contention that the matrilineate is primitive, the patrilineate intermediate, and bilateral descent associated with higher civilization.

Although early evolutionist theory has completely collapsed, a number of recent anthropologists, notably Lesser and White, have attempted to reinstate certain evolutionary principles. They have pointed out, for example, that hunting and gathering are earlier than herding and agriculture, that a stone age has everywhere preceded the use of metals, and that community organization antedates the development of any kind of complex political state. It is alleged that comparable evolutionary sequences can also be established in the field of social organization. The author has weighed a number of such suggestions against the data from his sample societies, but he has found none which accords with the ethnographic facts.

That the matrilineate is not inconsistent with political integration is demonstrated by the League of the Iroquois and the Creek Confederacy. That it can occur with an intense development of property rights and an elaborate structure of social classes is shown by the Haida, Tlingit, and Tsimshian of the Northwest Coast and by the Marshallese and other peoples of Micronesia. That the sib disappears with the development of the state is negated by the Chinese and the Manchus. Even in states founded upon feudal land tenure, unilinear kin groups may be strong, as in patrilineal West Africa and matrilineal Micronesia. The forms of social organization, indeed, appear to show a striking lack of correlation with levels or types of technology, economy, property rights, class structure, or political integration. As will appear below, an objective classification of societies in terms of their similarities in social structure results in grouping together under the same specific type and sub-type such dissimilar peoples as the New England Yankees and the forest-dwelling Negritoes of the Andaman Islands, the imperialistic Incas of Peru and the lowly Yaghan of Tierra del Fuego, the Chinese and the Vanimo Papuans of New Guinea, the Mayan Tzeltal of Yucatan and the backward Miwok of California, the civilized Nayars of India and the primitive nomadic Veddas of the interior of Ceylon. Nowhere does even a revised evolutionism find a shred of support.

The ethnographic evidence contradicting evolutionism in social

organization has long been available, and the line of critical argument adopted above is wholly consistent with the theoretical orientation of the American historical anthropologists influenced by Boas,[9]
who assumed as their principal scientific task the disproof of evolutionism in every aspect of culture. Out of excessive zeal, however,
they chose another course, and overreached themselves. Instead of
contenting themselves with a demonstration that matrilineal societies
are by no means universally more backward in culture than patrilineal societies, they sought to prove that patrilineal tribes are the
more primitive. And instead of showing that bilateral descent is as
characteristic of lower and intermediate as of higher cultures, they
tried to prove that it is peculiarly characteristic of the simplest
peoples and was historically antecedent to both types of unilinear
descent. What they really did, in short, was to reverse the matri-
lineal-patrilineal-bilateral sequence of the evolutionists and to produce an inverted image of the very dragon they sought to destroy.

This curious result, which was wholly at variance with the fundamental position of the authors and no doubt dialectic rather than
intentional, was wrought, not by youthful enthusiasts, but by the
soundest and most creative of American anthropologists. It began
with Swanton,[10] who attempted to prove that in aboriginal North
America the patrilineal tribes are in general culturally more backward than the matrilineal societies. His demonstration was appreciably facilitated by emphasizing the more advanced matrilineal
tribes of the Southwest, Southeast, and Northwest, by ignoring such
backward matrilineal peoples as the northwestern Athapaskans, by
denying that the Crow and Mandan of the Plains are really matrilineal, and by excluding entirely the patrilineal peoples of Mexico
with the highest civilization in native North America. Swanton
also sought to establish the relative cultural inferiority of the bilateral
tribes of North America. In each of his more advanced areas, however, there are bilateral as well as unilinear peoples of similar culture.
Thus the matrilineal Haida can be matched by the sibless Kwakiutl
in the Northwest Coast, the matrilineal Creek by the bilateral

[9] Cf. F. Boas, *The Mind of Primitive Man* (New York, 1911), p. 185.
[10] J. R. Swanton, "The Social Organization of American Tribes," *American
Anthropologist*, n.s., VI (1905), 663–73. Cf. also J. R. Swanton, "A Reconstruction of the Theory of Social Organization," *Boas Anniversary Volume*
(New York, 1906), pp. 166–78.

Catawba in the Southeast, and the matrilineal pueblo of Zuñi by the bilateral pueblo of Taos in the Southwest.

Lowie[11] uncritically accepts Swanton's conclusions with the allegation: "I am not aware of a single student in this field who has failed to accept his position." He then proceeds to extend the generalization to the entire world. In surveying the culturally most backward peoples of the earth in the effort to demonstrate that most of them lack unilinear kin groups, he scarcely does full justice to the facts when he dismisses as a special case the Australian aborigines with their double descent, when he ignores the matrilineal Vedda of Ceylon and the numerous lowly patrilineal and matrilineal societies of Amazonia and east central Brazil, when he mentions the bilateral Chukchee and Koryak but not the patrilineal Gilyak as representative of the Paleo-Siberian hunters, and when he denies sibs to the patrilineal Hottentots of South Africa and to the northern Athapaskans, of whom three out of the four tribes in our sample have matrilineal kin groups.[12]

This inverted evolutionistic scheme of a bilateral-patrilineal-matrilineal succession in the forms of social organization became an established dogma in American anthropology. It was accepted by Goldenweiser[13] as well as by Lowie. Kroeber[14] felt such confidence in it that he made it the basis of an "historical" interpretation: "The original Americans were non-exogamous, non-totemic, without sibs or unilateral reckoning of descent. The first institution of exogamic groups was on the basis of descent in the male line, occurred in or near Middle America, and flowed outward, though not to the very peripheries and remotest tracts of the continents. Somewhat later, perhaps also in Middle America, possibly at the same center, the institution was altered: descent became matrilinear. This new type of organization diffused, but in its briefer history traveled less far and remained confined to the tribes that were in most active cultural

---

[11] R. H. Lowie, *Primitive Society* (New York, 1920), pp. 150–5.

[12] With a scientist's respect for the facts, Lowie has corrected several of these errors in the second edition of *Primitive Society* (New York, 1947), p. 442a.

[13] A. A. Goldenweiser, "The Social Organization of the Indians of North America," *Journal of American Folk-Lore*, XXVII (1914), 436.

[14] A. L. Kroeber, *Anthropology* (New York, 1923), pp. 355–8. Kroeber's elaboration of the scheme is accepted in J. E. Thompson, *Mexico before Cortez* (New York, 1933), p. 105.

connection with Middle America." This theory rests on faith alone, for it is supported by not even a scrap of genuine historical evidence.

The most secure prop of the evolutionist theory of matrilineal priority, that which later anthropologists have had the greatest difficulty in removing, is the complete lack of historically attested, or even inferentially probable, cases of a direct transition from patrilineal to matrilineal descent.[15] No such case has been encountered in our sample, nor has the author ever encountered one in his ethnographic reading. As will shortly be demonstrated, the explanation turns out to be simple. There are no recorded cases of such a transition because it cannot occur. Every other major transition in descent—from bilateral to patrilineal, from patrilineal to bilateral, from bilateral to matrilineal, from matrilineal to bilateral, and from matrilineal to patrilineal—is possible, and historically attested instances can be adduced in fair number. Only the direct transition from patrilineal to matrilineal descent is impossible. With this fact established, the final bulwark of the evolutionist theory is destroyed, for the absence of contrary cases can no longer be regarded as evidence for the priority of the matrilineate.

Unaware of its impossibility, the American historical anthropologists sought desperately for instances of a transition from the patrilineate to the matrilineate as a final disproof of the evolutionist theory. Unsuccessful in their search, but secure in their convictions, they again allowed their zeal to warp their scientific judgment. Imagination discovered what research could not. Among the Kwakiutl of British Columbia Boas found what he thought was the needed evidence, and his discovery has been paraded in numerous subsequent works.[16] The allegedly patrilineal Kwakiutl are asserted to have borrowed a trait of matrilineal inheritance from their matrilineal neighbors to the north.

The facts are simple. Membership in a bilateral group called *numayn*, together with certain special privileges, ordinarily descends

---

[15] Cf. J. Kohler, "Zur Urgeschichte der Ehe," *Zeitschrift für vergleichende Rechtswissenschaft*, XII (1897), 62; R. L. Olson, "Clan and Moiety in Native America," *University of California Publications in American Archaeology and Ethnology*, XXXIII (1933), 410–11.

[16] See, for example, F. Boas *et al*, *General Anthropology* (Boston, etc., 1938), p. 425.

from a parent to the eldest child of either sex among the Kwakiutl, but these things can also be transmitted to a daughter's husband to hold in trust for his son. Since this exceptional mode of inheritance may pass through the husbands of a line of daughters, it is asserted to be in a sense matrilineal. Two significant points, however, are conveniently overlooked. First, the Kwakiutl, though they show certain incipient patrilineal features, are essentially bilateral in their social structure. Second, as is widely known, a man's matrilineal heirs include his siblings and his sisters' children but never his own children or his grandchildren. The alleged borrowing of a non-matrilineal trait by a non-patrilineal people has thus, through the magic of rationalization, undergone metamorphosis and emerged as the long-sought-for crucial case of a transition from the patrilineate to the matrilineate!

This curious obsession with an inverted evolutionism appears to have inhibited American anthropologists from advancing genuinely historical interpretations of social organization. The outstanding exception is Olson,[17] who has attempted to derive all unilinear institutions in North and South America from a single origin, dating back to the first peopling of the New World. "Unilateral institutions, wherever found," maintains Olson,[18] "represent deviations from the expectable, abnormalities in the social structure." They "are in themselves anomalous and artificial." Hence the fact that they are so regularly found associated with such phenomena as totemism, exogamy, comparable sib names, cross-cousin marriage, and reciprocal functions, thinks Olson, constitutes presumptive evidence of a common origin. In Chapter 3 and elsewhere in the present volume we demonstrate that unilinear descent is normal rather than "anomalous and artificial," and that the associated phenomena are not adventitious but expectable and often inevitable. If this is so, the entire basis of Olson's argument falls to the ground.

British diffusionists derive the matrilineate from a single origin in ancient Egypt [19] on evidence so unsatisfactory that the theory is now universally discredited. With much sounder scholarship the

[17] R. L. Olson, "Clan and Moiety in Native America," *University of California Publications in American Archaeology and Ethnology,* XXXIII (1933), 351–422.

[18] *Ibid.,* pp. 411, 409.

[19] Cf. W. J. Perry, *The Children of the Sun* (New York, 1923), pp. 252, 406. 428.

German and Austrian historical anthropologists associate unilinear institutions with a number of great complexes or *Kulturkreise* which are alleged to have diffused extensively over the world, e.g., the "patrilineal-household," the "exogamic-patrilineal," the "exogamic-matrilineal," the "free matrilineal," the "totemistic-matrilineal," and the "free patrilineal" complexes.[20] Though the methods of the several historical schools are susceptible to criticism, it is necessary here only to consider the general question of the extent to which the forms of social organization yield to exclusively historical methods of analysis.

Distributional studies by careful historical anthropologists have incontrovertibly shown that culture traits and trait-complexes tend to be found among contiguous or related peoples. They are usually exhibited by a cluster of tribes in a single culture area or in several adjacent areas, and are not scattered at random over the world. If they are found in more than one continental or insular area, they are attributed to diffusion if there is historical, geographical, or linguistic evidence of a former migration or other connection; to independent invention and diffusion from two or more centers if reasonable grounds for assuming a previous connection are lacking. Distributions conforming to such historical hypotheses have been established for complex artifacts (e.g., the loom, the outrigger canoe, the spear-thrower, the syringe, the wheel), for food crops (e.g., maize, manioc, wheat, rice, taro), for ceremonials (e.g., circumcision, the couvade, increase rites, the potlatch, the sun dance), and for numerous other aspects of culture. That they represent the normal in culture history can no longer be questioned.

One of the most extraordinary conclusions of the present study is that traits of social organization show practically no tendency to yield distributions of this type. Intertribal similarities are, to be sure, found in very restricted areas, where historical connections are indubitable, but rarely indeed do they extend to an entire culture area or to more than a minority of the tribes of a linguistic stock. Nor are they distributed in a few non-contiguous areas, as is characteristic

[20] See W. Schmidt and W. Koppers, *Völker und Kulturen* (Regensburg, 1924), pp. 194–351; W. Schmidt, *The Origin and Growth of Religion* (London, 1931), pp. 240–1.

in most instances of independent invention. On the contrary, they tend to occur widely over the entire earth in many disconnected areas almost as though their appearance were due to sheer chance. Their extraordinarily scattering distribution is revealed in Table 57, which indicates the incidence of the most important traits in each of the five major continental or insular areas of the world.

TABLE 57

Traits of Social Organization	Africa	Eurasia	North America	Oceania	South America
Forms of Marriage					
Monogamy	1	16	13	8	5
Limited polygyny	5	7	18	21	10
Preferential sororal polygyny	11	4	23	13	5
Non-sororal polygyny	45	6	13	11	1
Polyandry	0	1	0	1	0
Forms of the Family					
Independent nuclear	1	12	16	13	5
Independent polygynous	14	4	16	13	4
Independent polyandrous	0	1	0	1	0
Bilocal extended	1	1	3	3	1
Matrilocal extended	1	2	8	4	8
Avunculocal extended	2	0	4	1	0
Patrilocal extended	21	11	12	7	2
Types of Clans					
Matri-clans	0	1	3	6	1
Avuncu-clans	1	0	2	1	0
Patri-clans	32	12	2	24	2
Types of Bilateral Kin Groups					
Kindreds	5	3	12	13	0
Endogamous demes	1	1	8	1	4
Matri-demes	0	0	2	0	0
Patri-demes	0	1	8	1	3
Types of Moieties					
Matri-moieties	1	0	9	12	2
Patri-moieties	0	1	6	9	1

TABLE 57 — *Continued*

Traits of Social Organization	Africa	Eurasia	North America	Oceania	South America
Rules of Residence					
Bilocal	2	1	6	8	2
Neolocal	0	3	12	1	1
Matrilocal	3	2	16	8	9
Avunculocal	2	0	4	2	0
Matri-patrilocal	5	4	9	2	2
Patrilocal	53	24	23	39	7
Rules of Descent					
Bilateral	4	8	36	13	14
Matrilineal	11	2	20	15	3
Patrilineal	45	23	13	21	4
Double	5	1	1	11	0
Types of Cousin Terminology [21]					
Eskimo	6	9	6	2	4
Hawaiian	10	5	26	14	5
Iroquois	20	10	18	27	6
Sudanese	10	2	0	4	1
Omaha	10	6	8	4	1
Crow	7	0	12	7	3

A comparable scatter is observed when the data are analyzed by culture areas. To test this, it seems advisable to use areal criteria independent of those employed by the author in selecting his sample. For this purpose the most recent classification of American culture areas [22] has been adopted, although Kroeber differs from the present author, for example, in grouping the eastern Plains, the Northeast, and the Southeast in a single sub-area. Table 58 shows the rules of descent and residence and the types of cousin terminology which occur in each of the culture areas of South America and each of the sub-areas of North America.

The most indubitable evidence of a past historical connection between two tribes is the fact that they speak demonstrably related

[21] The several types of cousin terminology are precisely defined subsequently in the present chapter.

[22] A. L. Kroeber, *Anthropology* (rev. edit., New York, 1948), pp. 788–91.

TABLE 58

Culture Areas and Sub-Areas	Number of Tribes	Rules of Descent	Rules of Residence	Types of Cousin Terminology
Arctic Coast	2	B	N,P	E
Eastern-Northern				
Northern	8	B,M,P	A,B,P,T	C,H,I
Eastern	14	B,D,M,P	M,N,P,T	C,H,I,O
Plains	7	B,M	B,M,N,P	C,H
Northwest Coast	10	B,M,P	A,P	C,E,H,I,O
Intermediate				
Intermountain	6	B	B,M,N,P	E,H
California	7	B,P	N,P,T	H,I,O
Southwest				
Anasazi Sphere	9	B,M,P	B,M,N	C,E,H,I
Hohokam Sphere	6	B,P	B,N,P,T	H,I
Meso-America	1	P	T	O
Circum-Caribbean	3	B,M	M	C,H,I
Tropical Forest	8	B,P	B,M,P,T	C,E,H,I
Andean	4	B,P	B,P	E,H,O
Marginal	6	B,M,P	M,N,P,T	C,E,H,S

Symbols: Descent—B Bilateral, D Double, M Matrilineal, P Patrilineal
Residence—A Avunculocal, B Bilocal, M Matrilocal, N Neolocal, P Patrilocal, T Matri-patrilocal
Cousin terms—C Crow, E Eskimo, H Hawaiian, I Iroquois, O Omaha, S Sudanese

languages. Yet our survey shows that societies which belong to the same linguistic stock differ in social organization as much as do those which speak unrelated languages. A few examples will establish this point. The Mandan, Omaha, and Teton of the Plains area, who all speak Siouan languages, and who in addition are almost contiguous geographically, exemplify three different rules of descent (matrilineal, patrilineal, and bilateral) and as many distinct types of kinship systems (Crow, Omaha, and Iroquois). Of three nearly adjacent Sudanese tribes in Northern Nigeria, the Bachama are patrilineal and patrilocal, the Jukun bilateral and bilocal, and the Longuda matrilineal and avunculocal. Our sample includes three Malayo-Polynesian tribes from Sumatra: the patrilineal Batak, the bilateral Mentaweians, and the matrilineal Minangkabau. The almost unlimited variability in social forms among peoples of the same historical background is strikingly illustrated in the Malayo-Polynesian linguistic stock, which occupies most of the Pacific except for New Guinea and Australia. Representatives of this stock in our sample exhibit every possibility among the rules of residence and also, as is shown in Table 59, most of the possible combinations of rules of descent and types of kinship terminology.

TABLE 59

Types of Kinship Terminology	Bilateral Descent	Matrilineal Descent	Patrilineal Descent	Double Descent
Crow	....	Trobrianders	Seniang	Pentecost
Eskimo	Balinese	....	....	Pukapukans
Hawaiian	Samoans	Tetekantzi	Tikopia	Ontong-Javanese
Iroquois	Eromangans	Marshallese	Fijians	....
Omaha,				
Sudanese	Tokelau	....	Batak	Ranon

The scattering and almost random distribution of the traits of social organization, which is equally characteristic of remote or unrelated and of contiguous or related peoples, renders practically useless all historical interpretations based upon expectations of diffusion. Cultural similarities appear where they are not anticipated according to historical theory, and differences appear precisely where they are least expected. As a matter of fact, the forms of social organization seem singularly impervious to diffusion. Where similarities do occur among the societies of a restricted region, analysis reveals the probability that they are the result either of fission and migration or of independent adaptation to similar conditions rather than of diffusion in the ordinary sense. Traits of social structure appear to be borrowed, in general, only under conditions in which the same traits would be independently elaborated even in the absence of culture contacts.

If both historical and evolutionist interpretations fail so signally to account for the phenomena of social organization, is a solution perhaps to be found in the third major division of anthropological theory, that which its proponents have styled "functionalism"? Unfortunately not. Although the functional anthropologists have contributed greatly to our understanding of the interrelatedness of the elements of social organization, they have done little to illuminate the dynamics of cultural change. Indeed, so strongly have they emphasized the internal integration of social systems that they have made almost no theoretical provision for change. If nearly perfect integration is a universal characteristic of social structure, only additive change is possible. New elements, borrowed or invented can be adapted to existing configurations, but any fundamental revision or revolutionary modification of the basic pattern becomes impossible. Yet there is abundant historical evidence that such thoroughgoing changes in culture do occur. With respect to the mechanism, however, the functionalists have appreciably less to offer than do the historical anthropologists.

Since none of the three major bodies of anthropological theory contributes substantially to the solution of our problem, we must look elsewhere for helpful suggestions. Much excellent work has been done by recent anthropologists [23] on the factors and processes involved in cultural change. While our views accord substantially with theirs, the general theory of cultural change does not illuminate the particular problems of changing social structure. For the understanding of these, sociological and linguistic theory have proved especially helpful.

Among sociologists, Keller [24] has shown that cultural change is an adaptive process, largely accomplished through the blind trial-and-error behavior of the masses of a society. In this process, Sumner [25] has noted a "strain toward consistency," i.e., a trend toward the integration of the elements of culture. Unlike the functionalists in anthropology, however, Sumner does not regard integration as something regularly achieved; there is merely a tendency to approach an equilibrium, which is commonly interrupted by historical

[23] See especially H. G. Barnett, "Culture Processes," *American Anthropologist*, n.s., XLII (1940), 21–48; H. G. Barnett, "Invention and Cultural Change," *American Anthropologist*, n.s., XLIV (1942), 14–30; H. G. Barnett, "Personal Conflicts and Cultural Change," *Social Forces*, XX (1941), 160–71; J. Gillin, *The Ways of Men* (New York, 1948), pp. 532–69; A. I. Hallowell, "Sociopsychological Aspects of Acculturation," *The Science of Man in the World Crisis*, ed. R. Linton, pp. 171–200; A. L. Kroeber, *Anthropology* (rev. edit., New York, 1948), pp. 344–444; R. Linton, *The Study of Man* (New York, 1936), pp. 324–66; M. E. Opler, "Three Types of Variation and Their Relation to Cultural Change," *Language, Culture and Personality*, ed. L. Spier and others (Menasha, 1941), pp. 146–57.

[24] A. G. Keller, *Societal Evolution* (rev. edit., New York, 1931), pp. 78–251.

[25] W. G. Sumner, *Folkways* (Boston, 1906), pp. 5–6.

events which initiate trends toward new equilibria. Ogburn [26] has advanced the useful hypothesis of "cultural lag" in analyzing the gap which separates the beginning of a process of adaptive change from its accomplishment. Dollard [27] has shown how diffusion operates in this process, i.e., by providing possible solutions to cultural problems which can be borrowed far more readily than they can be evolved through trial and error, and which stand a better chance of success than alternative solutions since they have already been tested and found satisfactory by another society whose circumstances are similar. These theories are particularly applicable to the evolution of social organization, since this normally proceeds from one approximate equilibrium to another, and since it rarely involves cultural borrowing except as a short-cut to an internal reorganization which is already under way.

In studying changes in language, linguists have noted a phenomenon which is commonly called "drift." For reasons that are still very obscure, the speakers of one language will alter the articulation of, for example, a stop consonant. Comparable and compensatory shifts then occur in other consonants until a new equilibrium is achieved, and such changes commonly occur over considerable areas, apparently independently rather than through contact. The celebrated Grimm's Law [28] provides a striking example. The Proto-Germanic languages shifted the articulation of a series of stop consonants from the earlier Indo-European norms still exemplified in Greek and Latin, with the result that the voiceless stops of the latter were changed to the corresponding fricatives in many positions, the voiced stops to voiceless stops, and the fricatives to voiced stops. The High German languages subsequently made a second shift in the same direction, the voiced stops becoming voiceless stops, the fricatives voiced stops, and the voiceless stops fricatives. A comparison of the initial consonants in the names for the numerals 2 and 3 in Latin, English, and German reveals what has occurred: *duo, two, zwei; tres, three, drei.*

The phenomenon of linguistic drift exhibits numerous close

[26] W. F. Ogburn, *Social Change* (New York, 1922), pp. 200–80. Cf. also W. F. Ogburn and M. F. Nimkoff, *Sociology* (Boston, 1940), pp. 775–808.

[27] N. E. Miller and J. Dollard, *Social Learning and Imitation* (New Haven, 1941), pp. 253–73.

[28] Cf. L. Bloomfield, *Language* (New York, 1933), pp. 347–50.

parallels to the evolution of social organization, e.g., limitation in the possibilities of change, a strain toward consistency, shifts from one to another relatively stable equilibrium, compensatory internal readjustments, resistance to any influence from diffusion that is not in accord with the drift, and noteworthy lack of correlation with accompanying cultural norms in technology, economy, property, or government. The forms and structure of language are known to constitute a relatively independent body within culture as a whole, changing according to a dynamics of their own in response to causative factors that are exceedingly difficult to relate to social events or the environing culture. The present study has led to the conclusion that social organization is a semi-independent system comparable in many respects to language, and similarly characterized by an internal dynamics of its own. It is not, however, quite such a closed system, for it demonstrably does change in response to external events, and in identifiable ways. Nevertheless, its own structure appears to act as a filter for the influences which affect it.

In an admirable combination of functional and historical methods, and of field and library techniques, Spoehr [29] has analyzed the changes in kinship structure of a number of Muskogean tribes of the Southeast under the stimulus of contact with European civilization. His findings corroborate the conclusion of the present study that rules of descent, forms of familial and kin groupings, and kinship systems, under conditions of contact with other cultures, do not ordinarily change by direct diffusion but rather by a process of internal readjustment to altered conditions of life. The tribes in question entered the period of contact with kinship systems of the Crow type. As life conditions changed, affecting family organization, kinship terminology underwent a regular series of successive changes. It is significant that the same series of changes occurred quite independently in tribes or sections of tribes that were widely separated. It is perhaps even more significant that the end result in most cases was a system of the Hawaiian type and not one of the Eskimo type, which is the other major bilateral adjustment. Since the civilized whites, contact with whom initiated the changes, have a system of the Eskimo type, the acculturative reaction of the Indians

[29] A. Spoehr, "Changing Kinship Systems," *Field Museum of Natural History Anthropological Series*, XXXIII (1947), 176–8, 197.

was not one of direct borrowing but of internal reorganization leading to an alternative cultural solution.

The external factors which initiate changes in social structure must be such as will account for the peculiar spatial distribution of the forms of the latter. They must be able to explain both the differences among tribes that are geographically contiguous or linguistically related and the similarities among peoples who are scattered widely over the earth and characterized by markedly different types of culture. The evidence from our 250 societies supports the contention of the American historical anthropologists, against the evolutionists, that there is no inevitable sequence of social forms nor any necessary association between particular rules of residence or descent or particular types of kin groups or kinship terms and levels of culture, types of economy, or forms of government or class structure. On the other hand, it supports the evolutionists, against the several schools of historical anthropology, in the conclusion that parallelism or independent invention is relatively easy and common in the field of social organization, and that any structural form can be developed anywhere if conditions are propitious. The explanation seems to lie in the principle of limited possibilities, alluded to in the previous chapter. Unlike such cultural categories as language, technology, folklore, and ceremonial, where the possibilities of innovation are almost limitless, the various aspects of social organization admit of only a very few, relatively obvious, alternative variations.[30]

The present writer is unable to conceive of any single external factor or group of factors capable of producing similar effects in remote and diverse geographical areas among peoples of contrasting levels of culture while at the same time allowing for wide differentiation among tribes with demonstrably close historical connections. The only reasonable solution is to admit that quite different external influences are capable of producing an identical effect upon social organization, and that there are several series of multiple factors capable of producing different effects. If this is true, and our evidence strongly supports the hypothesis, the search for the sources of change must be shifted from the external factors to the social structure itself. We must look for some aspect of social organization

[30] Cf. G. P. Murdock, "The Common Denominator of Cultures," *The Science of Man in the World Crisis*, ed. R. Linton (New York, 1946), pp. 138–41.

which acts as a filter, which is capable of responding in only a limited number of ways but by each of them to a variety of quite diverse external stimuli. Such a structural feature must, in addition, be peculiarly sensitive to outside influences and at the same time be itself especially competent to effect compensatory readjustments elsewhere in the system.

Of the several major aspects of social structure, kinship terminology reacts very slightly if at all to external influences. As demonstrated in the previous chapter, it is determined primarily by the forms of familial and kin groupings. Rules of descent and the kin groups resulting therefrom are also relatively immune to forces from outside the social organization. There is abundant evidence that they tend long to outlast the influences which produce them, as is demonstrated by the frequent survival of matrilineal descent under patrilocal residence and by the continuation of consanguineal kin groups after the disappearance of the forms of family or clan organization which have presumably produced them. Extended families and clans are obviously dependent upon rules of residence; they appear only under an appropriate rule of residence and disappear almost immediately when residence changes. Types of marriage, on the other hand, can change in direct response to external causes. They are, for example, susceptible to influences from religion. Thus the Mohammedan preference for marriage with a father's brother's daughter has resulted in the loss of exogamy by the patri-sibs of both the Kababish in Africa and the Kurd in Asia, and Christianity has supplanted polygyny with monogamy in a number of the societies in our sample. However, the impact of a change in marriage upon other parts of the social structure is usually relatively slight as compared with other internal changes, and it will be subsequently demonstrated that marriage rules tend strongly to reflect other features of social organization rather than *vice versa*.

The one aspect of social structure that is peculiarly vulnerable to external influences is the rule of residence. While a number of earlier authorities [31] and at least one recent theorist [32] have suggested that

[31] Cf. E. B. Tylor, "On a Method of Investigating the Development of Institutions," *Journal of the Royal Anthropological Institute*, XVIII (1889), 245-69; P. Vinogradoff, *Outlines of Historical Jurisprudence*, I (New York, 1920), 195; E. Westermarck, *The History of Human Marriage* (5th edit., New York, 1922), I, 296-7.

an alteration in the prevailing rule of residence is the point of departure for nearly all significant changes in social organization, it is to Lowie [33] that we are primarily indebted for establishing this point and for specifying how changes in residence rules can disturb the equilibrium of a relatively stable social system and initiate a series of internal readjustments which may ultimately produce a new equilibrium. This is by far the most important contribution of any modern anthropologist to our knowledge of the evolution of social organization.

It is in respect to residence that changes in economy, technology, property, government, or religion first alter the structural relationships of related individuals to one another, giving an impetus to subsequent modifications in forms of the family, in consanguineal and compromise kin groups, and in kinship terminology. Patrilocal residence involves a man in lifelong residential propinquity and social participation with his father's patrilineal kinsmen; matrilocal residence associates him with the matrilineal relatives of his mother before marriage and with those of his wife after marriage; bilocal residence brings him into contact with a selected group of bilateral and/or affinal relatives; neolocal residence isolates him before marriage with his family of orientation and thereafter with his family of procreation; avunculocal residence aligns him physically and socially with his male matrilineal kinsmen and their families. Not only do his relations with his parents, his children, and other relatives differ profoundly under these various arrangements, but so do those with his wife. Either she or he may be isolated from his own relatives, while the other is surrounded and supported by sympathetic kinsmen, or both may be isolated together and made primarily dependent upon one another, or in special cases both may be amongst friendly kinsmen. So different are the circumstances of life for the individual under these several arrangements that it should occasion no surprise that the adoption by a society of a new rule of residence normally leads to far-reaching internal readjustments.

---

[32] M. Titiev, "The Influence of Common Residence on the Unilateral Classification of Kindred," *American Anthropologist,* n.s., XLV (1943), 511–30.

[33] R. H. Lowie, *Primitive Society* (New York, 1920), pp. 70–6, 122–37, 157–62, 166–85.

The conditions of existence in any society are always undergoing change—sometimes rapidly, sometimes slowly—in consequence of natural events such as famines and epidemics, of social events such as wars and revolutions, of biological influences such as increasing population density, of internal adaptations such as technological inventions, and of external contacts which may stimulate cultural borrowing. Many changes in fundamental life conditions may exert pressure in the direction of modifying the existing rule of residence. So diverse are the causal factors in social change, and so few are the alternatives in residence rules, that nearly any society, whatever its level of culture and existing forms of social organization, can probably encounter particular concatenations of circumstances that will favor the development of any one of the alternative rules of residence. It will be well to examine some of the conditions which seem to predispose societies on all levels to particular residence usages.

The development of neolocal residence, in societies following other rules, appears to be favored by any influence which tends to isolate or to emphasize the individual or the nuclear family. Since the nuclear family is somewhat submerged under polygyny, any factor which promotes monogamy will likewise favor neolocal residence. Examples of such factors include a sex division of labor in which the product of one woman's and that of one man's activities strike an approximately equal balance, widespread poverty which inhibits extensive wife-purchase, and the adoption of a religious or ethical system, such as Christianity, which forbids polygyny on principle. Since the nuclear family is also partially submerged in the presence of extended families or clans, any influence which tends to undermine or inhibit large local aggregations of kinsmen will create conditions favorable to neolocal residence. Political evolution from a gentile to a territorial form of the state, for example, has frequently been followed, in Africa, Asia, and Europe, by the disintegration of clans and the weakening of unilinear ties. Individualism in its various manifestations, e.g., private property, individual enterprise in the economic sphere, or personal freedom in the choice of marital partners, facilitates the establishment of independent households by married couples. A similar effect may be produced by overpopulation and other factors which stimulate individual migration, or by pioneer life in the occupation of new territory, or by the expansion of trade and industry, or by developing urbanization. A modification in inheritance rules, such as the replacement of primogeniture by the division of an estate among a number of heirs, can likewise favor neolocal residence. Even a change in architecture might exert an influence, e.g., the supplanting of large communal houses by a form of dwelling suited to the occupancy of a single family.

An equal variety of quite different factors can favor a transition to bilocal residence. On a relatively low level of culture, the adoption of a migratory life in unstable bands seems particularly conducive to this rule of residence. A family may pitch its tent or erect its hut near the father's relatives at one campsite and near the mother's at the next, or if they belong to different bands it may reside with either or shift from one to the other. On a higher cultural level, under sedentary conditions of life, an important contributory factor appears to be the approximate equality in status of the two sexes, especially with regard to the ownership and inheritance of property and privileges. Where women own and inherit property on a parity with men, it is common for a newly married couple to adopt the domicile of the spouse with the greater wealth or higher social status.[34] Differentiation in the status of children according to order of birth and primogeniture without regard to sex seems especially conducive to bilocal residence. Thus in Polynesia, where these customs are particularly common, a first-born child of either sex normally remains with his own family of orientation after marriage, the residence change being made by the spouse who is junior in status. Anything which lessens the strength of unilinear bonds favors bilocal residence, provided that kinship ties in general are not weakened. Factors that militate against neolocal residence must usually also be present, e.g., large or multi-family dwellings and collective rather than individual enterprise, so that bilaterally related nuclear families may be held together.

Still different are the factors that promote matrilocal residence. Lippert[35] has made the illuminating suggestion that matrilocal

[34] Cf. J. G. Frazer, *Totemism and Exogamy* (London, 1910), I, 72; P. Vinogradoff, *Outlines of Historical Jurisprudence*, I (New York, 1920), 195.

[35] J. Lippert, *The Evolution of Culture* (New York, 1931), p. 237.

residence is especially likely when the means of subsistence of a people depend primarily upon woman's activities in the division of labor by sex. The condition which most frequently lifts her economic contribution to a level above that of the man is the introduction of agriculture into a society previously dependent upon hunting and gathering. Since agriculture is usually woman's work, matrilocal residence and matrilineal descent tend to be particularly common among lower agricultural peoples.[36] Thurnwald [37] makes the point very clearly. Among bilateral hunting and collecting peoples, he says, "sons inherit the trapping and hunting gear of their fathers; daughters, the cooking utensils and food-gathering implements of their mother. When the women have advanced from collecting to agriculture, their property is augmented, and matrilineal inheritance consequently becomes the more important. Having at their disposal, as a result of agriculture, a more stable and often more abundant food supply than the men, their importance is further enhanced, and their superiority in the matter of property, including that in their children, finds widespread recognition in matrilineal descent."

A relatively high status of women, which favors bilocal residence, is also conducive to matrilocal residence. But whereas it is woman's comparative equality with man in property and other rights that promotes bilocal residence, it is her superiority to him, especially in production and in the ownership of the principal instrument thereof—land—that favors matrilocal residence. A contributory factor is the absence of movable property in herds, slaves, or other valuables; in the hands of the men these might challenge the preeminence of landed property and introduce the destructive factor of polygyny. Relative peacefulness is another contributory factor, for war enhances the importance of men and often brings them slave wives or booty with which to purchase women. Still another significant precondition is a relatively low level of political integration, particularly one which, as in Melanesia and among the Pueblo Indians, does not extend beyond the local community. Wider political authority brings to the holders, who are almost invariably

[36] Cf. R. H. Lowie, *Primitive Society* (New York, 1920), p. 160.
[37] R. C. Thurnwald, *Die menschliche Gesellschaft in ihren ethnosoziologischen Grundlagen*, II (Berlin, Leipzig, 1932), 193–4.

men, increased power, property, and prestige, which often spell doom to the matrilocal principle.

Patrilocal residence seems to be promoted by any change in culture or the conditions of life which significantly enhances the status, importance, and influence of men in relation to the opposite sex. Particularly influential is any modification in the basic economy whereby masculine activities in the sex division of labor come to yield the principal means of subsistence. "The nature of the economic activities does not affect the result; the only essential is their disparity." [38] The adoption of a pastoral economy has almost universally resulted in patrilocal residence.[39] A similar effect tends to appear where men supplant women as tillers of the soil, often in consequence of harnessing their domestic animals to the plow.[40] Even among hunters and gatherers the same result can be produced if a tribe moves into an area where game is plentiful and dependable, so that subsistence comes to depend primarily upon the chase rather than upon the collecting activities of the women. This possibly accounts for the prevalence of patrilocal residence in native Australia. It is significant that the Crow, who separated from the agricultural and matrilocal Hidatsa in late prehistoric times to adopt a buffalo-hunting economy on the Plains, have shifted to patrilocal residence though they still retain their matri-sibs.

Polygyny is relatively inconsistent with the individualism under neolocal residence and with the high and independent position of women under bilocal residence, and it is practically impossible, except in the sororal form, under matrilocal residence. It is, however, particularly congenial to patrilocal residence, where women are isolated from their kinsmen and tend to be economically and socially inferior to men. Hence anything which favors polygyny likewise favors the development of patrilocal residence. Even the introduction of a religious system which sanctions polygyny, e.g., Mohammedanism, may have such an effect.

Especially important is the development of any form of movable property or wealth which can be accumulated in quantity by men.

[38] J. Lippert, *The Evolution of Culture* (New York, 1931), p. 237.
[39] See L. T. Hobhouse, G. C. Wheeler, and M. Ginsberg, *The Material Culture and Social Institutions of the Simpler Peoples* (London, 1915), pp. 150-A
[40] Cf. R. H. Lowie, *Primitive Society* (New York, 1920), p. 194.

With such property, whether it be herds, slaves, money, or other valuables, prosperous men can offer a bride-price to the parents of girls which will induce them to part with their daughters. The concentration of property in the hands of men specifically facilitates a transition to patrilineal inheritance among peoples who have previously followed the rule of matrilineal inheritance, for men now have the power and the means to make effective their natural preference for transmitting their property to their own sons rather than to their sororal nephews. Warfare, slavery, and political integration all encourage patrilocal residence. War enhances men's influence and brings them captive (and hence patrilocal) wives and plunder wherewith to buy other women. Slavery provides a mechanism for purchasing women and enforcing patrilocal residence. Political expansion increases the power and prestige of the men and normally establishes a rule of patrilineal succession, both of which favor patrilocal residence.

Matri-patrilocal residence, which is merely a variant of patrilocal residence, is promoted by the same factors. The initial period of matrilocal residence before the patrilocal rule becomes established seems to result most commonly from one of two special factors. The first is bride-service, either as a supplement to or as a partial substitute for wife-purchase. The second is the adoption of the instalment plan for the payment of the bride-price; the husband resides with his wife's parents until he has paid the final instalment.

The case of avunculocal residence is particularly interesting. The evidence is overwhelming that it can never develop out of neolocal, bilocal, or patrilocal residence; it is only possible as a replacement for matrilocal residence. The identical factors which lead to patrilocal residence in a previously matrilocal society can also produce avunculocal residence. Under these circumstances the patrilocal and avunculocal rules are completely alternative to each other. They both result in social systems which are equivalent to one another in every respect except that the rule of descent is commonly patrilineal in the one instance and matrilineal in the other. Under both systems men live with their unilinear male relatives, whereas their wives are assembled from other localities and tend to be isolated from their kinsmen. Every advantage which males can achieve under patrilocal residence—polygyny, slaves, wealth, political power, military prestige—they can acquire equally well under avunculocal residence.

The only reason why avunculocal residence has appeared less frequently than patrilocal residence as a resolution of the problem created by increasing masculine influence under a matrilocal arrangement seems to be its dependence upon a somewhat unusual change of residence at or prior to marriage, namely, the requirement that a boy or youth leave his parental home and take up his domicile with a brother of his mother. Where such a residential shift is customary, as it is among the Haida of British Columbia, the Longuda of Nigeria, and the Trobrianders of Melanesia, any of the influences which would otherwise lead to patrilocal residence result in men bringing their wives, not to the home of the husband's parents but to the homes of the maternal uncles with whom they live.

A new rule of residence once established, what are its effects? In the first place, it begins to exert an influence on kinship terminology in accordance with the principles established in Theorems 6 to 12 under Postulate 1 in the previous chapter. Since, however, the relative efficacy of residence rules is not especially high, the expected changes in kinship nomenclature frequently do not appear until after the establishment of a new rule of descent. It is with respect to unilinear groupings of kinsmen that rules of residence exert their most important influence.

A transition from neolocal to bilocal residence, or *vice versa*, presents few difficulties. Both are normally associated with bilateral descent, and a change from one to the other merely produces a different type of bilateral organization. The shift to neolocal residence results in the emergence of the isolated nuclear family; that to bilocal residence facilitates the development of bilateral kin groups and the bilocal extended family.

A change to neolocal residence from any form of unilocal residence —matrilocal, patrilocal, or avunculocal—has a disruptive effect upon existing unilinear groupings. Clans are especially susceptible. Even if neolocal residence occurs in only a significant minority of cases, without really supplanting the prevailing unilocal rule, clans tend rapidly to disappear, leaving behind them only non-localized lineages and sibs. Unilocal extended families break up nearly as readily, giving way to independent polygynous or monogamous families.

Lineages, sibs, and moieties are more resistant, and if functionally important may survive for a considerable time. They are inevitably weakened, however, and tend eventually to disappear entirely. The final result of neolocal residence is thus always bilateral descent. Modern European societies provide a number of historical instances of this type of transition.

Bilocal residence exerts a comparable but less disruptive and more gradual influence upon unilinear institutions. Clans may survive for a period in a modified bilocal form, and may even become converted into kindreds. Unilocal extended families are transformed by easy gradations into bilocal extended families, and may continue to perform very similar functions. Lineages, sibs, and moieties, with their residential support gone, disappear gradually, much as they do under the impact of neolocal residence. The eventual result in both cases is bilateral descent. For one of the African societies in our sample, the Jukun of Northern Nigeria, there is explicit historical evidence of such a transition. Formerly matrilineal and matrilocal, the Jukun, under powerful influence from the patrilocal Fulani, adopted bilocal residence and bilateral descent as a compromise between opposing forces.

While neolocal and bilocal residence invariably result ultimately in the loss of unilinear descent, and appear to be the only means by which such loss can ordinarily occur, the adoption of unilocal residence in a bilateral society, though it favors the development of a corresponding unilinear rule of descent, by no means produces such a rule inevitably. As tabulations of our data will shortly show, both patrilocal and matrilocal residence are exceedingly common in each of the two major types of bilateral organization. Although unilocal residence does not necessarily lead to unilinear descent, the author must insist, in opposition to Lowie,[41] that unilinear descent can arise in no other way than through unilocal residence. Lowie's alternative factor, the division of labor by sex, does not exert its influence directly upon the rule of descent, but only indirectly through the residential alignment of unilinear kinsmen. If we reject the direct influences proposed by the evolutionists, especially the alleged ignorance of physical paternity and the asserted non-membership of the father in the primitive family, unilocal residence

[41] R. H. Lowie, *Primitive Society* (New York, 1920), pp. 159–60.

remains as the only factor known to be capable of creating the conditions out of which matrilineal and patrilineal kin groups can arise.

Unilocal residence does not produce lineages or sibs directly. It merely favors the development of extended families and exogamous demes with their characteristic unilinear alignment of kinsmen, and either of these in turn may lead to the recognition of non-localized kin groups. What matrilocal or patrilocal residence accomplishes is to assemble in spatial proximity to one another a group of uni-linearly related kinsmen of the same sex, together with their spouses. Local conditions may or may not favor the development of the particular kinds of social bonds between the members of such a group that would constitute them into an extended family or local-ized kin group. If such bonds are formed, and extended families or other residential kin groups make their appearance, the society is exceedingly likely to develop unilinear descent in due time. The Havasupai and Hupa, as was shown in Chapter 4, illustrate transi-tional stages in the development of patrilineal descent out of bilateral descent through the influence of patrilocal residence, the one by way of patrilocal extended families and the other by way of patri-demes.

Matri-sibs develop from matrilocal residence by way of matrilocal extended families, or occasionally matri-demes, in precisely similar fashion. Borneo provides an illuminating illustration, not only of the way in which this change can occur quite independently of any outside cultural contact, but also of the fact that such a development is by no means inevitable merely because matrilocal residence has been adopted. The matrilocal rule is nearly universal in Borneo, yet with a single exception all the tribes of the island are bilateral in descent. The Siong branch of the Maanyan tribe of south central Borneo, who are surrounded by sibless peoples whom they otherwise resemble in culture, alone have developed unilinear descent. From matrilocal residence they have evolved a system of true matri-sibs, each with its ceremonial center in a common ancestral tomb.[42]

[42] See J. Mallinckrodt, "De stamindeeling van de Maanjan-Sioeng-Dajaks," *Bijdragen tot de Taal-, Land-, en Volkenkunde van Nederlandsch Indië*, LXXXIII (1927), 561–4. The author is indebted to his colleague, Professor Raymond Kennedy, for calling this case to his attention.

When a matrilocal society with fully developed matrilineal kin groups encounters a combination of influences favorable to patrilocal residence and strong enough to alter the rule of residence, any of three different solutions is possible and can be illustrated from our sample tribes. If local circumstances permit boys to establish a domicile with their maternal uncles, avunculocal rather than patrilocal residence is adopted. The tribe retains such matrilineal lineages, sibs, and moieties as it may have, and its matrilocal extended families and matri-clans, if such exist, are either lost or become converted into avunculocal extended families and avuncu-clans. Eight societies in our sample—two in Africa, four in North America, and two in Oceania—appear to have experienced this transition.

If local circumstances do not favor avunculocal residence, a matrilineal society under strong patrilocal cultural pressure is likely to adopt patrilocal residence without giving up its matrilineal lineages, sibs, or moieties. Matri-clans and matrilocal extended families vanish almost immediately, but matrilineal kin groups of the non-localized or consanguineal type can survive for long periods provided their functions are not destroyed by the change in residence. Since patrilocal residence may scatter the members of a matri-sib over a considerable territory, any functions associated with a particular locality are necessarily lost. The function which best survives the shift in residence is that of the regulation of marriage, or exogamy. If this is lost, matrilineal descent speedily disappears, and the tribe becomes bilateral though patrilocal. If exogamy is retained, however, matrilineal descent is maintained despite the contradictory residence rule. This is the case with 14 societies in our sample—5 in Africa, 4 in North America, and 5 in Oceania. For some of them, e.g., the Crow of Montana, there is substantial historical evidence of such a transition.

A society of this type, if its matrilineal kin groups are exogamous and strongly functional, can subsequently undergo any of the changes that normally follow the introduction of patrilocal residence in a bilateral society, retaining throughout, however, its rule of matrilineal descent. It can, for example, develop patrilocal extended families, or adopt a rule of local exogamy, and on this basis eventually acquire genuine patri-lineages or patri-sibs. Acquisition of patrilineal descent in this manner, without loss of the earlier matrilineal kin groups, is the normal process by which double descent arises. Of our sample societies, 14 of those with double descent— 9 in Oceania, 4 in Africa, and 1 in Eurasia—have clearly undergone such a transition, and in 3 other instances it is possible if not probable. If the matrilineal heritage includes matri-moieties, the phenomenon of bilinear kin groups or "marriage classes" normally makes its appearance, as with the Ranon of the New Hebrides and many Australian tribes.

It may be pointed out incidentally that there is another, though much less common, origin of double descent. A bilateral society with distinct rules of inheritance for two types of property can evolve lineages on the basis of each type of ownership. Thus the Ontong-Javanese have land-holding patri-lineages and house-owning matri-lineages, and the double descent of the Pukapukans may well have had a similar origin. Such instances seem clearly distinguishable from the more usual type of double descent by the fact that the unilinear kin groups are lineages rather than sibs and that they tend to be non-exogamous.

Instead of becoming avunculocal, or patrilocal with matrilineal and perhaps eventual double descent, a matrilocal and matrilineal society under strong patrilocal cultural stresses may be transformed directly into a full-fledged patrilocal, patrilineal society. The rule of descent is altered along with or shortly after the rule of residence. Contact with specifically patrilineal neighbors appears to be a necessary precondition for the adoption of this third alternative, for only the presence of a model from whom to borrow can account for so rapid a development of a new rule of descent. Even under such favorable conditions, however, it is probable that a transitional period of bilateral descent, however brief, usually intervenes between the abandonment of the matrilineal and the adoption of the patrilineal rule.

Though perhaps comparatively rare, this type of transition is confirmed by dependable historical evidence for two of the African societies of our sample. The Henga of Nyasaland were matrilineal and matrilocal until relatively recently, and are known to have adopted patrilocal residence and patrilineal descent at approximately the same time as a result of invasions by the patrilineal Ngoni. Under similar stresses the Bena of Ubena first adopted patrilocal residence and then transformed their matri-sibs into patri-sibs, a change which has been completed only within the last few years. In this instance, however, the presence of bilateral kindreds suggests that there was at least a brief intermediate period of bilateral descent. In a number of other societies in our sample a comparable transition is indicated by internal evidence, e.g., the survival of special cases of matrilineal inheritance or of avunculocal residence in an otherwise completely patrilineal and patrilocal context.

The mechanics of such a transition cannot be fully understood except in reference to one fundamental difference between matrilineal and patrilineal organization. This difference rests upon a universal characteristic of the division of labor by sex. A study of the distribution of economic activities between the sexes in 224 tribes scattered throughout the world [43] has revealed that the tasks assigned to women in more than 75 per cent of the societies with relevant information are grain grinding, water carrying, cooking, the gathering of fuel and vegetable products, the manufacture and repair of clothing, the preservation of meat and fish, pottery making, weaving, and the manufacture of mats and baskets. It will be noted that most of these tasks can be carried on in the house or its immediate vicinity, and that none of them requires an intimate knowledge of the tribal terrain. The tasks assigned to men in more than 75 per cent of the sample societies, however, include the following: herding (84%), fishing (86%), lumbering (92%), trapping (95%), mining and quarrying (95%), hunting (98%), and the catching of sea mammals (99%). All of these activities, as well as the characteristically masculine pursuit of war, carry the men far from the dwelling and demand a thorough knowledge of the environs of the community and of the location of all its usable resources.

From these characteristics of the division of labor by sex it follows that a change of residence in marriage, if it involves a shift from one community to another, works far greater hardships on a man than on a woman. A woman can join her husband in another community and continue to carry on without handicap all the technical skills she has acquired since childhood. But a man who goes to a new community in matrilocal marriage has to master an entirely

[43] G. P. Murdock, "Comparative Data on the Division of Labor by Sex," *Social Forces*, XV (1937), 551–3.

new environment. All the knowledge he has gained as a boy and youth concerning the location of trails and landmarks, of mineral deposits, of superior stands of timber, of the haunts of game, and of the best grazing or fishing sites becomes largely useless, and must be painfully accumulated afresh for the new territory. These facts discourage a change of community in marriage on the part of the man, whereas they exert no such effect in the case of a woman. They do not prevent matrilocal residence *per se*, but they do impose limitations which do not exist for patrilocal residence.

Where residence is matrilocal, a man in marrying rarely settles in a new community. He merely takes his possessions from his parents' home and moves, so to speak, across the street to that part of the same village where his wife and her relatives live. In only three of the 25 matrilocal and matrilineal societies in our sample is there evidence that a man commonly changes his community when he marries, and in one of these cases, the Dobuans, he regularly spends half of his time in his own village and only half in his wife's. Among the Vedda of Ceylon and the Yaruro of Venezuela, the other two exceptional cases, the community is a migratory band, under which circumstances the reasons ordinarily militating against a man's change of residence do not apply. Moreover, the two bilateral societies, the Arapaho and Cheyenne, which combine matrilocal residence with a tendency toward local exogamy, are also organized in migratory bands. There is thus a nearly universal association between matrilocal residence in sedentary communities and local endogamy. Since there are rarely comparable reasons to prevent a woman from moving to a new community when she marries, such a shift is the rule in a substantial majority of the patrilocal and patrilineal societies in our sample (see Table 2 in Chapter 1).

One result of this distinction between the sexes with respect to change of community in marriage is that the conversion of an entire community into a patri-clan is both feasible and common. The case of the Hupa, for example, has shown how a patri-deme can develop into a patrilocal clan-community. The transformation of an entire community into a matri-clan, however, can apparently occur only under migratory conditions. An even more important result is the differential history of communities containing several clans after patrilineal or matrilineal descent and exogamy have become established.

As a community with several patri-clans grows and prospers, increasing population relative to the available means of subsistence normally results in the migration of a portion of the inhabitants to establish a new settlement. The fission of the community is likely to follow the existing cleavage between clans, so that those who leave will constitute one or more whole clans. After several such splits, both the home village and each of its daughter communities will tend to consist of a single clan. This explains why, among the 72 societies in our sample with patri-clans, 45 have clan-communities as opposed to only 27 with clan-barrios. This distribution contrasts sharply with that for matri-clans.

In a matrilineal and matrilocal society, fission cannot reduce the community to a single matri-clan, for this would require all men to leave their home community in marriage. Two matri-clans represent the irreducible minimum beyond which the fissive process cannot go. Any further emigration must consist of members of both kin groups, so that the men in both the parent and daughter communities can observe the rule of exogamy and marry matrilocally without leaving the village whose territory and resources they have come intimately to know.

This is, incidentally, the regular procedure by which matri-moieties are formed. The end result of fission is to leave two sibs in the parent community and to carry the matrilineal relatives of both to any new communities established by migration. If the rule of exogamy is retained, the original sibs become converted automatically into matri-moieties. This also explains why matri-moieties are so much more common than patri-moieties despite the considerably greater frequency of patrilineal descent. In our sample, for instance, only 17 of the 124 societies with patrilineal descent have patri-moieties, whereas matri-moieties occur in 24 of the 69 with matrilineal descent. The disparity becomes even greater when only moieties exhibiting at least a tendency toward exogamy are considered. Exogamous matri-moieties are found in 19 societies; exogamous patri-moieties in only 9, and 4 of these are tribes with double descent in which the earlier matri-moieties presumably served as the model upon which the patri-moieties were formed.

We are now in a position to examine the exact mechanics by which a transition to the patrilineate occurs in a previously matrilocal and matrilineal community. For demonstrative purposes we may conceive of such a community as a small settlement containing two matri-clans, each localized on one side of the main village thoroughfare. Before a change takes place, a man simply moves across the street when he marries, and settles in a hut belonging to his wife. He carries on all his economic activities in the same environing territory as before his marriage, and his closest relatives live just over the way, where he can visit them at any time and cooperate with them in the ways to which he became accustomed as a bachelor.

Let it be assumed that there now appears some factor which places a premium upon patrilocal residence—perhaps the introduction of cattle, or slaves, or shell money, accompanied by the idea that personal prestige can be enhanced through polygyny. One man after another, as he acquires wealth, is able to persuade other men to allow their daughters to remove to his home in marriage in return for the payment of a bride-price, and one man after another begins to leave some of his property to his own sons instead of bequeathing it all to his sisters' sons. Bit by bit, ties with patrilineal kinsmen are strengthened, while those with matrilineal relatives undergo a diminution in importance. Interpersonal relationships are readjusted gradually, naturally, and without strain.

Almost before the population of the village realizes that anything particularly significant has happened, they discover that the houses on one side of the street are now occupied by patrilineally related males with their wives and children, and that a similar group lives across the way. Patrilocal residence has become firmly established, patrilineal inheritance is accepted, and the former matri-clans have been transformed into incipient patri-clans. The situation is ripe for the development of patrilineal descent, and this may occur quite rapidly if there are patrilineal societies in the neighborhood to serve as models. Provided that matrilineal descent is lost in the process, a complete patrilineate can thus evolve out of the matrilineate through a succession of natural and almost imperceptible transitional steps.

A sharp contrast to the above is presented by a typical patrilocal and patrilineal community which experiences influences ordinarily conducive to matrilocal residence. The illustrative village may be assumed to be a patrilocal clan-community whose nearest neighbors are two similar settlements located six or eight miles distant, the one downstream on the opposite side of the same river, the other across the mountain in the next valley. It is from one or the other of these that the mothers and wives of the men in our village have come. If factors favorable to matrilocal residence make their appearance in such a setting, no easy and gradual transition is possible. A man cannot do much to strengthen the ties with his matrilineal relatives when they reside miles away, or to weaken those with his patrilineal kinsmen with whom he associates daily. No reasonable motive can induce him to bequeath his property to his sisters' sons in another village and to disinherit the sons in his own house. If he desires to live with his wife's relatives, he must move to another village and to a natural environment where most of his accumulated knowledge will go for naught. Moreover, he must forswear polygyny. The obstacles to matrilocal residence, in sum, are well-nigh insuperable.

If the forces favoring matrilocal residence are nevertheless irresistible, two solutions and only two are possible. First, an increasing number of men may brave the hardships involved and actually move to another village to live with their wives. But this merely institutes bilocal residence and initiates the series of changes already described by which the patrilineate gives way to bilateral descent. The second alternative is to defy the rule of exogamy and marry a woman of one's own village. If this becomes at all common, relationships are confused, the sib disintegrates through the removal of its residential and exogamic support, and the village becomes converted into an endogamous deme with bilocal and perhaps eventually matrilocal residence. A direct transition to the matrilineate is thus completely impossible for any typical patrilineal society, i.e., one which has evolved clan-communities.

In the minority of patrilocal and patrilineal societies which have only patrilocal extended families or clan-barrios, or which for some reason have lost all localized groupings of kinsmen, the introduction of matrilocal residence is opposed by polygyny. The only forms of marriage that are consistent with matrilocal residence are monogamy, polyandry, and exclusively sororal polygyny. Yet these forms occur in only 18 out of 97 patrilocal-patrilineal societies in our sample; 64 have general polygyny of non-sororal or mixed type, while 15 others allow it but do not practice it extensively. For such a society to become matrilocal, the men must renounce all plural marriages except sororal polygyny. They must also submit to other disadvantages, such as the lesser freedom they are likely to enjoy among their relatives-in-law than in their own homes. These factors render it highly improbable—even in the absence of clan-communities and under very strong pressure from forces favoring the matrilocal rule—that more than a fraction of the men will change their residence immediately to the homes of their wives' families. Unless all of them do so, however, residence becomes bilocal rather than matrilocal, unilinear institutions begin to disintegrate, and bilateral rather than matrilineal descent results.

Under matrilocal pressures, patrilineal societies can become bilateral, and thence perhaps eventually matrilineal. They cannot, however, undergo direct transition to a matrilineal form of organization. To be sure, exceptions are theoretically possible under extremely improbable combinations of circumstances. But if they actually occur at all, which has yet to be demonstrated, they are so rare that they may safely be ignored in a general hypothesis of the development of social organization.

The observation has often been made [44] that in many parts of the world patrilineal and matrilineal peoples are found side by side in restricted areas with cultures showing unmistakable evidences of historical connections. It should now be clear that wherever such a situation exists, if the two types of structure are in fact genetically related, the patrilineal tribes must have evolved from a matrilineal organization, and not *vice versa*. It must likewise be true that in all societies with full-fledged double descent the matrilineal kin groups were the first to be evolved, the rule of patrilineal descent representing a secondary development.[45] These generalizations, of course, can in no way be taken as supporting the evolutionist theory

[44] Cf. A. L. Kroeber, "The Societies of Primitive Man," *Levels of Integration in Biological and Social Systems*, ed. R. Redfield (Lancaster, 1942), p. 210.

[45] Emeneau is thus presumably in error in reversing this order for the Toda. See M. B. Emeneau, "Language and Social Forms: a Study of Toda Kinship," *Language, Culture and Personality*, ed. L. Spier and others (Menasha, 1941), pp. 173–5.

of the universal priority of the matrilineate. On the contrary, since the ancestors of nearly all groups which have survived until today must have undergone many changes in social organization during the long course of human history, the fact that the last transition in a particular series has been from matrilineal to patrilineal or double descent by no means implies that the matrilineate came first in the entire series.

The hypothesis of the evolution of social organization advanced in this chapter makes no assumptions about ultimate origins or over-all priorities among the several types of social structure. It is assumed only that the possibilities of change in any given instance are limited. From any type, only certain other types can be reached through direct transition, though any other type can be reached through a sufficient number of successive steps. Patrilineal societies, for example, can develop matrilineal institutions by way of intermediate bilateral forms. It is believed that the hypothesis accords in most important respects with the fundamental position of Boas and his followers, and might well have been developed by them had they not been misled into attempting to attack the evolutionist hypothesis by inverting it.

Along with the evolutionist assumption of the universal priority of the matrilineate, it is also necessary to reject the view of Lowie [46] that bilateral descent is universally antecedent to unilinear descent. It must be conceded, of course, that the family is primordial—pre-human and pre-cultural. It by no means follows from this, however, that bilateral descent is older than unilinear. All forms of descent are cultural, and none could have existed prior to the dawn of culture. All of them consist, as Rivers demonstrated, in the collective recognition of a principle whereby individuals are affiliated with particular groups of kinsmen. So far as the present author knows, there is no evidence to show that the first human society to achieve culture adopted a rule whereby the remoter relatives of both parents were discarded in forming the group to which a newborn child was assigned, instead of a rule by which the father's or the mother's relatives were chosen and the other group discarded. This is a question of fact, and until specific evidence is forthcoming it is impossible to reach a decision except through *a priori* reasoning.

[46] R. H. Lowie, *Primitive Society* (New York, 1920), pp. 146–57.

The proposed hypothesis of the evolution of social organization will be illustrated by a classification of the 250 sample societies into eleven major types of social structure, each with several sub-types. The validity of the classification and of the conclusions regarding the possibilities of transition from one type or sub-type to another is not susceptible to demonstration by any statistical method with which the author is familiar, since both synchronic and diachronic principles are inextricably interwoven in the hypothesis. All the relevant data, however, are summarized in tabular form under the several types, and the validation of the hypothesis must rest on the extent to which the actual data as tabulated correspond to theoretical expectations. It is believed that, of the approximately 2,500 separate items of data presented in the tables, there are hardly a dozen that are not reasonably accounted for by the theory, but the reader must of course reach his own decision.

Since the ethnographic reports consulted are by no means always clear on specific points, the author has frequently had to depend partly on inference in reaching a decision as to the classification of a trait. In doing so he has earnestly attempted to avoid letting his theoretical views influence the classification; indeed, for 220 of the 250 societies the classification of traits was made before the theory was formulated. Inferences were made only when they seemed reasonable from other evidence in the sources. Otherwise the item was left blank. As an example of the type of inference made we may cite the classification of residence among the Eyak of Alaska as avunculocal. This seemed reasonable from the fact that the authors, being unfamiliar with the category of avunculocal residence, devote considerable space to the conflicting statements of different informants as to whether the residence rule is matrilocal or patrilocal. Since a similar confusion is usual for demonstrably avunculocal societies, and since avunculocal residence is common in the region, being found for example among the Tlingit, it seemed likely that the Eyak follow the same rule. Further ethnographic work or superior analysis will certainly correct particular items in our lists, but it seems improbable that such corrections will significantly affect the theoretical implications of our data.

Emphasis should be laid upon the fact that our hypothesis is a dynamic one. It is concerned exclusively with evolution or cultural change, not with function. Any competent critic can point to instances where sub-types of one major type of organization create totally different conditions in the social life of the individuals who live under them, or where sub-types of different major types are functionally indistinguishable in the social conditions they set for individual participants. All that is claimed for the classification is that it represents, to the best of our ability, all the major possibilities of change in social structure, the order and sequence of such changes, and all the principal limitations thereupon. The classification may be regarded as a maze, in which a society can start at any given point and arrive at any other point whatsoever, but only by a limited number of possible routes. It is emphatically not to be viewed as an attempt to establish any single sequence, or even any series of alternative sequences, as the normal course of development over the span of man's history on earth.

Before the classification into types and the tabulation of data are presented, it will be well to summarize the general hypothesis as succinctly as possible. Assuming the relationships between residence and descent set forth in the present chapter and the dependence of kinship terminology upon both, as demonstrated in the theorems validating Postulate 1 in the preceding chapter, it makes the following generalizations regarding the normal order of change among the principal elements of social organization:

1. That when any social system which has attained a comparatively stable equilibrium begins to undergo change, such change regularly begins with a modification in the rule of residence.

2. That the development, disappearance, or change in form of extended families and clans ordinarily follows next in order after an alteration in the rule of residence, and is always consistent with the new rule.

3. That the development, disappearance, or change in form of consanguineal kin groups, particularly kindreds, lineages, and sibs, ordinarily follows next in order after a change in the localized aggregations of kinsmen, and is always consistent with the new status of the latter.

4. That adaptive changes in kinship terminology begin after steps 1 and 2, in accordance with the theorems of Postulate 1,

but are frequently not completed until the new rule of descent has become established, and sometimes not for a considerable period thereafter, so that they may continue for some time to reflect the previous form of social organization.

5. That at any time during or after such a sequence, historical and cultural influences originating outside the system of social organization can exert pressure in favor of a new rule of residence and thus initiate a new sequence, and that this, under conditions of rapid cultural change, can therefore sometimes overlap the previous sequence.

It will be noted that no place is allotted in this hypothesis to the influence of such factors as preferential marriage customs. Their effect is accepted to the extent demonstrated in the previous chapter, but it is considered to be distinctly secondary and not to affect in any significant way the interplay of the factors taken into account in the hypothesis.

The system of classification is derived from the theory. Since any sequence of change is assumed to have terminated when the adaptive modifications in kinship terms have been achieved, types of kinship terminology have been made one of the primary bases of classification. Since any sequence is assumed to begin with a change in residence, the several rules of residence have been adopted as the principal criteria for sub-types. Since rules of descent, though their change is commonly intermediate in any sequence, represent functionally the heart and core of the entire problem, the three principal rules—bilateral, patrilineal, and matrilineal descent—have been used, in conjunction with kinship terminology, to establish the primary types of social structure.

Selection of an appropriate typology for the classification of kinship terms has presented difficulties. The classification into lineal, generation, bifurcate merging, and bifurcate collateral types, proposed by Lowie and already found useful in the testing of theorems, offers certain advantages, and will be included with respect to the terms for aunts and nieces in the tables which follow. On Ego's generation, however, it unduly emphasizes the designation of parallel cousins, and fails to indicate whether cross-cousins on the father's and mother's sides are called by the same or different terms and whether either is classed with avuncular or nepotic relatives, both of which facts are known empirically to have diagnostic significance.

Terms for cross-cousins, as they are related to those for siblings, parallel cousins, and avuncular and nepotic relatives, were eventually chosen as the basis for establishing types of kinship terminology. They have the advantage of sampling rather fully the relatives in Ego's own generation, who are those with whom an individual in any society tends to have his strongest and most enduring relationships, and the further advantage of sampling those female relatives whom most societies either taboo or prefer most strongly as sex and marriage partners. Moreover, cross-cousin terminology has been used with considerable success by Spier [47] as the principal criterion of typology in what is certainly the most satisfactory classification of kinship nomenclature hitherto proposed.

The types of kinship terminology adopted are six in number. Four of them—the Crow, Eskimo, Iroquois, and Omaha types—are well established in the literature and correspond closely to those which Spier calls by the same names. For the fifth type, which embraces the Salish, Acoma, and Mackenzie Basin types of Spier and in part his Yuman type as well, we have adopted the name "Hawaiian," which also has some precedent in the literature. The sixth and last type has been called "Sudanese" from the area in which it is most prevalent. This type is unrepresented in Spier's system, and does not in fact occur in any of the 70 North American tribes in our sample. The six types, which are based exclusively on male-speaking terms for female relatives because of the limitations of our survey, are defined as follows:

Eskimo—FaSiDa and MoBrDa called by the same terms as parallel cousins but terminologically differentiated from sisters; the terms for the two cross-cousins are usually but not always the same.

Hawaiian—all cross and parallel cousins called by the same terms as those used for sisters.

Iroquois—FaSiDa and MoBrDa called by the same terms but terminologically differentiated from parallel cousins as well as from sisters; parallel cousins commonly but not always classified with sisters.

[47] L. Spier, "The Distribution of Kinship Systems in North America," *University of Washington Publications in Anthropology*, I (1925), 69–88.

Sudanese—FaSiDa and MoBrDa called by different terms and terminologically differentiated also from sisters, parallel cousins, aunts, and nieces; usually but not always associated with descriptive terminology.

Omaha—FaSiDa and MoBrDa called by different terms and terminologically differentiated from sisters and parallel cousins, but FaSiDa is terminologically classed with SiDa and/or MoBrDa with MoSi.

Crow—FaSiDa and MoBrDa called by different terms and terminologically differentiated from sisters and parallel cousins, but FaSiDa is terminologically classed with FaSi and/or MoBrDa with BrDa.

Eleven major types of social organization have been set up. Six of them are given the names of the types of kinship terminology normally associated with them. The other five, since they are differentiated from the foregoing in descent though characterized by similar kinship terms, are given different names: Dakota, Fox, Guinea, Nankanse, and Yuman. Dakota accords with established usage. Yuman is adapted from Spier's kinship type of the same name by excluding instances of unilinear descent and non-Iroquois cousin terminology. The other names are new, being derived from tribes or areas which exemplify the particular type. Table 60 lists the eleven major types of social structure with the rules of descent and types of cousin terminology by which they are defined.

TABLE 60

Primary Type of Social Organization	Associated Rule of Descent	Associated Type of Cousin Terminology
1 Eskimo	Bilateral	Eskimo
2 Hawaiian	Bilateral	Hawaiian
3 Yuman	Bilateral	Iroquois
4 Fox	Bilateral, Patrilineal	Crow, Omaha, Sudanese
5 Guinea	Patrilineal	Eskimo, Hawaiian
6 Dakota	Patrilineal	Iroquois
7 Sudanese	Patrilineal	Sudanese
8 Omaha	Patrilineal	Omaha
9 Nankanse	Matrilineal, Double	Eskimo, Hawaiian
10 Iroquois	Matrilineal, Double	Iroquois
11 Crow	Matrilineal, Double	Crow, Omaha, Sudanese

Eskimo and Hawaiian are the two common and stable types of bilateral organization. Yuman and Fox are transitional types, usually with bilateral descent. Guinea and Nankanse represent incipient unilinear structures, respectively patrilineal and matrilineal. Dakota and Omaha are the stable patrilineal types, to which correspond the Iroquois and Crow types for structures with matrilineal or double descent. Sudanese is a special patrilineal type which is either characterized by descriptive kinship terminology or transitional between Dakota and Omaha.

Under each primary type a separate sub-type is set up for each variation in residence rules or in descent. The sub-type from which the others seem usually to be derived—for Yuman and Fox that which is the most common—is designated as the normal sub-type. The others are denoted by prefixes indicating their deviant rules of residence, e.g., Patri-Eskimo, Matri-Hawaiian, Bi-Dakota, Neo-Omaha, and Avuncu-Crow, or their atypical rule of descent, e.g., Patri-Fox and Duo-Iroquois. The sub-types of the transitional Yuman and Fox types are related only in a descriptive sense, but those of other types are connected in a diachronic or evolutionary sense. Functional similarities, however, unite sub-types of different types when they have similar rules of residence and descent, rather than sub-types of the same type.

In order to facilitate the presentation of a very large mass of pertinent data in as compact a form as possible, a standard system of symbols has been adopted for tables 61 to 71. The meanings of the symbols in each column are as follows:

Descent: B—bilateral; Bd—double descent without exogamous kin groups; Bm—matrilineal descent without exogamous kin groups; Bp—patrilineal descent without exogamous kin groups; D—double descent with exogamous matrilineal and/or patrilineal kin groups; M—matrilineal descent with exogamy; P—patrilineal descent with exogamy.

Cousin Terms: C—Crow type; E—Eskimo type; H—Hawaiian type; I—Iroquois type; O—Omaha type; S—Sudanese type; double symbols indicate alternative usages or conflicting evidence.

Residence: A—avunculocal; B—bilocal; M—matrilocal; N—neolocal; P—patrilocal; T—matri-patrilocal; small letters indicate common alternative practices.

Clans and Demes: A—avuncu-clans; C—patrilocal clan-communities; D—endogamous demes; E—exogamous patri-demes; F—exogamous matri-demes; M—matri-clans; O—clans absent, demes absent or unreported; P—patri-clans other than clan-communities; U—clans unreported, demes absent.

Other Kin Groups: K—bilateral kindreds present; L—lineages the largest unilinear kin groups present; M—exogamous matri-moieties present; N—non-exogamous matri-moieties present; O—moieties absent, kindreds unreported; P—exogamous patri-moieties present; Q—non-exogamous patri-moieties present.

Exogamy and Other Extensions of Incest Taboos: B—bilateral extension of incest taboos (all first cousins ineligible in marriage under bilateral descent, all second cousins ineligible under unilinear descent); M—matrilineal extension of incest taboos (including matrilineal exogamy); O—no unilinear or bilateral extension of incest taboos beyond secondary relatives; P—patrilineal extension of incest taboos (including patrilineal exogamy); see Chapter 10 for an extended theoretical analysis and more refined definitions.

Marriage: M—exclusive monogamy; Mp—polygyny permitted but incidence below 20%; Ms—sororal polygyny permitted but incidence below 20%; P—general polygyny, non-sororal or unspecified; Ps—general polygyny with some preference for the sororal form; S—general polygyny, exclusively sororal; Y—general polyandry.

Family: A—avunculocal extended families; B—bilocal extended families; G—independent polygynous families; M—matrilocal extended families; N—independent nuclear families; P—patrilocal extended families; Y—independent polyandrous families; small letters indicate common alternative forms.

Aunt Terms: C—bifurcate collateral (distinct terms for Mo, MoSi, and FaSi); G—generation (identical terms for Mo, MoSi, and FaSi); L—lineal (one term for Mo, another for MoSi and FaSi); M—bifurcate merging (one term for Mo and MoSi, another for FaSi); double symbols indicate alternative usages, derivative terms, or conflicting evidence.

Niece Terms: C, G, L, and M as for aunt terms, but applying to Da, BrDa, and SiDa, respectively, instead of to Mo, MoSi, and FaSi.

TYPE 1: *THE ESKIMO TYPE OF SOCIAL ORGANIZATION*

For the benefit of readers unfamiliar with the social organization of other peoples, our classification begins with the type of structure prevailing in our own society. It should be emphasized, however, that this type is by no means characteristic of civilized as contrasted with primitive peoples, for in addition to the highly industrialized

Yankees of New England it includes such culturally diverse societies as the peasant Ruthenians of eastern Europe, the simple agriculturalists of Taos pueblo in the Southwest, the hunting and fishing Copper Eskimos of the far north, and the Andamanese pygmies of the tropical forest, a tribe so backward in culture that they may even have been ignorant of the generation of fire at the time of their discovery.

By definition, the Eskimo type includes all societies with Eskimo cousin terminology and no exogamous unilinear kin groups. In addition, as theory leads us to expect, it is characterized by monogamy, independent nuclear families, lineal terms for aunts and nieces, the bilateral extension of incest taboos, and the frequent presence of such bilateral kin groups as kindreds and demes, though these may often be unreported. In the variant sub-types, characterized by rules of residence other than the normal neolocal one, theory allows for the appearance of polygyny, the development of extended families, the loss of bilateral kin groups and of bilateral extension of incest taboos, the appearance of other terms for aunts and nieces (especially bifurcate collateral terms with patrilocal residence), and other changes representing departures from the norm as initial steps toward the development of other types. In short, the variant sub-types are expected to reveal various combinations of normal Eskimo traits and of traits of the types to which the altered rule of residence may eventually lead. Table 61 summarizes the relevant data for the 18 societies of our sample which have structures of the Eskimo type.

Examination of Table 61 reveals not a single trait that is at variance with theoretical expectations. The occasional appearance of bifurcate collateral terminology in normal or neolocal Eskimo societies presumably reflects former polygyny and patrilocal residence, as is attested for the Ruthenians by actual historical evidence. The non-exogamous patri-sibs and patri-moieties of the Tewa are obvious survivals of a previous patrilineal organization. That the Balinese may once have had an Hawaiian structure is suggested by the generation terms for aunts and the optional Hawaiian terms for cousins. All other deviations are in a theoretically anticipated direction.

TABLE 61

Sub-type and Tribe	Descent	Cousin Terms	Residence	Clans Demes	Kin Groups	Exogamy	Marriage	Family	Aunt Terms	Niece Terms
1. Normal Eskimo										
Andamanese	B	E	N	O	O	B	M	N	L	L
Copper Eskimo	B	E	N	O	O	B	Mp	N	.	C
Ruthenians	B	E	Np	D	K	B	M	N	CL	CL
Taos	B	E	N	D	O	B	M	N	LM	L
Tewa	Bp	E	N	O	Q	B	M	N	L	CL
Yankee	B	E	N	O	K	B	M	N	L	L
1B. Bi-Eskimo										
Cayapa	B	EH	Bn	O	O	B	M	Nb	L	GM
1M. Matri-Eskimo										
Tupinamba	B	E	M	O	O	O	Mp	M	L	L
1P. Patri-Eskimo										
Angmagsalik	B	E	Pn	O	K	B	Mp	N	.	.
Balinese	Bp	EH	P	O	L	O	Mp	P	G	.
Chukchee	B	E	T	O	O	O	P	P	L	L
Edo	B	E	P	O	O	P	P	.	C	L
Koryak	B	E	P	O	O	B	Mp	P	L	L
Kutenai	B	EH	P	O	O	B	P	.	C	C
Lapps	B	E	Tn	O	O	B	M	N	C	C
Ona	B	E	T	E	O	B	Ps	G	C	C
Quinault	B	EH	P	E	K	B	Ms	P	L	L
Semang	B	EH	Pb	O	O	B	Mp	N	L	.

Derivations of the type: from 2N; from 3N; from 4N; from 5N; from 9N; from 9P to 1P.

Possibilities of change: from 1B to 2; from 1M to 3M, 4M, or 9; from 1P to 3, 4, or 5.

TYPE 2: *THE HAWAIIAN TYPE OF SOCIAL ORGANIZATION*

Even commoner than the Eskimo type among bilateral peoples is the Hawaiian type of social structure. The reasons for its greater frequency presumably include those discussed under Proposition 16 in Chapter 7. By definition, this structural type embraces all societies possessing cousin terms of Hawaiian type and lacking exogamous unilinear kin groups. In addition, it is characterized by the exceedingly frequent appearance of limited polygyny, the bilocal extended family, generation terminology for aunts and nieces, bilateral extension of incest taboos, and bilateral kindreds or demes. In the variant sub-types, theory leads to the expectation that traits will often be modified in directions similar to those noted for the

Eskimo sub-types. Table 62 presents the data for the 45 societies in our sample which exhibit structures of the Hawaiian type. The Patri-Hawaiian sub-type, from the large number of cases, appears to be as stable as the normal or bilocal sub-type itself, and is doubtless the form from which a number of the tribes in the other sub-types have been derived.

TABLE 62

Sub-type and Tribe	Descent	Cousin Terms	Residence	Clans Demes	Kin Groups	Exogamy	Marriage	Family	Aunt Terms	Niece Terms
2.	*Normal Hawaiian*									
Eddystone	B	H	B	O	K	B	Mp	.	G	G
Ifugao	B	H	B	O	K	B	M	N	G	G
Ingassana	B	H	Ba	O	K	B	Mp	.	M	M
Jukun	B	H	Bp	O	K	B	P	B	G	G
Kaingang	B	H	B	O	O	O	Mp	B	G	G
Maori	B	EH	B	O	K	B	Mp	B	GL	L
Ontong-Javanese	Bd	H	B	O	KL	B	Mp	B	G	M
Samoans	B	H	B	O	K	B	Mp	B	GM	G
Shoshone	B	H	B	D	O	B	Ps	B	M	M
Sinkaietk	B	H	Bn	D	O	B	Ps	Bg	C	L
Tenino	B	H	Bp	O	K	B	P	G	C	C
2N.	*Neo-Hawaiian*									
Comanche	B	H	Np	D	O	B	S	G	M	M
Marquesans	B	H	N	O	O	O	Y	Y	.	.
Mataco	B	H	Np	O	O	B	Mp	N	L	L
Paiute	B	H	N	O	O	B	S	G	C	C
Tarahumara	B	H	N	O	O	B	M	N	C	C
2M.	*Matri-Hawaiian*									
Arapaho	B	H	M	F	O	B	S	M	M	M
Cheyenne	B	H	M	F	K	B	S	M	M	M
Chiricahua	B	H	M	D	O	B	Ms	M	C	C
Cuna	B	H	M	D	O	B	Ms	M	L	L
Kiowa Apache	B	H	Mb	D	O	B	S	M	CM	M
Washo	B	H	M	O	O	B	P	.	C	C
Wichita	B	H	M	D	O	B	S	G	L	M
2P.	*Patri-Hawaiian*									
Atsugewi	B	EH	T	O	O	B	S	P	C	CL
Aymara	B	.	P	D	O	B	Mp	P	M	.
Blackfoot	B	HS	P	E	O	B	Ps	P	M	L
Flathead	B	H	P	O	K	B	Ps	G	C	C
Futunans	B	EH	Pb	O	K	B	Mp	N	M	GM
Hawaiians	B	H	P	O	O	B	Mp	.	G	G
Hupa	B	H	Pb	E	O	B	P	P	C	C
Inca	B	H	P	D	O	O	Mp	P	M	M

TABLE 62 — *Continued*

Sub-type and Tribe	Descent	Cousin Terms	Residence	Clans Demes	Kin Groups	Exogamy	Marriage	Family	Aunt Terms	Niece Terms
Klallam	B	H	P	O	O	B	S	G	CL	L
Klamath	B	H	P	O	O	B	Ms	P	C	C
Kwakiutl	Bp	H	P	C	KL	B	P	P	L	L
Mangarevans	B	H	Pb	O	O	B	P	P	GL	L
Micmac	B	H	T	O	O	B	.	.	CM	CL
Nuba	B	H	Ta	D	K	B	Mp	N	G	M
Sekani	B	H	T	O	O	B	Ps	G	C	M
Syrian Christians	B	H	Pn	O	O	B	M	N	C	M
Tongans	Bp	H	P	P	KL	B	Ms	N	M	M
Tubatulabal	B	H	P	O	O	B	M	N	CM	M
Ulawans	B	H	P	O	K	B	Mp	.	G	M
Wishram	B	H	P	O	O	B	Ps	P	C	C
Yaghan	B	H	P	E	O	B	S	G	C	C
Yurok	B	H	Pb	E	O	B	P	P	L	L

Derivations of the type: from 1B; from 3B; from 4B; from 5B; from 9B; from 9P to 2P.

Possibilities of change: from 2M to 3M, 4M, or 9; from 2N to 1; from 2P to 3, 4, or 5.

The data in Table 62 conform throughout to theoretical expectations. All apparent deviations resolve themselves either into incipient developments toward another type consistent with the rule of residence, such as the non-exogamous patri-lineages and patri-clans of the Kwakiutl and Tongans, or into probable survivals from a previous type of organization. Among the examples of the latter we may note the bifurcate merging aunt and niece terminology and the alternative avunculocal residence rule of the Ingassana, which suggest derivation from some matrilineal type. The scattering lineal terms for aunts and nieces do not necessarily indicate a previous Eskimo structure, for there is evidence that lineal terminology may sometimes be as consistent with bilocal as with neolocal residence.

The occurrence of 11 tribes of the Malayo-Polynesian linguistic stock in Table 62, together with the frequent appearance of seemingly survivalistic generation terms for aunts and nieces in tribes of the same stock possessing other types of social structure, suggests that the Hawaiian system may have been characteristic of the ancestral Malayo-Polynesians (see Appendix A). If this is so, the variability of social structure among historically related peoples is strikingly illustrated by the fact that the Malayo-Polynesian tribes of our sample fall into no fewer than ten of our eleven major types of social organization today.

TYPE 3: *THE YUMAN TYPE OF SOCIAL ORGANIZATION*

Iroquois cousin terminology, which is one reflection of the bifurcate merging tendency, can develop on the basis of unilocal residence even before the appearance of unilinear descent, as was demonstrated in Theorems 8 and 9 of Postulate 1. It is therefore to be expected in a certain proportion of bilateral societies which are undergoing transition toward a unilinear organization through patrilocal or matrilocal residence. The Yuman type of social structure provides for such cases in its normal or patrilocal and its matrilocal sub-types. The former also accommodates societies with Iroquois cousin terms which have lost their matrilineal kin groups in consequence of a transition to patrilocal residence but have not yet evolved exogamous patrilineal kin groups.

The bilocal and neolocal sub-types provide for certain previously unilinear societies which have lost their kin groups or their exogamy in consequence of the adoption of bilocal or neolocal residence. Such a society, if characterized by Iroquois cousin terminology, will commonly become bilateral in descent before the kinship terms have completed the adaptive change to either the Eskimo or the Hawaiian type. Occasionally it may even undergo another change of residence before this occurs, thereby shifting to one of the other Yuman sub-types. Sometimes, too, a patrilineal or matrilineal tribe with Iroquois cousin terms may lose its rule of exogamy for other reasons than a shift in residence, and thus fall into a Yuman category.

The type is not stable, for all of its sub-types represent uncompleted transitions in descent. The number of cases is therefore small—only 16 in all. Because of its transitional character the type has no functional consistency and no criteria except those established by definition: Iroquois cousin terminology and the absence of exogamous unilinear kin groups. The theoretically expected characteristics are in each case the intermediate ones in the particular transition which is under way. The data, as summarized in Table 63, reveal no inconsistencies, with the possible exception of the Pima. The non-exogamous patri-sibs and patri-moieties of this tribe indicate derivation from some patrilineal type, either via Bi-Yuman or Neo-Yuman or by loss of exogamy in some other way.

TABLE 63

Sub-type and Tribe	Descent	Cousin Terms	Residence	Clans Demes	Kin Groups	Exogamy	Marriage	Family	Aunt Terms	Niece Terms
3. Normal Yuman										
Buin	B	I	P	O	O	O	P	P	C	M
Eromangans	B	I	P	E	O	BP	P	G	.	L
Havasupai	B	I	T	O	O	B	Mp	P	C	C
Nambikuara	B	I	Pb	O	O	O	Mp	N	M	M
Naskapi	B	I	Pb	O	O	O	P	G	C	.
Pima	Bp	I	P	O	KQ	B	P	G	C	C
Shasta	B	I	P	E	O	B	Mp	P	C	C
Teton	B	I	Pb	E	O	B	S	P	M	M
Tswana	Bp	I	P	P	KL	O	Ps	P	CM	CM
Walapai	B	I	T	E	O	O	Mp	N	C	C
Wapisiana	B	I	T	E	O	P	P	.	CM	.
3B. Bi-Yuman										
No instances										
3N. Neo-Yuman										
Wintu	B	I	N	O	O	B	Ms	N	C	C
3M. Matri-Yuman										
Carib	B	I	Mn	O	O	O	Ps	G	CM	M
Kallinago	Bm	I	M	O	L	O	Ms	M	M	M
Macusi	B	I	Mn	O	O	O	Mp	M	M	.
Mentaweians	B	I	M	D	O	O	M	N	C	C

Derivations of the type: from 1P; from 1M to 3M; from 2P; from 2M to 3M; from 6B to 3B; from 6N to 3N; from 10B to 3B; from 10N to 3N; from 10P.

Possibilities of change: from 3 to 6; from 3B to 2; from 3M to 10; from 3N to 1.

TYPE 4: *THE FOX TYPE OF SOCIAL ORGANIZATION*

The Fox type, with only 10 representatives in our sample, is even rarer than the Yuman type. Like the latter, it provides for cases of transition from one rule of descent to another, but whereas Yuman structures are characterized by symmetrical cross-cousin terminology those of Fox type have asymmetrical cross-cousin terms, i.e., Crow, Omaha, or Sudanese. The normal or patrilocal sub-type includes former matrilineal societies in transition to a patrilineal structure, former patrilineal societies which have lost their kin groups through causes other than a shift in residence, and bilateral societies which for special reasons have developed Omaha or Sudanese kinship terms on the basis of patrilocal residence before evolving patrilineal descent. The Matri-Fox sub-type embraces comparable transitions from matrilineal to bilateral descent or *vice versa*. The Bi-Fox and Neo-Fox sub-types provide for previously unilinear societies with asymmetrical cross-cousin terminology which have lost their kin groups or their exogamy in consequence of adopting bilocal or neolocal residence, and which have not yet developed a typical bilateral organization of Eskimo or Hawaiian type.

Patri-Fox is set up as a special sub-type, distinct from normal patrilocal Fox, to accommodate transitions from a matrilineal structure of Crow type to a patrilineal structure of Omaha or Sudanese type in which the original Crow terminology for cross-cousins has been retained even after the development of patrilineal descent. When a Crow tribe loses its matrilineal kin groups or exogamy in consequence of adopting patrilocal residence, it falls into the normal Fox type. Two internal readjustments then become probable: (1) the achievement of patrilineal descent; (2) the acquisition of a patrilineal type of asymmetrical cross-cousin terminology, i.e., Omaha or Sudanese. If the latter happens first, the classification does not change until the former occurs, when the structure becomes one of normal Omaha or Sudanese type. If, however, patrilineal descent is evolved before cousin terminology changes, the transition from Fox to Omaha or Sudanese is achieved through an intermediate Patri-Fox phase.

As in the case of Yuman, all of the Fox sub-types are ephemeral, and lack either structural or functional consistency. The type is defined by the presence of asymmetrical cross-cousin terminology and a rule of descent not ordinarily associated with cousin terms of the particular type. In other words, it includes all structures with asymmetrical cousin terminology which are not classifiable as Crow, Omaha, or Sudanese. As is apparent from Table 64, the traits occurring in Fox societies are rather diverse. In general, however, they accord with theoretical expectations for the particular transition exemplified.

TABLE 64

Sub-type and Tribe	Descent	Cousin Terms	Residence	Clans Demes	Kin Groups	Exogamy	Marriage	Family	Aunt Terms	Niece Terms
4. Normal Fox										
Kababish	Bp	S	P	C	O	O	P	P	C	.
Kurd	Bp	S	P	C	O	O	P	P	L	C
Takelma	B	O	P	E	O	B	P	.	C	C
4B. Bi-Fox										
Tokelau	B	O	B	O	K	B	M	N	GM	M
4N. Neo-Fox										
Fox	Bp	O	N	O	K	B	Ps	G	C	M
4M. Matri-Fox										
Pawnee	B	C	Mn	D	K	B	S	G	G	M
Siriono	B	C	M	D	O	O	Ps	M	M	GL
4P. Patri-Fox										
Bachama	P	C	P	C	O	P	.	P	GL	LM
Koranko	P	C	P	U	O	P	P	.	C	M
Seniang	P	C	P	C	O	BP	Ps	G	M	M

Derivations of the type: from 1P to 4; from 1M to 4M; from 2P to 4; from 2M to 4M; from 7B to 4B; from 7N to 4N; from 7 to 4P; from 8B to 4B; from 8N to 4N; from 8 to 4P; from 11P to 4; from 11B to 4B; from 11N to 4N; from 10D to 4P.

Possibilities of change: from 4 to 4P, 7, or 8; from 4B to 2; from 4M to 11; from 4N to 1; from 4P to 6, 7, or 8.

Because of their variability, the Fox tribes deserve individual comment. The Kababish and Kurd are clearly derived from Normal Sudanese, having lost their former sib exogamy in consequence of embracing Islam and adopting the Mohammedan preference for marrying a FaBrDa. Distributional evidence and the survival of bilateral extension of incest taboos indicate that the Takelma were formerly of Patri-Hawaiian type, and have acquired Omaha terminology on the basis of patrilocal residence. The Tokelau have made the same change, not, however, through a residence shift but because of certain peculiar patrilineal characteristics of their kindreds; affiliation with a kindred, here a discrete group which is practically a lineage, is always patrilineal for a chief's eldest son and for all eldest daughters, though dependent upon the residence of the parents in the case of other children. The Pawnee and Siriono were presumably once Matri-Hawaiian, having acquired Crow terminology on the basis of their residence rule. The non-exogamous patri-sibs of the Fox point to a former Omaha structure. The

Bachama, Koranko, and Seniang have doubtless evolved from Patri-Crow antecedents by way of Normal Fox, developing patrilineal descent in advance of an adaptive change in cousin terminology. With these interpretations all apparent discrepancies disappear.

TYPE 5: *THE GUINEA TYPE OF SOCIAL ORGANIZATION*

This type, which is named for its prevalence in West Africa, is transitional like the two preceding ones, but is commoner and seemingly more stable than either. It includes, by definition, all societies with exogamous patrilineal kin groups and cousin terminology of either the Eskimo or the Hawaiian type. It is devised to accommodate those tribes which formerly belonged to one of the stable bilateral types, Eskimo or Hawaiian, and which have evolved patrilineal descent on the basis of patrilocal residence without having

TABLE 65

Sub-type and Tribe	Descent	Cousin Terms	Residence	Clans Demes	Kin Groups	Exogamy	Marriage	Family	Aunt Terms	Niece Terms
5. *Normal Guinea*										
Albanians	P	E	P	U	O	P	M	P	C	L
Bolewa	P	HI	P	U	L	P	P	G	GM	G
Chawai	P	H	P	O	O	P	P	P	G	G
Ho	P	HI	P	O	O	P	Ps	P	C	C
Katab	P	H	P	C	O	BP	P	P	G	M
Kilba	P	H	Pb	P	O	P	P	P	G	M
Lakher	P	H	P	O	O	P	M	N	M	M
Lepcha	P	H	P	O	O	BP	Mp	P	L	L
Malabu	P	H	P	C	O	P	P	.	LM	.
Maricopa	P	H	Pn	O	O	BP	Mp	N	C	C
Mendi	P	E	P	U	O	P	P	.	G	L
Ngizim	P	H	P	C	O	P	P	.	G	M
Osset	P	E	P	C	O	P	S	P	C	C
Tikopia	P	H	P	P	K	BP	Ps	G	M	M
Timne	P	E	P	P	O	P	P	.	L	C
Vai	P	E	P	U	O	P	P	.	G	M
Xosa	P	E	P	C	O	BP	Ps	P	CM	CM
5B. *Bi-Guinea*										
Mabuiag	P	H	B	O	Q	BP	Ps	G	GM	M
5N. *Neo-Guinea*										
No instances.										

Derivations of the type: from 1P; from 2P; from 9D.

Possibilities of change: from 5 to 6, 7, or 8; from 5B to 2; from 5N to 1.

yet undergone the adaptive modifications in cross-cousin terms necessary to achieve a more typical patrilineal structure. The Bi-Guinea and Neo-Guinea sub-types provide for occasional instances where this transition is reversed in mid-course, bilocal or neolocal residence paving the way for a return to a stable bilateral structure.

In accordance with theoretical expectations, Guinea tribes are characterized by the development of polygyny, of patri-clans and/or patrilocal extended families, and of patrilineally extended incest taboos. Adaptive changes to bifurcate collateral or bifurcate merging terms appear in some instances, but the terminology for aunts and nieces usually shows the same conservatism as that for cross-cousins. Bilateral kin groups have vanished in nearly all instances, but there are occasional survivals of the bilateral extension of incest taboos. Table 65, which summarizes the data for the 18 Guinea tribes of our sample, reveals no genuine departure from theoretical expectations.

TYPE 6: *THE DAKOTA TYPE OF SOCIAL ORGANIZATION*

This stable type is the most widespread and typical form of patrilineal organization. The name Dakota, although established in the literature, is really a misnomer, for none of the Siouan tribes of North America, despite frequent allegations to the contrary, appears actually to be characterized by both patrilineal descent and Iroquois cousin terminology. The patrilineal tribes of this linguistic stock, like the Omaha and Winnebago, have Omaha structures; only its bilateral members, like the Teton, possess Iroquois or "Dakota" kinship systems.

The Dakota type of social structure includes, by definition, all patrilineal societies with Iroquois cousin terminology. In addition, it is widely characterized by non-sororal polygyny, by a family organization of either the independent polygynous or the patrilocal extended type, by patri-clans, by the patrilineal extension of incest taboos, and by bifurcate collateral or bifurcate merging terms for aunts and nieces, all of which traits are predicted by our theory. In the Bi-Dakota and Neo-Dakota sub-types, these traits may be expected to alter in the direction of bilateral characteristics. The

TABLE 60

Sub-type and Tribe	Descent	Cousin Terms	Residence	Clans Demes	Kin Groups	Exogamy	Marriage	Family	Aunt Terms	Niece Terms
6. **Normal Dakota**										
Abelam	P	I	P	P	O	P	Mp	N	M	M
Baiga	P	I	P	C	O	P	P	G	C	C
Banaro	P	I	P	P	O	P	Mp	.	GM	C
Bena	P	I	T	O	K	MP	Ps	G	M	M
Bhuïya	P	.	P	C	O	P	M	N	C	C
Chinese	P	HI	P	O	O	P	M	Pn	CM	C
Coorg	P	I	P	U	O	P	M	P	C	M
Epi	P	I	P	C	P	P	.	.	M	M
Fijians	P	I	T	P	O	P	Ps	P	CM	CM
Ganda	P	I	Pn	C	O	P	P	P	CM	M
Gond	P	I	P	C	O	P	Ps	P	C	M
Henga	P	I	P	U	O	P	P	.	M	M
Hottentot	P	I	T	C	O	P	Mp	P	M	M
Ibo	P	.	P	P	L	BP	P	P	L	CM
Keraki	P	I	P	C	P	P	P	G	C	CM
Kiwai	P	.	P	P	O	P	Mp	P	GL	M
Kutubu	P	I	P	U	O	P	P	.	C	G
Kyiga	P	I	P	C	O	P	P	.	CM	C
Luiseno	P	I	P	P	O	P	.		C	C
Manchu	P	I	P	C	O	P	M	P	C	CM
Masai	P	I	P	O	O	BP	P	.	GM	GM
Mikir	P	.	P	U	O	P	Mp	.	C	
Miriam	P	I	P	C	O	P	Mp	.	G	M
Orokaiva	P	I	P	C	O	P	Mp	N	M	M
Pedi	P	I	T	U	O	P	P	G	CM	.
Reddi	P	I	Pb	O	O	P	Mp	Np	CL	.
Susu	P	I	P	U	O	P	P	.	M	M
Swazi	P	I	P	C	O	P	Ps	P	M	GM
Tallensi	P	.	P	C	O	P	P	G	.	M
Tanala	P	I	P	P	O	MP	P	P	C	G
Tannese	P	I	P	U	O	P	P	G	M	M
Vanimo	P	I	P	P	O	P	M	N	C	C
Witoto	P	I	P	C	O	P	M	N	.	C
Zulu	P	I	P	C	O	BP	Ps	P	M	GM
6B. **Bi-Dakota**										
Chenchu	P	I	B	O	O	P	M	B	CM	M
Ojibwa	P	I	Bn	C	K	BP	Ps	G	C	C
Yuma	P	I	B	O	O	P	Mp	.	C	C
6N. **Neo-Dakota**										
No instances										

Derivations of the type: from 3; from 4P; from 5; from 10P; from 10D.

Possibilities of change: from 6 to 7; from 6 to 8; from 6B to 3B; from 6N to 3N.

Ojibwa, for example, have presumably acquired their kindreds and the bilateral extension of their sex prohibitions in consequence of their bilocal residence. Table 66 organizes the data for the 37 societies of our sample which have structures of the Dakota type. No matrilocal or avunculocal sub-types appear since they cannot develop out of a patrilocal and patrilineal organization.

Table 66 reveals no deviations from theoretical expectations. The occasional appearance of monogamy and the independent nuclear family accords with our previous admission that marriage forms as well as residence rules can respond directly to factors outside the social organization. The disappearance of clans, found in a few instances, is always possible after patri-sibs have developed, even without a fundamental modification in the rule of residence. The scattering generation or lineal terms for aunts or nieces are presumably survivals from a previous Guinea phase. The bilateral extension of incest taboos among the Ibo, Masai, and Zulu doubtless reflects prior bilateral organization, and the matrilineal extension of such taboos among the Bena and Tanala suggests a previous matrilineal structure, which is confirmed for the Bena by specific historical evidence. The fact that the Bena possess kindreds indicates that a bilateral Yuman phase, however brief, probably intervened between their loss of matrilineal descent and their acquisition of patri-sibs.

TYPE 7: *THE SUDANESE TYPE OF SOCIAL ORGANIZATION*

This type provides for two groups of patrilineal societies. The first includes those whose kinship terminology is primarily descriptive and who thus differentiate all four classes of first cousins from one another as well as from siblings. As has been pointed out elsewhere, these occur mainly in a band across central Africa from west to east on both sides of the boundary between the Bantu and Sudanese linguistic areas. Although many tribes in the same area do not exhibit this tendency toward the extreme use of descriptive terminology, the distribution nevertheless suggests that some obscure historical or linguistic cause has been operative. The second group embraced in the Sudanese category consists of those patrilineal societies which have developed asymmetrical cross-cousin terminology without arriving at the more characteristic Omaha pattern.

The criteria for the Sudanese type are identical with those for the Dakota type except for the difference in cousin terminology. The data for the 13 societies of our sample which possess structures of the Sudanese type, assembled in Table 67, reveal no departures from theoretical expectations. The bilocal and neolocal sub-types are purely theoretical, since we have discovered no actual cases.

TABLE 67

Sub-type and Tribe	Descent	Cousin Terms	Residence	Clans Demes	Kin Groups	Exogamy	Marriage	Family	Aunt Terms	Niece Terms
7. *Normal Sudanese*										
Awuna	P	S	P	P	O	P	P	.	C	CG
Azande	P	S	P	U	O	BP	P	G	M	.
Batak	P	S	P	C	O	P	P	.	M	M
Cherente	P	S	P	P	P	P	Ms	N	M	C
Dahomeans	P	S	P	P	O	P	P	G	C	.
Dinka	P	S	P	P	O	BP	P	.	CM	.
Gesu	P	ES	P	C	O	P	P	.	C	M
Gilyak	P	S	P	O	O	P	S	G	M	M
Limba	P	S	P	U	O	P	P	.	CG	GL
Mailu	P	S	P	P	O	P	M	P	M	G
Sabei	P	S	P	C	O	P	P	.	C	M
Shilluk	P	S	P	P	O	MP	Ps	G	C	.
Yakut	P	HS	T	C	O	P	P	G	CL	.
7B. *Bi-Sudanese*										
No instances										
7N. *Neo-Sudanese*										
No instances										

Derivations of the type: from 4; from 4P; from 5; from 6.

Possibilities of change: from 7 to 8; from 7B to 4B; from 7N to 4N.

TYPE 8: *THE OMAHA TYPE OF SOCIAL ORGANIZATION*

Patrilineal societies with Omaha cousin terminology fall by definition into the Omaha type of social structure. The criteria for this type and its sub-types with variant residence rules are identical with those for the Dakota and Sudanese types except with respect to cross-cousin terms. The pertinent data are assembled in Table 68. Not a single item deviates from theoretical expectations.

The fact that 25 societies in our sample, representing nearly every

TABLE 68

Sub-type and Tribe	Descent	Cousin Terms	Residence	Clans Demes	Kin Groups	Exogamy	Marriage	Family	Aunt Terms	Niece Terms
8. Normal Omaha										
Acholi	P	O	P	U	O	P	P	.	.	.
Angami	P	O	P	P	Q	P	M	N	M	C
Ao	P	O	P	P	O	P	M	N	CM	M
Arapesh	P	O	P	P	Q	P	P	.	C	CM
Araucanians	P	O	P	U	L	P	Ps	G	M	.
Bari	P	O	P	O	O	BP	P	G	M	M
Dorobo	P	O	P	C	O	P	.	P	C	M
Iatmul	P	O	P	U	P	P	P	P	.	M
Kitara	P	O	P	U	O	P	Mp	P	CM	M
Kwoma	P	O	P	C	O	P	P	G	C	M
Lango	P	O	P	C	O	P	P	G	M	M
Lenge	P	O	P	C	O	P	P	.	M	M
Lhota	P	O	T	U	O	P	P	G	CM	M
Miwok	P	O	P	U	P	P	Ps	.	C	M
Nandi	P	O	P	U	O	P	P	.	M	M
Rengma	P	O	P	P	O	P	M	.	M	M
Sema	P	O	P	C	O	P	Mp	N	M	M
Shona	P	O	P	C	O	BP	Ps	P	M	M
Soga	P	O	P	U	O	BP	Ps	G	C	CM
Thado	P	O	P	U	O	P	P	.	C	.
Thonga	P	O	P	C	O	P	Ps	P	M	.
Tzeltal	P	O	T	O	O	P	M	.	CM	CM
Winnebago	P	O	T	O	P	P	Ms	P	CM	M
8B. Bi-Omaha										
No instances										
8N. Neo-Omaha										
Kickapoo	P	O	Np	O	O	BP	P	G	CM	M
Omaha	P	O	Nt	O	Q	BP	Ms	N	M	M

Derivations of the type: from 4; from 4P; from 5; from 6; from 7.
Possibilities of change: from 8B to 4B; from 8N to 4N.

region of the world, have structures of Omaha type demonstrates that this form of social organization is very far from being the anomaly that certain authors have called it. White [48] probably comes very close to the truth when he characterizes it as typical of the patrilineate in its most highly developed form. Our data enable us to test White's hypothesis. If it is essentially correct, most Omaha

[48] L. A. White, "A Problem in Kinship Terminology," *American Anthropologist*, n.s., XLI (1939), 569–70.

societies will have passed through a prior Dakota or Sudanese phase and will thus have possessed patrilineal descent for a longer period, on the average, than patrilineal societies of other types. They will consequently have had more opportunity, by and large, to lose the factors which originally gave rise to the patrilineal rule, notably patri-clans and patri-families. Our data confirm this expectation. Patrilocal clans and extended families are absent or unreported in 36 per cent of the normal Omaha tribes in our sample but in only 26 per cent of the normal Dakota and Sudanese societies.

According to White's theory there should also be more survivals of non-patrilineal structures in Dakota and Sudanese than in Omaha societies. In harmony with this expectation, our tables show 15 patrilocal Dakota and Sudanese tribes with at least alternative aunt or niece terms of generation or lineal type, which are characteristic of bilateral organization, but such survivals do not appear in a single one of our normal Omaha societies. Again, since moieties are presumably the last type of unilinear kin group to be developed, White's hypothesis would lead us to expect patri-moieties more frequently in Omaha than in Dakota or Sudanese societies. As a matter of fact, they occur in 6 of our 28 Omaha tribes but in only 3 of the 50 with Dakota or Sudanese organization. The view that Omaha structure represents a mature form of the patrilineate thus receives substantial confirmation.

TYPE 9: *THE NANKANSE TYPE OF SOCIAL ORGANIZATION*

This is an incipient and transient type of matrilineal organization corresponding precisely to the Guinea type of patrilineal structure. It is defined by the presence of matrilineal or double descent and of Eskimo or Hawaiian cousin terminology, and is in general transitional between stable bilateral structures and more mature types of matrilineal organization. Only five societies in our sample fall into the Nankanse category. This doubtless results from the fact that conditions throughout the world in recent centuries have not been conducive to the appearance of the matrilineate, so that mature types are more frequent than incipient forms.

As in all basically matrilineal types of social organization, it is necessary to allow not only for the usual bilocal, neolocal, and patrilocal sub-types but also for sub-types with avunculocal residence and double descent. Avunculocal residence can develop only from a prior matrilocal rule, and double descent can appear only in a society with matrilineal descent which adopts patrilocal residence and on this basis evolves patrilineal kin groups without losing its previous matrilineal kin groups. The Avuncu-Nankanse sub-type, as well as Bi-Nankanse and Neo-Nankanse, is unrepresented in our sample, but its prior existence is attested by the presence of alternative avunculocal residence in two of the five tribes. Of the two Duo-Nankanse tribes, the Pukapukans are shown by distributional evidence to have derived their structure from an Hawaiian antecedent form.

Theoretical considerations lead to the expectation that Nankanse structures will reveal matrilineal features, survivals of bilateral characteristics, and special traits associated with the prevailing rule of residence. Table 69, which summarizes the meager evidence, reveals no apparent contradictions.

TABLE 69

	Sub-type and Tribe	De-scent	Cousin Terms	Resi-dence	Clans Demes	Kin Groups	Exog-amy	Mar-riage	Fam-ily	Aunt Terms	Niece Terms
9.	*Normal Nankanse*										
	Apinaye	M	E	M	O	N	M	M	M	CM	M
9A.	*Avuncu-Nankanse*										
	No instances										
9B.	*Bi-Nankanse*										
	No instances										
9N.	*Neo-Nankanse*										
	No instances										
9P.	*Patri-Nankanse*										
	Sherbro	M	EH	P	O	O	BM	P	.	G	L
	Tetekantzi	M	H	Pa	O	M	M	.	.	G	M
9D.	*Duo-Nankanse*										
	Nankanse	D	H	Pa	C	O	MP	P	P	CM	CG
	Pukapukans	D	E	P	P	KN	BM	M	N	G	G

Derivations of the type: from 1M; from 2M.

Possibilities of change: from 9B to 2; from 9D to 5; from 9N to 1; from 9P to 1P, 2P, or 9D.

It should be pointed out that the classification of the Apinaye in Table 69 is dubious. The ethnographer, who leaves a number of questions unanswered, reports that descent is patrilineal for males and matrilineal for females, and that marriages cycle through the four sibs. Double descent is apparently excluded by the fact that there seems to be only a single set of sibs, not two sets with differing rules of descent. On the other hand, the phenomenon of cycling, which depends upon the restriction of marriage to a single kin group other than one's own, is normally characteristic only of structures with double descent. It is not inconceivable that this rule, coupled with bilinear kin groups, once prevailed among the Apinaye but has degenerated. This would agree with the presence of matri-moieties, though these are not now exogamous. The fact that the Apinaye are the only society in our entire sample of 250 whose social organization appears genuinely anomalous on the basis of existing reports suggests the desirability of further field research to clarify the situation. In the meantime they have been tentatively classed as matrilineal rather than patrilineal because (1) residence is matrilocal, (2) the moieties are matrilineal, and (3) female relatives, with whom the present study is exclusively concerned, are matrilineally rather than patrilineally aggregated.

TYPE 10: *THE IROQUOIS TYPE OF SOCIAL ORGANIZATION*

The matrilineal analogue of Dakota organization is the Iroquois type of social structure. By definition this includes all matrilineal societies with Iroquois cousin terminology, including those which also have patrilineal descent. The normal or matrilocal sub-type is also characterized by monogamy or sororal polygyny, by matri-clans and/or matri-families, by the matrilineal extension of incest taboos, and by aunt and niece terms of bifurcate merging type, all of which traits are anticipated by our theory. In the sub-types with variant residence rules, non-sororal polygyny and bifurcate collateral terminology are to be expected with avunculocal or patrilocal residence, generation terminology and bilateral characteristics with bilocal residence, and the disappearance of clans and extended families with all residence changes except that to the avunculocal rule.

The Duo-Iroquois sub-type accommodates societies with Iroquois

TABLE 70

Sub-type and Tribe	Descent	Cousin Terms	Residence	Clans Demes	Kin Groups	Exogamy	Marriage	Family	Aunt Terms	Niece Terms
10. Normal Iroquois										
Arosi	M	I	M	M	O	M	Ps	.	G	M
Chewa	M	I	M	U	O	M	P	.	CM	.
Cochiti	M	HI	M	U	O	M	M	.	G	GM
Dobuans	M	CI	Ma	O	O	M	M	M	M	M
Iroquois	M	I	M	M	KM	M	M	M	GM	M
Lesu	M	I	M	M	M	M	P	G	M	M
Marshallese	M	I	Mn	M	O	M	Mp	N	G	G
Minangkabau	M	.	M	M	O	M	Mp	M	G	.
Nauruans	M	I	M	O	K	M	Ps	M	G	M
Navaho	M	I	M	M	O	M	S	Mn	CM	CM
Nayar	M	I	M	O	KL	M	Ms	M	CM	.
Vedda	M	I	M	M	O	M	M	M	C	M
Yao	M	I	M	U	O	M	P	.	M	M
10A. Avuncu-Iroquois										
Eyak	M	I	A	O	M	M	P	A	C	CM
Tsimshian	M	I	A	O	O	M	Ps	A	M	M
10B. Bi-Iroquois										
Kurtatchi	M	I	Bm	M	K	BM	S	G	G	M
10N. Neo-Iroquois										
Jemez	M	I	N	O	O	M	M	N	M	.
10P. Patri-Iroquois										
Carrier	M	I	T	O	O	M	P	.	C	C
Getmatta	M	I	P	O	O	M	Mp	.	G	M
Ila	M	I	P	O	O	M	P	G	GM	M
Kutchin	M	I	Pb	O	O	M	Mp	N	C	C
Lamba	M	I	Tb	O	O	M	Mp	.	M	C
Mbundu	M	I	P	O	O	M	P	G	M	C
Santa Cruz	M	I	P	O	O	M	.		M	M
Tismulun	M	I	P	O	O	M	.	.	M	M
10D. Duo-Iroquois										
Arunta	D	I	P	C	MP	MP	Ps	G	M	M
Dieri	D	I	P	C	M	MP	S	.	M	M
Herero	D	I	P	C	O	MP	P	.	.	C
Kamilaroi	D	I	P	C	MP	MP	Mp	.	M	M
Kariera	D	I	P	C	MP	MP	Ps	G	M	M
Toda	D	I	P	C	O	MP	Y	Y	M	M
Venda	D	I	P	C	O	P	Ps	P	CM	M
Wogeo	D	I	P	P	M	MP	Ps	G	GM	.

Derivations of the type: from 3M; from 9; from 9A to 10A; from 9D to 10D; from 9P to 10P.

Possibilities of change: from 10 to 11; from 10A to 11A: from 10B to 3B; from 10N to 3N; from 10D to 6; from 10P to 10D or 3.

cousin terminology and double descent. That residence is patrilocal in all such cases confirms our own hypothesis and that of Lawrence [49] that such a structure can arise only in a matrilineal society which has become patrilocal and has thereby acquired patrilineal kin groups without losing its previous matrilineal ones. If matri-moieties are present, as in native Australia, the phenomenon of "marriage classes" tends to appear. Otherwise the structure resembles that of the Dakota type except for the addition of matrilineal descent. Table 70 presents the data from the 33 societies of our sample with an Iroquois type of organization.

There are no serious discrepancies in Table 70. The frequent appearance of generation terms for aunts and cousins presumably reflects the comparative recency of a prior bilateral organization, and the occurrence of kindreds in some instances may be subject to a similar interpretation. Among societies like the Iroquois and Nayar that have long been in contact with higher bilateral civilizations, however, kindreds are at least equally likely to reflect a late acculturative change. The reported non-sororal polygyny of the Chewa, Lesu, and Yao, which is inconsistent with matrilocal residence, may be due either to unrevealed alternatives in residence or to the common failure among ethnographers to record whether the polygyny they report is sororal. The alternative Crow cousin terms and avunculocal residence among the Dobuans suggest an incipient transition toward an Avuncu-Crow structure. The Venda are presumably in the process of evolving a Dakota structure, since matrilineal exogamy has already disappeared and the surviving matri-sibs retain only religious functions.

TYPE 11: *THE CROW TYPE OF SOCIAL ORGANIZATION*

This type of organization, for matrilineal societies, corresponds to the Omaha type for patrilineal tribes. By definition it is characterized by matrilineal or double descent and asymmetrical cross-cousin terminology. The cousin terms are regularly of Crow type except with double descent, where Omaha and Sudanese terms appear under the influence of patrilocal residence and patrilineal kin groups.

[49] W. E. Lawrence, "Alternating Generations in Australia," *Studies in the Science of Society*, ed. G. P. Murdock (New Haven, 1937), pp. 345-6.

The other traits associated with a Crow structure are typically the same as in Iroquois societies. When tribes of the Duo-Crow subtype lose their matrilineal kin groups they fall into either the Patri-Fox, the Normal Sudanese, or the Normal Omaha category, depending upon the kind of asymmetrical cousin terminology they possess. Table 71 summarizes the data for the 30 societies of our sample which have structures of the Crow type.

The number and wide distribution of societies of the Crow type indicate that it is a recurrent phenomenon and not an anomaly. White [50] has suggested that it is the most highly developed form of matrilineal organization. When we compare the Crow and Iroquois societies of our sample, we find that a larger proportion of the former lack matri-clans and matri-families, indicating a greater average lapse of time since the origin of matrilineal descent; that fewer of them have generation terms for aunts or nieces, which are presumptive survivals from a former bilateral organization, and that more of them possess matri-moieties, which are presumably a late development. These facts lend considerable support to White's theory of the relative maturity of Crow organization. The greater frequency of avunculocal residence might be regarded as additional evidence.

The data in Table 71 conform in general to theoretical expectations. The kindreds and bilateral extension of incest taboos among the Hopi justify the inference that this tribe was formerly bilateral in organization, which accords with distributional studies [51] and with the fact that most of the other Shoshonean societies in our sample have bilateral structures of the Hawaiian type. A parallel interpretation is probably not warranted, however, in the case of the Choctaw and Creek, whose bilateral extension of incest taboos may well be attributable to the strong acculturative influences which these tribes have encountered.

Several of the Duo-Crow societies require special comment. The Pentecost are specifically reported to have six sections, with marriage forbidden into all except one. They thus resemble the Ranon, but

---

[50] L. A. White, "A Problem in Kinship Terminology," *American Anthropologist*, n.s., XLI (1939), 569–70.

[51] Cf. W. D. Strong, "An Analysis of Southwestern Society," *American Anthropologist*, n.s., XXIX (1917), 1–61.

TABLE 71

Sub-type and Tribe	Descent	Cousin Terms	Residence	Clans Demes	Kin Groups	Exogamy	Marriage	Family	Aunt Terms	Niece Terms
11. Normal Crow										
Cherokee	M	C	M	U	N	M	M	N	M	M
Choctaw	M	C	M	U	M	BM	Ms	.	M	M
Creek	M	C	M	M	M	BM	Ms	M	CM	M
Daka	M	C	M	O	O	M	M	M	G	M
Hopi	M	C	M	O	K	BM	M	N	M	M
Kaska	M	C	M	O	M	M	M	N	M	G
Ramkokamekra	M	C	M	O	O	M	M	M	M	M
Trukese	M	C	M	M	O	M	M	M	G	G
Yaruro	M	CS	M	M	M	M	M	M	M	.
Zuni	M	C	M	O	O	M	M	M	M	M
11A. Avuncu-Crow										
Haida	M	C	A	A	M	M	Mp	A	M	C
Longuda	M	C	A	A	N	M	P	A	GM	M
Mota	M	C	Ap	U	M	M	Ps	A	G	M
Ndoro	M	C	A	U	O	M	.	A	G	M
Tlingit	M	C	A	A	M	M	.	A	CM	M
Trobrianders	M	C	A	A	O	M	Mp	N	M	M
11B. Bi-Crow										
Acoma	M	CH	Bn	O	O	M	M	B	GM	M
11N. Neo-Crow										
Mandan	M	C	N	O	N	M	S	G	M	M
11P. Patri-Crow										
Crow	M	C	P	O	O	M	S	G	M	M
Kongo	M	C	P	O	O	M	Ps	G	M	.
Natchez	M	C	T	O	O	M	Ms	N	C	M
Rossel	M	C	P	O	O	M	Mp	N	CM	.
Twi	M	CS	P	O	O	M	P	G	M	M
11D. Duo-Crow										
Ashanti	D	S	P	O	O	MP	P	P	M	C
Manus	D	C	P	P	O	MP	Mp	N	CM	M
Murngin	D	S	T	C	MP	MP	Ps	G	M	M
Pentecost	D	C	P	U	M	MP	.	.	GM	M
Ranon	D	S	P	U	M	MP	.	.	M	C
Yako	D	.	P	P	O	MP	P	P	G	.
Yuchi	D	O	P	O	Q	M	P	G	CM	CM

Derivations of the type: from 4M; from 9; from 9A to 11A; from 9D to 11D; from 9P to 11P; from 10; from 10A to 11A; from 10D to 11D; from 10P to 11P.

Possibilities of change: from 11B to 4B; from 11N to 4N; from 11P to 4; from 11D to 4P, 7, or 8.

the available evidence is so scanty that their classification must be regarded as tentative. Since cousin terminology is not available on the Yako they have been assigned to Duo-Crow only on the basis of distributional probabilities, and may actually be Duo-Nankanse or Duo-Iroquois in structure. Double descent has been ascribed to the Yuchi because, in addition to exogamous matri-sibs, they are reported to possess moieties which are apparently patrilineal though their functions are purely political and ceremonial in nature and not concerned with the regulation of marriage. The alternative would be to assign them to the Patri-Crow sub-type. There is historical evidence [52] that they have shifted from Crow to Omaha cousin terminology in post-Columbian times in consequence of contacts with the Shawnee. This provides a good example of the manner in which diffusion can accelerate a process of adaptive change, for patrilocal residence and patri-moieties paved the way for the adoption of a characteristically patrilineal type of asymmetrical cross-cousin terminology. Diffusion cannot, however, reverse a trend or produce arbitrary changes.

The inadequacy of diffusionistic interpretations of social structure is strikingly revealed by an analysis of the distribution of the eleven major types of social organization. In our sample of 250 societies, representatives of all eleven types occur in both Africa and Oceania. North America lacks the Sudanese and Nankanse types; South America, the Guinea and Iroquois types; Eurasia, the Yuman, Nankanse, and Crow types. All these gaps are explicable in terms either of the rarity of the type or of the smallness of our sample in particular regions. Table 72 shows the numerical distribution of the eleven types of social organization with respect to the five major continental and insular areas of the world.

The various types of social organization with their sub-types admit of so many combinations of traits, especially when allowance is made for survivals of past structural types and anticipations of future ones, that the reader may have gathered the impression that any combination is possible. This is, however, definitely not the case. A very large number of combinations not expected according to our theory do not occur in fact in any of the 250 societies. For

[52] See F. Eggan, "Historical Changes in the Choctaw Kinship System," *American Anthropologist*, n.s., XXXIX (1937), 46–7.

TABLE 72

Type of Structure	Africa	Eurasia	North America	Oceania	South America	Total
Eskimo	1	7	6	1	3	18
Hawaiian	3	1	24	11	6	45
Yuman	1	..	7	3	5	16
Fox	3	1	3	2	1	10
Guinea	10	5	1	2	..	18
Dakota	13	9	3	11	1	37
Sudanese	8	2	..	2	1	13
Omaha	10	6	5	3	1	25
Nankanse	2	..	..	2	1	5
Iroquois	7	3	8	15	..	33
Crow	7	..	13	8	2	30
TOTALS	65	34	70	60	21	250

example, matrilocal extended families are never associated with patrilineal or double descent, nor exogamous moieties with bilocal or neolocal residence, nor bilateral kindreds with avunculocal residence, nor patrilineal extension of incest taboos with exclusively matrilineal descent, nor lineal terminology for aunts or nieces with double descent, nor avunculocal residence with Eskimo, Hawaiian, Omaha, or Sudanese terms for cousins, nor matrilocal residence with patrilineal or double descent, nor monogamy with avunculocal residence, nor Omaha or Sudanese cousin terminology with matriclans or matrilocal extended families, nor patri-lineages, patri-sibs, or patri-moieties with matrilocal or avunculocal residence. Such absences of association are inconsistent with theories which assume that "historical accident" can produce any assembly of traits.

The insistence of certain functionalists upon synchronic integration, which would permit only the association of compatible traits, fails equally to accord with the evidence. Among our 250 societies, for example, there are 15 which combine exclusive matrilineal descent with patrilocal or matri-patrilocal residence, 52 which associate unilocal residence with bilateral descent, and 22 which combine unilinear descent with typically bilateral (i.e., Eskimo or Hawaiian) terms for cousins. Though perhaps logically incompatible, such trait associations are both consistent with and expected by our theory, which allows for particular inharmonious combinations during transitions from one relatively stable structural equilibrium to another. Contradictory combinations, however, do not occur at random, but only where theoretically anticipated.

The principal derivations of each major type of social structure and the commonest transitional steps from one to another have been noted in the tables. When they are put together there emerges a comprehensive picture of the possibilities and limitations of change in the evolution of social organization. This is done in Table 73, which lists every transition for which there is internal evidence, actual or inferential historical testimony, or a reasonable possibility on theoretical grounds. Asterisks mark changes which are presumably rare or exceptional. It is assumed that certain shifts in residence cannot occur directly, but only through some other intermediate rule. These are the changes from neolocal to bilocal, from patrilocal to matrilocal, from avunculocal to bilocal or matrilocal, and from any type except matrilocal to avunculocal.

In Table 73, transitions are assumed to take place by modification of a single trait at a time. Thus the evolution from Patri-Hawaiian to Dakota requires two steps, the transition occurring via either Normal Yuman or Normal Guinea depending upon whether the first adaptive adjustment to the rule of patrilocal residence is the development of Iroquois cousin terminology or of patrilineal descent. Sometimes, of course, both modifications may occur simultaneously or nearly so, in which case the double transition is accomplished in a single step.

The principal conclusion from the foregoing analysis is that the evolution of social organization is always channelized by the characteristics of the existing structure, which regularly limits the possibilities of change and in some instances also predetermines its direction. Sometimes the alternatives are exceedingly few. Thus, with rare exceptions, an avunculocal structure can only become patrilocal, and an Omaha structure only bilateral. In other cases the range of possibilities is wide. Thus a Patri-Nankanse structure can, with almost equal facility, become transformed directly into another sub-type characterized by either bilateral, patrilineal, matrilineal, or double descent.

Mere similarity between two types of organization, whether structural or functional, does not mean that transition is equally easy or direct in either direction. The Duo-Iroquois and Normal Dakota sub-types provide an excellent example. They are functionally very similar, especially if moieties are not present, and they differ structurally only in the fact that the former has matrilineal as well as patrilineal kin groups. A Duo-Iroquois society can acquire a Normal Dakota structure directly through the loss of matrilineal descent, which is not difficult under patrilocal residence. A Normal Dakota society, on the other hand., can be transformed into a Duo-Iroquois structure only through a long and circuitous series of steps, of which the most typical would be the following:

1. A residence shift to Bi-Dakota.
2. Loss of patrilineal descent, producting a Bi-Yuman structure.
3. An adjustment in cousin terminology, yielding a Normal Hawaiian structure.
4. A residence shift to Matri-Hawaiian.
5. Development of matrilineal descent, producing a Normal Nankanse organization.
6. An adjustment in cousin terminology, yielding a Normal Iroquois structure.
7. A residence shift to Patri-Iroquois.
8. Acquisition of patrilineal without loss of matrilineal descent.

Analysis of Table 73 will reveal numerous comparable examples.

The structural limitations upon the possibilities of change in social organization have important implications for historical anthropology. They mean that any existing social system can have been preceded by one of only a very few possible forms. By excluding the vast majority of conceivable antecedents, and concentrating upon the few genuine alternatives, it often becomes possible to make dependable inferences as to specific earlier forms. As a result of cultural lag, social systems very commonly include elements developed during previous phases which have not yet completed the adaptive modifications necessary to integrate them into a new equilibrium. These become highly diagnostic when the types of structure from which they can have been derived are reducible to a very small number. If, for example, a particular survivalistic trait is a normal accompaniment of four types of social organization, only one of

TABLE 73

Types and Sub-types	Transitions by Residence Changes	Transitions by Descent Changes	Transitions by Changes in Cousin Terms
1. ESKIMO			
Normal Eskimo	Matri-Eskimo Patri-Eskimo	None possible	None probable
Bi-Eskimo	Normal Eskimo Matri-Eskimo Patri-Eskimo	None possible	Normal Hawaiian
Matri-Eskimo	*Normal Eskimo Bi-Eskimo Patri-Eskimo	Normal Nankanse	Matri-Yuman *Matri-Fox
Patri-Eskimo	Normal Eskimo Bi-Eskimo	Normal Guinea	Normal Yuman *Normal Fox
2. HAWAIIAN			
Normal Hawaiian	Neo-Hawaiian Matri-Hawaiian Patri-Hawaiian	None possible	None probable
Neo-Hawaiian	Matri-Hawaiian Patri-Hawaiian	None possible	Normal Eskimo
Matri-Hawaiian	Normal Hawaiian *Neo-Hawaiian Patri-Hawaiian	Normal Nankanse	Matri-Yuman *Matri-Fox
Patri-Hawaiian	Normal Hawaiian Neo-Hawaiian	Normal Guinea	Normal Yuman *Normal Fox

252

TABLE 73 (Con't)

3. YUMAN

Normal Yuman	*Bi-Yuman	Normal Dakota	*Normal Fox
	Neo-Yuman	None possible	Normal Hawaiian
Bi-Yuman	Normal Yuman		
	*Neo-Yuman		
Neo-Yuman	Matri-Yuman	None possible	Normal Eskimo
	Normal Yuman		
Matri-Yuman	*Matri-Yuman	Normal Iroquois	*Matri-Fox
	*Normal Yuman		
	*Bi-Yuman		
	*Neo-Yuman		

4. FOX

Normal Fox	*Bi-Fox	Patri-Fox	*Normal Yuman
	*Neo-Fox	Normal Sudanese	
		Normal Omaha	
Bi-Fox	Normal Fox	None possible	Normal Hawaiian
	*Neo-Fox		
	Matri-Fox		
Neo-Fox	Normal Fox	None possible	Normal Eskimo
	*Matri-Fox		
Matri-Fox	Normal Fox	Normal Crow	*Matri-Yuman
	*Bi-Fox		
	*Neo-Fox		
Patri-Fox	*Bi-Fox	*Normal Fox	*Normal Dakota
	*Neo-Fox		Normal Sudanese
			Normal Omaha

253

TABLE 73 (Con't)

Types and Sub-types	Transitions by Residence Changes	Transitions by Descent Changes	Transitions by Changes in Cousin Terms
5. GUINEA			
Normal Guinea	*Bi-Guinea	*Patri-Eskimo	Normal Dakota
	*Neo-Guinea	*Patri-Hawaiian	Normal Sudanese
			Normal Omaha
Bi-Guinea	*Normal Guinea	Normal Hawaiian	None probable
	*Neo-Guinea		
Neo-Guinea	*Normal Guinea	Normal Eskimo	None probable
6. DAKOTA			
Normal Dakota	Bi-Dakota	*Normal Yuman	Normal Sudanese
	Neo-Dakota		Normal Omaha
Bi-Dakota	*Normal Dakota	Bi-Yuman	Bi-Guinea
Neo-Dakota	*Normal Dakota	Neo-Yuman	Neo-Guinea
7. SUDANESE			
Normal Sudanese	Bi-Sudanese	*Normal Fox	*Normal Dakota
	Neo-Sudanese		Normal Omaha
Bi-Sudanese	*Normal Sudanese	Bi-Fox	Bi-Guinea
Neo-Sudanese	*Normal Sudanese	Neo-Fox	Neo-Guinea

254

TABLE 73 (Con't)

8. OMAHA

Normal Omaha	Bi-Omaha	*Normal Fox	*Normal Dakota
	Neo-Omaha		*Normal Sudanese
Bi-Omaha	*Normal Omaha	Bi-Fox	Bi-Guinea
Neo-Omaha	*Neo-Omaha	Neo-Fox	Neo-Guinea
	*Normal Omaha		

9. NANKANSE

Normal Nankanse	Avuncu-Nankanse	*Matri-Eskimo	Normal Iroquois
	Bi-Nankanse	*Matri-Hawaiian	Normal Crow
	Neo-Nankanse		
	Patri-Nankanse		
Avuncu-Nankanse	Neo-Nankanse	None possible	Avuncu-Iroquois
	Patri-Nankanse		Avuncu-Crow
			None probable
Bi-Nankanse	*Normal Nankanse	Normal Hawaiian	
	*Neo-Nankanse		
	Patri-Nankanse		
Neo-Nankanse	*Normal Nankanse	Normal Eskimo	None probable
	Patri-Nankanse		
Patri-Nankanse	*Bi-Nankanse	Patri-Eskimo	Patri-Iroquois
	*Neo-Nankanse	Patri-Hawaiian	
		Normal Guinea	
		Duo-Nankanse	
		Normal Guinea	
Duo-Nankanse	*Bi-Nankanse		Duo-Iroquois
	Neo-Nankanse		*Duo-Crow

TABLE 73 (Con't)

Types and Sub-types	Transitions by Residence Changes	Transitions by Descent Changes	Transitions by Changes in Cousin Terms
10. IROQUOIS			
Normal Iroquois	Avuncu-Iroquois	*Matri-Yuman	Normal Crow
	Bi-Iroquois		
	Neo-Iroquois		
	Patri-Iroquois		
Avuncu-Iroquois	Neo-Iroquois	None possible	Avuncu-Crow
	Patri-Iroquois		
Bi-Iroquois	*Normal Iroquois	Bi-Yuman	Bi-Nankanse
	*Neo-Iroquois		
	Patri-Iroquois		
Neo-Iroquois	*Normal Iroquois	Neo-Yuman	Neo-Nankanse
	Patri-Iroquois		
Patri-Iroquois	*Bi-Iroquois	Normal Yuman	*Patri-Crow
	*Neo-Iroquois	Normal Dakota	
		Duo-Iroquois	
Duo-Iroquois	*Bi-Iroquois	Normal Dakota	Duo-Crow
	*Neo-Iroquois		

TABLE 73 (Con't)

11. CROW

Normal Crow	Avuncu-Crow	Bi-Crow	Neo-Crow	Patri-Crow	Duo-Crow		
Avuncu-Crow	*Normal Crow	Normal Crow	*Bi-Crow	*Bi-Crow		*Matri-Fox	*Normal Iroquois
Bi-Crow	*Neo-Crow	Patri-Crow	*Neo-Crow	Neo-Crow		None possible	*Avuncu-Iroquois
Neo-Crow	Patri-Crow					Bi-Fox	Bi-Nankanse
Patri-Crow						Normal Fox	Neo-Nankanse
Neo-Crow						Patri-Fox	*Patri-Iroquois
Patri-Crow						Duo-Crow	Duo-Iroquois
						Patri-Fox	
						Normal Sudanese	
						Normal Omaha	

which is included among the three possible antecedents of the social system in question, its occurrence points to that particular type as the one from which the system has been derived. When several such inferences agree, little doubt remains as to the historically antecedent structure.

The author has analyzed all the societies of his sample for such inferences. He has discovered (1) that whenever there are two or more independent sources of inference in the unintegrated features of a particular social structure they nearly always point in the same direction; (2) that whenever the ethnographer presents actual historical evidence as to the preexisting structure it nearly always supports the inferences from internal evidence; (3) that whenever reasonable inferences can be drawn from ethnographic or linguistic distributions by established anthropological methods these inferences nearly always accord with those from the social structure itself. So generally do inferences from the internal analysis of social organization agree both with one another and with all available historical evidence that the author has systematized them in the form of a special technique for historical reconstruction.

This technique is naturally of no avail in a perfectly integrated social system, i.e., one in which marriage, family organization, kin groups, exogamy, kinship terminology, and rules of residence, inheritance, and descent have all been brought into complete consistency with one another in one of the more stable structural types. Perfect integration is, however, the exception. Often, indeed, survivals make it possible to infer with a high degree of assurance not merely the type of structure immediately preceding the one described by the ethnographer, but two, three, or even more antecedent steps and the order of their succession. The Nankanse, who fall into the Duo-Nankanse sub-type, will serve as an example. The preceding structure was Patri-Nankanse because double descent requires a matrilineal antecedent and there is no other alternative. The second previous structure was Avuncu-Nankanse because of the survivalistic alternative of avunculocal residence, which can have had no other origin. The third antecedent structure was Normal Nankanse because this is the only possible source of Avuncu-Nankanse. The fourth previous structure was Matri-Hawaiian, for no other derivation is consistent with the surviving Hawaiian cousin terminology and the alternative generation terms for nieces. The fifth antecedent structure was presumably Normal Hawaiian because this is the usual derivation of the Matri-Hawaiian sub-type. This inferential sequence is consistent at all points with the distributional evidence on West African social organization. For additional examples the reader is referred to Appendix A, where the proposed technique for historical reconstruction is fully described and illustrated.

The theory of social change propounded in this chapter, the associated typology, and the technique for historical reconstruction derived from them represent completely unanticipated products of the present study. The research was undertaken with the exclusive aim of determining whether the forms of social structure operate to channelize patterned sex behavior. Repeated handling of masses of cases, however, engendered an increasing realization of the striking frequency of parallelism in the forms of social organization and led to an attempt to discover whether the number of possible configurations might not be finite. A few trial-and-error classifications, guided largely by suggestions from Lawrence and Lowie, yielded such promising results that the endeavor was carried through to the conclusions presented above. These add manifest confirmation to the impression from other portions of the work that cultural forms in the field of social organization reveal a degree of regularity and of conformity to scientific law not significantly inferior to that found in the so-called natural sciences.

9

THE REGULATION OF SEX

THE IMPERIOUS drive of sex is capable of impelling individuals, reckless of consequences while under its spell, toward behavior which may imperil or disrupt the cooperative relationships upon which social life depends. The countless interpersonal bonds out of which human association is forged, complex and often delicately balanced, can ill suffer the strain of the frustrations and aggressions inevitably generated by indiscriminate competition over sexual favors. Society, therefore, cannot remain indifferent to sex but must seek to bring it under control. Possibly in man's long history there have been peoples who have failed to subject the sexual impulse to regulation. If so, none has survived, for the social control of sex is today a cultural universal.[1] Our sample societies reveal not a single exception.

Regulation must not, however, be carried too far. To survive, any society must grant to the individual at least sufficient expression of the sexual impulse to maintain reproduction and prevent population decline. Still further concessions are presumably also necessary. While the sex drive may be more capable than others, such as hunger and thirst, of being diverted into substitutive forms of expression, or sublimations,[2] the clinical evidence strongly suggests

[1] Cf. B. Z. Seligman, "Incest and Descent," *Journal of the Royal Anthropological Institute*, LIX (1929), 239.

[2] Even this widely accepted view has been challenged, with an impressive array of evidence, in A. C. Kinsey, W. B. Pomeroy, and C. E. Martin, *Sexual Behavior in the Human Male* (Philadelphia, 1948), pp. 205–13.

that excessive sexual deprivation produces personality maladjustments that are inimical to satisfactory social relationships. A society must therefore permit sufficient sexual gratification to maintain the mental health and efficiency of its members as well as their numbers.

All societies have faced the problem of reconciling the need of controlling sex with that of giving it adequate expression, and all have solved it by some combination of cultural taboos, permissions, and injunctions.[3] Prohibitory regulations curb the socially more disruptive forms of sexual competition. Permissive regulations allow at least the minimum impulse gratification required for individual well-being. Very commonly, moreover, sex behavior is specifically enjoined by obligatory regulations where it appears directly to subserve the interests of society.

An analysis of sex behavior is prerequisite to an understanding of sex regulation. For present purposes it will not be necessary to consider so-called "unnatural practices," such as auto-eroticism and homosexuality, nor sexual sublimations such as dancing and droll stories, nor various other aspects of sex behavior. Attention will be focused exclusively on overt heterosexual relations within and outside of marriage. Socially considered, any act of sexual intercourse may be regarded as falling into one of seven major categories. When engaged in by a married couple observing all social proprieties, it may be termed *marital sexuality*. When it takes place outside of marriage between two persons of whom at least one is married to another person, it is called *adultery*. If its participants are related to one another by a real, assumed, or artificial bond of kinship which is culturally regarded as a bar to sex relations, it is classed as *incest*. If the couple belong to different social classes, castes, races, or ethnic or national groups between which sex relations are culturally forbidden, it may be called *mismating*. If either party occupies a social status in which permanent chastity is required, e.g., a priest in our own society or a widow in certain others, sexual intercourse may be termed *status unchastity*. If either or both is violating social

---

[3] Merton distinguishes between "prescription, proscription, preference, and permission" in reference to the regulation of marriage; see R. K. Merton, "Intermarriage and the Social Structure: Fact and Theory," *Psychiatry*, IV (1941), 364.

proprieties or cultural taboos, such as the temporary injunction of continence during a ceremonial fast or when the woman is menstruating or pregnant, the act may be called *incontinence*. The final category of *fornication* includes all other instances of sexual intercourse, i.e., all sex relations that are neither marital, adulterous, incestuous, mismated, ritually unchaste, nor incontinent. It applies to intercourse which conforms to social conventions in all respects except that the partners are not married.

The foregoing classification suggests the principal foci of sex regulation, which are marital status, kinship, social stratification (including ethnic differences), special social statuses, particular events and circumstances, and, finally, sex in general. With respect to any of these, regulation may be prohibitory, permissive, or obligatory; sex behavior may be forbidden, allowed, or required. Kinship and social stratification, moreover, play a prominent role in the regulation of marriage, and incest and mismating apply to marital as well as sexual unions. Table 74 summarizes the more important types of sex regulation.

TABLE 74

Referment of Regulation	Prohibitory Regulations	Permissive Regulations	Obligatory Regulations
Sex in general	Prohibition of fornication	Permissive promiscuity	Sexual hospitality
Marital status	Prohibition of adultery	Premarital license	Marital duty
Kinship	Incest taboos and exogamy	Privileged relationships	Preferential mating
Social stratification	Caste, class, and ethnic endogamy	Permissive miscegenation	Hypergamy
Special statuses	Status chastity and celibacy	Sexual prerogatives	Special sex obligations
Particular circumstances	Ritual continence and reproductive sex taboos	Ceremonial license	Obligatory sex rites

Our own culture includes a blanket taboo against fornication, an over-all prohibition of all sexual intercourse outside of the marital relationship. To a member of our society, consequently, sex itself seems the obvious focus of sex regulation. Not only the man in the street but most of our serious scholars unconsciously assume that sex regulation in other societies must have the same basis, and the literature on the subject is largely written from this point of view. Actually, the assumption is demonstrably false. To the overwhelming majority of the peoples of the world, the point of departure for the regulation of sex is not sexual intercourse *per se* but one or more other social phenomena with respect to which sex is important, notably marriage, kinship, social status, reproduction, and ceremonial. Instead of a generalized sex taboo, what the ethnographer and the historian usually encounter is a series of sex restrictions, permissions, and obligations in relation to these other phenomena. The evidence from our worldwide sample of 250 societies which bears upon the prevalence of a generalized taboo against all sex relations outside of marriage is compiled in Table 75.

TABLE 75

Information on Sex Taboos	Number of Societies
Indications of probable presence of a generalized sex taboo	3
Definite evidence of absence of a generalized sex taboo	
Permissive premarital unchastity	49
Fully or conditionally permitted adultery	3
Privileged relationships	23
Two or all three of the above	40
TOTAL	115
Inadequate information	
No data on premarital unchastity	7
No data on premarital or postmarital relationships	35
TOTAL	42
No relevant data whatsoever	90
TOTAL	250

The societies with a probable general sex taboo, in addition to the New England Yankees, are the Ashanti and Timne of West Africa, and for the latter of these the information is far from complete. Of the 42 societies with inadequate information, a general sex taboo is reasonably probable for the Syrian Christians of India and the Tarahumara of Mexico, and is possible in a few other instances. From available evidence, however, it seems unlikely that a general prohibition of sex relations outside of marriage occurs in as many as five per cent of the peoples of the earth.

The bias of our own highly aberrant traditional sex mores has not only distorted the analysis of sexual restrictions but has led generations of writers to postulate for early man or for primitive peoples the antithesis of our own type of regulation, namely, a generalized sexual permissiveness variously called "hetairism," "primitive promiscuity," or "sexual communism." [4] The factual support for this assumption is as insubstantial as for its opposite. Only two of our sample societies, the Kaingang of Brazil and the Todas of southern India, approach a general lack of sex restrictions sufficiently closely to justify speaking of them as promiscuous. In neither, however, is there complete unregulation. The Todas, for example, observe incest taboos, sib exogamy, and moiety endogamy despite their indifference to adultery.

Generalized obligatory regulations such as wife lending and sexual hospitality [5] are also exceedingly infrequent. Our sample reveals only twelve instances, in nearly all of which the practice is highly restricted. The conclusion is thus inescapable that sex regulation hinges only rarely on the fact of sex itself. To few peoples is sex an evil, albeit a necessary one, and thus to be confined exclusively within the limits of the one social relationship vested with the responsibility for reproduction.

[4] Cf. J. J. Bachofen, *Das Mutterrecht* (Stuttgart, 1861); L. H. Morgan, *Ancient Society* (New York, 1877), p. 416; J. Kohler, "Studien über Frauengemeinschaft, Frauenraub und Frauenkauf," *Zeitschrift für vergleichende Rechtswissenschaft*, V (1884), 336; J. Lubbock, *The Origin of Civilisation and the Primitive Condition of Man* (5th edit., New York, 1892), pp. 86–98; J. G. Frazer, *Totemism and Exogamy* (London, 1910), IV, 151; L. F. Ward, *Pure Sociology* (2nd edit., New York, 1921), pp. 340–1; W. H. R. Rivers, *Social Organization* (New York, 1924), p. 80; R. Briffault, *The Mothers* (New York, 1927), I, 614–781; W. G. Sumner and A. G. Keller, *The Science of Society* (New Haven, 1927), III, 1547.

[5] For illustrative cases see E. Westermarck, *The History of Human Marriage* (5th edit., New York, 1922), I, 225–30; R. Briffault, *The Mothers* (New York, 1927), I, 635–40.

The marital relationship is a major focus of regulation. Within this relationship, sexual intercourse is normally not merely permissive but obligatory. Taboos on adultery are extremely widespread, though sometimes more honored in the breach than in the observance. They appear in 120 of the 148 societies in our sample for which data are available. In 4 of the remaining 28, adultery is socially disapproved though not strictly forbidden; it is conditionally permitted in 19 and freely allowed in 5. It should be pointed out, however, that these figures apply only to sex relations with an unrelated or distantly related person. A substantial majority of all societies, as will be demonstrated below, permit extramarital relations with certain affinal relatives.

Sex freedom before marriage is consistent with the marital basis of sex regulation. Among the sample societies for which information is available, non-incestuous premarital relations are fully permitted in 65 instances, and are conditionally approved in 43 and only mildly disapproved in 6, whereas they are forbidden in only 44. In other words, premarital license prevails in 70 per cent of our cases. In the rest, the taboo falls primarily upon females and appears to be largely a precaution against childbearing out of wedlock [6] rather than a moral requirement.

Ethnic differences and social stratification frequently constitute a basis for sex regulation. Most societies confine sex relations and marriage within specified social limits through rules of endogamy. Sometimes endogamy applies to the local community, sometimes to the tribe or nation, sometimes to members of the same race. The Quinault of coastal Washington are unique among the societies of our sample in actually preferring marriages into other tribes. Many primitive peoples with sexual practices that are otherwise quite lax impose strong taboos upon sex relations with Europeans, thus paralleling exactly the ethnocentric tendency of the white man to forbid intermarriage and to disapprove illicit relations with members of the darker races. Only a minority of human societies appear to give full sanction to miscegenation.

When a society is stratified into social classes or castes, the cultural differences and "social distance" [7] ordinarily characteristic of

[6] Cf. H. Webster, *Taboo* (Stanford University, 1942), pp. 146–8.

[7] This apt term is adopted from the sociologist E. S. Bogardus.

geographically separated groups are commonly manifested by groups that are only socially and hierarchically distinct. Endogamous preferences thus become associated with caste and class strata. Most of the sample societies with complex social stratification exhibit either a strict rule or a marked preference for caste and class endogamy. In some cases, however, sexual and marital unions between members of different social strata are not regarded as mismating, and in a few instances there actually appear rules prescribing caste or class exogamy, e.g., hypergamy. Among the Natchez of the lower Mississippi, for example, a woman of any of the three noble classes—the Suns, Nobles, and Honored People—is required to marry a commoner, a man of the Stinkard class.

Sex regulation may attach not only to general but also to special social statuses. The commonest restrictive regulation of this type is the requirement of celibacy and often also of chastity in priests and other religious functionaries.[8] In some societies a similar taboo is imposed upon widows. Special social status may also be associated with permissive regulations. One of the best known is the *jus primae noctis*,[9] the right of a feudal lord, priest, or other male in a position of authority to have sexual intercourse with a bride on her wedding night before her husband is allowed access to her. Another instance is the special prerogative of violating the usual incest taboos which certain societies accord to persons of exceptionally high status. The most famous examples are the brother-sister marriages which were not merely tolerated but preferred in the royal families of Incaic Peru and Ptolemaic Egypt. Our own sample reveals three cases of such a disregard for primary incest taboos: the right of certain high Azande nobles to wed their own daughters and the preference for marriages between brother and sister in the old Hawaiian aristocracy and in the Inca royal family. Status prerogatives shade imperceptibly into special sex obligations, as when the "right of the first night" becomes an onerous duty rather than a privilege.

Events in the reproductive cycle are widely associated with sex restrictions. Most societies impose a taboo against sexual intercourse during a woman's menstrual periods, during at least the later months

---

[8] See J. Main (E. C. Parsons), *Religious Chastity* (New York, 1913).

[9] Cf. K. Schmidt, *Jus primae noctis* (Freiburg, 1881); E. Westermarck, *The History of Human Marriage* (5th edit., New York, 1922), I, 166–96.

of pregnancy, and for a period immediately following childbirth.[10] Many extend the latter taboo throughout most or all of the period of lactation.[11] These prohibitions doubtless contribute significantly to the widespread notion of the uncleanness of women.[12] Sexual intercourse is occasionally made obligatory in the belief that it is beneficial to reproduction. Thus the Azande and the Kiwai enjoin copulation during pregnancy in order to promote the development of the fetus.

Sex regulation is frequently associated with other events of social and ceremonial significance. Many of the societies in our sample require strict continence before, during, and sometimes immediately after a military expedition, a harvest, a hunting, fishing, or collecting trip, or engaging in particular manufacturing processes.[13] Abstention from sex as well as from food and labor is a normal concomitant of ritual fasting and particular religious ceremonies. Many societies require a newly married couple to remain continent for one night or longer after their wedding.[14] The ceremonial regulation of sex may also be permissive. Thus a number of societies sanction either general sexual license or a substantial slackening of ordinary restrictions on the occasion of weddings, funerals, festivals, or religious ceremonies.[15] Obligatory sex regulations of a ceremonial nature are illustrated by orgiastic fertility rites.

Common as are many of the prohibitions, permissions, and obligations outlined above, the only type of sex regulation which is genuinely universal is that associated with kinship. The prohibitory regulations of this type fall into two principal categories: incest taboos and exogamous restrictions. Incest taboos prevent sexual intercourse or marriage between persons who are believed to be closely akin, whether they are actually close relatives or whether the kinship bond between them is merely a conventional one. It is

[10] Cf. C. S. Ford, "A Comparative Study of Human Reproduction," *Yale University Publications in Anthropology*, XXXII (1945), 12, 48-9, 67.

[11] *Ibid.*, pp. 80-1.

[12] Cf. H. Webster, *Taboo* (Stanford University, 1942), pp. 110-21.

[13] See also C. S. Ford, "A Comparative Study of Human Reproduction," *Yale University Publications in Anthropology*, XXXII (1945), 28-9.

[14] Cf. H. Webster, *Taboo* (Stanford University, 1942), pp. 155-7.

[15] Cf. W. G. Sumner and A. G. Keller, *The Science of Society* (New Haven, 1927), III, 1550-3; IV, 852-8.

notable that nearly all societies interpose an incest taboo between such artificial relatives as adoptive parents and adopted children, stepparents and stepchildren, godparents and godchildren, and persons who become brother and sister through the establishment of a bond of blood-brotherhood. Exogamous restrictions appear to be merely another extension of incest taboos [16]—usually to an entire lineage, sib, or other consanguineal kin group but sometimes to a community or other local group. In either case the basis of the taboo is the belief or fiction that all the members are related to one another too closely to permit intercourse or marriage between them. Incest taboos and their extensions are explained in Chapter 10.

Obligatory regulations based on kinship refer almost exclusively to marriage rather than to sexual intercourse. The commonest type is *preferential mating* [17] or a cultural preference for marriage between persons who stand in particular kin relationships to one another, such as cross-cousins or siblings-in-law of opposite sex. Permissive regulations with respect to kinship fall mainly into the category of *privileged relationships,* within which sexual intercourse is permitted before marriage and frequently afterwards as well. Privileged relationships commonly reveal a close connection with preferential mating. Thus of the tribes in our sample for which information is available, 11 allow premarital intercourse with FaSiDa and 14 with MoBrDa, as compared with 38 which forbid it in the former case and 37 in the latter.

The most illuminating of privileged relationships, however, are those between siblings-in-law of opposite sex, who are, of course, frequently potential spouses under the sororate and levirate. Nearly two thirds of the sample societies for which data are available permit sexual intercourse after marriage with a brother-in-law or a sister-in-law.

Facts of this kind have frequently been misinterpreted as evidences of group marriage or of polyandry (see Chapter 2). Actually, however, they are merely one reflection of the fact that the vast majority of human societies make no attempt to confine sexual intercourse to marriage through a generalized sex taboo. Premarital

[16] Cf. B. Z. Seligman, "Incest and Descent," *Journal of the Royal Anthropological Institute,* LIX (1929), 253.

[17] Cf. R. H. Lowie, *Primitive Society* (New York, 1920), pp. 26-38.

license and privileged relationships are the commonest, though by no means the only, cultural provisions for extending sexual rights outside of matrimony. Like polygyny, privileged relationships serve to counteract the sexual deprivations that men would otherwise suffer in those societies which impose prolonged continence during pregnancy and nursing. In addition, they clearly operate equally to the advantage of women. They not only provide sexual variety and relief but also help to offset individual differences in sex potential,[18] and they accomplish these results without threatening the disruption of marital ties.

Privileged relationships and preferred marriages of the sororate and levirate type are explicable as extensions of the marital relationship. In all human societies husband and wife are privileged to cohabit sexually, however restricted or extensive other sexual outlets may be either before or after marriage. Incest taboos prevent the extension of this marital privilege to any other relationship within the nuclear family. If it is to be extended at all, the psychological principle of generalization [19] would lead us to anticipate its extension to those persons outside of the nuclear family who most closely resemble the spouse in significant characteristics, and the same similarities would be expected to influence the selection of a second spouse.

The persons who universally reveal the most numerous and detailed resemblances to a spouse are the latter's siblings of the same sex. These siblings are likely to have similar physical characteristics since they are biologically more closely akin to the spouse than anyone else of the same generation. In addition, they have almost identical social statuses since they necessarily belong to the same kin groups—family of orientation, kindred, sib, etc. These likenesses provide the requisite conditions for the generalization of behavior patterns, including sex responses, and often also for the reinforcement and fixation of the generalized responses. We should therefore expect a widespread tendency for sex relations to be extended to

[18] The extraordinary range of individual variation in this respect has been convincingly demonstrated for our own society. See A. C. Kinsey, W. B. Pomeroy, and C. E. Martin, *Sexual Behavior in the Human Male* (Philadelphia, 1948), pp. 193–217.

[19] Cf. C. L. Hull, *Principles of Behavior* (New York, 1943), pp. 183–203.

the spouse's siblings of the same sex, and for the same persons to be preferred in secondary marriages.

The data from our sample societies abundantly bear out this theoretical expectation. Since a wife's sister most closely resembles a wife, and a husband's brother (to whom the woman is his brother's wife) most closely resembles a husband, we find that true sororate and levirate unions are the most common of preferential secondary marriages and that the most frequent privileged relationships are, from the point of view of a male, those with WiSi and BrWi. The frequencies of permissive and forbidden extramarital sex relations and marriage with various affinal relatives in our 250 societies are shown in Table 76. The frequencies for permitted premarital relations with BrWi, FaWi, FaBrWi, and MoBrWi are fractionally higher than for extramarital intercourse.

TABLE 76

	Extramarital Sex Relations		Marriage	
Relative	Freely or Conditionally Permitted	Forbidden or Disapproved	Freely or Conditionally Permitted	Forbidden or Disapproved
BrWi	34	22	153	32
WiSi	28	15	133	27
WiBrWi	1	14	2	30
FaWi	3	26	29	43
FaBrWi	3	18	17	38
MoBrWi	6	13	33	34
WiMo	2	29	1	54
SoWi	3	29	5	45
WiDa	1	10	10	25
WiSiDa	1	12	5	26
WiBrDa	1	10	20	31

In a comparison of BrWi and WiSi with all other affinal relatives, permissions average 63 per cent for the former as against only 12 per cent for the latter in respect to extramarital relations, and 83 as against 27 per cent for marriage. Even if one compares BrWi, as lower than WiSi in permissive frequency, with MoBrWi, as revealing by far the highest permissive frequency among the other relatives in the table, the disparity in favor of the former is very great. The degree to which permission is associated with BrWi and prohibition with MoBrWi can be expressed statistically by coefficients of association of $+.54$ for extramarital relations and $+.66$ for marriage,[20] and all other comparisons would show appreciably higher coefficients. The frequency of permitted premarital relations with BrWi is very nearly as high as with an unrelated unmarried woman—60 and 62 per cent, respectively—while that of permitted extramarital relations is vastly higher than with an unrelated woman (24 permissions, 124 prohibitions).

Secondary marriages tend to be channelized by unilinear groupings of kinsmen. Thus a widow is likely to marry the son of her husband by another wife or the son of her husband's brother where descent is patrilineal, or the sister's son of her husband under matrilineal descent. Similarly if a man is to take a second wife from the generation below his own, she is likely to be a close unilinear relative of the first, e.g., his WiBrDa under patrilineal descent or his WiSiDa under matrilineal descent. The evidence is presented in Table 77. The statistical indices, which are the same as those employed in Chapter 7, confirm the theoretical expectation with high and consistent positive coefficients of association and with indices of reliability that are surprisingly large in view of the small size of the samples.

TABLE 77

	Marriage Permitted		Marriage Forbidden		Statistical Indices	
Relative	Patrilineal Descent	Other Rules of Descent	Patrilineal Descent	Other Rules of Descent	Q	χ^2
FaWi	22	7	15	29	$+.72$	100
FaBrWi	10	7	10	28	$+.60$	20
WiBrDa	11	9	9	23	$+.51$	10
	(Matrilineal Descent)		(Matrilineal Descent)			
MoBrWi	15	18	7	27	$+.53$	10
WiSiDa	2	3	2	24	$+.78$	2

Future marriages may be said to cast their shadows before them. A relative eligible for marriage is likely to be a permissible sex

[20] These coefficients are reliable, respectively, at the five per cent and at the one-tenth-of-one per cent level of confidence, using the chi square index of reliability described in Chapter 7.

object in advance of marriage, whereas a relative with whom marriage is forbidden tends to be ineligible also for premarital relations. The data on cross-cousins, presented in Table 78, substantiate this point with maximal positive coefficients of association that are highly reliable, even though χ^2 indices are not appropriate.

TABLE 78

Relative	Cross Cousin Marriage Allowed		Cross Cousin Marriage Forbidden		Statistical Indices	
	Premarital Intercourse Permitted	Premarital Intercourse Forbidden	Premarital Intercourse Permitted	Premarital Intercourse Forbidden	Q	χ^2
FaSiDa	11	2	0	37	+1.00	*
MoBrDa	13	3	0	35	+1.00	*

The extension of sexual privileges from the marital to other kin relationships follows principles which correspond exactly to those governing the extension of incest taboos from members of the nuclear family to other kinsmen. Since these will be fully expounded and amply substantiated in Chapter 10, they need not be considered here. Some of the more pertinent evidence, however, has been presented above.

A special aspect of sex regulation is revealed in the formal patterns of behavior that prevail between kinsmen of opposite sex. It has been observed [21] that such patterns form a continuum from complete avoidance of speech and physical contact at one pole to extreme license or obligatory joking and horseplay at the other. This continuum may conveniently be divided into five segments, as follows:

1. From complete avoidance to marked restraint.
2. From respect to moderate reserve.
3. From informality to intimacy.
4. From familiarity to privileged joking.
5. From obligatory joking to extreme license.

Patterned behavior between kinsmen of the same sex also falls into the same categories. Nevertheless, with the possible exception of intermediate informal relations, the factor of sex appears always to

[21] F. Eggan, "The Cheyenne and Arapaho Kinship System," *Social Anthropology of North American Tribes*, ed. F. Eggan (Chicago, 1937), p. 76.

be involved in some manner in the reciprocal behavior of male and female relatives.

Patterned avoidance behavior has frequently been ascribed the function of protecting or reinforcing incest taboos.[22] If this were a sufficient explanation, avoidance should be associated particularly with the relationships in which incest taboos are regularly the strongest, namely, those with Mo, Si, and Da, whereas it actually occurs more frequently with such secondary and tertiary relatives as WiMo, SoWi, and WiBrWi. Nevertheless, the suggestion is not wholly without merit. The author has gathered a distinct impression from the ethnographic literature that societies fall into two groups with respect to the manner in which they handle incest and other sexual taboos. One group seems to depend primarily upon the strong internalization of sexual prohibitions during the socialization process. The taboos are so thoroughly instilled by precept and sanction that they become "second nature." The very thought of violating them arouses a sense of guilt in the socialized individual, with the result that the society can afford to depend mainly on the consciences of its members to prevent deviations. The other group of societies apparently succeeds less well in internalizing sexual prohibitions. Consequently they cannot rely upon individual conscience for the enforcement of taboos, and are compelled to bulwark these with external precautionary safeguards such as avoidance rules.

Our own society clearly belongs to the former category. So thoroughly do we instill our sex mores in the consciences of individuals that we feel quite safe in trusting our internalized sanctions. We allow brother and sister to associate freely with one another, and even to live together and have intimate physical contacts, without fear that these conditions of sexual stimulation will produce violations of our incest taboos. Similarly we accord to women a maximum of personal freedom, knowing that the internalized ethics of premarital chastity and postmarital fidelity will ordinarily suffice to prevent abuse of their liberty through fornication or adultery

---

[22] Cf. J. G. Frazer, *The Golden Bough* (3rd edit., 12 vols., London, 1922), Vol. III: *Taboo and the Perils of the Soul*, pp. 85-6, n.6; W. H. R. Rivers, "Kin; Kinship," *Encyclopaedia of Religion and Ethics*, ed. J. Hastings, VII (New York, 1915), 706.

whenever a favorable opportunity presents itself. Societies of the other type commonly attempt to inhibit incest by avoidance restrictions which keep brother and sister apart and thus prevent sexual provocation. They attempt to preserve premarital chastity by secluding their unmarried girls or providing them with duennas or other protective escorts when they go out in public, and to check adultery by such external devices as veiling, seclusion in harems, or constant surveillance.

If this hypothesis is correct, societies should tend to require similar behavior toward all tabooed primary relatives, either allowing relatively informal relations alike with mother, sister, and daughter or insisting upon avoidance or marked respect toward all three. To be sure, the relationship with the mother differs somewhat from the other two. It is almost necessarily intimate or marked by a minimum of reserve in consequence of the close physical contact of the mother with her son during the nursing period and of her provision of food and housekeeping services during his later childhood. Thus in our sample societies there is no instance in which greater respect or restraint is shown toward a mother than toward both sister and daughter, and only four cases in which it is reported to exceed either. Hence the father-daughter and brother-sister relationships are more comparable to one another than is either to the mother-son relationship, although our evidence shows that the latter is nearly always consistent with the others. We shall therefore use only the two former relationships as a test case.

Behavior toward both sister and daughter is characterized by avoidance or marked respect in 17 of our sample societies: Ao, Batak, Chiricahua, Fijians, Fox, Haida, Jukun, Kiowa Apache, Minangkabau, Navaho, Ojibwa, Rossel, Syrian Christians, Toda, Tongans, Trukese, and Wintu. Informal or only mildly respectful behavior toward both relatives prevails in 8 societies: Ashanti, Kababish, Kwoma, Lamba, Manus, Shilluk, Tikopia, and Yankee. Respect for a sister is coupled with informality toward a daughter in 6 instances: Arapaho, Cheyenne, Kurtatchi, Lepcha, Lesu, and Sinkaietk. Informality with a sister but respect for a daughter are found in two societies: Cherokee and Dahomeans. These findings corroborate, by a coefficient of association of $+.84$ reliable to the ten per cent level, our hypothesis that some societies depend in general on the internalization of sex taboos whereas others find it necessary to support them by institutionalized restraints. Further information must be gathered and additional tests made, however, before confirmation can be considered complete.

Lowie [23] denies that avoidance customs have anything to do with the prevention of incest. All cultures, he says, divide persons of opposite sex into two groups, those who are sexually accessible and those who are not. From this dichotomy develop differences in attitude "which in the one case may degenerate into license, and in the other assume the grotesque prudery of avoidance." If this were true, the distribution of behavior patterns among different relatives should be purely random, which the evidence of our survey, shortly to be tabulated, demonstrates decisively is not the case. The hypothesis is particularly inapplicable in certain instances. Why, for example, is the mother, who is always taboo as a sex object, never avoided? And why are grandmothers and granddaughters, surely the least desirable and available of female relatives, more regularly associated with joking behavior than any others?

Eggan [24] regards avoidance and license as alternative solutions to the problem of resolving serious potential conflicts between kinsmen, the former being especially characteristic of relatives of different generations, the latter of those on the same generation level. Respect and mild joking he considers to replace avoidance and license respectively when the potentialities of conflict are slighter. This interpretation has the virtue of introducing psychological factors such as ambivalence into the analysis of patterned behavior. The present writer believes that here is one aspect of social organization where psychoanalytic theory, despite its unfortunate lack of precision, has an especially important contribution to make. Eggan's hypothesis has, on the other hand, a number of disadvantages. If not over-simple, it is certainly difficult to apply objectively, and it depends too heavily upon a Radcliffe-Brownian verbalism, in this case the "social necessity for avoiding or minimizing conflict if the household organization is to function properly."

[23] R. H. Lowie, *Primitive Society* (New York, 1920), pp. 104–5.
[24] F. Eggan, "The Cheyenne and Arapaho Kinship System," *Social Anthropology of North American Tribes*, ed. F. Eggan (Chicago, 1937), pp. 77–81.

A number of authorities [25] have advanced an hypothesis, to which Brant [26] has added substantial factual support, that "the joking relationship tends to obtain between relatives standing in a potential sexual relationship to each other." Though incomplete, this theory is confirmed by our own evidence. Before an attempt is made to formulate a broader interpretation, however, it will be well to summarize the data from our 250 sample societies. Table 79 presents the distribution of patterned behavior between a male Ego and all female relatives for whom evidence is available from at least ten tribes, the listing being approximately in the descending order of avoidance.

The wide range of variation which Table 79 reveals in the distribution of behavior patterns among different kinsmen suggests that no simple hypothesis can adequately account for all cases. Different explanations are probable for different relatives. The author will therefore consider separately the groups of kinship categories which differ markedly from one another in the incidence of different norms of behavior and probably therefore also in the interpretations thereof. He will advance some evidence in support of his conclusions, but his analysis is frankly exploratory rather than definitive.

Given the universality of intra-family incest taboos, which will be explained in the next chapter, the patterned behavior reported for mother, sister, and daughter seems consistent with the hypothesis already expressed, namely, that incest prohibitions require external support from rules of avoidance or exaggerated respect in some societies but not in others where they are more strongly internalized and ingrained in the individual conscience. Differences in the social conditions normally affecting the three relatives would account for the decreasing frequency of avoidance and respect as one passes from sister first to daughter and then to mother. The distribution of patterned behavior for FaDa, MoDa, FaBrDa, and MoSiDa closely resembles that for Si; that for BrDa and WiSiDa is like

[25] Cf. E. D. Chapple and C. S. Coon, *Principles of Anthropology* (New York, 1942), pp. 312–13; R. H. Lowie, *Primitive Society* (New York, 1920), p. 104; A. R. Radcliffe-Brown, "On Joking Relationships," *Africa*, XIII (1940), 195–210.

[26] C. S. Brant, "On Joking Relationships," *American Anthropologist*, n.s., L (1948), 161.

TABLE 79

Relative	Avoidance or Marked Restraint	Respect or Reserve	Informality or Intimacy	Joking or Familiarity	License or Extreme Joking
WiMo	78	33	26	–	–
WiBrWi	12	5	1	1	–
SoWi	35	29	22	2	–
MoDa	10	11	3	1	–
FaDa	10	11	4	3	–
Si	30	29	17	3	–
MoSiDa	17	24	9	3	–
FaBrDa	15	24	11	4	–
Da	2	28	11	–	–
BrDa	2	15	6	2	–
WiSiDa	1	4	5	–	–
FaSi	6	30	5	9	–
MoBrWi	7	8	7	5	1
MoBrDa	11	19	9	13	1
FaSiDa	13	17	7	15	2
MoSi	1	13	13	–	–
Mo	–	22	20	–	–
FaBrWi	2	4	10	–	–
FaWi	–	4	6	–	–
YoBrWi	18	16	16	13	8
WiElSi	14	17	16	16	9
SiDa	2	14	13	10	–
Wi	–	5	16	–	–
MoMo	–	16	14	14	–
FaMo	–	16	13	15	–
ElBrWi	10	15	16	20	8
WiYoSi	8	14	19	20	9
WiBrDa	2	1	7	4	1
SoDa	1	6	12	13	–
DaDa	–	7	13	14	–

that for Da; that for MoSi, FaWi, and FaBrWi is almost identical
with that for Mo. In all these instances the social characteristics
and classification of the secondary and tertiary relatives mentioned are normally very similar to those of the primary relative.
Hence just as the kinship terms and incest taboos associated with
the latter are regularly generalized or extended to the former,
so also are other patterned norms of behavior.

The wife stands in a special non-tabooed relationship. The fact that neither avoidance, nor joking, nor license is associated with the spouse in any of our sample societies reflects the economic cooperation, sexual cohabitation, and partnership in child-rearing that are universally characteristic of this relationship. The only types of behavior that are consistent with these functions are intimacy, informality, and a reasonable measure of mutual respect.

The patterned behavior exhibited toward FaMo, MoMo, SoDa, and DaDa may be considered together, since that in the first two instances is nearly reciprocal with that in the second two, and since the tabulated evidence is strikingly similar for all four. The principal difference is the relatively greater frequency of respect behavior toward grandmothers, as is consistent with their age advantage. All four relationships are marked by an absence of extremes in behavior—both license and, with a single exception, avoidance. What characterizes them most strikingly, however, is the high frequency of permissive joking. This may well relate to the separation of grandparents from grandchildren by two generations. Intermediate between them falls a man or a woman who is a child of the one and a parent of the other. As psychoanalysis has shown, the reciprocal attitudes of parent and child are necessarily ambivalent because the former not only rewards the latter by providing food and other comforts but also frustrates and punishes him in the course of the process of socialization. Grandparent and grandchild are drawn together by the fact that each can expect from the other an unconscious sympathy for his own dissatisfactions with the intervening relative. The relationship between them is thus likely to be positive rather than ambivalent. The tolerant affection of grandparent for grandchild and the unalloyed pleasure of the latter in the former, so familiar in our own society, are apparently exceedingly widespread.

From this basis of warm congeniality it is an easy step to a mild joking relationship. Our cases reveal that the jesting revolves largely around the subject of sex. Each party delights in calling the other his husband or wife, in accusing him of sexual advances, and in playfully initiating erotic overtures of his own. This doubtless provides both with some substitutive gratification, and the age disparity makes it apparent to everyone that the behavior is merely "good clean fun" with no ulterior overtones. As we shall see below, joking relations with other kinsmen of opposite sex reveal quite a different emotional quality.

The relatively extraordinary frequency of avoidance with WiBrWi, apparently hitherto unnoticed in the literature, challenges special attention. It cannot be explained by the fact that under the fairly common circumstance of cross-cousin marriage Ego's WiBrWi can be his own sister, for the behavior is appreciably more extreme than is usually the case with a sister. It is possibly a corollary of the special relationship that commonly prevails between brothers-in-law. Although the author unfortunately did not gather data on social behavior between male relatives, he has a distinct impression from general reading that the relations between brothers-in-law are commonly characterized by respect or reserve, especially by a marked tendency to avoid mentioning matters of sexual import. This is not unnatural in view of the fact that, with respect to the same woman, one of the two men enjoys unrestrained sexual freedom whereas the other must observe one of the strictest of incest taboos. Any allusion to sex by the former is likely to arouse unconscious anxieties in the latter, whereas an allusion by the latter might imply to the former a lack of respect for the woman who unites them or even suggest the possibility of an unpardonable incestuous connection with her. For the former to have relations with the wife of the latter would be to flaunt the fact of sex in his face as no merely verbal impropriety could possibly do. The patterned avoidance of WiBrWi provides a social mechanism whereby such an outrageous event can be prevented from occurring.

The classic avoidance relationship is that with the wife's mother. In only 19 per cent of the 137 societies for which evidence is available is behavior toward a mother-in-law reported as informal, and in no instance does either joking or license occur. The incidence of respect is 24 per cent and of true avoidance 57 per cent. The writer sees no reason for doubting the common allegation that mother-in-law taboos have the function of preventing sexual intercourse under circumstances peculiarly disruptive of intra-family cooperation. This interpretation is supported by the fact that only an insignificant number of polygynous societies permit marriage with both a mother and her daughter. For a man to have sexual intercourse with his mother-in-law would be to inject into his wife's nuclear family of orientation the kind of sexual rivalry that all societies have found it necessary to prevent through incest taboos. To the mother-in-law he would seem analogous both to a son who is having intercourse with his sister and to a husband who has seduced his daughter. To the wife he would seem symbolically like a brother who is having incestuous relations with both her and her mother at the same time. The sex taboo between man and mother-in-law probably thus derives from an exaggeration of the same forces which have everywhere produced intra-family incest taboos [27] (see Chapter 10), and the widespread prevalence of mother-in-law avoidance is readily understandable as a social device to prevent violations. Identical factors in reverse presumably explain avoidance and reserve between a father-in-law and his son's wife, which are only slightly less general than mother-in-law taboos.

For each of the several groups of relatives hitherto considered, a single fairly simple explanation accounts satisfactorily for the patterns of kinship behavior found all over the world. The essential conditions determining them are practically identical everywhere. They are, in short, the universal ones of the nuclear human family, which Freud took as the basis for his psychology. We now come to a series of relatives for whom the conditions underlying kinship behavior differ significantly from society to society. In nearly all of them, it will be noted, the patterned norms reported run the full gamut from avoidance to license. Discrimination with respect to social situations becomes imperative if sense is to be made of such variations.

Relations with FaSi offer a case in point. Five of the six cases of avoidance and eight of the cases of respect occur in tribes allowing cross-cousin marriage with FaSiDa. They are thus attributable to the fact that the paternal aunt in these societies tends to be the same person as the mother-in-law and is consequently treated like the latter. Moreover, six of the nine instances of joking are found in tribes, five of them matrilineal, which also prescribe joking toward the non-marriageable FaSiDa, suggesting that this type of behavior is matrilineally transmitted as a feature of the reciprocal interaction

[27] This is essentially the interpretation reached in B. Z. Seligman, "Incest and Descent," *Journal of the Royal Anthropological Institute*, LIX (1929), 255, 269.

with women of the father's matrilineal descent line. If these 19 cases are eliminated from our tabulation, the distribution of patterned reactions toward FaSi approximates fairly closely those with MoSi and is presumably due to similar causes.

In the case of MoBrWi, similarly, at least four and perhaps six of the seven instances of avoidance and three of respect occur in conjunction with cross-cousin marriage with MoBrDa, which would equate MoBrWi with WiMo and produce comparable behavior. Moreover, in three of the five instances of joking the maternal uncle's wife is a potential levirate spouse, like BrWi, and is accorded similar treatment. With these special cases excluded, the distribution of behavior approximates that toward FaBrWi.

With reference to SiDa and WiBrDa, analysis of the data does not suggest any satisfactory explanation for the wide scatter of patterned behavior. The two kin-types show a similar distribution and presumably belong together. Both are equated with SoWi under cross-cousin marriage; this may account for several instances of avoidance and respect behavior, but it only differentiates both relatives still further from BrDa and WiSiDa. Joking is unusually prevalent in both instances, but it occurs in tribes so diverse in social structure as to offer no obvious clues toward an interpretation. In the absence of factual support we will refrain from theorizing.[28]

Patterned behavior toward siblings-in-law of opposite sex appears to depend almost exclusively upon whether or not preferential mating with such relatives is prescribed. All of the instances of license with WiSi and BrWi, and all except an average of three instances of joking with each, occur in the presence of preferential sororate or levirate usages respectively.[29] The higher incidence of joking with WiYoSi and ElBrWi merely reflects the preference for junior sororate or junior levirate. If all instances of preferential mating with siblings-in-law are eliminated from our tabulation, the

[28] For the reader who may wish to tackle this problem for himself, our tribes with data on behavior toward WiBrDa are: (with avoidance) Ashanti, Wichita; (with respect) Trukese; (with informality) Acholi, Chiricahua, Dobuans, Kwoma, Miwok, Murngin, Yankee; (with joking) Cheyenne, Kiowa Apache, Tenino, Thonga; (with license) Fox. Evidence on behavior toward SiDa is more widely available.

[29] Cf. C. S. Brant, "On Joking Relationships," *American Anthropologist*, n.s., L (1948), 160–2.

remaining distribution of behavior patterns is almost identical with that for sisters and parallel cousins.

True license is confined almost exclusively to siblings-in-law who are potential secondary spouses. Moreover, the joking associated with these relatives is qualitatively different from that manifested toward grandparents and grandchildren of opposite sex, being commonly of a rougher and more compulsive nature. Both joking and license nearly always include a degree of physical contact and of coarse or sexual humor which would be considered highly indecent with any other relative of opposite sex. The relative with whom one jokes or engages in wrestling or horseplay is not merely a potential future spouse but usually also a currently accessible sex partner. Of the tribes which prescribe joking or license toward WiSi or BrWi, evidence on premarital and extramarital relations is available for nearly half. With the exception of BrWi among the Thonga and ElBrWi among the Ngizim, both premarital and extramarital relations are fully or conditionally permitted with the sister-in-law in every instance.

Under such circumstances several factors conspire to encourage excessive familiarity and coarse jesting. Since the sister-in-law is a permissible sex object, such behavior is not inhibited by social sanctions. It provides not only substitutive gratification in itself but also an opportunity for making actual erotic overtures or arranging assignations. Nor should one lose sight of the fact that, even though sexual intercourse is permitted between the pair, the primary sex object is in one case the man's own wife and in the other the woman's own husband. In consequence, relations between them are likely to be only semi-sanctioned, or to be dependent upon circumstances, or to be subject, so to speak, to a higher priority. In any case, physical expression is likely to suffer frustration, and the resulting aggression will tend to be directed, at least unconsciously, toward the primary obstacle, the intervening spouse. Public joking and license provide a socially acceptable channel for expressing such aggression along with sexual impulses, and this may well account for the rough and compulsive nature of the behavior.

Under preferential cross-cousin marriage, every FaSiDa and/or MoBrDa whom Ego does not himself marry is likely to be or become a sister-in-law, and thus to be subject to joking or license where these forms of behavior are exhibited toward WiSi or BrWi. When the societies which practice cross-cousin marriage are excluded from our tabulation, a majority of the cases of joking and license with FaSiDa and MoBrDa disappear, and the distribution of patterned behavior in the remaining instances parallels very closely that reported for parallel cousins and is presumably explicable on similar grounds.

If the foregoing analysis of patterned kinship behavior is valid, it demonstrates that attitudes and reaction tendencies succumb as readily to scientific investigation as do the structured forms of social organization. Here, too, order and conformity to law prove to be as characteristic of cultural phenomena as they are of the data with which the natural sciences deal. Our findings suggest that a high degree of precision and predictability is possible in the social sciences, and that allegations of indeterminacy, complaints about undue complexity, and special pleading for intuitive methods are as unwarranted in anthropology, psychology, and sociology as they are in physics, chemistry, and biology.

10

INCEST TABOOS AND THEIR EXTENSIONS

THE AIM of the present chapter is to formulate and test an hypothesis explanatory of the prohibitory regulations of the sex drive that have a kinship basis. Like permissive and obligatory regulations associated with particular kin-types, they appear to be grounded in the constitution of the nuclear family. Privileged relationships and preferential mating were shown in Chapter 9 to be derived by extension from the sanctioned sex relations of married spouses. Similarly, incest taboos and exogamous restrictions of whatsoever sort seem clearly to be extensions of the sex taboos between parent and child and between brother and sister in the nuclear family. The universality and importance of incest taboos were noted in Chapter 1. Their origin and function, however, still require explanation.

An acceptable theory of incest taboos and their varying incidence in different societies must, in the first place, be consistent with the known facts and, in the second, provide a satisfactory explanation for all or most of them. A consideration of existing theories will therefore be postponed until the most important empirical conclusions of the present study have been set forth. These are eight in number.

Our first conclusion is that, with the exception of married parents, incest taboos apply universally to all persons of opposite sex within the nuclear family. The data from our 250 societies, as summarized in Chapter 1, reveal not a single instance in which sexual intercourse or marriage is generally permissible between mother and son, father and daughter, or brother and sister. Aside from a few rare and highly restricted exceptions, there is complete universality in this respect.

A second factual conclusion is that incest taboos do not apply universally to any relative of opposite sex outside of the nuclear family. Though nowhere may a man marry his mother, his sister, or his daughter, he may contract matrimony with any other female relative in at least some of the societies surveyed for the present work. To give but a few examples, he may marry his paternal aunt among the Marquesans and Yaruro, his maternal aunt among the Osset and Sema, his half sister by the same mother among the Lakher and Mentaweians, his half sister by the same father among the Edo and Minangkabau, either parallel cousin (FaBrDa or MoSiDa) among the Balinese and Chukchee, his sororal niece among the Carib and Keraki, and his fraternal niece among the Haida and Kababish.

While anthropologists usually record marriage rules in full, comparatively few of them give adequate data on the restrictions and permissions governing sex relations between specific relatives outside of marriage. Even the fragmentary evidence, however, is conclusive. The Kiowa Apache and numerous other tribes allow complete sexual freedom between a man and his sister-in-law. The Shilluk wink at affairs with a stepmother, and the Baiga at those with a maternal aunt, while the Trobrianders positively encourage them with a paternal aunt. A Marquesan may cohabit with his mother-in-law or his daughter-in-law in the absence of his wife. The Tupinamba permit sex relations with a sororal niece, the Kaingang with a fraternal niece, the Bari with the mother's brother's wife, the Lepcha with the father's brother's wife. There is, in short, no relative outside of the nuclear family with whom intercourse or marriage is not allowed in at least one of our 250 societies. Table 80 summarizes the evidence for aunts, nieces, and first cousins.

A third empirical conclusion from our survey is that incest taboos are never confined exclusively to the nuclear family. Universally they apply to at least some secondary and tertiary relatives. Even the Kaingang of Brazil, who come closest to constituting an excep-

TABLE 80

	Premarital Intercourse		Marriage	
Relative	Forbidden or Disapproved	Conditionally or Freely Permitted	Forbidden or Disapproved	Conditionally or Freely Permitted
FaSi	63	2	181	5
MoSi	58	1	167	3
FaBrDa	75	1	205	10
FaSiDa	38	11	136	65
MoBrDa	37	14	122	79
MoSiDa	69	1	185	13
BrDa	60	1	170	4
SiDa	51	2	151	8

tion, refrain from marrying a son's wife and rarely wed a half sister. Of the societies in our sample, 232 extend incest taboos to embrace one or more first cousins, whereas only 8 do not, and two of the latter, including the Yankees, disapprove of unions between first cousins.

Our fourth conclusion is that incest taboos tend to apply with diminished intensity to kinsmen outside of the nuclear family, even though they are designated by the same kinship terms as primary relatives. From the point of view of a male Ego, the prohibitions against sexual intercourse and marriage with an own mother, sister, and daughter are the strongest of all incest taboos. Other relatives may fall under an equally severe ban, but analysis of our data reveals no instance where a relative outside the nuclear family is more stringently tabooed than one within it. The reverse, however, is often the case. Of the handful of ethnographers who give adequate information on the differential intensity of incest taboos, all report for their respective tribes that, for example, the taboos apply more strongly to own than to "classificatory" sisters, to half sisters than to cousins, to first than to second or remoter cousins, and so on. It must not be assumed, however, that the diminution in intensity is the same in all directions, for inequality in this respect is the rule.

A fifth conclusion is that incest taboos, in their application to persons outside of the nuclear family, fail strikingly to coincide with nearness of actual biological relationship. Regulations vary widely in different cultures; relatives with whom intercourse and marriage

are strictly forbidden in one society are often privileged or preferred mates in another. Even within the same society, taboos frequently apply to certain distant relatives but not to other kinsmen
who are genealogically closer. In approximately one fourth of our
tribes, for example, certain second cousins are subject to rigid
marital prohibitions while first cousins of particular types are
allowed or even encouraged to marry. Very commonly, in fact,
incest taboos exempt certain close consanguineal kinsmen but apply
to adoptive, affinal, or ceremonial relatives with whom no biological
kinship can be traced. The controversy over marriage with a deceased wife's sister, which shook Victorian England, shows that
such inconsistencies are not confined to primitive cultures. The rules
governing marriages with first cousins will serve as a test case. Since
the daughters of the father's brother, father's sister, mother's brother,
and mother's sister are consanguineally related to a male Ego in
exactly the same degree, all intra-cultural differences in marriage
regulations applying to the several types of cousins represent
divergences from biological expectations. As compiled in Table 81,
such differences are found to be numerous.

TABLE 81

Pairs of Cousins	Similar Marriage Regulations	Variant Marriage Regulations	Opposite Marriage Regulations
FaBrDa-FaSiDa	124	10	47
FaBrDa-MoBrDa	113	10	56
FaBrDa-MoSiDa	161	4	11
FaSiDa-MoBrDa	156	15	19
FaSiDa-MoSiDa	125	6	47
MoBrDa-MoSiDa	119	7	49

A sixth conclusion is that incest taboos are highly correlated with
purely conventional groupings of kinsmen. They tend to apply, for
example, to all relatives called by a classificatory kinship term which
includes sexually tabooed primary relatives. A survey of the terms
used for secondary and tertiary relatives of Ego's generation in the
250 sample societies reveals that in 441 cases they are designated
by terms that are also applied to either mother, sister, or daughter,
and that in 971 instances they are called by other terms. In the
former group, incest taboos apply to 417 and do not apply to 24; in

the latter, they apply to 351 and do not apply to 620. The tendency of incest taboos to be associated with those relatives who are called "mother," "sister," or "daughter" is expressed by a coefficient of association of $+.94$, reliable at the maximal level of one tenth of one per cent. Incest taboos also tend to be coextensive with membership in consanguineal kin groups. Sibs will serve as an example. Out of 161 of the sample societies possessing true sibs, incest taboos apply to all sib members in 129, and in 24 others there is a tendency toward exogamy; six societies have non-exogamous sibs, and evidence is lacking in two cases. Abundant additional data will be presented elsewhere in this chapter.

A seventh conclusion is that incest taboos and exogamous restrictions, as compared with other sexual prohibitions, are characterized by a peculiar intensity and emotional quality. Among other sexual prohibitions, only menstrual taboos exhibit the same characteristic at all frequently, and they by no means universally. In none of the societies surveyed, we believe, do taboos against adultery or fornication exceed in strength the strictest incest taboos prevalent in the same society, and rarely if ever do they equal or even approach the latter in intensity. The foregoing statement, of course, involves a qualitative judgment and is not easily susceptible to proof, but it is believed that any impartial reader of the ethnographic evidence will be forced to the same conclusion. Again and again there will be brought home to him something of the sense of grisly horror with which most peoples invest the very idea of incest. He will be impressed by the frequency of an invariable death penalty for this breach of the mores. Even more convincing, however, is the fact that there is often no legal sanction at all; the taboo is so strongly internalized, the idea is so deeply repressed, that the act is considered simply unthinkable, and, if it occurs, is attributed to supernatural intervention and its punishment left exclusively to inexorable fate or divine vengeance. The emotional quality attaching to prohibitions of fornication and adultery is usually quite different. Any male in our own society can sense this for himself by fantasying an intrigue with his secretary or a business associate's wife on the one hand and an amour with his own mother or sister on the other.

Our eighth and last empirical conclusion is that violations of incest taboos do occur. Despite the strength of cultural barriers and their internalization in the consciences of individuals, sporadic instances of incestuous intercourse are reported in most of our sample societies for which ethnographers have investigated the subject. There is, of course, abundant clinical and criminological evidence of the actual occurrence of incest in our own and related societies.[1] It is clear, therefore, that close relatives enjoy no natural immunity to the sex drive, and that even the strongest of cultural restraints are only imperfectly successful.

No theory of the regulation of incest can be regarded as valid unless it is consistent with all the foregoing factual conclusions, nor as satisfactory unless it accounts for all of them. Several of the more widely accepted hypotheses may be subjected to analysis from this point of view. No attention will be paid to the numerous bizarre theories on the subject.[2]

A theory commonly advanced by earlier writers attributes incest taboos to the intelligent recognition by primitive man of the biological dangers of close inbreeding. Ethnography, however, gives little evidence of a precise knowledge of the reproductive process or of the principles of heredity among simple peoples. It is particularly hard to understand, for example, how a tribe ignorant of the very fact of physical paternity, like the Arunta or the Trobrianders, could have arrived at prohibitions on such a basis. Moreover, the theory does not account for the peculiar intensity of incest taboos. The violation of other biologically protective taboos is normally associated with a sense, not of horror but of anxiety or fear. The theory is quite inconsistent with our fifth empirical conclusion. If incest taboos spring from rational biological knowledge, why do they fail so strikingly to correlate with nearness of actual relationship? Often, in fact, they do not prevent inbreeding but positively encourage it, as when they result in a preference for

---

[1] Cf. A. T. Bingham, *Determinants of Sex Delinquency in Adolescent Girls* (New York, 1923), pp. 34–41; L. J. Doshay, *The Boy Offender and His Later Career* (New York, 1943), pp. 77, 149; A. C. Kinsey, W. B. Pomeroy, and C. E. Martin, *Sexual Behavior in the Human Male* (Philadelphia, 1948), p. 558; S. Riemer, "A Research Note on Incest," *American Journal of Sociology*, XLV (1940), 566–75; J. B. Tomkins, "Penis Envy and Incest," *Psychoanalytic Review*, XXVII (1940), 319.

[2] For example, Lord Raglan, in *Jocasta's Crime* (London, 1933), derives all incest taboos from "a very ancient magical belief that it is dangerous to have intercourse with a woman who lives on the same side of the stream" (p. 191).

marriage with a first cousin. When this is the case, as with 56 of our sample societies, extreme inbreeding may actually coexist with strong incest taboos.

Modern developments in the science of genetics, finally, cast serious doubt on the assumption of the biological harm of close inbreeding itself. Recessive traits come to light, or are emphasized, in the offspring of near relatives. If such traits are undesirable, inbreeding is harmful. If, however, they are desirable, as is equally possible, inbreeding may be positively advantageous, and it is often, in fact, purposely practiced by animal breeders. In itself, inbreeding seems to be neither good nor bad; its results depend exclusively on the particular hereditary qualities resident in the stock. If the alleged biological harm of inbreeding is not a fact, then primitive peoples could not have discovered or recognized it, and the theory of incest avoidance based on this assumption can have no validity.[3]

A second theory, accepted at one time by Lowie,[4] attributes incest prohibitions to instinct. Though perhaps consistent with the universal application of incest taboos within the nuclear family, and with their diminution in intensity outside thereof, this view fails to account for or even to harmonize with the other empirical conclusions. If it were instinctive, the avoidance of incest would be automatic. There would be no horror of an impulse not felt and no clinical and criminological evidence of incestuous desires and acts.[5] The diversity of incest taboos, their lack of correlation with actual consanguinity, and their agreement with cultural categories seem impossible to explain by an instinctive principle alone, and when other factors are introduced to account for them the need of invoking an instinct vanishes. The fallacy of attributing highly variable social phenomena to relatively stable biological factors is today generally recognized, and instinctivist interpretations are no longer admissible in any of the sciences dealing with human behavior.[6]

[3] See W. G. Sumner and A. G. Keller, *The Science of Society* (New Haven, 1927), III, 1571–94, for an extended argument against this theory of incest taboos and for references to the relevant authorities.

[4] R. H. Lowie, *Primitive Society* (New York, 1920), pp. 15, 105. This view was subsequently retracted in R. H. Lowie, "The Family as a Social Unit," *Papers of the Michigan Academy of Sciences*, XVIII (1933), 67.

[5] Cf. R. Fortune, "Incest," *Encyclopaedia of the Social Sciences*, VI (1932), 620.

[6] Cf. L. L. Bernard, *Instinct* (New York, 1924).

Westermarck rejects the instinctive theory and regards prohibitions of incest as habits formed during childhood—a position fully consistent with the varied application and cultural diversity of incest taboos. He goes further than this, however, and maintains that these habits of avoidance result from the dulling of the sexual appetite through prolonged association.[7] One feels no erotic attraction, he alleges, for a person of opposite sex with whom one has grown up in the same household from childhood. This theory does not explain the wider extensions of incest taboos. It does not harmonize with the not infrequent ethnographic cases where marriage with a housemate is actually favored; among the Angmagsalik, for example, "it is by no means uncommon for children who have been brought up together to marry."[8] It is inconsistent with the widespread preference for levirate and sororate unions, which often involve members of the same extended family. It is contradicted by the enduring attachments between husband and wife which occur in most societies, for instead of these it would lead us to expect sexual indifference and ultimate aversion as the normal result of marital cohabitation. Above all, the theory flagrantly overlooks, and even inverts, the vast body of clinical evidence which shows that incestuous desires are regularly engendered within the nuclear family and are kept in restraint only through persistent social pressure and individual repression.

The only other theory of the origin of incest taboos which deserves serious consideration is that of Freud.[9] Like Westermarck, Freud believes that such taboos are learned or acquired rather than innate or instinctive. They have their genesis in the universal conditions of the nuclear family—in the Œdipus situation, to use Freud's term. The child's infantile sexual attraction to the parent of opposite sex encounters frustrations and rebuffs from parents and rival siblings as an inevitable consequence of the conditions of family life. Ambivalence is generated, and the impulse is repressed. Though no

---

[7] E. Westermarck, *The History of Human Marriage* (5th edit., New York, 1922), II, 192. This view is also adopted in H. Ellis, *Psychology of Sex* (London, 1934), p. 80.

[8] G. Holm, "Ethnological Sketch of the Angmagsalik Eskimo," *Meddelelser om Grønland*, XXXIX (1914), 65.

[9] For an extended exposition see S. Freud, *A General Introduction to Psychoanalysis* (Garden City, 1938), pp. 186–7, 291–6.

longer consciously acknowledged, the impulse is by no means annihilated, and its expression must be curbed by unconscious mechanisms. The emotional intensity of incest taboos and the horror associated with the idea of their violation are thus interpreted as normal "reaction formations" to a repressed impulse, as unconscious defenses against genuine temptation.

In addition to accounting for the emotional quality of incest taboos, Freud's theory explains the universality of incest avoidance by relating it to a universal condition of human social life, the nuclear family. It does not, however, account for the extension of such taboos beyond the immediate family nor for their diverse application in different societies. It does not even suggest why they are so regularly a part of culture. Many if not most Freudian mechanisms and their products, e.g., regression, the displacement of aggression, projection, and sadistic behavior, are ordinarily opposed or at best barely tolerated by culture. Incest avoidance, on the other hand, universally receives the approval of society and is specifically incorporated everywhere in sanctioned cultural norms. Though helpful, Freudian theory alone is incapable of accounting for the facts revealed by ethnographers. Moreover, without detracting in the slightest from Freud's extraordinary insight into individual psychology or from his revolutionary contributions in this field, we must admit that his ventures into cultural theory are little short of fantastic.

No unitary theory of incest taboos appears capable of accounting for all aspects of the phenomenon of incest prohibitions. For a satisfactory interpretation it is necessary to draw upon the scientific contributions of several disciplines which have concerned themselves with human behavior. A full explanation, indeed, requires a synthesis of the products of no fewer than four distinct fields of scientific endeavor, namely, psychoanalysis, sociology, cultural anthropology, and behavioristic psychology. When specific contributions from all four of these disciplines are put together, a complete and adequate theory emerges. When any one of the four essential elements is omitted, however, the phenomenon remains mysterious and unexplained. In other words, a satisfactory theory of incest taboos has had to await the recent development of interdisciplinary and integrative research in the several sciences that deal with human behavior.

Freud's theory, as previously suggested, provides the only available explanation of the peculiar emotional intensity of incest taboos. Also, by starting with conditions that are universal, i.e., those prevailing within the nuclear family, it accounts for the occurrence in all societies of tendencies in individual behavior which cultures can seize upon and institutionalize. While it does not help us to understand why all cultures have done this, it does provide a basis for assuming that all peoples have the essential behavioral ingredients out of which taboos can be fashioned. Without the contribution of Freud, the universality of incest prohibitions would be incomprehensible. If they depended upon the chance appearance of particular constellations of behavior, or upon local circumstances, they should be no more widespread than, for example, cannibalism, the potlatch, or the couvade.

Explanation must begin with the conditions in the nuclear family which generate incest avoidance habits in the developing child. These habits must be conceived as, at first, merely the products of individual learning, not yet socially sanctioned or culturally patterned. What are the circumstances that lead the maturing child to inhibit the direct expression of his sex drive within the family?

Every normal infant will inevitably develop approach tendencies toward his parents and elder siblings in consequence of the nourishment, care, and manifold other gratifications which they provide him. Without committing ourselves to Freud's position on infantile sexuality, we must nevertheless admit that many of the approach responses which a child learns to make toward the parent or sibling of opposite sex will, through accident or imitation, resemble sexual responses and be so interpreted by adults. As sex typing is learned and maturation proceeds, these approaches will tend to be more and more specifically sexual and to be strengthened by generalization from other reinforced responses. Unless extinguished or inhibited, they would prepare the child for fully genital incestuous intercourse at the onset of puberty.

Inevitably, however, the sexual responses of children within the family encounter discouragement. The preoccupation of the parents with one another, with other children, and with various adult activities results necessarily in rebuffs to the child's approach responses, and these frustrations become more frequent with increasing age and self-sufficiency. Moreover, inhibitions acquired during the inculcation of cleanliness, temper control, and other cultural restraints doubtless generalize in some measure to the sex impulse. Most important of all, however, are the punishments which the child receives from other members of the family, and later from the community, when he exhibits approach responses toward parent or sibling of opposite sex that are interpreted as sexual. In consequence of frequent rebuffs, frustrations, and punishments he learns to inhibit his incest strivings, to repress them, and to subject them to the rein of a strong internalized restraint.

The crucial factor in the development of incest avoidance in the child is the discouraging attitude and punitive behavior of its parents. The father, as a sexually experienced adult, will feel an attraction toward his daughter in which there will necessarily be a specifically erotic component, unconscious and repressed if not acknowledged, and the mother will feel similarly drawn to her son. As socialized beings with internalized restraints, both parents will experience anxiety over these attachments and will therefore tend to curb any overt expression in both themselves and their children. Moreover, the mother's attachment to her son will constitute a threat, symbolic if not real, to the father and to his relationship with her. Any overtly sexual manifestation thereof will constitute a frustration to him, will arouse his aggression in the form of jealousy,[10] and will prompt him to take retaliatory measures which will have an inhibiting influence upon both mother and son. In like fashion a mother will resent and seek to thwart any unduly intimate behavior between father and daughter. Erotic approaches between son and daughter, furthermore, will threaten the unconscious attachments of both parents to their children of opposite sex and will similarly evoke resentment and punishment. The very structure of the family, in short, favors the individual learning of sexual restraint in all primary relationships except that between husband and wife, even in the absence of a specific cultural taboo.

Such tendencies, recurring in numerous individual instances, are, moreover, certain to receive the sanction and support of society. Freudian theory fails us at this point, and we must turn to social

[10] Cf. G. B. Vetter, "The Incest Taboos," *Journal of Abnormal and Social Psychology*, XXIII (1928), 232–40.

science for assistance. There are cogent sociological reasons why human societies lend their support to the observance and inculcation of incest avoidance within the nuclear family, and why they universally elevate these tendencies to cultural norms and invest them with social sanctions. Over and above the fact that their members have themselves been socialized, have thus acquired an abhorrence of incest, and are consequently motivated to discourage and punish it, the prohibitions themselves have genuine social value.

The family, as was seen in Chapter 1, subserves a number of important societal needs—economic cooperation, reproduction, education, and socialization—and no society has discovered another means as satisfactory in fulfilling them. Anything that weakens the family, therefore, weakens the body politic by stifling cooperation, lowering reproduction, raising the infant mortality rate, or increasing the proportion of incapable and undersocialized or criminal members. Conflict within the family is a source of weakness, as is abundantly demonstrated by the current sociological literature on family disorganization. No form of conflict is more disruptive than sexual competition and jealousy. The reduction of sexual rivalry between parents and children and between siblings consolidates the family as a cooperative social group, promotes the efficiency of its societal services, and thus strengthens the society as a whole.

Moreover, as Brenda Seligman [11] has pointed out, sex relationships between parent and child would destroy the authority of the former, so necessary both to social order and to the transmission of culture. Renunciation of incest, on the other hand, makes possible the continued cooperation of adolescent and adult children with their parents and one another, and promotes social unity by removing sources of rivalry. Societal advantage thus supplements individual self-interest and assures that sexual restraints within the family will become culturally normative and be supported by the various mechanisms of social control.

The social advantages of incest taboos are doubtless in part consciously perceived, as modern Europeans are aware of the dangers of rising divorce and declining birth rates, and to this extent societal enforcement of family mores, including incest taboos, may be re-

[11] B. Z. Seligman, "Incest and Descent," *Journal of the Royal Anthropological Institute*, LIX (1929), 243–5.

garded as rational. But whether or not they are consciously perceived, the advantages nevertheless become effective. Those societies
which do not, through irrational as well as rational beliefs and
practices, succeed in reducing intra-family conflicts to a level that
will not interfere with the satisfactory performance of the family's
societal services, will tend over time to decline and disappear in
their competition with others. Presumably only those societies that
have solved this problem in the one obvious and satisfactory manner,
namely, through incest taboos, have survived to be studied by
modern ethnographers.[12] Irrespective, then, of their possible but
dubious biological value, incest prohibitions have a social value of
such unquestionable importance as to account for their presence
in all known cultures and for their enforcement by all known
societies.

A powerful additional advantage of incest taboos from the stand-
point of societal survival is somewhat less obvious. Every family is
a distinct social group and as such has its distinct culture.[13] Even
though its members share an overwhelming proportion of their
collective habits with individuals in other families throughout the
society, they always have at least a few habits characteristic of
themselves alone. Even in a modern American family there are
usually a few home remedies, cooking recipes, minor technological
skills, private superstitions, and divers other bits of standardized
behavior which its members share with one another but not with
outsiders. Petty inventions often gain their first social acceptance
within the family. Incest taboos, by compelling marriage outside
of the family, result automatically in the diffusion of such elements
of culture. Every child grows up in a group which combines two
family cultures—those of the families of orientation of the father
and the mother—and which forms its own family culture by selection
of the most advantageous elements from both sources as well as by
borrowing and invention. Incest taboos thus promote the cultural
processes of internal diffusion and selective elimination, and a society
possessing them, other things being equal, will progress more rapidly

[12] Cf. B. Z. Seligman, "Incest and Descent," *Journal of the Royal Anthropological Institute*, LIX (1929), 239.
[13] Cf. J. M. Roberts, *The Navaho Household* (unpublished doctoral dissertation, Yale University).

and become culturally better equipped than one which lacks them.[14]

In the absence of incest taboos, many if not most marriages would take place between brothers and sisters or between parents and adult children. Under such circumstances, intra-group diffusion would operate more slowly and differences in family cultures would grow increasingly pronounced with the passage of time. Since cultural differences promote ethnocentrism and militate against social cohesion, societies practicing incestuous marriages would be less capable than others of developing unity and cooperation in crises and would thus be more likely to be destroyed or absorbed by their rivals. Intermarriage, on the other hand, promotes social solidarity. European history gives repeated examples of the cementing of international alliances by dynastic marriages. What occurs on a grand scale also happens in miniature. Through intermarriage, families establish new bonds of relationship and cooperation which increase the cohesion and strength of the entire society and lead to still further cultural cross-fertilization and progress.

Whatever their biological value, the social advantages of incest taboos are enormous. They suffice to fix and perpetuate restrictions on intra-family sexuality wherever these appear. Since Freudian principles assure their appearance in all societies, incest taboos are universal. The recognized principles governing individual behavior and cultural change are quite sufficient to account for this universality without invoking dubious new hypotheses of primitive rationality, instinctive horror, or sexual indifference through habituation.

Though psychoanalytic and sociological theory, in combination, account satisfactorily for the universal appearance of incest avoidance tendencies and for their establishment as socially sanctioned taboos within the nuclear family in all known societies, they provide no explanation of why incest taboos are so regularly associated with secondary and remoter relatives or why their incidence among such relatives is so extraordinarily diverse in different societies. For an understanding of the reasons for the extension of incest taboos it is necessary to turn to other bodies of social science theory.

[14] Cf. W. G. Sumner and A. G. Keller, *The Science of Society* (New Haven, 1927), III, 1617-20.

The tendency for incest taboos to be extended beyond the nuclear family is explained by the principle of "stimulus generalization" from behavioristic psychology.[15] According to this principle, any habitual response, learned in connection with one stimulus or situational configuration, will tend to be evoked by other stimuli or situations in proportion to their similarity to the former. To the extent, therefore, that any secondary or remoter relative resembles a sexually tabooed member of the nuclear family, the avoidance behavior will tend to be extended to him. The mother's sister, for example, is likely to resemble the mother in many respects. They belong to the same generation, and as full siblings are likely to possess similar features and other physical traits. They commonly belong to the same social groups. Thus both have the same family of orientation and belong to the same consanguineal kin groups, whether kindred, lineage, sib, or moiety. Under matrilocal residence or sororal polygyny they are likely to be housemates and members of the same larger family group. Where the sororate prevails, the mother's sister may at any time assume the actual role of mother. Very frequently, as we have already seen, the same kinship term is applied to the two women, and similar patterned behavior is exhibited toward both. In view of such far-reaching similarities it should occasion no surprise that the incest taboo universally associated with a man's own mother is widely extended to her sister as well.

Psychological behavior theory, however, merely accounts for the tendency for incest taboos to be generalized to relatives outside of the nuclear family and provides the mechanism by which such extension can take place. It cannot explain why extension occurs in some instances and not in others, in particular societies and not in all. For this we must draw upon the analysis of social structure which generations of cultural anthropologists have worked out. Anthropology alone can reveal the differential conditions under which extension does or does not take place. It alone can show what social usages and configurations create a degree of similarity between primary and other relatives sufficient to generalize incest taboos from the former to the latter, and what other social practices and forms establish differences adequate to inhibit generalization.

[15] Cf. C. L. Hull, *Principles of Behavior* (New York, 1943), pp. 183–203.

The anthropological principles necessary to supplement psychological theory and to account for the differential conditions under which learning mechanisms operate have already been set forth in Chapter 7.

A complete explanation is still not at hand. Even when we are given the psychological tendency to generalization and the cultural conditions that will facilitate it, generalized responses will not actually become established as social norms unless they are rewarded or reinforced. If they do not prove gratifying or useful, "discrimination" [16] will occur; the responses will be inhibited or extinguished, and will be replaced by behavior of a different kind. In short, though intra-family incest taboos may show an initial tendency to be extended to secondary and remoter kinsmen who significantly resemble some member of the nuclear family, this tendency will be counteracted and will not actually produce extended incest taboos or exogamous rules unless these have at least some measure of utility.

That extended incest taboos do commonly have genuine social utility has been recognized by both anthropologists [17] and sociologists.[18] The reasons run parallel to those already indicated for intrafamily incest taboos. Just as the latter curb sexual rivalries and jealousy within the family, so do the former within the kindred, lineage, sib, extended family, clan, or community. The unity or social solidarity of these groups is thereby enhanced, and the cooperation of their members in the performance of other functions is facilitated. Moreover, out-marriage makes possible the establishment of friendly relations between groups and helps to bind them together in larger political units, with a resultant competitve advantage over other societies which have not developed intra-group or intergroup bonds of this type. Finally, intermarriage and the resulting peaceful relations between groups foster the reciprocal borrowing of culture traits, promote the "cross-fertilization of cultures," and accelerate social adaptation and cultural progress. These

[16] Cf. C. L. Hull, *Principles of Behavior* (New York, 1943), p. 266.

[17] Cf. B. Z. Seligman, "Incest and Descent," *Journal of the Royal Anthropological Institute*, LIX (1929), 271-2; E. B. Tylor, "On a Method of Investigating the Development of Institutions," *Journal of the Royal Anthropological Institute*, XVIII (1889), 267-8.

[18] Cf. W. G. Sumner and A. G. Keller, *The Science of Society* (4 vols., New Haven, 1927), III, 1617-21.

advantages seem sufficient to account for the fixation of extended incest taboos as group norms in a large proportion of the instances where social structure favors psychological generalization.

It thus appears that a complete scientific explanation of incest taboos and exogamous rules emerges from a synthesis of the theories of four separate disciplines that deal with human behavior. Psychoanalytic theory accounts for the peculiar emotional quality of such taboos; for the occurrence of violations, which neither an instinct hypothesis nor Westermarck's theory of acquired aversion explains; for the diminished intensity of taboos outside of the nuclear family; and for the universal occurrence of incest avoidance tendencies which serve as a basis for cultural elaboration. Sociological theory demonstrates the social utility of both intra-family and extended incest taboos and thus accounts for their universality. Psychological behavior theory reveals the mechanism by which extension occurs and that by which social utility becomes translated into custom, thus supplying an essential part of the reasons for both the universality and the variety of extended taboos. Cultural anthropology, finally, contributes to our explanation the varied conditions of social structure and usage which channelize generalization or produce discrimination, and thus accounts for the differential incidence of exogamous rules and extended incest taboos, for their correlation with conventional groupings of kinsmen, and for their lack of correspondence with nearness of actual biological relationship.

Without any one of these four systems of social science theory an adequate explanation is impossible. All previous hypotheses concerning incest taboos have drawn upon only one or at most two of the relevant disciplines, and have thus failed to account for significant segments of observed fact. A reasonably complete interpretation has thus had to await the day when interdisciplinary knowledge and research in the social sciences had advanced to the point where the intellectual tools of four separate bodies of systematic theory could be brought to bear concurrently upon a single problem of human behavior. If we have succeeded, there is ground for hope that other hitherto insoluble problems of social science may yield to a comparable joint attack.

The portion of our composite hypothesis which concerns the reasons for the universality of intra-family incest taboos cannot be subjected to independent test by any methods at our disposal, since the very universality of both the taboos and the family organization with which they are associated deprives us of independent variables to correlate. The validity of this part of our interpretation thus rests only on such evidence as has been adduced by the psychoanalysts and sociologists upon whose theories we draw. The portion of our hypothesis which deals with the extension of incest taboos to relatives outside of the nuclear family, on the other hand, can be tested by the data from our 250 societies, since both the extensions and the conditions that are presumed to produce and fix them are variable.

Analysis of the principles governing the extension of incest taboos beyond the nuclear family should begin with consanguineal relatives. Here the causal factors are simple and readily demonstrated. In the case of affinal relatives, however, additional factors are involved, and consideration of them will therefore be deferred.

Extended incest taboos—or exogamous rules, as they are frequently called—ordinarily apply alike to sexual intercourse before marriage, to extramarital sex relations, and to marriage. In only a handful of our sample societies is their incidence for these three types of behavior reported to differ in any significant respect. In a few cases, premarital but not extramarital relations are permitted with particular relatives, and somewhat more frequently marriage is allowed although premarital and adulterous relations are forbidden. Identity in the three rules is so general, however, that the few exceptions can be safely disregarded in most statistical tests. This is fortunate since it enables us to use marriage rules, which are reported nearly thrice as often in the literature, as representative of all types of extended sexual prohibitions. Except in crucial tests, therefore, only data on marriage rules will be presented.

In nearly all the societies of our sample there is a preference for marrying within the same generation. Secondary marriages, to be sure, frequently occur between persons of different generations, and in a number of tribes even primary marriages across generation lines are fairly common. Only among the Lesu, however, are first marriages regularly of this type, the preferred spouse of a male Ego being the daughter of a female cross-cousin. The general preference for marriage on the same generation level simplifies the problem of analysis and demonstration, since it makes possible the adequate testing of hypotheses with the data for cousins of varying degrees.

Partly because of this generation preference and partly because of their close association and kinship with members of Ego's nuclear family, secondary consanguineal relatives like aunts, nieces, and half sisters are rarely eligible as spouses. In our entire sample, marriage is permitted with FaSi in only five societies, with MoSi in only three, with BrDa in four, with SiDa in eight, with FaDa and with MoDa in only three each. For none of these relatives is either premarital or extramarital intercourse reported as permissible in more than two societies. Significant differences between societies in the extension of incest taboos to consanguineal relatives begin, therefore, with first cousins.

Beyond secondary relatives, extensions of primary incest taboos differ in two respects—in direction and in distance. In direction they can take any of three different paths, which correspond closely with the three major rules of descent. Prohibitions can ramify symmetrically and equally along all lines of consanguineal connection like bilateral descent, or they can extend asymmetrically and unequally, like matrilineal or patrilineal descent, along consanguineal connections through one sex only. Our entire sample of 250 societies reveals not a single instance of a type of extension to cousins that is not symmetrically bilateral, asymmetrically patrilineal, asymmetrically matrilineal, or a combination of some two of these three. Deviations are rare and usually of a compromise character, as where a particular cross or parallel cousin is assimilated to one of the opposite instead of its own type.

With respect to the distance to which any of these three types of extension may be carried there are innumerable gradations, but analysis reveals four modal distances for each type. Combinations of the three directions with the four modal distances yield twelve classes of extensions, which may be numbered, named, and defined as follows:

B1. *Bilateral Non-Extension*—absence of any bilateral extension of marriage prohibitions beyond secondary relatives; marriage fully sanctioned with some or all first cousins.

B2. *Minimal Bilateral Extension*—marriage forbidden or disapproved with all first cousins but permitted with at least some second cousins.

B3. *Normal Bilateral Extension*—marriage forbidden or disapproved with all second cousins but allowed with at least some remote cousins with whom an actual genealogical connection can be traced.

B4. *Maximal Bilateral Extension*—marriage forbidden with any relative, however remote, with whom an actual genealogical connection can be traced in any line.

M1. *Matrilineal Non-Extension*—absence of any tendency to extend marriage prohibitions further in the female line than in any other.

M2. *Minimal Matrilineal Extension*—marriage prohibitions extended further in the female line than in at least some other, but not further than an actual genealogical connection can be traced.

M3. *Normal Matrilineal Extension*—marriage prohibitions extended matrilineally to sibmates or other persons with whom kinship is assumed but cannot be actually traced genealogically.

M4. *Maximal Matrilineal Extension*—marriage prohibitions extended to the actual or assumed matrilineal kinsmen of the father, as well as to those of Ego and his mother.

P1. *Patrilineal Non-Extension*—absence of any tendency to extend prohibitions further in the male line than in any other.

P2. *Minimal Patrilineal Extension*—prohibitions extended further in the male line than in some other, but not further than actual genealogical connections can be traced.

P3. *Normal Patrilineal Extension*—prohibitions extended patrilineally to sibmates or others with whom kinship is assumed but cannot be actually traced.

P4. *Maximal Patrilineal Extension*—prohibitions extended to the actual or assumed patrilineal kinsmen of the mother, as well as to those of Ego and his father.

The direction of the extension of incest taboos depends almost exclusively upon the presence, absence, or conjunction of particular types of consanguineal kin groups. The underlying principles are similar to those governing the extension of kinship terms from primary to secondary and remoter relatives, as demonstrated in the validation of Postulate 1 in Chapter 7. In the present instance, however, there is only one significant social equalizer, namely, participation in the same consanguineal kin group as a tabooed primary relative. Residential propinquity and other equalizers, though doubtless not without effect, are so overshadowed by the influence of kindreds, lineages, sibs, and moieties, that it is not even necessary to consider them.

The distance to which incest taboos are extended appears to be primarily a function of the time which has elapsed since the establishment of the kin groups that have channeled them. It is presumably also correlated with the functional significance of the kin groups in question and with the degree to which primary incest taboos have been internalized in the socialization process, but at least the former of these is also largely dependent upon the time factor.

The process of change is an adaptive or evolutionary one, beginning with an alteration in the structure of consanguineal kin groups. Owing usually to a change in the rule of residence, existing kin groups disappear or new types are evolved. Social similarities between particular secondary or remoter relatives and those to whom primary incest taboos apply are reduced or enhanced as former ties of kin group participation are lost or new ones develop, and tendencies toward exogamy wane or wax accordingly. Such change must in general be relatively rapid, for non-agreement between consanguineal kin groups and rules of exogamy occurs in remarkably few instances. The cases are just numerous enough, however, to indicate that exogamy is not an inherent aspect of kin group structure, and to demonstrate that the usual consistency between them is achieved only with the passage of finite periods of time.

Matrilineal extension of incest taboos follows inevitably after the introduction of matrilineal descent, patrilineal extension after the establishment of patrilineal descent. As time proceeds, exogamy encompasses first the lineage, then the sib, and ultimately the phratry or moiety. In this manner the unilinear kinsmen of Ego's mother and sister are brought under the exogamous taboos in matrilineal societies, and those of Ego's sister and daughter in patrilineal societies. The last phase of unilinear extension consists in generalizing also the father-daughter taboo under matrilineal descent and the mother-son taboo under patrilineal descent. This final step, producing maximal matrilineal or patrilineal extension respectively, is accomplished by applying the rule of exogamy to the father's matrilineal kinsmen under matrilineal descent or to the mother's patrilineal kinsmen under patrilineal descent, in addition to the members of Ego's own unilinear kin group.

Bilateral extension follows the establishment of bilateral kin groups. The mother-son, father-daughter, and brother-sister taboos are extended first throughout the kindred, then ultimately throughout the deme or to all known consanguineal relatives, or even in extreme instances, as among the Quinault, throughout the entire tribe. In the absence of any type of consanguineal kin group, either unilinear or bilateral, there is little tendency to extend primary incest taboos beyond secondary relatives; exogamy in any form is usually completely absent.

The statistical validation of these interpretations will follow a tabulation of the evidence from our 250 sample societies, presented for the benefit of specialists who may wish to check our information or may be in a position to correct it. With the aid of inferences in certain cases, it has proved possible to classify all of our sample societies according to the number, direction, and distance of their extensions of marriage prohibitions. Minimal bilateral extension in the presence of extensions of unilinear type is ignored in the classification, since in a majority of cases it is purely incidental. Thus it is produced almost automatically by the prohibition of cross-cousin marriage, which results inevitably from maximal unilinear extension and usually from Crow or Omaha terminology (because of the extension to cross-cousins of kinship terms for primary and/or secondary relatives). The classification is as follows:

Non-Extension (B1-M1-P1): Balinese, Buin, Carib, Chukchee, Inca, Kababish, Kaingang, Kallinago, Kurd, Macusi, Marquesans, Mentaweians, Nambikuara, Naskapi, Siriono, Tupinamba, Tswana, Walapai. Total: 18.

Bilateral Extension

Minimal (B2-M1-P1): Andamanese, Angmagsalik, Aymara, Cayapa, Comanche, Copper Eskimo, Futunans, Jukun, Kiowa Apache, Koryak, Kutenai, Kwakiutl, Lapps, Mangarevans, Maori, Mataco, Micmac, Paiute, Ruthenians, Sekani, Semang, Tarahumara, Tenino, Teton, Tewa, Washo, Wichita, Yankee. Total: 28.

Normal (B3-M1-P1): Atsugewi, Chiricahua, Cuna, Flathead, Havasupai, Hupa, Ifugao, Ingassana, Ona, Ontong-Javanese, Pawnee, Pima, Samoans, Shasta, Syrian Christians, Takelma, Taos, Tokelau, Tongans, Tubatulabal, Ulawans, Wintu, Yaghan. Total: 23.

Maximal (B4-M1-P1): Arapaho, Blackfoot, Cheyenne, Eddystone, Fox, Hawaiians, Klallam, Klamath, Nuba, Quinault, Shoshone, Sinkaietk, Wishram, Yurok. Total: 14.

Bilateral and Patrilineal Extension (with M1): Azande (B3-P4), Bari (B4-P4), Dinka (B3-P3), Eromangans (B3-P2), Ibo (B3-P2), Katab (B3-P3), Kickapoo (B3-P3), Lepcha (B3-P4), Mabuiag (B3-P3), Maricopa (B4-P3), Masai (B3-P2), Ojibwa (B3-P3), Omaha (B4-P4), Seniang (B4-P4), Shona (B3-P3), Soga (B3-P3), Tikopia (B3-P3), Xosa (B4-P3), Zulu (B4-P4). Total: 19.

Bilateral and Matrilineal Extension (with P1): Choctaw (B3-M3), Creek (B3-M4), Hopi (B3-M4), Kurtatchi (B3-M3), Pukapukans (B3-M2), Sherbro (B3-M3). Total: 6.

Matrilineal Extension

Minimal (M2-P1-B1 or B2): Longuda, Mandan, Mbundu, Twi. Total: 4.

Normal (M3-P1-B1 or B2): Apinaye, Arosi, Carrier, Chewa, Daka, Eyak, Getmatta, Haida, Ila, Iroquois, Kaska, Kongo, Kutchin, Lamba, Lesu, Marshallese, Minangkabau, Mota, Natchez, Nauruans, Nayar, Ndoro, Ramkokamekra, Rossel, Santa Cruz, Tetekantzi, Tismulun, Tlingit, Trobrianders, Tsimshian, Vedda, Yao, Yaruro, Yuchi. Total: 34.

Maximal (M4-P1-B2): Acoma, Cherokee, Cochiti, Crow, Dobuans, Jemez, Navaho, Trukese, Zuñi. Total: 9.

Matrilineal and Patrilineal Extension (with B1 or B2): Ashanti (M3-P3), Arunta (M3-P4), Bena (M2-P3), Dieri (M3-P3), Herero (M3-P3), Kamilaroi (M3-P3), Kariera (M3-P3), Manus (M2-P3), Murngin (M3-P4), Nankanse (M2-P4), Pentecost (M3-P3), Ranon (M3-P4), Shilluk (M2-P3), Tanala (M2-P2), Toda (M3-P3), Wogeo (M3-P2), Yako (M3-P3). Total: 17.

Patrilineal Extension

Minimal (P2-M1-B1 or B2): Arapesh, Araucanians, Bolewa, Chawai, Edo, Fijians, Kilba, Lakher, Manchu, Nandi, Tannese, Thonga, Venda, Wapisiana. Total: 14.

Normal (P3-M1-B1 or B2): Abelam, Acholi, Albanians, Angami, Ao, Awuna, Bachama, Baiga, Banaro, Batak, Bhuiya, Chenchu, Cherente, Chinese, Coorg, Dahomeans, Dorobo, Epi, Ganda, Gesu, Gilyak, Gond, Henga, Ho, Hottentot, Iatmul, Keraki, Koranko, Kyiga, Lenge, Lhota, Limba, Mailu, Malabu, Mendi, Mikir, Miwok, Ngizim, Orokaiva, Osset, Pedi, Reddi, Rengma, Sabei, Sema, Susu, Swazi, Tallensi, Thado, Timne, Tzeltal, Vai, Vanimo, Winnebago, Witoto, Yakut, Yuma. Total: 57.

Maximal (P4-M1-B2): Kitara, Kiwai, Kutubu, Kwoma, Lango, Luiseno, Miriam. Total: 7.

The hypothesis that the direction of the extension of incest taboos is determined primarily by the presence of consanguineal kin groups is readily validated in the case of unilinear descent. Table 82 shows that matrilineal extension is strongly associated with the presence of matrilineal kin groups, patrilineal extension with patrilineal kin groups, and extension in both directions with the presence of double descent. The relationship is measured in each instance by a maximally reliable coefficient of association of $+ .99$. The extreme magni-

TABLE 82

Exogamous Extensions and Unilinear Kin Groups	Number of Societies
Matrilineal Extension	
Present, matrilineal kin groups being present	67
Present, matrilineal kin groups being absent	3
Absent, matrilineal kin groups being present	4
Absent, matrilineal kin groups being absent	176
Statistical indices: $Q + .99$; χ^2 1000	
Patrilineal Extension	
Present, patrilineal kin groups being present	113
Present, patrilineal kin groups being absent	3
Absent, patrilineal kin groups being present	14
Absent, patrilineal kin groups being absent	120
Statistical indices: $Q + .99$; χ^2 1000	
Matrilineal and Patrilineal Extension	
Both present, double descent being present	15
Both present, double descent being absent	3
Either or both absent, double descent being present	5
Either or both absent, double descent being absent	227
Statistical indices: $Q + .99$; χ^2 1000	

tude in the statistical indices is attained, it should be noted, despite the fact that every doubtful case has been construed negatively. Thus the religious moieties of the Longuda, the political and ceremonial moieties of the Yuchi, and the descent groups of the Washo which oppose one another in games have been classed as patrilineal kin groups, and the matrilineally inherited totems of the Buin as matri-lineages. The demonstration is so overwhelming that further evidence need not be adduced.

The dependence of bilateral extension upon the presence of bilateral kin groups cannot be demonstrated quite so conclusively, since the incompleteness of the ethnographic coverage in the case of kindreds necessitates using unreported instances rather than reported absences as negative cases. Despite the fact that this might be expected seriously to reduce the magnitude of coefficients, the compilation of data in Table 83 still shows that bilateral extension is associated with the presence of kindreds, and non-extension with the absence or unreported presence of all consanguineal kin groups, by maximally reliable coefficients of association of approximately the magnitude of $+.80$. The role of kindreds in producing bilateral extension, even in unilinear societies, is strikingly instanced by the Hopi, Kurtatchi, Ojibwa, Pukapukans, and Tikopia.

TABLE 83

Exogamous Extensions and Kin Groups	Number of Societies
Bilateral Extension	
Present, kindreds being reported	26
Present, kindreds being unreported	64
Absent, kindreds being reported	5
Absent, kindreds being unreported	155
Statistical indices: $Q+.83$; x^2 1000	
Non-Extension beyond Secondary Relatives	
No extension, no kin groups being reported	12
No extension, kin groups being reported	6
Extension, no kin groups being reported	44
Extension, kin groups being reported	188
Statistical indices: $Q+.79$; x^2 1000	

The validation of that portion of the hypothesis which concerns the distance of extension presents somewhat greater difficulties. Maximal extension is to be expected, according to our theory, in societies in which matrilineal, patrilineal, or bilateral organization has been long established and has attained a high level of integration. Criteria for the relative age or degree of development of a social system are difficult to establish, and thus far in the present volume evidence has been discovered for only one. This is White's hypothesis, corroborated in Chapter 8, that among the various types of unilinear structure those with Crow and Omaha kinship terminology are the most highly developed, and hence in general the oldest. As applied to our theory, this would lead us to expect maximal matrilineal extension to be substantially associated with Crow terminology and maximal patrilineal extension with Omaha terminology. This theoretical expectation is borne out by the data presented in Table 84. The coefficients of association are high, positive, and consistent, but the small size of the samples results in low indices of reliability. In both tests, however, the latter actually attain the 25 per cent level of confidence.

TABLE 84

Direction of Extension	Maximal Extension		Minimal or Normal Extension		Statistical Indices	
	Omaha or Crow Terms	Other Terms	Omaha or Crow Terms	Other Terms	Q	χ^2
Patrilineal	6	6	23	58	+.43	2
Matrilineal	7	4	16	26	+.48	2

That the distance to which primary incest taboos are extended depends primarily upon the time factor is rendered probable by our evidence, but further research will be necessary before the conclusion can be considered firmly established. That the direction of extension is determined by the prevailing consanguineal kin groups, however, has been conclusively demonstrated. Those consanguineal relatives of Ego who belong to his kindred, lineage, or sib form, as we have seen, his second line of defense. It is to them that he turns for help or support when his primary relatives, i.e., his own family, are unable to supply what he needs. It is scarcely surprising, therefore, that the consanguineal kin group acquires some of the characteristics of the nuclear family. Primary kinship terms tend to be extended to its members, as was seen in Chapter 7, and with them tend to be generalized the incest taboos everywhere generated within the family. Exogamous rules are less universal than primary incest taboos, therefore, only to the extent that consanguineal kin groups are lacking in a few societies and in a few others are too recent to have exerted a significant influence.

The problem of the extension of primary incest taboos to affinal relatives, though more complex than in the case of consanguineal relatives, involves no principles not already adumbrated. The cases fall into three categories. The first includes certain affinal relatives, notably WiMo, SoWi, and WiBrWi, for whom special factors lead to the prohibition of sex relations and marriage and to the strengthening of these taboos through rules of avoidance, as was shown in Chapter 9 (see Table 79).

The second category includes affinal relatives who happen, in consequence of the characteristics of the social structure of the society in question, to be members of the same consanguineal kin group as Ego. Exogamous restrictions tend to be extended to such kinsmen in precisely the same manner as to consanguineal relatives in general. Table 85 demonstrates that both marriage and extramarital relations with affinal relatives of this category are almost universally prohibited. The coefficients of association are extraordinarily high, as is also the over-all reliability.

TABLE 85

Relative and Relationship	Same Kin Group as Ego		Different Kin Group		Statistical Indices	
	Relation Forbidden	Relation Allowed	Relation Forbidden	Relation Allowed	Q	χ^2
FaWi—marriage	19	0	24	27	+1.00	*
FaWi—extramarital	10	0	15	2	+1.00	*
FaBrWi—marriage	20	0	18	15	+1.00	*
FaBrWi—extramarital	10	0	10	3	+1.00	*
MoBrWi—marriage	11	1	23	33	+.88	100
MoBrWi—extramarital	4	0	11	6	+1.00	*
WiBrDa—marriage	17	0	13	20	+1.00	*
WiBrDa—extramarital	7	0	2	0	.00	*
WiSiDa—marriage	13	0	13	5	+1.00	*
WiSiDa—extramarital	5	0	3	1	+1.00	*

The third category of affinal relatives includes those who belong to the same consanguineal kin group as Ego's spouse. It was shown in Chapter 9 (see Tables 76 and 77) that the permissive sex relationship between husband and wife tends to be extended to the consanguineal relatives of each in precisely the same manner as the incest taboos between father and daughter, mother and son, and brother and sister are extended along channels of kin group affiliation. The evidence for the most striking instances, namely, BrWi and WiSi, has already been presented in Table 76. The data with respect to marriage are assembled for other affinal kinsmen in Table 86, where theoretical expectations are confirmed by high, positive, and consistent coefficients of association of moderate reliability.

TABLE 86

	Same Kin Group as Wife		Different Kin Group		Statistical Indices	
Relative	Marriage Allowed	Marriage Forbidden	Marriage Allowed	Marriage Forbidden	Q	χ^2
FaWi	5	22	3	40	+ .50	2
FaBrWi	2	13	3	35	+ .35	—
MoBrWi	8	26	3	31	+ .52	2
WiBrDa	15	5	8	23	+ .79	100
WiSiDa	3	2	4	22	+ .76	5

From the foregoing evidence it is possible to formulate a general rule governing the extension of incest taboos to affinal relatives. Extension tends to occur to the extent that the relative in question is a member of any consanguineal kin group to which Ego belongs, or is segregated from Ego by a rule of avoidance, and to be inhibited to the extent that he or she is affiliated with the same consanguineal kin group as Ego's spouse.

That sex behavior and marriage are channelized in very large measure by the forms of social structure is by now quite apparent. Attention has been directed mainly to the canalizing effect of consanguineal kin groups because it is so spectacular and so readily demonstrated. But other features of social organization clearly exert an auxiliary influence. There are, for example, demonstrable relationships between kinship terminology and sex behavior. Thus any relative called by a kinship term that is also applied to a kinsman who is genealogically closer to Ego, and with whom marriage or sex relations are forbidden, tends to be placed in a similar taboo category. This is shown in Table 87, which presents the data on marriage and on premarital and extramarital sex relations for all secondary and tertiary relatives for whom ten or more permissions are recorded in the 250 sample societies. Theoretical expectations are borne out by uniformly high, positive, and consistent coefficients of association, supported in most instances by substantial indices of reliability.

TABLE 87

Relative and Relationship	Kinship Term That of a Closer Tabooed Kinsman		Kinship Term Not That of a Closer Tabooed Kinsman		Statistical Indices	
	Relation Forbidden or Disapproved	Relation Allowed or Conditional	Relation Forbidden or Disapproved	Relation Allowed or Conditional	Q	χ^2
FaBrWi—marriage	26	7	3	6	+.72	20
MoBrWi—marriage	20	15	11	16	+.32	2
FaBrDa—marriage	164	6	38	4	+.48	2
FaSiDa—premarital	21	2	19	8	+.63	5
FaSiDa—marriage	89	15	44	47	+.73	1000
MoBrDa—premarital	21	3	17	11	+.64	10
MoBrDa—marriage	69	18	49	57	+.63	1000
MoSiDa—marriage	153	5	24	5	+.73	100
BrWi—premarital	3	1	19	23	+.57	—
BrWi—extramarital	3	2	17	24	+.36	—
BrWi—marriage	5	3	24	125	+.79	100
WiSi—extramarital	3	0	14	25	+1.00	*
WiSi—marriage	5	3	22	116	+.80	100
WiBrDa—marriage	13	4	4	11	+.86	20

Numerous other tabulations have been made which show comparable relationships between kinship structure and sex behavior. They are not presented here because the forms of familial and kin groupings have been shown independently to exert a channelizing or determining influence on both kinship terminology and sex behavior, so that associations between the latter may reflect merely the parallel effects of common causes. While we suspect that kinship structure exerts an auxiliary influence on sex relationships, and does so to a somewhat greater extent than it is reciprocally influenced by them, we know of no means by which this can be conclusively demonstrated from ethnographic data. It is rendered probable, however, by recent psychological experiments [19] which show that, with human subjects, responses are more likely to be transferred from one stimulus to another when they are given the same name than when they are given different names.

Cross-cultural analysis clearly demonstrates that patterns of sex behavior neither reflect "historical accident" nor constitute a closed system within human cultures, but are everywhere molded and directed by the prevailing forms of social organization. So marked is their dependence upon the latter, indeed, that they can be predicted to a notable degree if the structural forms are known. Moreover, as our final chapter will attempt to illustrate, there may even be a possibility of organizing the governing principles into scientific laws of considerable complexity.

[19] Cf. J. S. Birge, *The Role of Verbal Response in Transfer* (unpublished doctoral dissertation, Yale University).

11

SOCIAL LAW OF SEXUAL CHOICE

IN THIS brief concluding chapter an attempt will be made to synthesize the various theoretical and factual conclusions of the present volume as they relate to the selection of sexual and marriage partners in human societies. Since these principles will be expressed in terms of a series of reciprocally interacting gradients of attraction and repulsion which are believed to operate in all societies, and each of which is capable of fairly precise measurement for any particular society, they may in their entirety be regarded, if the reader likes, as a universal social law of sexual choice. The author himself cares little whether this or a less pretentious name is applied to them, since his purpose is merely to point up some of the conclusions of the volume and not to advance anything new in fact or theory.

Human beings everywhere appear to select their mates for any sexual purpose in accordance with a limited number of fundamental criteria, some of them negative and some positive. Each of these criteria represents a continuum of differential characteristics which range from a pole of maximum attraction or repulsion to zero. Factors of culture and personality, however, lead different societies to vary somewhat the stress they lay on particular criteria, with the result that these become effective at different points on the several continua. Cross-cultural comparisons show that these varying degrees of emphasis tend to cluster at certain modal points, which make it possible to establish standard steps or gradations along each continuum. Factors of social organization often deflect the direction of particular gradients or otherwise affect their incidence. In consequence, the points at which the various gradients intersect differ from society to society. In any individual case, however, it is usually possible to determine within fairly narrow limits a particular group or groups of persons who are not excluded by negative criteria and who rank highest according to the positive criteria as locally applied. It is these persons who constitute the preferred sex and marriage partners in that society.

1. The Negative Gradient of Ethnocentrism. Life in society, or association, has two fundamental aspects: an obverse side of social cooperation and positive "we-feeling" and a reverse side of antagonism and "ethnocentrism" toward non-members. As it affects sex and marriage preferences, ethnocentrism establishes a negative gradient of ethnic endogamy which operates with increasing force in proportion to social distance, i.e., in relation to the diminution of social ties and the multiplication of cultural differences. The principal gradations in this continuum appear to be the following:

1. Lower animals. The widespread taboo on bestiality reflects this pole of repulsion.
2. Persons of alien culture and nationality. A minority of societies, including our own, make a distinction between culture and race in this and subsequent levels, rejecting persons of different culture more strongly if they also differ markedly in physical characteristics.
3. Members of alien tribes or nations with cultures not dissimilar to that of Ego's own society.
4. Members of groups within Ego's own tribe or nation who are characterized by different cultures, e.g., castes and ethnic minorities.
5. Members of groups within Ego's tribe or nation who are characterized by different sub-cultures, e.g., social classes and geographical regions.
6. Fellow citizens who do not exhibit significant cultural differences.

In most societies preferred mates are found in the sixth of the above groups, with specific taboos applying to all who fall into or above a particular higher level and with those on intermediate levels ranking in decreasing order of preference from bottom to top. The only exceptions occur when one or more levels at the bottom are excluded by the extension to them of the negative gradient of exogamy. Thus where castes are exogamous units of the order of sibs, as happens occasionally, the requirement of hypergamy may exclude the fifth and sixth levels and result in the preferred mate being found on the fourth level. Even more extreme is the case of the Quinault, who carry the fear of incest to the point of preferring to marry outside of the tribe, i.e., on the third level in the above list.

2. *The Negative Gradient of Exogamy.* The manner in which intra-family incest taboos are extended to relatives outside the family along channels determined by the prevailing rules of descent has already been fully described in Chapter 10. The modal distances to which such extensions are carried constitute the principal steps in the gradient of exogamy:

1. Primary consanguineal relatives.
2. Secondary consanguineal relatives. A very few societies exempt particular secondary relatives from extended incest taboos, e.g., SiDa in certain tropical lowland tribes of South America. Special principles of extension commonly include in this category certain secondary affinal relatives, e.g., WiMo and SoWi.
3. Relatives embraced by minimal extensions of primary incest taboos, i.e., tertiary consanguineal relatives under bilateral descent and lineage mates under unilinear descent.
4. Relatives embraced by normal exogamous extensions, i.e., quaternary and quinary consanguineal relatives under bilateral descent and sibmates under unilinear descent.
5. Relatives embraced by maximal exogamous extensions, i.e., all traceable consanguineal relatives under bilateral descent and the unilinear kinsmen of both parents under matrilineal or patrilineal descent.
6. Non-relatives.

All levels to which exogamous restrictions are not extended coalesce.

Thus in the absence of even minimal extensions of any sort, persons in the third to fifth level inclusive are equated with non-relatives insofar as sex and marriage preferences are concerned.

3. *The Negative Gradient of Adultery.* The universality of marriage and of the special sexual privilege associated with this relationship, coupled with the jealousy with which this privilege is normally guarded, results in widespread disapproval of adulterous as opposed to non-adulterous relations. As was shown in Chapter 9, however, there are certain affinal relationships to which a measure of the marital sex privilege is commonly extended. In such instances adultery is less disfavored than with an unrelated person, and may even be fully permitted. This results in a gradient of adultery, the principal steps in which are the following:

(For an Unmarried Person)	(For a Married Person)
1. Spouses of non - relatives and of distant relatives.	Non-relatives and distant relatives.
2. Spouses of members of Ego's own consanguineal kin group.	Members of the consanguineal kin group to which Ego's spouse belongs.
3. Spouses of own siblings.	Siblings of own spouse.
4. Unmarried persons.	(No equivalent).

The third and fourth levels may sometimes be transposed, as in a society which recognizes privileged relationships but disapproves of premarital sex relations.

4. *The Negative Gradient of Homosexuality.* The fourth gradient is presumably derived from the biological fact of bisexuality and the universal value set on reproduction. In consequence thereof, nearly all societies seek to confine marriage and sex relations to persons of complementary sex. Some permit homosexuality in specifically delimited contexts, and a very few manifest wide latitude in this regard. Among the latter, however, it is noteworthy that homosexual relations conform to the other regulative gradients, e.g., moiety exogamy among the Keraki. The principal gradations appear to be three in number:

1. Persons of Ego's own sex.
2. Persons of opposite sex exhibiting marked cross-sex charac-

teristics, e.g., transvestites, effeminate men, and masculine women.

3. Typical representatives of the opposite sex.

The positive or attractive gradients, shortly to be described, exert steady pressure against the foregoing negative or repelling gradients. In consequence of this pressure, undersocialized or criminal individuals, oversocialized or neurotic persons, and others under strong emotional or situational stress are prone to disregard the taboos and engage in mismating, incest, adultery, or overt homosexuality.

5. *The Positive Gradient of Propinquity.* The first of three positive gradients is based upon the factor of opportunity for sexual expression. It is called the gradient of propinquity because physical nearness is unquestionably the predominant element in opportunity. The following principal gradations may be noted:

1. Member's of Ego's community, i.e., those persons with whom regular face-to-face relationships are maintained. In accordance with this preference, most marriages and sexual liaisons tend to take place between residents of the same community in all societies where the community is not regularly a clan or an exogamous deme.

2. Residents of adjacent communities. Preferred sex and marriage partners will be found at this level when the negative gradients of exogamy and adultery operate to exclude persons on the first level, as in societies organized into exogamous demes or clan-communities.

3. Residents of remote communities. At this point the negative gradient of ethnocentrism commonly begins to exert an opposing influence.

6. *The Positive Gradient of Appropriate Age.* Differences in age between potential sex or marriage partners constitute a positive gradient ranging from age relationships considered especially appropriate to those culturally defined as inappropriate. This gradient applies principally to primary marriages, and appreciably less rigorously to premarital and extramarital sex relations. It exerts comparatively little influence on secondary marriages, where other

factors more strongly affect sexual choice. The gradient appears to be based, like that of propinquity, on the element of opportunity. Age stratification, which occurs in all societies, tends to bring persons of the same generation into closest contact. Moreover, when a girl or youth attains marriageable age, most persons of older generations are already preempted in marriage, while those of younger generations are as yet ineligible. Thus with rare exceptions, notably the Lesu in our sample, primary marriages tend predominantly to occur within the same generation. Since females mature somewhat earlier than males, it is usually considered appropriate in a first marriage for the groom to be somewhat older than the bride. The most typical gradations, therefore, appear to be the following:

1. Persons of the same generation and of similar age, the male being older where there is an appreciable age difference.
2. Persons of the same generation but of dissimilar age, the female being older or the male much older.
3. Persons of adjacent generations, the male being older.
4. Persons of adjacent generations, the female being older, or of non-adjacent generations.

7. *The Positive Gradient of Kinship.* The seventh and last gradient is that of kinship. Although the fact is obscured by the opposing gradient of exogamy, people in all societies unquestionably tend to select sex and marriage partners in direct proportion to the nearness of their actual or conventional kinship. The tendency has two sources. One is the unconscious incestuous attraction toward primary relatives which, as psychoanalysis has demonstrated, is inevitably generated within the nuclear family. The other is the "we-feeling" or "consciousness of kind" developed within all social groups as the opposite pole to ethnocentrism. The more social relationships one has with others, and the more groups one participates in with them, the greater by and large is one's sense of cohesion with them and attraction toward them. The largest number and variety of social ties are shared with the members of one's own nuclear family, and in most societies these diminish in close proportion to genealogical distance. Gradations of actual and conventional kinship thus serve as a measure of the degree of both incestuous attraction and social affiliation. The following are widely distinguishable:

1. Primary relatives. All except the spouse, who is universally a preferred sex object, are regularly excluded by the negative gradient of exogamy, specifically by primary incest taboos. The strength of the attraction between them is nevertheless revealed, not only by criminological and clinical evidence, but also by such special cultural exceptions as dynastic incest, which occur in precisely the situations where those concerned possess power and prestige enough to exempt themselves with impunity from even this strongest of all sex taboos.

2. Secondary and tertiary relatives. All except affinal relatives in this category are excluded by minimal or greater bilateral extensions of exogamous taboos and by maximal matrilineal or patrilineal extension. Those not excluded, except in some instances by the negative gradient of adultery, embrace siblings-in-law and other close affinal relatives, who are the commonest objects of privileged sex relationships and preferred secondary marriages, and under unilinear descent also cross-cousins, who are the commonest objects of preferential primary marriages and often of premarital liaisons as well.

3. Distant relatives with whom a genealogical connection is traceable. Affinal relatives in this category tend to be excluded by the negative gradient of adultery. Consanguineal relatives tend to be excluded, or at least reduced to the level of non-relatives, by the negative gradient of exogamy in societies with bilateral kin groups. In matrilineal and patrilineal societies, however, second and remoter cross-cousins are not affected by unilinear exogamous extensions and actually tend to be preferred sex objects when closer kinsmen are excluded by maximal extensions.

4. Persons whose kinship to Ego is merely conventional or traditional, e.g., members of the same deme or tribe.

The gradient of kinship obviously runs directly counter to that of ethnocentrism. On the other hand, it runs closely parallel to that of propinquity, though it usually descends more steeply. They nearly coincide in societies organized into demes or clan-communities. The gradient of kinship is especially effective where communities are segmented, but it tends to be largely superseded by the gradient of propinquity in societies like our own where kin groups are not localized and kinsmen are scattered.

Analysis of the social organization of any society in terms of the seven above-mentioned gradients enables one, it is believed, to predict with a high degree of probable accuracy precisely what categories of persons will be preferred as sex objects and in marriage. Our own society may serve as an example. Gradient 1, which is rather strongly emphasized, excludes all aliens and all fellow citizens of different caste, class, or ethnic group. Gradient 2, which in world perspective is rather less stressed than average, excludes all consanguineal relatives of primary, secondary, and tertiary degree. Gradient 3, which we accentuate to an unusual degree, bars all adulterous unions of any type and tends even to be extended by anticipation to premarital sex relations. Gradient 4, which is fairly strongly stressed, excludes for a male Ego all males and masculine females. Gradient 5, though probably less effective than average because of our geographical mobility, favors residents of the same town and especially of the same neighborhood within it. Gradient 6, which is perhaps normally elaborated, militates against marriage, and to a lesser extent against fornication, between a man and a woman older or much younger than himself. Gradient 7 does not significantly affect marriage choices in our own society because, with bilateral descent and non-localization of kin groups, it yields precedence to the gradient of propinquity.

In summary, the law of sexual choice, which in another society might lead to cross-cousin marriage, when it operates in the context of our own particular social structure predisposes the unmarried American male to prefer, both in marriage and in informal sex liaisons, a woman of his own age or slightly younger, with typically feminine characteristics, who is unmarried, resides in his own neighborhood or at least in his own town, belongs to his own caste and social class, and exhibits no alien cultural traits. To a married man, such a sex object is subject to only one higher preference, namely, his wife. These predictions are, of course, fully supported by the sociological literature on marriage preferences and by what we ourselves, as "participant observers," know of sex behavior in the culture in which we live.

An eminent predecessor,[1] in the final paragraph of what is certainly the outstanding work heretofore written in the field of social structure, reaches a conclusion about our own civilization which he emphasizes by dubbing it "that planless hodgepodge, that thing of shreds and patches." To the implication of these words the whole import of our own work is diametrically opposed. In the present chapter, as throughout the volume, we have found that sex behavior and the forms of social organization in our own society exhibit the same regularities and conform to the same scientific principles as do comparable phenomena among the simpler peoples of the earth.

[1] R. H. Lowie, *Primitive Society* (New York, 1920), p. 441. In his *Social Organization* (New York, 1948), published after the manuscript of the present work was completed, Lowie modifies virtually every statement or position in his earlier work with which we have been compelled to take issue. Though it offers little that is novel in theory, it is to be recommended for its breadth, its scope, and its judgment.

APPENDIX A: A TECHNIQUE OF HISTORICAL RECONSTRUCTION

HIS APPENDIX is addressed primarily to historians and to anthropologists with historical interests. As is well known, the records of departed civilizations, archeological and documentary, are relatively rich in evidences as to technology, economics, religion, and government but poor in information as to rules of descent, kinship terminology, and other aspects of social organization. If a technique were available whereby a social system fully described at some recent date or during an historical period of rich documentation could be subjected to analysis in such manner as to reveal its antecedent structural forms with a high degree of probability, it might prove exceedingly useful. Given an inferred sequence of earlier forms of organization, the historian might find enough evidence in oblique literary references, or the archeologist in such data as house sites, to establish a probable association between a particular historical period or archeological horizon and a specific type of social structure. Considerably greater time depth might thus be achieved for an aspect of culture which has hitherto proved singularly refractory to historical reconstruction.

Such a technique is suggested by the theories of the determination of kinship terminology, the evolution of social organization, and the extension of incest taboos validated in Chapters 7, 8, and 10. The fact that a considerable period of time must ordinarily elapse before all adaptive readjustments have been completed in the transition from one form of social organization to another—the phenomenon known as "cultural lag"—results in the presence of "survivals" from previous forms of organization in most social systems. Analysis of these can frequently yield reliable indications of historically antecedent types of social structure. Such deductions from internal evidence have been found to agree strikingly with actual historical evidence, with analyses of linguistic relationships, and with the results of distributional studies where any of these is available. It seems desirable,

323

therefore, to systematize them and thereby formulate a technique for historical reconstruction which may supplement other methods and even provide insight into the past when other evidence is lacking.

When this proposed method is applied to the 250 societies of our sample, the inferences from internal evidence are found to converge toward the past in the direction of a single original type of social organization for each recognized linguistic stock, which must of course have had a single historical origin. This provides validation of a specifically historical character, not only for the proposed technique of reconstruction but also for the entire body of theory from which it is derived. Historical and comparative tests thus offer parallel confirmation of the essential validity of the hypotheses advanced in this volume.

The proposed technique of historical reconstruction will utilize two tables which summarize conclusions that have been reached in various places in the text. The limited possibilities in the evolution of social organization, established in Chapter 8, are brought together in Table A, which lists every sub-type in our system of classification with an indication of all the other sub-types from which each can be immediately derived. The possibilities are presented in approximately the order of their probability. The derivations enclosed in parentheses are so improbable, on theoretical grounds and the evidence of our sample societies, that they can be ignored in applying the method unless specific indications of such a derivation are present.

TABLE A

Structural Sub-Types	Probable and Possible Derivations
Normal Eskimo	Patri-Eskimo, Neo-Yuman, Neo-Fox, Neo-Hawaiian, (Neo-Guinea), (Neo-Nankanse), (Matri-Eskimo), (Bi-Eskimo).
Bi-Eskimo	Matri-Eskimo, Patri-Eskimo, (Normal Eskimo).
Matri-Eskimo	Bi-Eskimo, Normal Eskimo.
Patri-Eskimo	Normal Eskimo, Patri-Nankanse, Bi-Eskimo, (Matri-Eskimo).
Normal Hawaiian	Patri-Hawaiian, Matri-Hawaiian, Bi-Nankanse, Bi-Guinea, Bi-Yuman, Bi-Fox, Bi-Eskimo.
Matri-Hawaiian	Normal Hawaiian, (Normal Nankanse), (Neo-Hawaiian).
Neo-Hawaiian	Patri-Hawaiian, Normal Hawaiian, Matri-Hawaiian.
Patri-Hawaiian	Normal Hawaiian, Patri-Nankanse, Neo-Hawaiian, (Patri-Guinea), (Matri-Hawaiian).

Structural Sub-Types	*Probable and Possible Derivations*
Normal Yuman	Patri-Hawaiian, Patri-Iroquois, Patri-Eskimo, (Normal Dakota), (Bi-Yuman), (Neo-Yuman), (Normal Fox).
Bi-Yuman	Bi-Dakota, Bi-Iroquois, (Normal Yuman), (Matri-Yuman).
Matri-Yuman	Matri-Hawaiian, Matri-Eskimo, (Normal Iroquois), (Bi-Yuman), (Neo-Yuman), (Matri-Fox).
Neo-Yuman	Neo-Dakota, Neo-Iroquois, (Normal Yuman), (Matri-Yuman), (Bi-Yuman).
Normal Fox	Patri-Hawaiian, Patri-Crow, Patri-Eskimo, (Normal Omaha), (Normal Sudanese), (Bi-Fox), (Neo-Fox), (Normal Yuman).
Bi-Fox	Bi-Omaha, Bi-Crow, Bi-Sudanese, (Normal Fox), (Matri-Fox).
Matri-Fox	Matri-Hawaiian, Matri-Eskimo, (Bi-Fox), (Normal Crow), (Neo-Fox), (Matri-Yuman).
Neo-Fox	Neo-Omaha, Neo-Crow, Neo-Sudanese, (Normal Fox), (Matri-Fox), (Bi-Fox).
Patri-Fox	Duo-Crow, Normal Fox, (Patri-Crow).
Normal Guinea	Patri-Hawaiian, Patri-Eskimo, Duo-Nankanse, (Bi-Guinea), (Neo-Guinea), (Patri-Nankanse).
Bi-Guinea	Normal Guinea, Bi-Dakota, Bi-Omaha, Bi-Sudanese.
Neo-Guinea	Normal Guinea, Neo-Dakota, Neo-Omaha, Neo-Sudanese.
Normal Dakota	Normal Guinea, Normal Yuman, Duo-Iroquois, (Patri-Fox), (Bi-Dakota), (Neo-Dakota), (Normal Omaha), (Normal Sudanese), (Patri-Iroquois).
Bi-Dakota	Normal Dakota.
Neo-Dakota	Normal Dakota, (Bi-Dakota).
Normal Sudanese	Normal Dakota, Normal Guinea, Normal Fox, Duo-Crow, (Bi-Sudanese), (Neo-Sudanese), (Normal Omaha), (Patri-Fox).
Bi-Sudanese	Normal Sudanese.
Neo-Sudanese	Normal Sudanese, (Bi-Sudanese).
Normal Omaha	Normal Dakota, Normal Fox, Normal Guinea, Normal Sudanese, Duo-Crow, (Bi-Omaha), (Neo-Omaha), (Patri-Fox).
Bi-Omaha	Normal Omaha.
Neo-Omaha	Normal Omaha, (Bi-Omaha).

Structural Sub-Types	Probable and Possible Derivations
Normal Nankanse	Matri-Hawaiian, Matri-Eskimo, (Bi-Nankanse), (Neo-Nankanse).
Avuncu-Nankanse	Normal Nankanse.
Bi-Nankanse	Normal Nankanse, Bi-Iroquois, Bi-Crow, (Patri-Nankanse).
Duo-Nankanse	Patri-Nankanse.
Neo-Nankanse	Normal Nankanse, Neo-Iroquois, Neo-Crow, (Patri-Nankanse), (Avuncu-Nankanse), (Bi-Nankanse).
Patri-Nankanse	Bi-Nankanse, Avuncu-Nankanse, (Neo-Nankanse), (Normal Nankanse).
Normal Iroquois	Normal Nankanse, Matri-Yuman, (Bi-Iroquois), (Neo-Iroquois), (Normal Crow).
Avuncu-Iroquois	Normal Iroquois, (Avuncu-Nankanse).
Bi-Iroquois	Normal Iroquois, (Patri-Iroquois).
Duo-Iroquois	Patri-Iroquois, Duo-Nankanse, (Duo-Crow).
Neo-Iroquois	Normal Iroquois, (Patri-Iroquois), (Avuncu-Iroquois), (Bi-Iroquois).
Patri-Iroquois	Bi-Iroquois, Avuncu-Iroquois, (Patri-Nankanse), (Neo-Iroquois), (Normal Iroquois), (Patri-Crow).
Normal Crow	Normal Iroquois, Matri-Fox, Normal Nankanse, (Bi-Crow), (Neo-Crow).
Avuncu-Crow	Normal Crow, (Avuncu-Iroquois), (Avuncu-Nankanse).
Bi-Crow	Normal Crow, (Patri-Crow).
Duo-Crow	Patri-Crow, Duo-Iroquois, (Duo-Nankanse).
Neo-Crow	Normal Crow, (Patri-Crow), (Avuncu-Crow), (Bi-Crow).
Patri-Crow	Bi-Crow, Avuncu-Crow, (Neo-Crow), (Patri-Iroquois), (Normal Crow).

Table B lists the features of social organization from which inferences as to antecedent structural forms can be drawn. Each is designated by a letter which is the same, except in a few cases of conflict, as the symbol used for the feature in earlier tables in this volume, and they are arranged, for the sake of reference, in alphabetical rather than logical order. The reasons for the inferences have been made clear in the text, and are summarized only in complex instances.

TABLE B

A. *Avunculocal residence* as an alternative to a normal patrilocal rule indicates derivation, not necessarily immediate, from a structure with regular avunculocal residence. See under R for inferences from normal avunculocal residence.

B. *Bilateral extension* of incest taboos, if normal or maximal, in a unilinear structure with unilocal residence indicates derivation from a bilateral structure. It normally arises with bilocal or neolocal residence and especially in conjunction with kindreds. When bilateral exogamy is reported for strongly acculturated societies like the Creek, the inference should not be drawn without corroborative evidence.

C. *Bifurcate collateral terms* for aunts and/or nieces, if general polygyny is lacking and the residence rule is other than patrilocal, indicate derivation, immediate or proximate, from a patrilocal structure.

D. *Descent rules* admit of numerous inferences. Of the three principal classificatory factors, descent usually changes later than residence (R) but earlier than cousin nomenclature (N) in transitions from one stable structural equilibrium to another. Hence the types of structure in which descent is likely to have been the most recent of the three factors to change are those in which it is consistent with residence but inconsistent with nomenclature. (By consistency we mean the particular associations of residence, descent, and nomenclature that occur in the normal sub-types of the Eskimo, Hawaiian, Dakota, Sudanese, Omaha, Iroquois, and Crow types.) Changes in descent naturally mark only transitions between sub-types characterized by the same nomenclature and residence rule, e.g, Patri-Eskimo to Normal Guinea, Patri Crow to Normal Fox, Duo-Iroquois to Normal Dakota. Bilateral descent can be derived directly from either matrilineal or patrilineal but not from double descent. Matrilineal descent can evolve only out of bilateral descent. Patrilineal descent can arise not only from bilateral but also from matrilineal descent, though in the latter case nearly always by way of an intermediate phase, however brief, of bilateral or double descent. The patrilocal sub-types of Eskimo, Hawaiian, Yuman, and Fox, and the double-descent sub-types of Nankanse, Iroquois, and Crow thus constitute normal intermediate steps in the various possible transitions from a matrilineal to a patrilineal structure. Double descent can ordinarily evolve only from a matrilineal structure, though in rare instances it can arise in a bilateral structure on the basis of varying rules of inheritance for different kinds of property. Such cases, however, are revealed by the fact that the unilinear kin groups tend to be lineages rather than sibs, and to be non-exogamous.

E. *Eskimo cousin terms*, when alternative to the terms by which the system is classed, suggest ultimate derivation from a Normal Eskimo structure. However, the inference is not strong enough, especially in an Hawaiian structure, to be given weight unless there are corroborative indications. See under N for inferences from regular Eskimo terminology.

F. *Bifurcate merging terms* for aunts and/or nieces, if sororal polygyny is lacking and the rule of residence is other than matrilocal, indicate derivation from a matrilocal structure. Corroborative evidence is required, however, if the structure is strictly patrilineal, since an alternative explanation is possible in such instances.

G. *Generation terms* for aunts and/or nieces, if the residence rule is other than bilocal, indicate derivation from a bilateral structure, and usually specifically from Normal Hawaiian.

H. *Hawaiian cousin terms*, when alternative to the terms by which the system is classed, suggest ultimate derivation from a Normal Hawaiian structure. However, the inference is not strong enough, especially in an Eskimo structure, to be given weight unless there are corroborative indications. See under N for inferences from regular Hawaiian terminology.

I. *Matrilineal inheritance* of property owned by men and/or matrilineal succession to positions of authority, whether either is the exclusive rule or merely an important alternative, indicates derivation from a matrilineal structure in any society which lacks consanguineal kin groups of matrilineal type.

K. *Kindreds* normally develop either with bilocal residence or with neolocal residence and bilateral descent, and are therefore especially characteristic of bilateral structures. Hence their presence in a unilocal sub-type of Eskimo or Hawaiian structure indicates derivation from the normal sub-type of the same type; their presence in unilocal sub-types of Yuman or Fox indicates derivation from Eskimo or Hawaiian unless specific contrary evidence of unilinear derivation is present; and their presence in a unilocal sub-type of any unilinear type ordinarily indicates ultimate derivation from a bilateral structure.

L. *Lineal terms* for aunts and/or nieces, if the residence rule is other than neolocal, indicate derivation from a neolocal structure, and usually specifically from Normal Eskimo. However, lineal terms are not seriously inconsistent with other bilateral structures and do not negate indications of derivation from an Hawaiian structure.

M. *Matrilineal extension* of incest taboos in any structure which lacks consanguineal kin groups of matrilineal type, provided the rule of residence is other than matrilocal, indicates derivation from a matrilineal structure.

N. *Nomenclature for cross-cousins* admits of numerous inferences. Since it usually changes later than both residence (R) and descent (D) in transitions from one stable structural equilibrium to another, it is particularly likely to have been the last of the three classificatory features to change in situations where all three are consistent with one another. Cross-cousin terminology is an especially clear indicator of specific derivations, notably, Dakota from Yuman or Iroquois, Sudanese or Omaha from Fox, Guinea or Nankanse from Hawaiian or Eskimo, Yuman from Dakota or Iroquois, Fox from Sudanese, Omaha, or Crow. Moreover, immediate or proximate derivation from the normal sub-type of the same type is almost universal for the variant sub-types of the Dakota, Sudanese, Omaha, Iroquois, and Crow types.

P. *Patrilineal extension* of incest taboos in any structure which lacks consanguineal kin groups of patrilineal type indicates derivation from a patrilineal structure, provided the rule of residence is other than patrilocal or matri-patrilocal.

R. *Residence rules* admit of numerous inferences. Since residence is normally the first of the three main classificatory factors to change in transitions from one stable structural equilibrium to another, it is particularly likely to have been the latest of the three to change when it is not consistent with the rule of descent. Although the possible antecedents for every residential sub-type are enumerated in Table A, the general principles governing the succession of residence rules may be stated here. Avunculocal residence can develop only from a matrilocal structure. Bilocal residence can evolve, with rare exceptions, only from a matrilocal or a patrilocal structure. Matrilocal residence can, in general, develop only from a bilocal structure, although a neolocal origin is not unknown. Neolocal residence ordinarily evolves from a patrilocal basis, although both matrilocal and avunculocal origins are possible. Patrilocal residence can arise in a structure with any other rule of residence, but with few exceptions the transition from matrilocal to patrilocal residence is effected by way of an intermediate bilocal phase, however transitory.

S. *Sororal polygyny* as a preferred form of marriage, since it is peculiarly consistent with matrilocal residence, tends to indicate, when found with any other rule of residence, immediate or proximate derivation from a prior matrilocal structure. Since it constitutes merely presumptive evidence, however, it must not be accepted unless the indicated derivation is, on other grounds, at least as probable as alternative ones.

T. *Matri-patrilocal residence* indicates immediate or proximate derivation from a matrilocal structure. As Tylor suggested, it normally arises as an adjustive expedient in the transition from matrilocal to patrilocal residence.

U. *Unilinear kin groups* make possible at least two types of inference. Since their normal development is from lineages or localized sibs to larger and more extended sibs and ultimately to phratries and moieties, the presence of lineages in a unilinear structure, but not of sibs or moieties, indicates recent derivation from a bilateral structure unless there is specific evidence of a transition from matrilineal to patrilineal descent. Since the decadence of unilinear descent, as through the loss of exogamy, affects kin groups of all sizes nearly equally, the presence of non-exogamous sibs or moieties in any bilateral structure (Eskimo, Hawaiian, Yuman, or Fox) indicates ultimate derivation from a unilinear structure with the same rule of descent.

V. *Variant survivals,* or special deviations from normal features of social structure which appear in circumstances especially conducive to conservative retention, frequently provide clues as to prior structural forms. We shall consider only a few variants pointing to possible antecedent matrilineal descent which are reported in isolated areas (e.g., matrilocal residence in remote Jukun districts), in special circumstances (e.g., particular Dahomean marriage forms involving matrilocal residence and matrilineal descent), or in a religious context (e.g., matrilineal inheritance of totems among the Buin). The user of this method, however, should be on the alert for a wide variety of variant usages from which inferences as to prior forms of social organization might be made.

To apply the proposed technique in reconstructing the structural prehistory of a particular society, the following steps should be taken in order:

1. Classify the structure by its prevailing cousin nomenclature, rule of descent, and rule of residence, establishing the type and sub-type to which it belongs according to the system of classification presented in Chapter 8.

2. Look under the appropriate sub-type in Table A, and note the other sub-types from which the one in question can be immediately derived. If there is only one alternative, it is the antecedent structure sought, and Steps 3 and 4 can be skipped. If there are several

alternative derivations, Steps 3 and 4 are designed to indicate which is the more probable.

3. Examine the existing structure for survivals, i.e., elements which are inconsistent with the rest of the structure or which may have been retained from earlier forms of organization because of their known conservatism or for other reasons.

4. Look up the survivals in Table B to determine which of the possible antecedent forms they tend to be consistent with. If they support one of the alternatives, as usually happens, this can be assumed to be the actual antecedent.

5. If a probable antecedent structure has been determined in Step 2 or Step 4, make the change in cousin terminology, descent, or residence which will convert the existing structure into the indicated antecedent sub-type.

6. Refer again to Table A for possible sub-types from which the antecedent structure could have been immediately derived. If there is more than one of these, repeat Steps 3 and 4 to determine which is the more probable. This, if discoverable, can be assumed to be the structure which existed immediately prior to the antecedent one.

7. Repeat Step 6 for evidence as to which forms probably existed at three, four, or more removes before the present one. The process should be continued until a point is reached where no one earlier structural sub-type can be determined by internal evidence to be more probable than its alternatives, or even further if there is conclusive evidence of a still earlier form derivable by alternative routes.

To illustrate the proposed technique, the above criteria and rules will be applied below in an attempt to reconstruct the social prehistory of all our 250 societies. For each of them, all reconstructed antecedent forms will be listed in inverse order of succession, with the reasons for each inference indicated by symbols from Table B or by the symbol O if there are no indications except the inherent limitations noted in Table A. Since the data were assembled without any anticipation that they would be used for historical inferences, it is certain that the author has missed innumerable valuable clues. It is hoped that critics will correct manifest errors, and that interested specialists will try out the method on societies which they know well, especially where there is actual or inferential evidence against which to test the conclusions, for only thus can the method be invalidated or substantiated, refined, and improved.

Abelam: Normal Dakota, from Normal Guinea, Normal Yuman, or Duo-Iroquois (O).

Acholi: Normal Omaha, from Normal Dakota, Normal Fox, Normal Guinea, Normal Sudanese, or Duo-Crow (O).

Acoma: Bi-Crow, from Normal Crow (FR). Aunt and cousin terms indicate an incipient transition via Bi-Nankanse to Normal Hawaiian.

Albanians: Normal Guinea, from Patri-Eskimo (DLN), from Normal Eskimo (L).

Andamanese: Normal Eskimo, from Patri-Eskimo, Neo-Yuman, Neo-Fox, or Neo-Hawaiian (O).

Angami: Normal Omaha, from Normal Dakota, Normal Fox, Normal Guinea, Normal Sudanese, or Duo-Crow (O).

Angmagsalik: Patri-Eskimo, from Normal Eskimo (KNR).

Ao: Normal Omaha, from Normal Dakota, Normal Fox, Normal Guinea, Normal Sudanese, or Duo-Crow (O).

Apinaye: Normal Nankanse, perhaps from Matri-Eskimo (DN), from Normal Eskimo (RN). This typical reconstruction, however, ignores the anomalous social structure of the Apinaye, with patrilineal descent for males, matrilineal descent for females, matri-moieties, and cycling of marriages through the four sibs. These might be interpreted as survivals of an Australian-like system with double descent and bilinear kin groups, i.e., Duo-Crow, Duo-Iroquois, or Duo-Nankanse, by way of an unusual bilocal transitional phase. This would also account for the presence of two minor patrilocal or patrilineal traits, namely, the alternative bifurcate collateral terms for aunts and an alternative Omaha usage for FaSiDa.

Arapaho: Matri-Hawaiian, from Normal Hawaiian (R).

Arapesh: Normal Omaha, from Normal Dakota, Normal Fox, Normal Guinea, Normal Sudanese, or Duo-Crow (O).

Araucanians: Normal Omaha, from Normal Fox (U).

Arosi: Normal Iroquois, from Normal Nankanse (N), from Matri-Hawaiian (DGN), from Normal Hawaiian (GR).

Arunta: Duo-Iroquois, from Patri-Iroquois (D), from Bi-Iroquois (R), from Normal Iroquois (RS), from Normal Nankanse or Matri-Yuman (O).

Ashanti: Duo-Crow, from Patri-Crow (DF), from Bi-Crow (FR), from Normal Crow (FR).

Atsugewi: Patri-Hawaiian, from Normal Hawaiian (R), from Matri-Hawaiian (RST), from Normal Hawaiian (R), from Bi-Eskimo (ELN), from Matri-Eskimo or Patri-Eskimo (ELR), from Normal Eskimo (EL). Beyond Matri-Hawaiian the reconstruction is increasingly speculative.

Awuna: Normal Sudanese, from Normal Guinea (N), from Patri-Hawaiian (D), from Normal Hawaiian (GR). Though based on the single slim survival of alternative generation terms for nieces, this reconstruction accords with West African distributions.

Aymara: possibly Patri-Hawaiian from Normal Hawaiian, but cousin terms are lacking.

Azande: Normal Sudanese, from Normal Fox (BN).

Bachama: Patri-Fox, from Normal Fox (D), from Bi-Fox (GR), from Bi-Crow (IR), from Normal Crow (FN).

Baiga: Normal Dakota, from Normal Guinea, Normal Yuman, or Duo-Iroquois (O).

Balinese: Patri-Eskimo, from Normal Eskimo (R), from Neo-Hawaiian (GHN), probably from Normal Hawaiaan (GH). The patri-lineages indicate an incipient transition toward Patri-Guinea.

Banaro: Normal Dakota, from Normal Guinea, Normal Yuman, or Duo-Iroquois (O).

Bari: Normal Omaha, from Normal Fox (B), from Patri-Hawaiian or Patri-Eskimo (B). The retention of maximal bilateral extension suggests this most direct derivation from a full-fledged bilateral structure.

Batak: Normal Sudanese, from Normal Dakota, Normal Guinea, Normal Fox, or Duo-Crow (O).

Bena: Normal Dakota, from Normal Yuman (K), from Bi-Yuman (KR), from Bi-Iroquois (DMNT), from Normal Iroquois (FRV), from Normal Nankanse or Matri-Yuman (O). Most of the above steps are attested by actual historical evidence.

Bhuiya: possibly Normal Dakota, but cousin terms are lacking.

Blackfoot: Patri-Hawaiian, from Normal Hawaiian (BR).

Bolewa: Normal Guinea, from Patri-Hawaiian (DU), from Normal Hawaiian (GNR). The alternative Iroquois cousin terms indicate an incipient transition toward Normal Iroquois.

Buin: Normal Yuman, from Patri-Iroquois (V), from Bi-Iroquois (R), from Normal Iroquois (FR), from Normal Nankanse or Matri-Yuman (O).

Carib: Matri-Yuman, from Matri-Hawaiian or Matri-Eskimo (O).

Carrier: Patri-Iroquois, from Bi-Iroquois (R), from Normal Iroquois (RT), from Normal Nankanse or Matri-Yuman (O).

Cayapa: Bi-Eskimo, from Matri-Eskimo (FR), from Normal Eskimo (O). Alternative niece and cousin terms indicate an incipient transition toward Normal Hawaiian.

Chawai: Normal Guinea, from Patri-Hawaiian (D), from Normal Hawaiian (G).

Chenchu: Bi-Dakota, from Normal Dakota (R).

Cherente: Normal Sudanese, from Duo-Crow (S), from Patri-Crow (D), from Bi-Crow (R), from Normal Crow (RS). This reconstruction is consistent with the distributional evidence, e.g., from the Ramkokamekra.

Cherokee: Normal Crow, from Normal Iroquois, Matri-Fox, or Normal Nankanse (O).

Chewa: Normal Iroquois, from Normal Nankanse or Matri-Yuman (O).

Cheyenne: Matri-Hawaiian, from Normal Hawaiian (KR).

Chinese: Normal Dakota, from Normal Guinea (HN), from Patri-Hawaiian (D), from Normal Hawaiian (H). This reconstruction is based on admittedly slight evidence, namely, that cross-cousin terms are compounded from sibling terms.

Chiricahua: Matri-Hawaiian, from Normal Hawaiian (R), from Patri-Hawaiian (C).

Choctaw: Normal Crow, from Matri-Fox, Normal Iroquois, or Normal Nankanse (O). If bilateral extension is old, and not a recent acculturative phenomenon, the derivation from Matri-Fox is indicated.

Chukchee: Patri-Eskimo, from Bi-Eskimo (R), from Matri-Eskimo (RT), probably from Normal Eskimo (L).

Cochiti: Normal Iroquois, from Normal Nankanse (N), from Matri-Hawaiian (D), from Normal Hawaiian (GHR).

Comanche: Neo-Hawaiian, from Matri-Hawaiian (S), from Normal Hawaiian (R).

Coorg: Normal Dakota, from Normal Guinea, Normal Yuman, or Duo-Iroquois (O).

Copper Eskimo: Normal Eskimo, from Patri-Eskimo (C).

Creek: Normal Crow, from Matri-Fox, Normal Iroquois, or Normal Nankanse (O). If bilateral extension is old, and not a recent acculturative phenomenon, the derivation from Matri-Fox is indicated.

Crow: Patri-Crow, from Bi-Crow (R), from Normal Crow (RS). This reconstruction is confirmed by historical evidence that the Crow split off from the Hidatsa tribe.

Cuna: Matri-Hawaiian, probably from Neo-Hawaiian (L).

Dahomeans: Normal Sudanese, from Duo-Crow (V), from Patri-Crow (DV), from Bi-Crow (R), from Normal Crow (RV). This reconstruction accords with that from the Ashanti, although an alternative derivation via Normal Guinea and Duo-Nankanse from Normal Nankanse would also agree with distributional evidence.

Daka: Normal Crow, from Normal Nankanse (N), from Matri-Hawaiian (D), from Normal Hawaiian (GR).

Dieri: Duo-Iroquois, from Patri-Iroquois (D), from Bi-Iroquois (R), from Normal Iroquois (RS), from Normal Nankanse or Matri-Yuman (O).

Dinka: Normal Sudanese, from Normal Fox (BN).

Dobuans: Normal Iroquois, from Normal Nankanse or Matri-Yuman (O). Alternating avunculocal residence and alternative Crow cousin terms indicate an incipient transition toward Avuncu-Crow, the structure of the neighboring Trobrianders.

Dorobo: Normal Omaha, from Normal Dakota, Normal Fox, Normal Guinea, Normal Sudanese, or Duo-Crow (O).

Eddystone: Normal Hawaiian, from Patri-Hawaiian, Matri-Hawaiian, Bi-Nankanse, Bi-Guinea, Bi-Yuman, or Bi-Eskimo (O).

Edo: Patri-Eskimo, from Normal Eskimo (L). Patrilineal inheritance of food taboos and a theoretical exogamy associated therewith indicate an incipient transition toward Normal Guinea.

Epi: Normal Dakota, from Normal Guinea, Normal Yuman, or Duo-Iroquois (O).

Eromangans: Normal Yuman, from Patri-Eskimo (B), from Normal Eskimo (LN). The development of patrilineal extension, even if not associated with kin groups, indicates an incipient transition toward Normal Dakota.

Eyak: Avuncu-Iroquois, from Normal Iroquois (FR), from Normal Nankanse or Matri-Yuman (O).

Fijians: Normal Dakota, from Normal Yuman (patrilineal descent is incipient), from Patri-Iroquois (D), from Bi-Iroquois (R), from Normal Iroquois (RST), from Normal Nankanse or Matri-Yuman (O).

Flathead: Patri-Hawaiian, from Normal Hawaiian (K), probably from Matri-Hawaiian (RS).

Fox: Neo-Fox, from Neo-Omaha (DU), from Normal Omaha (R). Sororal polygyny might reflect an ultimate derivation from a matrilineal structure, e.g., Normal Crow via Normal Fox and Patri-Crow, or alternatively the kindreds and bilateral exogamy might indicate some bilateral antecedent.

Futunans: Patri-Hawaiian, from Normal Hawaiian (GK), probably from Matri-Hawaiian (FR).

Ganda: Normal Dakota, from Normal Yuman (D), from Patri-Iroquois (V), from Bi-Iroquois (R), from Normal Iroquois (FR), from Normal Nankanse or Matri-Yuman (O).

Gesu: Normal Sudanese, from Normal Dakota, Normal Guinea, Normal Fox, or Duo-Crow (O). The Eskimo aspect of cousin terminology merely reflects the method of composition in forming descriptive terms and does not indicate an Eskimo derivation.

Getmatta: Patri-Iroquois, from Bi-Iroquois (R), from Normal Iroquois (R), from Normal Nankanse (N), from Matri-Hawaiian (D), from Normal Hawaiian (GR).

Gilyak: Normal Sudanese, from Normal Dakota, Normal Guinea, Normal Fox, or Duo-Crow (O). Sororal polygyny suggests possible derivation from a matrilocal structure.

Gond: Normal Dakota, from Normal Guinea, Normal Yuman, or Duo-Iroquois (O). Sororal polygyny suggests a possible ultimate matrilocal derivation.

Haida: Avuncu-Crow, from Normal Crow (FR).

Havasupai: Normal Yuman, from Patri-Hawaiian, Patri-Iroquois, or Patri-Eskimo (O). Matri-patrilocal residence suggests an ultimate matrilocal derivation, but this could equally well be Matri-Hawaiian, Normal Iroquois, or Matri-Eskimo.

Hawaiians: Patri-Hawaiian, from Normal Hawaiian (G).

Henga: Normal Dakota, from Normal Yuman or Duo-Iroquois (D), from Patri-Iroquois (DV), from Bi-Iroquois (R), from Normal Iroquois (FR). Historical evidence indicates an almost direct transition from Iroquois to Dakota.

Herero: Duo-Iroquois, from Patri-Iroquois (DI), from Bi-Iroquois (R), from Normal Iroquois (R), from Normal Nankanse or Matri-Yuman (O).

Ho: Normal Guinea, from Patri-Hawaiian (DN), from Normal Hawaiian (N). Cousin terms are possibly Iroquois, in which case sororal polygyny might indicate ultimate derivation from Normal Iroquois.

Hopi: Normal Crow, from Normal Nankanse (N), from Matri-Hawaiian (BD), from Normal Hawaiian (BKR). This reconstruction is confirmed by Shoshonean distributions.

Hottentot: Normal Dakota, from Normal Yuman or Duo-Iroquois (D), from Patri-Iroquois (D), from Bi-Iroquois (R), from Normal Iroquois (FRT).

Hupa: Patri-Hawaiian, from Normal Hawaiian (N).

Iatmul: Normal Omaha, from Normal Dakota, Normal Fox, Normal Guinea, Normal Sudanese, or Duo-Crow (O).

Ibo: Normal Dakota, from Normal Guinea (N), from Patri-Eskimo (BDU), from Normal Eskimo (LN).

Ifugao: Normal Hawaiian, from Patri-Hawaiian, Matri-Hawaiian, Bi-Nankanse, Bi-Guinea, Bi-Yuman, Bi-Fox, or Bi-Eskimo (O).

Ila: Patri-Iroquois, from Bi-Iroquois (R), from Normal Iroquois (FNR), from Normal Nankanse or Matri-Yuman (O). Alternative generation terms for aunts suggest a possible ultimate derivation from Normal Hawaiian.

Inca: Patri-Hawaiian, from Normal Hawaiian (NR), from Matri-Hawaiian (FR).

Ingassana: Normal Hawaiian, from Patri-Hawaiian (R), from Patri-Nankanse (D), from Avuncu-Nankanse (A), from Normal Nankanse (FR). An Iroquois or Crow derivation is almost equally probable.

Iroquois: Normal Iroquois, from Normal Nankanse (N), from Matri-Hawaiian (DK), from Normal Hawaiian (GKR). This reconstruction is merely weakened, not altered, if the kindreds prove to be recent products of acculturation.

Jemez: Neo-Iroquois, from Normal Iroquois (FNR), from Normal Nankanse or Matri-Yuman (O).

Jukun: Normal Hawaiian, from Bi-Nankanse (IV), from Normal Nankanse (RV), from Matri-Hawaiian or Matri-Eskimo (O). Actual historical evidence corroborates much of this reconstruction.

Kababish: Normal Fox, from Normal Sudanese (NU). This transition clearly resulted from the introduction of Islam with preferred marriage with FaBrDa.

Kaingang: Normal Hawaiian, from Patri-Hawaiian, Matri-Hawaiian, Bi-Nankanse, Bi-Guinea, Bi-Yuman, Bi-Fox, or Bi-Eskimo (O).

Kallinago: Matri-Yuman, from Matri-Hawaiian or Matri-Eskimo (O). Matri-lineages indicate an incipient transition toward Normal Iroquois.

Kamilaroi: Duo-Iroquois, from Patri-Iroquois (D), from Bi-Iroquois (R), from Normal Iroquois (RS), from Normal Nankanse or Matri-Yuman (O).

Kariera: Duo-Iroquois, from Patri-Iroquois (D), from Bi-Iroquois (R), from Normal Iroquois (RS), from Normal Nankanse or Matri-Yuman (O).

Kaska: Normal Crow, from Normal Nankanse (N), from Matri-Hawaiian (D), from Normal Hawaiian (GR).

Katab: Normal Guinea, from Patri-Hawaiian (BD), from Normal Hawaiian (BG).

Keraki: Normal Dakota, from Normal Guinea, Normal Yuman, or Duo-Iroquois (O).

Kickapoo: Neo-Omaha, from Normal Omaha (NR). The kindreds are presumably a product of acculturation.

Kilba: Normal Guinea, from Patri-Hawaiian (D), from Normal Hawaiian (GR).

Kiowa Apache: Matri-Hawaiian, from Normal Hawaiian (N), probably from Patri-Hawaiian (CR).

Kitara: Normal Omaha, from Normal Dakota, Normal Fox, Normal Guinea, Normal Sudanese, or Duo-Crow (O).

Kiwai: possibly Normal Dakota, though cousin terms are lacking.

Klallam: Patri-Hawaiian, from Neo-Hawaiian (L), from Matri-Hawaiian (S), from Normal Hawaiian (NR).

Klamath: Patri-Hawaiian, from Normal Hawaiian (N).

Kongo: Patri-Crow, from Bi-Crow (R), from Normal Crow (NRS).

Koranko: Patri-Fox, from Normal Fox (D), from Patri-Crow (D), from Bi-Crow (R), from Normal Crow (FNR).

Koryak: Patri-Eskimo, from Normal Eskimo (N).

Kurd: Normal Fox, from Normal Sudanese (NU). The lineal terms for aunts may possibly indicate an ultimate derivation from Normal Eskimo. The transition from Sudanese to Fox reflects the loss of exogamy resulting from the introduction of Islam and preferential marriage with FaBrDa.

Kurtatchi: Bi-Iroquois, from Normal Iroquois (RS), from Normal Nankanse (N), from Matri-Hawaiian (B), from Normal Hawaiian (GKR). The bilateral features are too numerous to be attributed to recent bilocal residence.

Kutchin: Patri-Iroquois, from Bi-Iroquois (R), from Normal Iroquois (NR), from Normal Nankanse or Matri-Yuman (O).

Kutenai: Patri-Eskimo, probably from Normal Eskimo (N). The structure might equally well be classed as Patri-Hawaiian, or might be derived from Normal Hawaiian (H).

Kutubu: Normal Dakota, from Normal Guinea (N), from Patri-Hawaiian (D), from Normal Hawaiian (G).

Kwakiutl: Patri-Hawaiian, from Normal Hawaiian (KLN). Patri-lineages indicate an incipient transition toward Normal Guinea.

Kwoma: Normal Omaha, from Normal Dakota, Normal Fox, Normal Guinea, Normal Sudanese, or Duo-Crow (O).

Kyiga: Normal Dakota, from Normal Guinea, Normal Yuman, or Duo-Iroquois (O).

Lakher: Normal Guinea, from Patri-Hawaiian (D), from Normal Hawaiian (N).

Lamba: Patri-Iroquois, from Bi-Iroquois (RT), from Normal Iroqouis (FRT), from Normal Nankanse or Matri-Yuman (O).

Lango: Normal Omaha, from Normal Dakota, Normal Fox, Normal Guinea, Normal Sudanese, or Duo-Crow (O).

Lapps: Patri-Eskimo, from Bi-Eskimo (R), from Matri-Eskimo (RT), from Normal Eskimo (N).

Lenge: Normal Omaha, from Normal Dakota, Normal Fox, Normal Guinea, Normal Sudanese, or Duo-Crow (O).

Lepcha: Normal Guinea, from Patri-Hawaiian (BD), from Normal Hawaiian (BGN).

Lesu: Normal Iroquois, from Normal Nankanse or Matri-Yuman (O).

Lhota: Normal Omaha, from Normal Fox (D), from Patri-Crow (D), from Bi-Crow (R), from Normal Crow (FNRT). There are alternative, but slightly less direct, transitions from other matrilineal structures, which are almost equally probable.

Limba: Normal Sudanese, from Normal Guinea (N), from Patri-Hawaiian (D), from Normal Hawaiian (GN).

Longuda: Avuncu-Crow, from Normal Crow (FR), from Normal Nankanse (N), from Matri-Hawaiian (D), from Normal Hawaiian (GNR). Though this reconstruction is based on the slim evidence of alternative generation terminology for aunts, it accords with West African distributions.

Luiseno: Normal Dakota, from Normal Guinea or Normal Yuman (O). Since the patri-sibs are clearly incipient, being very small and strictly localized, the derivation from Normal Hawaiian via Normal Guinea and Patri-Hawaiian is highly probable, and would be supported by Shoshonean distributions.

Mabuiag: Bi-Guinea, from Normal Guinea (R), from Patri-Hawaiian (BD), from Normal Hawaiian (BGN), from Matri-Hawaiian (RS). The bilateral traits are too numerous to be attributed to bilocal residence alone, and must be survivals.

Macusi: Matri-Yuman, from Matri-Hawaiian or Matri-Eskimo (O).

Mailu: Normal Sudanese, from Normal Guinea (N), from Patri-Hawaiian (D), from Normal Hawaiian (GN).

Malabu: Normal Guinea, from Patri-Hawaiian (D), from Normal Hawaiian (N).

Manchu: Normal Dakota, from Normal Guinea, Normal Yuman, or Duo-Iroquois (O).

Mandan: Neo-Crow, from Normal Crow (FNRS).

Mangarevans: Patri-Hawaiian, from Normal Hawaiian (GN).

Manus: Duo-Crow, from Patri-Crow (D), from Bi-Crow (R), from Normal Crow (FNR).

Maori: Normal Hawaiian. Kinship terms, which reveal an almost even balance between the two bilateral types, might reflect a derivation either from Normal Eskimo or from Neo-Hawaiian, of which the latter would be far more in accord with Polynesian distributions. However, kinship evidence is always dubious in inferring derivations of either major bilateral structure from the other.

Maricopa: Normal Guinea, from Patri-Hawaiian (BD), from Normal Hawaiian (BN).

Marquesans: Neo-Hawaiian, from Normal Hawaiian (NR).

Marshallese: Normal Iroquois, from Normal Nankanse (N), from Matri-Hawaiian (D), from Normal Hawaiian (GNR).

Masai: Normal Dakota, from Normal Guinea (N), from Patri-Hawaiian (BD), from Normal Hawaiian (BG).

Mataco: Neo-Hawaiian, from Patri-Hawaiian, Normal Hawaiian, or Matri-Hawaiian (O).

Mbundu: Patri-Iroquois, from Bi-Iroquois (R), from Normal Iroquois (FR), from Normal Nankanse or Matri-Yuman (O).

Mendi: Normal Guinea, from Patri-Eskimo (D), from Normal Eskimo (LN), perhaps from Bi-Eskimo (G).

Mentaweians: Matri-Yuman, probably from Matri-Hawaiian (O), from Normal Hawaiian (NR), from Patri-Hawaiian (CR). The clan-like extended families indicate an incipient transition toward Normal Iroquois.

Micmac: Patri-Hawaiian, from Normal Hawaiian (NR), from Matri-Hawaiian (FRT).

Mikir: possibly Normal Dakota, but cousin terms are lacking.

Minangkabau: possibly Normal Iroquois, but cousin terms are lacking. An ultimate derivation from Normal Hawaiian, however, is probable (G).

Miriam: Normal Dakota, from Normal Guinea (N), from Patri-Hawaiian (D), from Normal Hawaiian (G).

Miwok: Normal Omaha, from Normal Dakota, Normal Fox, Normal Guinea, Normal Sudanese, or Duo-Crow (O).

Mota: Avuncu-Crow, from Normal Crow (FNRS), from Normal Nankanse (N), from Matri-Hawaiian (D), from Normal Hawaiian (GNR).

Murngin: Duo-Crow, from Patri-Crow (D), from Bi-Crow (R), from Normal Crow (FRST). The alternative derivation from Normal Iroquois via Patri-Iroquois and Duo-Iroquois to Duo-Crow is almost equally probable on internal evidence and more probable on distributional evidence.

Nambikuara: Normal Yuman, from Patri-Iroquois (D), from Bi-Iroquois (R), from Normal Iroquois (FNR), from Normal Nankanse or Matri-Yuman (O).

Nandi: Normal Omaha, from Normal Dakota, Normal Fox, Normal Guinea, Normal Sudanese, or Duo-Crow (O).

Nankanse: Duo-Nankanse, from Patri-Nankanse (D), from Avuncu-Nankanse (A), from Normal Nankanse (FR), from Matri-Hawaiian (D), from Normal Hawaiian (GNR).

Naskapi: Normal Yuman, probably from Patri-Hawaiian (O). Of the two alternative derivations, Patri-Eskimo is statistically less probable and Patri-Iroquois is unlikely because of the lack of matrilocal-matrilineal survivals. The Patri-Hawaiian derivation, moreover, accords with distributional evidence.

Natchez: Patri-Crow, from Bi-Crow (R), from Normal Crow (RST).

Nauruans: Normal Iroquois, from Normal Nankanse (N), from Matri-Hawaiian (DK), from Normal Hawaiian (GNR).

Navaho: Normal Iroquois, from Normal Nankanse or Matri-Yuman (O). The alternative bifurcate collateral aunt and niece terms possibly reflect some earlier patrilocal structure.

Nayar: Normal Iroquois, from Normal Nankanse or Matri-Yuman (O). There. are indications of derivation from a bilateral (KU) and perhaps even patrilocal (C) structure.

Ndoro: Avuncu-Crow, from Normal Crow (FR), from Norman Nankanse (N), from Matri-Hawaiian (D), from Normal Hawaiian (GNR).

Ngizim: Normal Guinea, from Patri-Hawaiian (D), from Normal Hawaiian (GN).

Nuba: Patri-Hawaiian, from Patri-Nankanse (I), from Avuncu-Nankanse (A), from Normal Nankanse (FRT), from Matri-Hawaiian (D), from Normal Hawaiian (GKNR).

Ojibwa: Bi-Dakota, from Normal Dakota (R), from Normal Guinea or Normal Yuman (O). If the kindreds and bilateral extension are due either to acculturation or to bilocal residence, the probable derivation is via Yuman from Iroquois (S); otherwise via Guinea from Hawaiian or Eskimo (BK).

Omaha: Neo-Omaha, from Normal Omaha (R). The kindreds are presumably a product of acculturation. The occurrence of sororal polygyny may reflect an ultimate matrilocal derivation.

Ona: Patri-Eskimo, from Matri-Eskimo via Bi-Eskimo or from Normal Nankanse via Patri-Nankanse (RST).

Ontong-Javanese: Normal Hawaiian, from Matri-Hawaiian (DF). Double descent with non-exogamous matri-lineages and patri-lineages is presumably a product of dual inheritance, matrilineal for dwellings and patrilineal for land.

Orokaiva: Normal Dakota, from Normal Guinea, Normal Yuman, or Duo-Iroquois (O).

Osset: Normal Guinea, from Patri-Eskimo (D), from Normal Eskimo (N). Sororal polygyny suggests derivation from a matrilocal structure, perhaps Matri-Eskimo.

Paiute: Neo-Hawaiian, from Matri-Hawaiian (S), from Normal Hawaiian (R), from Patri-Hawaiian (CR).

Pawnee: Matri-Fox, from Matri-Hawaiian (K), from Normal Hawaiian (BGR).

Pedi: Normal Dakota, from Normal Yuman (D), from Patri-Iroquois (D), from Bi-Iroquois (R), from Normal Iroquois (FRT), from Normal Nankanse or Matri-Yuman (O).

Pentecost: Duo-Crow, from Patri-Crow (D), from Bi-Crow (R), from Normal Crow (FNR), from Normal Nankanse (N), from Matri-Hawaiian (D), from Normal Hawaiian (GR). The derivation beyond Normal Crow depends upon the slight evidence of alternative generation terms for aunts, but it nevertheless has distributional support.

Pima: Normal Yuman, from Neo-Yuman or Bi-Yuman (O), from Neo-Dakota or Bi-Dakota (DU), from Normal Dakota (NR).

Pukapukans: Duo-Nankanse, from Patri-Nankanse (D), from Bi-Nankanse (R), from Normal Nankanse (R), from Matri-Eskimo or Matri-Hawaiian (BDGKN). Cousin terms suggest a further derivation from Normal Eskimo, aunt and niece terms from Normal Hawaiian. The latter would accord with Polynesian distributions.

Quinault: Patri-Eskimo, from Normal Eskimo (KL), possibly from Neo-Hawaiian (H). Sororal polygyny suggests a possible ultimate matrilocal derivation, e.g., Matri-Hawaiian.

Ramkokamekra: Normal Crow, from Normal Iroquois, Matri-Fox, or Normal Nankanse (O).

Ranon: Duo-Crow, from Patri-Crow (D), from Bi-Crow (R), from Normal Crow (FR).

Reddi: Normal Dakota, from Normal Guinea, Normal Yuman, or Duo-Iroquois (O). The lineal terms for FaYoSi and MoYoSi might conceivably, though improbably, reflect Eskimo antecedents.

Rengma: Normal Omaha, from Normal Dakota, Normal Fox, Normal Guinea, Normal Sudanese, or Duo-Crow (O).

Rossel: Patri-Crow, from Bi-Crow (R), from Normal Crow (FNR).

Ruthenians: Normal Eskimo, from Patri-Eskimo (C). Actual historical evidence confirms this reconstruction.

Sabei: Normal Sudanese, from Normal Dakota, Normal Guinea, Normal Fox, or Duo-Crow (O).

Samoans: Normal Hawaiian, possibly from Matri-Hawaiian (F).

Santa Cruz: Patri-Iroquois, from Bi-Iroquois (R), from Normal Iroqouis (FNR), from Normal Nankanse or Matri-Yuman (O).

Sekani: Patri-Hawaiian, from Normal Hawaiian (N), from Matri-Hawaiian (ST). Derivation from some matrilineal structure via Patri-Nankanse is equally probable.

Sema: Normal Omaha, from Normal Dakota, Normal Fox, Normal Guinea, Normal Sudanese, or Duo-Crow (O).

Semang: Patri-Eskimo, from Normal Eskimo (LN).

Seniang: Patri-Fox, from Normal Fox (BD), from Patri-Crow (D), from Bi-Crow (R), from Normal Crow (NRS).

Shasta: Normal Yuman, from Patri-Hawaiian, Patri-Iroquois, or Patri-Eskimo (O).

Sherbro: Patri-Nankanse, from Bi-Nankanse (R), from Normal Nankanse (R), from Matri-Eskimo or Matri-Hawaiian (BD), from Normal Eskimo (EL) or Normal Hawaiian (GH). The indications of Eskimo and Hawaiian derivation are evenly balanced.

Shilluk: Normal Sudanese, from Duo-Crow (DM), from Patri-Crow (D), from Bi-Crow (R), from Normal Crow (RS).

Shona: Normal Omaha, from Normal Fox (BD), from Patri-Crow (D), from Bi-Crow (R), from Normal Crow (NRS). Several alternative derivations from a matrilineal by way of a bilateral structure are equally possible.

Shoshone: Normal Hawaiian, from Matri-Hawaiian (RS).

Sinkaietk: Normal Hawaiian, from Matri-Hawaiian (RS), perhaps from Neo-Hawaiian (L).

Siriono: Matri-Fox, from Matri-Hawaiian (G) or Matri-Eskimo (L).

Soga: Normal Omaha, from Normal Fox (BD), from Patri-Crow (D), from Bi-Crow (R), from Normal Crow (NRS). Other derivations from a matrilineal by way of a bilateral structure are equally possible.

Susu: Normal Dakota, from Normal Guinea, Normal Yuman, or Duo-Iroquois (O).

Swazi: Normal Dakota, from Normal Yuman (D), from Patri-Iroquois (D), from Bi-Iroquois (R), from Normal Iroquois (NRS). Alternative generation terminology for nieces may indicate an ultimate derivation from Hawaiian.

Syrian Christians: Patri-Hawaiian, from Normal Hawaiian (N), possibly from Matri-Hawaiian (FR).

Takelma: Normal Fox, from Patri-Hawaiian or Patri-Eskimo (B).

Tallensi: possibly Normal Dakota, but cousin terms are lacking.

Tanala: Normal Dakota, from Duo-Iroquois (DM), from Patri-Iroquois (DMV), from Bi-Iroquois (R), from Normal Iroquois (NR), from Normal Nankanse (N), from Matri-Hawaiian (D), from Normal Hawaiian (GNR). Despite its extraordinary length of eight successive structural stages, this reconstruction does no violence either to the reported ethnographic facts or to known Malayan distributions.

Tannese: Normal Dakota, from Normal Guinea, Normal Yuman, or Duo-Iroquois (O).

Taos: Normal Eskimo, possibly from Matri-Eskimo (F).

Tarahumara: Neo-Hawaiian, from Patri-Hawaiian (CR), from Normal Hawaiian (N).

Tenino: Normal Hawaiian, from Patri-Hawaiian (CR).

Tetekantzi: Patri-Nankanse, from Avuncu-Nankanse (A), from Normal Nankanse (FR), from Matri-Hawaiian (N), from Normal Hawaiian (GNR).

Teton: Normal Yuman, from Patri-Iroquois (D), from Bi-Iroquois (R), from Normal Iroquois (NRS), from Normal Nankanse or Matri-Yuman (O).

Tewa: Normal Eskimo, from Neo-Fox (N), from Neo-Omaha (DU), from Normal Omaha (CR). Patri-moieties make Omaha the most probable former patrilineal structure.

Thado: Normal Omaha, from Normal Dakota, Normal Fox, Normal Guinea, Normal Sudanese, or Duo-Crow (O).

Thonga: Normal Omaha, from Normal Fox (D), from Patri-Crow (D), from Bi-Crow (R), from Normal Crow (RS). This reconstruction depends on the rather slim evidence from sororal polygyny.

Tikopia: Normal Guinea, from Patri-Hawaiian (BDK), from Normal Hawaiian (KN), from Matri-Hawaiian (RS).

Timne: Normal Guinea, from Patri-Eskimo (D), from Normal Eskimo (LN).

Tismulun: Patri-Iroquois, from Bi-Iriquois (R), from Normal Iroquois (FNR), from Normal Nankanse or Matri-Yuman (O).

Tlingit: Avuncu-Crow, from Normal Crow (FNR).

Toda: Duo-Iroquois, from Patri-Iroquois (D), from Bi-Iroquois (R), from Normal Iroquois (FR).

Tokelau: Bi-Fox, from Normal Hawaiian (BGK), perhaps from Matri-Hawaiian (FR). The unusual transition from Normal Hawaiian directly to Bi-Fox is rendered probable by the strong patrilineal bias of the kindred, which might well suffice to produce a transition from Hawaiian to Omaha kinship terminology. Such a derivation, moreover, accords completely with Polynesian distributions as well as with the internal evidence from strong bilateral traits.

Tongans: Patri-Hawaiian, from Normal Hawaiian (KN), from Matri-Hawaiian (RS).

Trobrianders: Avuncu-Crow, from Normal Crow (FNR).

Trukese: Normal Crow, from Normal Nankanse (N), from Matri-Hawaiian (D), from Normal Hawaiian (GR).

Tsimshian: Avuncu-Iroquois, from Normal Iroquois (NRS), from Normal Nankanse or Matri-Yuman (O).

Tswana: Normal Yuman, from Patri-Iroquois (D), from Bi-Iroquois (R), from Normal Iroquois (NRS), from Normal Nankanse or Matri-

Yuman (O). The ill-defined kindreds are probably not an indication of derivation from one of the basic bilateral types. The patrilineages indicate incipient transition toward a Dakota structure.

Tubatulabal: Patri-Hawaiian, from Normal Hawaiian (N), from Matri-Hawaiian (F).

Tupinamba: Matri-Eskimo, from Normal Eskimo (LN).

Twi: Patri-Crow, from Bi-Crow (R), from Normal Crow (FRN).

Tzeltal: Normal Omaha, from Normal Fox (D), from Patri-Crow (D), from Bi-Crow (R), from Normal Crow (FRT).

Ulawans: Patri-Hawaiian, from Normal Hawaiian (GK), from Matri-Hawaiian (FR).

Vai: Normal Guinea, from Patri-Eskimo (D), from Bi-Eskimo (GR), from Matri-Eskimo (FR), from Normal Eskimo (N).

Vanimo: Normal Dakota, from Normal Guinea, Normal Yuman, or Duo-Iroquois (O).

Vedda: Normal Iroquois, from Normal Nankanse or Matri-Yuman (O). Bifurcate collateral terms for aunts may indicate some prior patrilocal structure.

Venda: Duo-Iroquois, from Patri-Iroquois (D), from Bi-Iroquois (R), from Normal Iroquois (NRS), from Normal Nankanse or Matri-Yuman (O).

Walapai: Normal Yuman, from Patri-Hawaiian, Patri-Iroquois, or Patri-Eskimo (O). Matri-patrilocal residence suggests a former matrilocal structure, but there is no internal evidence indicating whether it belonged to a bilateral or a matrilineal type.

Wapisiana: Normal Yuman, from Patri-Iroquois (D), from Bi-Iroquois (R), from Normal Iroquois (FNRT), from Normal Nankanse or Matri-Yuman (O).

Washo: Matri-Hawaiian, from Normal Hawaiian (NR), from Patri-Hawaiian (C).

Wichita: Matri-Hawaiian, from Normal Hawaiian (NR).

Winnebago: Normal Omaha, from Normal Fox (D), from Patri-Crow (D), from Bi-Crow (R), from Normal Crow (RST).

Wintu: Neo-Yuman, from Neo-Dakota (D), from Normal Dakota (CNR). Sororal polygyny is too sporadic to support the alternative derivation from Normal Iroquois.

Wishram: Patri-Hawaiian, from Normal Hawaiian (N), from Matri-Hawaiian (S).

Witoto: Normal Dakota, from Normal Guinea, Normal Yuman, or Duo-Iroquois (O).

Wogeo: Duo-Iroquois, from Patri-Iroquois (D), from Bi-Iroquois (R), from Normal Iroquois (NRS), from Normal Nankanse (N), from

Matri-Hawaiian (D), from Normal Hawaiian (GR). Beyond Normal Iroquois the reconstruction is dependent upon alternative generation terms for aunts.

Xosa: Normal Guinea, from Patri-Eskimo (BD), from Bi-Eskimo (R) or Patri-Nankanse (D). Sororal polygyny suggests an ultimate matrilocal derivation, which might be either Matri-Eskimo or some matrilineal-matrilocal structure.

Yaghan: Patri-Hawaiian, from Normal Hawaiian (N), from Matri-Hawaiian (RS).

Yako: possibly Duo-Crow, but cousin terms are lacking.

Yakut: Normal Sudanese, from Normal Guinea (N), from Patri-Hawaiian (D), from Normal Hawaiian (H), from Matri-Hawaiian (RT).

Yankee: Normal Eskimo, from Patri-Eskimo, Neo-Yuman, or Neo-Fox (O). Patrilineally inherited names may indicate an ultimate derivation from a patrilineal structure.

Yao: Normal Iroquois, from Normal Nankanse or Matri-Yuman (O).

Yaruro: Normal Crow, from Normal Iroquois, Matri-Fox, or Normal Nankanse (O).

Yuchi: Duo-Crow, from Patri-Crow (D), from Bi-Crow (R), from Normal Crow (FR). This reconstruction is confirmed by historical evidence of a former Crow structure, the Omaha cousin terminology being borrowed from the Shawnee.

Yuma: Bi-Dakota, from Normal Dakota (CNR).

Zulu: Normal Dakota, from Normal Guinea (N), from Patri-Hawaiian (BD), from Normal Hawaiian (BG), from Matri-Hawaiian (RS). An alternative derivation from Normal Eskimo via Normal Yuman is equally in accordance with the evidence.

Zuñi: Normal Crow, from Normal Iroquois, Matri-Fox, or Normal Nankanse (O).

In the foregoing reconstructions the author has purposely pushed his internal evidence to the extreme. Although this sometimes leads to inferences, particularly as to structural forms far removed from the present, that are very tenuous, it offers the maximum opportunity for testing the method. Even if the technique is sound, the reconstructions must include many errors—some due to faults in the sources and some to the author's failure to note relevant items of information. Doubtless, too, some of the criteria used are of uncertain reliability, and will require correction and refinement.

If, however, the method has any validity, this should be demonstrable from the mass implications of the reconstructions. Linguistic stocks provide an ideal means of making a test. An irresistible conclusion from demonstrated linguistic relationships is that the ancestors of the peoples now speaking related languages must once have formed a single linguistic community, which must also have had a common culture including a common social organization. As the descendants of the speakers of the ancestral language subsequently spread into different regions, they must necessarily have undergone modifications in culture and social structure as well as in language. By and large, therefore, we should expect differences in social organization among linguistically related peoples to decrease as we go backward in time, and to disappear as our time depth approaches the period of original linguistic community. Unless our reconstructions tend to show such a convergence in the past within individual linguistic stocks, the method must be presumed faulty. The evidence for each stock which is represented in our sample by three or more societies will therefore be subjected to analysis.

Algonquian. The eight tribes of the Algonquian linguistic stock appear to converge in the past toward a common ancestral structure of Hawaiian type. Four of them—the Arapaho, Blackfoot, Cheyenne, and Micmac—are still Hawaiian and show no survivals of any other structure. The Naskapi, who are now Yuman in structure, are shown by both internal and distributional evidence to have been Hawaiian at one time. For the Ojibwa, who are Dakota in type, Hawaiian is a probable though alternative derivation. Only the Fox and the Kickapoo, respectively of the Fox and Omaha types, cannot be derived with confidence from Hawaiian antecedents. It may well be, however, that the marked bilateral features in both societies, which the author has assumed to be the result of acculturation, may actually represent survivals of a former bilateral structure of Hawaiian type.

Athapaskan. The eight Athapaskan societies of the sample also appear to derive from a common Hawaiian origin. The Chiricahua, Hupa, Kiowa Apache, and Sekani, who live in four different culture areas, give no evidence of ever having had any other type of structure. The other four representatives of the stock are today matrilineal, but one of them, the Kaska, gives specific indications of Hawaiian antecedents and makes a similar derivation quite probable for the neighboring Carrier and Kutchin. The Navaho, finally, are shown by the distributional evidence from their Apache neighbors and kinsmen to be almost certainly derived from an Hawaiian structure, even though internal analysis reveals no survivals.

Australian. The five Australian tribes, all characterized today by double descent, clearly derive from matrilineal antecedents. That the ancestral structure was of the Iroquois type is specifically indicated for the Arunta, Dieri, Kamilaroi, and Kariera, and for the Murngin is as probable as the alternative derivation from a Crow structure.

Bantu. The 23 Bantu tribes, rather surprisingly for an area so notoriously patriarchal, give clear evidence of converging in the past toward a matrilineal structure, probably of Iroquois type. Only the Chewa, Ila, Kongo, Lamba, Mbundu, and Yao are strictly matrilineal today with no evidence of a former structure other than Iroquois or Crow. There are clear internal evidences of a similar antecedent structure, however, among the Herero and Venda with double descent, the Tswana with a Yuman structure, the Bena, Ganda, Henga, Pedi, and Swazi with Dakota structures, and the Shona, Soga, and Thonga with Omaha structures. This renders it highly probable that the Kyiga with a Dakota structure, the Gesu with a Sudanese structure, and the Kitara and Lenge with an Omaha structure have a similar matrilineal derivation, especially since all of them reveal bifurcate merging terminology, a matrilocal indicator, for aunts and/or nieces. The remaining tribes, the Xosa and Zulu, are also patrilineal today, though our reconstructions indicate for them an Eskimo and Hawaiian origin respectively. If the bilateral exogamous extensions on which these reconstructions are largely based should be attributable to acculturative influences, a matrilineal derivation would become probable even for them, and our cases would reveal no deviations from theoretical expectations.

Cariban. The three tribes of this stock—the Carib, Kallinago, and Macusi—are all Yuman in structure, and give no internal evidence of derivation from either a unilinear or a more basic bilateral structure.

Dravidian. Among the 10 Dravidian tribes, the Nayar and Vedda have Iroquois structures, the former being apparently derivable from Hawaiian antecedents. The Toda, with double descent, are in process of evolution to a Dakota from an Iroquois structure. The Baiga, Bhuiya, Chenchu, Coorg, Gond, and Reddi are of Dakota type without survivals, and may have followed the same transition as the Toda. The Ho, though classed as Guinea in type on the basis of similarly spelled terms for sister and cross-cousin, may actually be of Dakota type and susceptible to a similar interpretation. Except perhaps for the indicated antecedents of the Nayar, the data are consistent with an original Iroquois structure for all the Dravidian peoples and with the later emergence of a Dakota sub-group in the northern part of their habitat.

Ge. Of the four Ge tribes in our sample, the Ramkokamekra have a Crow structure with no indications of another derivation, the Cherente with a Sudanese structure show evidence of Crow antecedents, and the Apinaye with their anomalous Nankanse structure are at least matrilineal today and quite conceivably could once have had a Crow organization. Only the Kaingang with their Hawaiian structure are really divergent, and this may be due to the fact that the particular group studied gives clear evidence of cultural disintegration. It is not improbable, therefore, that all the Ge peoples may have had a Crow organization at the time that they formed a linguistic community.

Indo-European. Four of the major divisions within the Indo-European linguistic stock are represented in our sample—the Germanic division by the Yankees, the Slavic by the Ruthenians, the Thraco-Illyrian by the Albanians, and the Indo-Iranian by the Kurds and Ossets. Two of the five societies, the Ruthenians and Yankees, have social structures of Eskimo type without internal evidence of any other derivation. Two of the others, the Albanians and Ossets, are characterized today by structures of the Guinea type, but with survivals pointing to Eskimo antecedents. With the sole exception of the Kurds, therefore, all the evidence indicates convergence toward an Eskimo type of social structure in the prehistory of the Indo-European peoples. Even for the Kurds, with their Fox organization, the same ultimate derivation is by no means improbable, as witness their lineal terminology for aunts.

Malayo-Polynesian. The most striking confirmation of the method comes from the Malayo-Polynesian stock, of which our sample includes 42 societies stretching halfway around the earth from Hawaii to Madagascar. Of those in the Malayan division, the Ifugao are Hawaiian in structure without other indicated antecedents, while the Balinese with an Eskimo structure, the Mentaweians with a Yuman structure, the Minangkabau with a presumptive Iroquois structure, and the Tanala with a Dakota structure all show internal evidences of an Hawaiian derivation, leaving only the Sudanese Batak without clear survivals of a similar origin. In the Micronesian division, all three tribes—the Marshallese, Nauruans, and Trukese—give unmistakable evidence of Hawaiian antecedents, though all possess matrilineal organizations of Crow or Iroquois type today. In the Polynesian division, the Pukapukans with their Nankanse structure, the Tikopia with their Guinea structure, and the Tokelau with their Fox structure have all clearly sprung from an Hawaiian background, and all of the remaining eight representatives—the Futunans, Hawaiians, Mangarevans, Maori, Marquesans, Ontong-Javanese, Samoans, and Tongans—are still Hawaiian in structure with no internal indications of any other derivation. Only within the Melanesian division does evidence of a common Hawaiian structural prototype fall short of being conclusive. Even here the Hawaiian type is the earliest that can be inferred for the Eddystone and Ulawans, who are still Hawaiian in structure, for the Tetekantzi with a present Nankanse structure, for the Arosi, Getmatta, and Kurtatchi with Iroquois structures, and for the Mota and Pentecost with Crow structures. For fourteen other Melanesian tribes, however, internal evidence points no farther than a Yuman, Fox, Dakota, Iroquois, or Crow origin. In some of them, presumably, an earlier Hawaiian structure has left no survivals. But in many cases it is probable that the ancestors of the present population once spoke another language and acquired their present Malayo-Polynesian dialects through contact with a wave of later immigrants, as is indeed suggested by the survival of so-called "Papuan" languages in the interior of several of the larger Melanesian islands. Under these circumstances, survivals of a still earlier Malayo-Polynesian social structure would not be expected. It may be concluded, therefore, that our reconstructions provide overwhelming support for the hypothesis that the original Malayo-Polynesian speech community had a social organization of Hawaiian type.

Natchez-Muskogean. The three tribes of this linguistic stock—the Choctaw, Creek, and Natchez—agree in revealing a Crow structure with no internal evidence of other antecedents.

Papuan. Whether the natives of New Guinea fall into one or many linguistic stocks is still not known. Excluding inhabitants of offshore islands, however, our sample reveals no Papuan tribe with other than a patrilineal structure—Omaha among the Arapesh, Iatmul, and Kwoma, Sudanese among the Mailu, and Dakota among the Abelam, Banaro, Keraki, Kiwai, Kutubu, Orokaiva, and Vanimo. While there are suggestions of possible bilateral derivation for the Kutubu and Mailu, the evidence is so slight in both cases as to justify assuming a very old patrilineal structure throughout the area.

Salishan. The four Salishan tribes of the sample appear to derive from an ancestral Hawaiian structure. The Flathead, Klallam, and Sinkaietk still preserve organizations of this type, while the Eskimo structure of the Quinault contains intimations of a derivation from the Hawaiian type.

Sinitic. The ten Sinitic tribes unfortunately do not adequately represent the main divisions of this linguistic stock since eight of them are from Assam. A patrilineal structure is universal—in Assam nearly always of Omaha type without indications of other antecedents. A bilateral derivation is possible, however, for the Chinese, Lakher, and Lepcha. The evidence on the whole is inconclusive.

Siouan. Of the five tribes which speak Siouan languages, the Crow and Mandan are matrilineal, the Teton bilateral, and the Omaha and Winnebago patrilineal. Internal evidence, however, makes an original matrilineal organization, presumably of Crow type, possible for the Omaha and probable for the other four tribes. Despite the fact that Siouan and Algonquian tribes, where they have lived as neighbors in historical times, commonly reveal very similar social structures, analysis of these structures suggests sharply divergent antecedents for the two stocks.

Sudanese. Linguistic relationships in the Sudan, as in New Guinea, are little known and probably complex. Though they cannot be used to test our reconstructions, it may be of interest to note that these suggest an original Sudanese or Omaha core in the Nilotic area, an Eskimo core in Sierra Leone, Liberia, and coastal Nigeria, a Crow core in Ashanti and Dahomey, and an Hawaiian core in Northern Nigeria.

Tanoan. The evidence from our three Tanoan tribes is contradictory. Iroquois antecedents are indicated for the matrilineal Jemez and an Omaha origin for the patrilineal but non-exogamous Tewa, while the Taos reveal no survivals of a structure differing from their present Eskimo one. This is the only linguistic stock for which the evidence is definitely inconsistent with our hypothesis. However, this may result primarily from the fact that we have followed Harrington rather than Parsons on the rule of descent in Tewa sibs.

Ural-Altaic. The three tribes of this stock represent different major divisions within it—the Finnic (Lapps), the Turkic (Yakut), and the Tungusic (Manchu). The Lapps have a social structure of stable Eskimo type, the Yakut a Sudanese structure apparently derived from Hawaiian, and the Manchu a Dakota structure without survivals. This diversity in social organization, however, may not be significant since linguists are still in dispute as to the unity of the stock. The major divisions, therefore, may actually be independent stocks, or they may be related so remotely that convergence in social structure is not to be expected.

Uto-Aztecan. The eight representatives of this stock clearly show convergence toward an ancestral Hawaiian structure. The Comanche, Paiute, Shoshone, Tarahumara, and Tubatulabal, who are scattered in four culture areas, are still Hawaiian in structure without internal evidences of any other derivation. The Dakota organization of the Luiseno and the Crow organization of the Hopi both reveal traces of Hawaiian antecedents. Only the Pima, with a Yuman structure presumably derived from Dakota, show no unmistakable survivals of the presumably original Hawaiian structure. Conceivably, however, patrilineal descent in this tribe is incipient rather than decadent, having been borrowed from the neighboring Yuman tribes on the basis of the existing rule of patrilocal residence.

Yuman. Of the four tribes representing this stock, the Yuma are Dakota in structural type, while the other three tribes reveal clear evidences of development toward the same structure, the Havasupai and Walapai being Yuman and the Maricopa Guinea in type. Only the Maricopa show internal evidence of a prior organization, in their case presumably Hawaiian. The total impression is of a group of tribes with a recent or incipient patrilineate evolving from patrilocal residence out of a formerly bilateral and probably Hawaiian structure.

Despite errors and oversights with their necessarily blurring effect, the foregoing survey of our reconstructions by linguistic stocks strikingly confirms the theoretically expected tendency toward convergence as one moves backward in time, and hence validates the method. Since the method is based squarely upon our hypotheses concerning the interrelationships of structural traits and the evolution of social organization as a whole, these theories, too, are validated. To their statistical support is now added a demonstration which rests exclusively on historical rather than cross-cultural assumptions. Historical and comparative tests lead to the same conclusion. The sociologist or functional anthropologist who suspects the one, and the historian or historical anthropologist who suspects the other, may each exercise his private choice. The social scientist, presumably, can accept both and take comfort that they are in complete agreement.

BIBLIOGRAPHY

All the ethnographic sources utilized for data on the 250 sample societies are listed below in alphabetical order of the societies for which they were consulted. An asterisk before a tribal name indicates that the sources were consulted in the files of the Cross-Cultural Survey. Works of a theoretical nature are not listed, since complete references are given in footnotes at the points where they are cited.

Abelam
  Kaberry, P. M. "The Abelam Tribe, Sepik District, New Guinea." *Oceania*, XI, 233–257, 345–367. 1941.

Acholi
  Seligman, C. G. *Pagan Tribes of the Nilotic Sudan,* pp. 113–134. London, 1932.

Acoma
  Kroeber, A. L. "Zuñi Kin and Clan." *Anthropological Papers of the American Museum of Natural History*, XVIII, 83–87. 1917.
  Parsons, E. C. "The Kinship Nomenclature of the Pueblo Indians." *American Anthropologist*, n.s., XXXIV, 377–389. 1932.
  White, L. A. "The Acoma Indians." *Annual Reports of the Bureau of American Ethnology*, XLVII, 17–192. 1930.

Albanians
  Durham, M. E. *Some Tribal Origins, Laws and Customs of the Balkans.* London, 1928.

Andamanese
  Man, E. H. *On the Aboriginal Inhabitants of the Andaman Islands.* London, 1882.
  Radcliffe-Brown, A. R. *The Andaman Islanders.* Second edit. Cambridge, 1933.

Angami
  Hutton, J. H. *The Angami Nagas.* London, 1921.

Angmagsalik

Holm, G. "Ethnological Sketch of the Angmagsalik Eskimo." *Meddelelser om Grønland*, XXXIX, 1–147. 1914.

Ao

Mills, J. P. *The Ao Nagas.* London, 1926.

*Apinaye

Nimuendajú, C. "The Apinayé." *Catholic University of America Anthropological Series*, VIII, 1–189. 1939.

Arapaho

Eggan, F. "The Cheyenne and Arapaho Kinship System." *Social Anthropology of North American Tribes*, ed. F. Eggan, pp. 33–95. Chicago, 1937.

Arapesh

Mead, M. "The Mountain Arapesh." *Anthropological Papers of the American Museum of Natural History*, XXXVI, 139–349; XXXVII, 317–451; XL, 183–419. 1940–47.

Araucanians

Cooper, J. M. "The Araucanians." *Bulletin of the Bureau of American Ethnology*, CXLIII, ii, 687–760. 1946.

Hallowell, A. I. "Araucanian Parallels to the Omaha Kinship Pattern." *American Anthropologist*, n.s., XLV, 489–491. 1943.

Arosi

Fox, C. E. "Social Organization in San Cristoval, Solomon Islands." *Journal of the Royal Anthropological Institute*, XLIX, 94–120. 1919.

*Arunta

Spencer, B., and Gillen, F. J. *The Arunta.* 2 vols. London, 1927.

*Ashanti

Rattray, R. S. *Ashanti.* Oxford, 1923.

——. *Ashanti Law and Constitution.* Oxford, 1929.

Atsugewi

Garth, T. R. "Kinship Terminology, Marriage Practices and Behavior toward Kin among the Atsugewi." *American Anthropologist*, n.s., XLVI, 348–361. 1944.

Awuna (Fera group)

Rattray, R. S. *The Tribes of the Ashanti Hinterland.* 2 vols. Oxford, 1932.

Aymara

Tschopik, H. "The Aymara." *Bulletin of the Bureau of American Ethnology*, CXLIII, ii, 501–573. 1946.

Azande

Seligman, C. G. *Pagan Tribes of the Nilotic Sudan*, pp. 495–539. London, 1932.

Bachama
   Meek, C. K. *Tribal Studies in Northern Nigeria*, I, 1–57. London, 1931.
Baiga
   Elwin, V. *The Baiga.* London, 1939.
Balinese
   Belo, J. "A Study of a Balinese Family." *American Anthropologist*, n.s.,
      XXXVIII, 12–31. 1936.
   Covarrubias, M. *Island of Bali.* New York, 1937.
Banaro
   Thurnwald, R. "Banaro Society." *Memoirs of the American Anthro-
      pological Association*, III, 251–391. 1916.
Bari
   Seligman, C. G. *Pagan Tribes of the Nilotic Sudan*, pp. 239–296.
      London, 1932.
Batak (Toba group)
   Loeb, E. M. "Patrilineal and Matrilineal Organization in Sumatra: the
      Batak and the Minangkabau." *American Anthropologist*, n.s., XXXV,
      16–50. 1933.
Bena
   Culwick, A. T. and G. M. *Ubena of the Rivers.* London, 1936.
Bhuiya
   Sarat Chandra Roy. *The Hill Bhuiyas of Orissa.* Ranchi, 1935.
Blackfoot (Piegan group)
   Josselin de Jong, J. P. B. de. "Social Organization of the Southern
      Piegans." *Internationales Archiv für Ethnographie*, XX, 191–197.
      1912.
   Michelson, T. "Notes on the Piegan System of Consanguinity." *Holmes
      Anniversary Volume*, pp. 320–333. Washington, 1916.
   Spier, L. "Blackfoot Relationship Terms." *American Anthropologist*,
      n.s., XVII, 603–607. 1915.
   Wissler, C. "The Social Life of the Blackfoot Indians." *Anthropological
      Papers of the American Museum of Natural History*, VII, 1–64. 1912.
Bolewa
   Meek, C. K. *Tribal Studies in Northern Nigeria*, II, 288–310. London,
      1931.
Buin
   Rivers, W. H. R. *The History of Melanesian Society*, I, 258–261. Cam-
      bridge, 1914.
   Thurnwald, H. "Woman's Status in Buin Society." *Oceania*, V, 142–
      170. 1934.
Carib (Barama River group)
   Gillin, J. "The Barama River Caribs of British Guiana." *Papers of the*

Peabody Museum of American Archaeology and Ethnology, Harvard University, XIV, No. 2. 1936.

Carrier

Morice, A. G. "The Western Dénés." *Proceedings of the Canadian Institute,* series 3, VII, 109–174. 1890.

*Cayapa

Barrett, S. A. "The Cayapa Indians of Ecuador." *Indian Notes and Monographs,* XL, Parts 1–2. 1925.

Chawai

Meek, C. K. *Tribal Studies in Northern Nigeria,* II, 145–164. London, 1931.

Chenchu

Fürer-Haimendorf, C. von. *The Chenchus.* London, 1943.

*Cherente

Nimuendajú, C. "The Šerente." *Publications of the Frederick Webb Hodge Anniversary Publication Fund,* IV, 1–106. 1942.

Cherokee (Eastern group)

Gilbert, W. H., Jr. "Eastern Cherokee Social Organization." *Social Anthropology of North American Tribes,* ed. F. Eggan, pp. 285–338. Chicago, 1937.

*Chewa

Steytler, J. G. Ethnographic Report on the Achewa Tribe of Nyasaland. Unpublished manuscript.

Cheyenne

Eggan, F. "The Cheyenne and Arapaho Kinship System." *Social Anthropology of North American Tribes,* ed. F. Eggan, pp. 35–95. Chicago, 1937.

Chinese

Chen, T. S., and Shryock, J. K. "Chinese Relationship Terms." *American Anthropologist,* n.s., XXXIV, 623–669. 1932.

Feng, H. Y. "Teknonymy as a Formative Factor in the Chinese Kinship System." *American Anthropologist,* n.s., XXXVIII, 59–66. 1936.

Kroeber, A. L. "Process in the Chinese Kinship System." *American Anthropologist,* n.s., XXXV, 151–157. 1933.

Latourette, K. S. *The Chinese, Their History and Culture.* 2 vols. New York, 1934.

Chiricahua

Opler, M. E. "An Outline of Chiricahua Apache Social Organization." *Social Anthropology of North American Tribes,* ed. F. Eggan, pp. 171–239. Chicago, 1937.

Choctaw
Eggan, F. "Historical Change in the Choctaw Kinship System." *American Anthropologist*, n.s., XXXIX, 34–52. 1937.
Swanton, J. R. "Source Material for the Social and Ceremonial Life of the Choctaw Indians." *Bulletin of the Bureau of American Ethnology*, CIII, 1–282. 1931.

°Chukchee
Bogoras, W. "The Chukchee," Part II. *Memoirs of the American Museum of Natural History*, XI, 277–733. 1907.

Cochiti
Goldfrank, E. S. "The Social and Ceremonial Organization of Cochiti." *Memoirs of the American Anthropological Association*, XXXIII, 1–129. 1927.
Parsons, E. C. "The Kinship Nomenclature of the Pueblo Indians." *American Anthropologist*, n.s., XXXIV, 377–389. 1932.

Comanche
Hoebel, A. E. "Comanche and H3kandika Shoshone Relationship Systems." *American Anthropologist*, n.s., XLI, 440–457. 1939.

Coorg
Emeneau, M. B. "Kinship and Marriage among the Coorgs." *Journal of the Royal Asiatic Society of Bengal, Letters*, IV, 123–147. 1939.

°Copper Eskimo
Jenness, D. "The Life of the Copper Eskimos." *Report of the Canadian Arctic Expedition*, 1913–18, XII, A, 1–277. Ottawa, 1922.

°Creek
Swanton, J. R. "Social Organization and Social Usages of the Indians of the Creek Confederacy." *Annual Reports of the Bureau of American Ethnology*, XLII, 23–472. 1928.

°Crow
Lowie, R. H. *The Crow Indians*. New York, 1935.
——. "The Kinship Systems of the Crow and Hidatsa." *Proceedings of the International Congress of Americanists*, XIX, 340–343. 1917.
——. "Social Life of the Crow Indians." *Anthropological Papers of the American Museum of Natural History*, XXV, 179–248. 1922.
——. "Supplementary Notes on the Social Life of the Crow." *Anthropological Papers of the American Museum of Natural History*, XXI, 53–86. 1917.
Voget, F. W. Unpublished field notes.

°Cuna
Nordenskiöld, E. "An Historical and Ethnological Survey of the Cuna Indians," ed. H. Wassén. *Comparative Ethnographical Studies*, X, 1–686. Göteborg, 1938.

*Dahomeans
  Herskovits, M. J. *Dahomey, an Ancient West African Kingdom.* 2 vols. New York, 1938.
Daka (Dirrim group)
  Meek, C. K. *Tribal Studies in Northern Nigeria,* I, 394–412. London, 1931.
*Dieri
  Elkin, P. A. "The Dieri Kinship System." *Journal of the Royal Anthropological Institute,* LXI, 493–498. 1931.
  Howitt, A. W. *The Native Tribes of South-East Australia.* London, 1904.
Dinka
  Seligman, C. G. *Pagan Tribes of the Nilotic Sudan,* pp. 135–205. London, 1932.
*Dobuans
  Fortune, R. F. *Sorcerers of Dobu.* New York, 1932.
Dorobo
  Huntingford, G. W. B. "The Social Organization of the Dorobo." *African Studies,* I, 183–200. 1942.
Eddystone
  Rivers, W. H. R. *The History of Melanesian Society,* I, 251–255. Cambridge, 1914.
  ——. *Psychology and Ethnology,* pp. 71–94. London, 1926.
Edo
  Thomas, N. W. *Anthropological Report of the Edo-speaking Peoples of Nigeria.* London, 1910.
Epi
  Deacon, A. B. "Notes on Some Islands of the New Hebrides." *Journal of the Royal Anthropological Institute,* LIX, 498–506. 1929.
Eromangans
  Humphreys, C. B. *The Southern New Hebrides.* Cambridge, 1926.
Eyak
  Birket-Smith, K., and De Laguna, F. *The Eyak Indians of the Copper River Delta, Alaska.* København, 1938.
Fijians (Lau group)
  Hocart, A. M. "Lau Islands, Fiji." *Bulletin of the Bernice P. Bishop Museum,* LXII, 1–240. 1929.
Flathead
  Turney-High, H. H. "The Flathead Indians of Montana." *Memoirs of the American Anthropological Association,* XLVII, 1–161. 1937.
Fox
  Tax, S. "The Social Organization of the Fox Indians." *Social Anthro-*

pology of North American Tribes, ed. F. Eggan, pp. 243–282. Chicago, 1937.

Futunans
Burrows, E. G. "Ethnology of Futuna." *Bulletin of the Bernice P. Bishop Museum,* CXXXVIII, 1–239. 1936.

Ganda
Roscoe, J. *The Baganda.* London, 1911.

Gesu
Roscoe, J. *The Bagesu and Other Tribes of the Uganda Protectorate,* pp. 1–50. Cambridge, 1924.

Getmatta
Chinnery, E. W. P. "Certain Natives in South New Britain and Dampier Straits." *Territory of New Guinea Anthropological Reports,* III, 1–102. 1927.

*Gilyak
Sternberg, L. *Semya i Rod u Narodov Severo-Vostochnoi Azii.* Leningrad, 1933.

*Gond (Maria group)
Grigson, W. V. *The Maria Gonds of Bastar.* London, 1938.

Haida
Murdock, G. P. "Kinship and Social Behavior among the Haida." *American Anthropologist,* n.s., XXXVI, 355–385. 1934.
—. *Our Primitive Contemporaries,* pp. 221–263. New York, 1934.

Havasupai
Spier, L. "Havasupai Ethnography." *Anthropological Papers of the American Museum of Natural History,* XXIX, 81–392. 1928.
—. "A Suggested Origin for Gentile Organization." *American Anthropologist,* n.s., XXIV, 487–489. 1922.

Hawaiians
Emory, K. P. Personal communication.
Morgan, L. H. "Systems of Consanguinity and Affinity of the Human Family." *Smithsonian Contributions to Knowledge,* XVII, 1–590. 1870.
Rivers, W. H. R. *The History of Melanesian Society,* I, 374–387. Cambridge, 1914.

Henga (Tumbuka group)
Sanderson, M. "The Relationship Systems of the Wangonde and Wahenga Tribes, Nyasaland." *Journal of the Royal Anthropological Institute,* LIII, 448–459. 1923.
Young, T. C. *Notes on the Customs and Folklore of the Tumbuka-Kamanga Peoples.* Livingstonia, 1931.

Herero

Luttig, H. G. *The Religious System and Social Organization of the Herero.* Utrecht, 1934.

Ho

Chatterjee, A., and Das, T. "The Hos of Seraikella." *Anthropological Papers of the University of Calcutta,* n.s., I, 1–94. 1927.

*Hopi

Beaglehole, P. "Notes on Personal Development in Two Hopi Villages." *Memoirs of the American Anthropological Association,* XLIV, 25–65. 1935.

Eggan, F. R. *The Kinship System of the Hopi Indians.* Chicago, 1936.

Lowie, R. H. "Hopi Kinship." *Anthropological Papers of the American Museum of Natural History,* XXX, 361–397. 1929.

Parsons, E. C. "The Kinship Nomenclature of the Pueblo Indians." *American Anthropologist,* n.s., XXXIV, 377–389. 1932.

Simmons, L. W. Unpublished field notes.

Titiev, M. "The Problem of Cross-Cousin Marriage among the Hopi." *American Anthropologist,* n.s., XL, 105–111. 1938.

*Hottentot (Nama group)

Hoernlé, A. W. "The Social Organization of the Nama Hottentots of Southwest Africa." *American Anthropologist,* n.s., XXVII, 1–24. 1925.

Schultze, L. *Aus Namaland und Kalahari.* Jena, 1907.

Hupa

Gifford, E. W. "Californian Kinship Terminologies." *University of California Publications in American Archaeology and Ethnology.* XVIII, 17–18. 1922.

Goddard, P. E. "Life and Culture of the Hupa." *University of California Publications in American Archaeology and Ethnology,* I, 1–88. 1903.

Kroeber, A. L. "Yurok and Neighboring Kin Term Systems." *University of California Publications in American Archaeology and Ethnology,* XXXV, 15–22. 1934.

*Iatmul

Bateson, G. *Naven.* Cambridge, 1936.

——. "Social Structure of the Iatmül People of the Sepik River." *Oceania,* II, 245–291, 401–451. 1932.

Ibo

Meek, C. K. *Law and Authority in a Nigerian Tribe.* London, 1937.

*Ifugao

Barton, R. F. "Ifugao Law." *University of California Publications in American Archaeology and Ethnology,* XV, 1–186. 1919.

——. *Philippine Pagans.* London, 1938.

Lambrecht, F. "The Mayawyaw Ritual." *Publications of the Catholic Anthropological Conference,* IV, 169–325. 1935.

Ila

Smith, E. W., and Dale, A. M. *The Ila-speaking Peoples of Northern Rhodesia.* 2 vols. London, 1920.

Inca

Rowe, J. H. "Inca Culture at the Time of the Spanish Conquest." *Bulletin of the Bureau of American Ethnology,* CXLIII, ii, 183–330. 1946.

Ingassana

Seligman, C. G. *Pagan Tribes of the Nilotic Sudan,* pp. 429–437. London, 1932.

Iroquois (Seneca group)

Goldenweiser, A. A. "On Iroquois Work." *Summary Report of the* [Canada] *Geological Survey, Department of Mines,* 1912, 464–475; 1913, 363–372.

Morgan, L. H. *League of the Ho-Dé-No-Sau-Nee or Iroquois,* ed. H. M. Lloyd. 2 vols. New York, 1901.

——. "Systems of Consanguinity and Affinity of the Human Family." *Smithsonian Contributions to Knowledge,* XVII, 150–169, 291–382. 1871.

Jemez

Parsons, E. C. "Kinship Nomenclature of the Pueblo Indians." *American Anthropologist,* n.s., XXXIV, 377–389. 1932.

——. *The Pueblo of Jemez.* New Haven, 1925.

*Jukun

Meek, C. K. *A Sudanese Kingdom: an Ethnographical Study of the Jukun-speaking Peoples of Nigeria.* London, 1931.

*Kababish

Seligman, C. G. and B. Z. "The Kabâbîsh, a Sudan Arab Tribe." *Harvard African Studies,* II, 105–185. 1918.

Kaingang

Henry, J. *Jungle People.* New York, 1941.

Kallinago

Kirchhoff, P. "Die Verwandtschaftsorganisation der Urwaldstämme Südamerikas." *Zeitschrift für Ethnologie,* LXIII, 137–141. 1931.

Taylor, D. "Kinship and Social Structure of the Island Carib." *Southwestern Journal of Anthropology,* II, 180–212. 1946.

*Kamilaroi

Howitt, A. W. *The Native Tribes of South-East Australia.* London, 1904.

Radcliffe-Brown, A. "Notes on the Social Organization of Australian Tribes." *Journal of the Royal Anthropological Institute*, LIII, 424–446. 1923.
*Kariera
Radcliffe-Brown, A. R. "Three Tribes of Western Australia." *Journal of the Royal Anthropological Institute*, XLIII, 143–170. 1913.
Kaska
Honigmann, J. J. Kaska Ethos. Unpublished doctoral dissertation.
Katab
Meek, C. K. *Tribal Studies in Northern Nigeria*, II, 1–90. London, 1931.
*Keraki
Williams, F. E. *Papuans of the Trans-Fly*. Oxford, 1936.
*Kickapoo
Hockett, C. F. Unpublished field notes.
Jones, W. "Kickapoo Ethnological Notes." *American Anthropologist*, n.s., XV, 332–335. 1913.
Morgan, L. H. "Systems of Consanguinity and Affinity of the Human Family." *Smithsonian Contributions to Knowledge*, XVII, 291–382. 1871.
Kilba
Meek, C. K. *Tribal Studies in Northern Nigeria*, I, 181–213. London, 1931.
Kiowa Apache
McAllister, J. G. "Kiowa-Apache Social Organization." *Social Anthropology of North American Tribes*, ed. F. Eggan, pp. 97–169. Chicago, 1937.
Kitara
Roscoe, J. *The Bakitara or Banyoro*. Cambridge, 1923.
*Kiwai
Landtman, G. *The Kiwai Papuans of British New Guinea*. London, 1927.
Klallam
Gunther, E. "Klallam Ethnography." *University of Washington Publications in Anthropology*, 1, 171–314. 1927.
Klamath
Spier, L. "Klamath Ethnography." *University of California Publications in American Archaeology and Ethnology*, XXX, 1–338. 1930.
Kongo
Weeks, J. H. *Among the Primitive Bakongo*. London, 1914.
Koranko
Thomas, N. W. *Anthropological Report on Sierra Leone*. London, 1916.

Koryak
Jochelson, W. "The Koryak." *Memoirs of the American Museum of Natural History*, Vol. X. 1905–08.

*Kurd (Rowanduz group)
Leach, E. R. "Social and Economic Organization of the Rowanduz Kurds." London School of Economics and Political Science, *Monographs on Social Anthropology*, III, 1–74. 1940.

*Kurtatchi
Blackwood, B. *Both Sides of Buka Passage*. Oxford, 1935.

*Kutchin (Peel River group)
Osgood, C. "Contributions to the Ethnography of the Kutchin." *Yale University Publications in Anthropology*, XIV, 1–189. 1936.

Kutenai
Boas, F. "Kinship Terms of the Kutenai Indians." *American Anthropologist*, n.s., XXI, 98–101. 1919.

Chamberlain, A. F. "Report on the Kootenay Indians of South-Eastern British Columbia." *Reports of the British Association for the Advancement of Science*, LXII, 549–614. 1892.

Sapir, E. "Kinship Terms of the Kootenay Indians." *American Anthropologist*, n.s., XX, 414–418. 1918.

Kutubu
Williams, F. E. "Natives of Lake Kutubu, Papua." *Oceania*, XI, 121–157, 259–294, 374–401; XII, 49–74, 134–154. 1940–41.

*Kwakiutl
Boas, F. "The Social Organization and the Secret Societies of the Kwakiutl Indians." *Report of the United States National Museum*, 1895, 311–738.

——. "The Social Organization of the Kwakiutl Indians." *American Anthropologist*, n.s., XXII, 111–126. 1920.

——. "Tsimshian Mythology." *Annual Reports of the Bureau of American Ethnology*, XXXI, 494–495. 1916.

Ford, C. S. *Smoke from Their Fires*. New Haven, 1941.

*Kwoma
Whiting, J. W. M. *Becoming a Kwoma*. New Haven, 1941.

——. Unpublished field notes.

Whiting, J. W. M., and Reed, S. W. "Kwoma Culture." *Oceania*, IX, 170–216. 1938.

Kyiga
Roscoe, J. *The Bagesu and Other Tribes of the Uganda Protectorate*, pp. 162–183. Cambridge, 1924.

*Lakher
Parry, N. E. *The Lakhers*. London, 1932.

*Lamba
Doke, C. M. *The Lambas of Northern Rhodesia.* London, 1931.
*Lango
Driberg, J. H. *The Lango.* London, 1923.
——. "Some Aspects of Lango Kinship." *Sociologus,* VIII, 44–61. 1932.
*Lapps
Bernatzik, H. A. *Overland with the Nomad Lapps.* New York, 1938.
Nielsen, K. "Lappisk Ordbok." *Institutet for Sammenlignende Kultur-forskning,* series B, XVII, 1–718. Oslo, 1934.
Nordström, E. B. *Tent Folk of the Far North.* London, 1930.
Lenge
Earthy, E. D. *Valenge Women.* London, 1933.
*Lepcha
Gorer, G. *Himalayan Village.* London, 1938.
*Lesu
Powdermaker, H. *Life in Lesu.* New York, 1933.
Lhota
Mills, J. P. *The Lhota Nagas.* London, 1922.
Limba
Thomas, N. W. *Anthropological Report on Sierra Leone.* London, 1916.
Longuda
Meek, C. K. *Tribal Studies in Northern Nigeria,* II, 331–368. London, 1931.
Luiseno
Gifford, E. W. "Clans and Moieties in Southern California." *University of California Publications in American Archaeology and Ethnology,* XIV, 155–219. 1918.
Kroeber, A. L. "California Kinship Systems." *University of California Publications in American Archaeology and Ethnology,* XII, 339–396. 1917.
Mabuiag
Haddon, A. C., ed. *Reports of the Cambridge Anthropological Expedition to Torres Straits,* Vol. V. Cambridge, 1904.
*Macusi
Farabee, W. C. "The Central Caribs." *University of Pennsylvania Museum Anthropological Publications,* X, 13–152. 1924.
Kirchhoff, P. "Die Verwandtschaftsorganisation der Urwaldstämme Südamerikas." *Zeitschrift für Ethnologie,* LXIII, 101–117. 1931.
*Mailu
Malinowski, B. "The Natives of Mailu." *Transactions and Proceedings of the Royal Society of South Australia,* XXXIX, 494–706. 1915.

Malabu

Meek, C. K. *Tribal Studies in Northern Nigeria,* I, 91–113. London, 1931.

Manchu

Shirokogoroff, S. M. "Social Organization of the Manchus." *Royal Asiatic Society (North China Branch), Extra Volume,* III, 1–194. Shanghai, 1924.

°Mandan

Lowie, R. H. "Social Life of the Mandan." *Anthropological Papers of the American Museum of Natural History,* XXI, 7–16. 1917.

Will, G. F., and Spinden, H. J. "The Mandans." *Papers of the Peabody Museum of American Archaeology and Ethnology,* Harvard University, III, 81–219. 1906.

Mangarevans

Buck, P. H. "Ethnology of Mangareva." *Bulletin of the Bernice P. Bishop Museum,* CLVII, 1–519. 1938.

°Manus

Mead, M. "Kinship in the Admiralty Islands." *Anthropological Papers of the American Museum of Natural History,* XXXIV, 181–337. 1933.

°Maori

Best, E. *The Maori.* 2 vols. Wellington, 1924.

——. "Maori Marriage Customs." *Transactions and Proceedings of the New Zealand Institute,* XXXVI, 14–67. 1903.

——. "Maori Nomenclature." *Journal of the Royal Anthropological Institute,* XXXII, 182–201. 1902.

Firth, R. *Primitive Economics of the New Zealand Maori.* New York, 1929.

°Maricopa

Spier, L. *Yuman Tribes of the Gila River.* Chicago, 1933.

Marquesans

Handy, E. S. C. "The Native Culture in the Marquesas." *Bulletin of the Bernice P. Bishop Museum,* IX, 1–358. 1923.

Linton, R. "Marquesan Culture." *The Individual and His Society,* by A. Kardiner, pp. 137–196. New York, 1939.

°Marshallese

Murdock, G. P., Ford, C. S., and Whiting, J. W. M. "Marshall Islands." United States Navy, Office of Chief of Naval Operations, *Military Government Handbooks,* I, 1–113. 1943.

Wedgwood, C. H. "Notes on the Marshall Islands." *Oceania,* XIII, 1–23. 1942.

*Masai

Hollis, A. C. "A Note on the Masai System of Relationship and Other Matters connected therewith." *Journal of the Royal Anthropological Institute*, XL, 473–482. 1910.

Leakey, L. S. B. "Some Notes on the Masai of Kenya Colony." *Journal of the Royal Anthropological Institute*, LX, 185–209. 1930.

Merker, M. *Die Masai*. Berlin, 1904.

*Mataco

Hunt, R. J. "Mataco-English and English-Mataco Dictionary." *Ethnological Studies*, V, 1–98. Göteborg, 1937.

Karsten, R. "Indian Tribes of the Argentine and Bolivian Chaco." *Societas Scientiarum Fennica, Commentationes Humanorum Litterarum*, IV, i, 1–236. 1932.

Métraux, A. Unpublished field notes.

*Mbundu

Hambly, W. D. "The Ovimbundu of Angola." *Field Museum of Natural History Anthropological Series*, XXI, 89–362. 1934.

Tastevin. "La famille 'Nyaneka.'" *Semaine Internationale d'Ethnologie Religieuse*, V, 269–287. 1929.

Mendi

Thomas, N. W. *Anthropological Report on Sierra Leone*. London, 1916.

Mentaweians (North Pageh group)

Loeb, A. M. "Mentawei Social Organization." *American Anthropologist*, n.s., XXX, 408–433. 1928.

Micmac

Le Clercq, C. "New Relations of Gaspesia," ed. W. F. Ganong. *Publications of the Champlain Society*, V, 1–452. Toronto, 1910.

Morgan, L. H. "Systems of Consanguinity and Affinity of the Human Family." *Smithsonian Contributions to Knowledge*, XVII, 291–382. 1871.

Parsons, E. C. "Micmac Notes." *Journal of American Folk-Lore*, XXXIX, 460–485. 1926.

Speck, F. G. "Beothuk and Micmac." *Indian Notes and Monographs*, series 2, XXII, 1–187. 1921.

——. "Kinship Terms and the Family Band among the Northeastern Algonkian." *American Anthropologist*, n.s., XX, 143–161. 1918.

Mikir

Stack, E. *The Mikirs*. London, 1908.

Minangkabau

Loeb, E. M. "Patrilineal and Matrilineal Organization in Sumatra." *American Anthropologist*, n.s., XXXVI, 26–56. 1934.

*Miriam
   Haddon, A. C., ed. *Reports of the Cambridge Anthropological Expedition to Torres Straits*, Vol. VI. Cambridge, 1908.
Miwok
   Gifford, E. W. "Miwok Moieties." *University of California Publications in American Archaeology and Ethnology*, XII, 139–194. 1916.
Mota
   Codrington, R. H. *The Melanesians*. Oxford, 1891.
   Rivers, W. H. R. *The History of Melanesian Society*, I, 20–176. Cambridge, 1914.
*Murngin
   Lawrence, W. E., and Murdock, G. P. "Murngin Social Organization." *American Anthropologist*, n.s., Vol. LI. 1949.
   Warner, W. L. *A Black Civilization*. New York, 1937.
   Webb, T. T. Personal communication, 1938.
Nambikuara
   Levi-Strauss, C. "The Social and Psychological Aspect of Chieftainship in a Primitive Tribe." *Transactions of the New York Academy of Sciences*, series 2, VII, 16–32. 1944.
   ——. "The Social Use of Kinship Terms among Brazilian Indians." *American Anthropologist*, n.s., XLV, 398–409. 1943.
Nandi
   Hollis, A. C. *The Nandi, Their Language and Folk-Lore*. Oxford, 1909.
Nankanse
   Rattray, R. S. *The Tribes of the Ashanti Hinterland*. 2 vols. Oxford, 1932.
*Naskapi (Northern group)
   Hallowell, A. I. "Kinship Terms and Cross-Cousin Marriage of the Montagnais and the Cree." *American Anthropologist*, n.s., XXXIV, 171–199. 1932.
   Speck, F. G. "Kinship Terms and the Family Band among the Northeastern Algonquians." *Proceedings of the International Congress of Americanists*, XIX, 143–161. 1918.
   Strong, W. D. "Cross-Cousin Marriage and the Culture of the Northeastern Algonquian." *American Anthropologist*, n.s., XXXI, 277–288. 1929.
*Natchez
   Haas, M. R. "Natchez and Chitimacha Clans and Kinship Terminology." *American Anthropologist*, n.s., XLI, 597–610. 1939.
   Swanton, J. R. "Indian Tribes of the Lower Mississippi Valley." *Bulletin of the Bureau of American Ethnology*, XLIII, 1–274. 1911.
   ——. "Social Organization and Social Usages of the Indians of the

Creek Confederacy." *Annual Reports of the Bureau of American Ethnology*, XLII, 23–472. 1925.

Nauruans

Wedgwood, C. "Report on Research Work in Nauru Island, Central Pacific." *Oceania*, VI, 359–391; VII, 1–33. 1936.

*Navaho

Carr, M., Spencer, K., and Woolley, D. "Navaho Clans and Marriage at Pueblo Alto." *American Anthropologist*, n.s., XLI, 245–257. 1939.

Opler, M. E. "The Kinship Systems of the Southern Athabaskan-speaking Tribes." *American Anthropologist*, n.s., XXXVIII, 620–633. 1936.

Reichard, G. A. "Social Life of the Navajo Indians." *Columbia University Contributions to Anthropology*, VII, 1–239. 1928.

Nayar

Fawcett, F. "Nayars of Malabar." *Bulletin of the Madras Government Museum*, III, 185–322. 1901.

Panikkar, K. M. "Some Aspects of Nayar Life." *Journal of the Royal Anthropological Institute*, XLVII, 254–293. 1918.

Ndoro

Meek, C. K. *Tribal Studies in Northern Nigeria*, II, 589–605. London, 1931.

Ngizim

Meek, C. K. *Tribal Studies in Northern Nigeria*, II, 247–269. London, 1931.

Nuba (Lafofa group)

Seligman, C. G. *Pagan Tribes of the Nilotic Sudan*, pp. 366–412. London, 1932.

Ojibwa

Landes, R. "Ojibwa Sociology." *Columbia University Contributions to Anthropology*, XXIX, 1–144. 1937.

*Omaha

Dorsey, J. O. "Omaha Sociology." *Annual Reports of the Bureau of American Ethnology*, III, 205–370. 1884.

Fletcher, A. C., and La Flesche, F. "The Omaha Tribe." *Annual Reports of the Bureau of American Ethnology*, XXVII, 17–654. 1911.

Fortune, R. F. "Omaha Secret Societies." *Columbia University Contributions to Anthropology*, XIV, 1–193. 1932.

Ona

Gusinde, M. *Die Feuerland-Indianer*, Vol. I: "Die Selk'nam." Mödling bei Wien, 1931.

Ontong-Javanese

Hogbin, H. I. "The Social Organization of Ontong Java." *Oceania*, I, 399–425. 1931.

*Orokaiva

Williams, F. E. Orokaiva Society. London, 1930.

*Osset

Kovalesky, M. Coutume contemporaine et loi ancienne: droit coutoumier Ossetien. Paris, 1893.

——. "The Customs of the Ossetes." Journal of the Royal Asiatic Society, n.s., XX, 344–412. 1888.

——. "La famille matriarchale au Caucase." L'Anthropologie, IV, 259–278. 1893.

*Paiute (Surprise Valley group)

Kelly, I. T. "Ethnography of the Surprise Valley Paiute." University of California Publications in American Archaeology and Ethnology, XXXI, 67–210. 1932.

Kroeber, A. L. "California Kinship Systems." University of California Publications in American Archaeology and Ethnology, XII, 358–362. 1917.

Pawnee (Skidi group)

Dorsey, G. A. "Social Organization of the Skidi Pawnee." Proceedings of the International Congress of Americanists, XV, ii, 71–77. 1906.

Grinnell, G. B. "Marriage among the Pawnees." American Anthropologist, IV, 275–281. 1891.

Lesser, A. "Levirate and Fraternal Polyandry among the Pawnees." Man, XXX, 98–101. 1930.

Morgan, L. H. "Systems of Consanguinity and Affinity of the Human Family." Smithsonian Contributions to Knowledge, XVII, 291–382. 1871.

Pedi

Harries, C. L. The Laws and Customs of the Bapedi and Cognate Tribes of the Transvaal. Johannesburg, 1929.

Warmelo, N. J. van. "Kinship Terminology of the South African Bantu." Union of South Africa Department of Native Affairs Ethnological Publications, II, 1–119. 1931.

Pentecost

Rivers, W. H. R. The History of Melanesian Society, I, 189–212. Cambridge, 1914.

Seligman, B. Z. "Asymmetry in Descent, with Special Reference to Pentecost." Journal of the Royal Anthropological Institute, LVIII, 533–558. 1928.

*Pima

Parsons, E. C. "Notes on the Pima, 1926." American Anthropologist, n.s., XXX, 445–464. 1928.

370 SOCIAL STRUCTURE

Russell, F. "The Pima Indians." *Annual Reports of the Bureau of American Ethnology*, XXVI, 3–390. 1908.

*Pukapukans

Beaglehole, E. and P. "Ethnology of Pukapuka." *Bulletin of the Bernice P. Bishop Museum*, CL, 1–419. 1938.

Quinault

Olson, R. L. "The Quinault Indians." *University of Washington Publications in Anthropology*, VI, 1–190. 1936.

Ramkokamekra

Nimuendajú, C. "The Eastern Timbira." *University of California Publications in American Archaeology and Ethnology*, XLI, 1–358. 1946.

Ranon

Deacon, A. B. "The Regulation of Marriage in Ambrym." *Journal of the Royal Anthropological Institute*, LVII, 325–342. 1947.

Radcliffe-Brown, A. R. "The Regulation of Marriage in Ambrym." *Journal of the Royal Anthropological Institute*, LVII, 343–348. 1927.

Seligman, B. Z. "Bilateral Descent and the Formation of Marriage Classes." *Journal of the Royal Anthropological Institute*, LVII, 349–375. 1927.

Reddi

Fürer-Haimendorf, C. von. *The Reddis of the Bison Hills*. London, 1945.

Rengma

Mills, J. P. *The Rengma Nagas*. London, 1937.

Rossel

Armstrong, W. E. *Rossel Island*. Cambridge, 1928.

Ruthenians

Koenig, S. "Marriage and the Family among the Galician Ukrainians." *Studies in the Science of Society*, ed. G. P. Murdock, pp. 299–318. New Haven, 1937.

Sabei

Roscoe, J. *The Bagesu and Other Tribes of the Uganda Protectorate*, pp. 51–90. Cambridge, 1924.

Samoans

Mead, M. "Social Organization of Manua." *Bulletin of the Bernice P. Bishop Museum*, LXXVI, 1–218. 1930.

Santa Cruz

Codrington, R. H. *The Melanesians*. Oxford, 1891.

Rivers, W. H. R. *The History of Melanesian Society*, I, 217–223. Cambridge, 1914.

Sekani
Jenness, D. "The Sekani Indians of British Columbia." *Bulletin of the Canada Department of Mines and Resources* (National Museum of Canada), LXXXIV, 1–82. 1937.
Sema
Hutton, J. H. *The Sema Nagas*. London, 1921.
Semang
Evans, I. H. N. *The Negritos of Malaya*. Cambridge, 1937.
Schebesta, P. *Among the Forest Dwarfs of Malaya*. London, 1927.
Seniang
Deacon, A. B. *Malekula*. London, 1934.
Shasta
Dixon, R. B. "The Shasta." *Bulletin of the American Museum of Natural History*, XVII, 381–498. 1907.
Gifford, E. W. "Californian Kinship Terminologies." *University of California Publications in American Archaeology and Ethnology*, XVIII, 35–37. 1922.
Sherbro
Hall, H. U. *The Sherbro of Sierra Leone*. Philadelphia, 1938.
Thomas, N. W. *Anthropological Report on Sierra Leone*. London, 1916.
Shilluk
Seligman, C. G. *Pagan Tribes of the Nilotic Sudan*, pp. 37–105. London, 1932.
Shona
Bullock, C. *The Mashona*. Cape Town, 1928.
Seed, J. H. "The Kinship System of a Bantu Tribe." *Southern Rhodesia Native Affairs Department Annual*, X, 65–73; XI, 35–56. 1932–33.
Shoshone (Hekandika group)
Hoebel, E. A. "Comanche and H3kandika Shoshone Relationship Systems." *American Anthropologist*, n.s., XLI, 440–457. 1939.
Sinkaietk
Cline, W., Commons, R. S., Mandelbaum, M., Post, R. H., and Walters, L. V. W. "The Sinkaietk or Southern Okanagon of Washington," ed. L. Spier. *General Series in Anthropology*, VI, 1–262. 1938.
Siriono
Holmberg, A. R. *Nomads of the Long Bow*. (In press, Smithsonian Institution.)
Soga
Roscoe, J. *The Bagesu and Other Tribes of the Uganda Protectorate*, pp. 97–136. Cambridge, 1924.

Susu

Thomas, N. W. *Anthropological Report on Sierra Leone*. London, 1916.

Swazi

Marwick, B. A. *The Swazi*. Cambridge, 1940.

Syrian Christians

Anantha Krishna Ayyar, L. K. *Anthropology of the Syrian Christians*. Ernakulam, 1926.

Behanan, K. T. Personal communication, 1939.

Takelma

Sapir, E. "Notes on the Takelma Indians of Southwestern Oregon." *American Anthropologist*, n.s., IX, 250–275. 1907.

Tallensi

Fortes, M. "Kinship, Incest and Exogamy of the Northern Territories of the Gold Coast." *Custom is King*, ed. L. H. D. Buxton, pp. 237–256. London, 1936.

Tanala

Linton, R. "The Tanala." *Field Museum of Natural History Anthropological Series*, XXII, 1–334. 1933.

Tannese (Whitesands group)

Humphreys C. B. *The Southern New Hebrides*. Cambridge, 1926.

Taos

Parsons, E. C. "The Kinship Nomenclature of the Pueblo Indians." *American Anthropologist*, n.s., XXXIV, 377–389. 1932.

——. "Taos Pueblo." *General Series in Anthropology*, II, 1–121. 1936.

Tarahumara

Bennett, W. C., and Zingg, R. M. *The Tarahumara*. Chicago, 1935.

Lumholtz, C. *Unknown Mexico*. 2 vols. New York, 1902.

Tenino

Murdock, G. P. Unpublished field notes.

Tetekantzi

Hogbin, H. I. "The Hill People of North-Eastern Guadalcanal." *Oceania*, VIII, 62–89. 1936.

Teton

Hassrick, R. B. "Teton Dakota Kinship Terminology." *American Anthropologist*, n.s., XLVI, 338–347. 1944.

Tewa

Harrington, J. P. "Tewa Relationship Terms." *American Anthropologist*, n.s., XIV, 472–498. 1912.

Parsons, E. C. "The Social Organization of the Tewa of New Mexico." *Memoirs of the American Anthronological Association*, XXXVI, 1–309. 1929.

———. "Tewa Kin, Clan, and Moiety." *American Anthropologist*, n.s., XXVI, 333–339. 1924.

Thado

Shaw, W. *Notes on the Thadou Kukis*. London (?), 1929.

Thonga

Junod, H. *The Life of a South African Tribe*. Second edit. 2 vols. London, 1927.

Tikopia

Firth, R. *We the Tikopia*. New York, 1936.

Timne

Thomas, N. W. *Anthropological Report on Sierra Leone*, Part I: "Law and Custom of the Timne and Other Tribes." London, 1916.

Tismulun

Deacon, A. B. "Notes on Some Islands of the New Hebrides." *Journal of the Royal Anthropological Institute*, LIX, 480–495. 1929.

Tlingit

Oberg, K. "Crime and Punishment in Tlingit Society." *American Anthropologist*, n.s., XXXVI, 145–156. 1934.

Swanton, J. R. "Social Condition, Beliefs, and Linguistic Relationship of the Tlingit Indians." *Annual Reports of the Bureau of American Ethnology*, XXVI, 391–485. 1908.

Toda

Emeneau, M. B. "Toda Marriage Regulations and Taboos." *American Anthropologist*, n.s., XXXIX, 103–112. 1937.

Rivers, W. H. R. *The Todas*. London, 1906.

Tokelau

Macgregor, G. "Ethnology of Tokelau Islands." *Bulletin of the Bernice P. Bishop Museum*, CXLVI, 1–183. 1937.

Tongans

Collocott, E. E. V. "Marriage in Tonga." *Journal of the Polynesian Society*, XXXII, 221–228. 1923.

Gifford, E. W. "Tongan Society." *Bulletin of the Bernice P. Bishop Museum*, Vol. LXI. 1929.

Rivers, W. H. R. *The History of Melanesian Society*, I, 363–368. Cambridge, 1914.

Trobrianders

Malinowski, B. *Coral Gardens and Their Magic*. 2 vols. New York, 1935.

———. *The Sexual Life of Savages in North Western Melanesia*. 2 vols. New York, 1929.

Trukese

Murdock, G. P., and Goodenough, W. H. "Social Organization

of Truk." *Southwestern Journal of Anthropology*, III, 331–343. 1947.

Tsimshian

Durlach, T. M. "The Relationship Systems of the Tlingit, Haida and Tsimshian." *Publications of the American Ethnological Society*, XI, 1–177. 1928.

Garfield, V. E. "Tsimshian Clan and Society." *University of Washington Publications in Anthropology*, VII, 167–340. 1939.

Tswana

Schapera, I. *A Handbook of Tswana Law and Custom*. London, 1938.

Warmelo, N. J. van. "Kinship Terminology of the South African Bantu." *Union of South Africa Department of Native Affairs Ethnological Publications*, II, 72–87. 1931.

*Tubatulabal

Gifford, E. W. "Tübatulabal and Kawaiisu Kinship Terms." *University of California Publications in American Archaeology and Ethnology*, XII, 219–248. 1917.

Voegelin, E. W. "Tübatulabal Ethnography." *Anthropological Records*, II, i, 1–82. 1938.

*Tupinamba

D'Anchieta, J. "Informaçao dos casamentos dos Indios do Brasil." *Revista Trimensal de Historia e Geographia*, VIII, 254–262. 1846.

D'Evreux, P. *Voyage au Brésil exécuté dans les années 1612 et 1613*, ed. F. Denis. Paris, 1864.

Staden, H. *The True Story of His Captivity*, ed. M. Letts. London, 1928.

Twi

Mead, M. "A Twi Relationship System." *Journal of the Royal Anthropological Institute*, LXVII, 297–304. 1937.

Tzeltal

Holmes, C. G. "Clanes y sistema de parentesco de Cancuc (México). *Acta Americana*, V, 1–17. 1947.

Rojas, A. V. "Kinship and Nagualism in a Tzeltal Community." *American Anthropologist*, n.s., XLIV, 578–587. 1947.

Ulawans

Ivens, W. G. *Melanesians of the South-East Solomon Islands*. London, 1927.

Vai

Ellis, G. W. *Negro Culture in West Africa*. New York, 1914.

Thomas, N. W. *Anthropological Report on Sierra Leone*. London, 1916.

Vanimo
Thomas, K. H. "Notes on the Natives of the Vanimo Coast, New Guinea." *Oceania*, XII, 163–186. 1941.

*Vedda
Seligman, C. G. and B. Z. *The Veddas*. Cambridge, 1911.

*Venda
Stayt, H. A. *The Bavenda*. London, 1931.

Walapai
Kroeber, A. L., ed. "Walapai Ethnography." *Memoirs of the American Anthropological Association*, XLII, 1–293. 1935.

*Wapisiana
Farabee, W. C. "The Central Arawaks." *University of Pennsylvania Museum Anthropological Publications*, IX, 13–131. 1918.

Washo
Barrett, S. A. "The Washo Indians." *Bulletin of the Public Museum of the City of Milwaukee*, II, 1–52. 1917.

Kroeber, A. L. "California Kinship Systems." *University of California Publications in American Archaeology and Ethnology*, II, 362–365. 1917.

Lowie, R. H. "Ethnographic Notes on the Washo." *University of California Publications in American Archaeology and Ethnology*, XXXVI, 301–352. 1939.

Siskin, E. L. Unpublished field notes.

Wichita
Lesser, A. "Levirate and Fraternal Polyandry among the Pawnees." *Man*, XXX, 98–101. 1930.

Spier, L. "Wichita and Caddo Relationship Terms." *American Anthropologist*, n.s., XXVI, 259–263. 1924.

Winnebago
Eggan, F. Unpublished notes on a manuscript by R. Commons on Winnebago kinship.

Radin, P. "The Social Organization of the Winnebago Indians." *Museum Bulletin of the Canada Department of Mines, Geological Survey*, X, 1–40. 1915.

——. "The Winnebago Tribe." *Annual Reports of the Bureau of American Ethnology*, XXXVII, 35–560. 1923.

Wintu
Du Bois, C. "Wintu Ethnography." *University of California Publications in American Archaeology and Ethnology*, XXXVI, 1–148. 1935.

Gifford, E. W. "California Kinship Terminologies." *University of California Publications in American Archaeology and Ethnology*, XVIII, 102–104. 1922.

Wishram

Spier, L., and Sapir, E. "Wishram Ethnography." *University of Washington Publications in Anthropology*, III, 151–300. 1930.

°*Witoto*

Murdock, G. P. "The Witoto Kinship System." *American Anthropologist*, n.s., XXXVIII, 525–527. 1936.

Whiffen, T. *The North-West Amazons*. London, 1915.

Wogeo

Hogbin, H. I. "Marriage in Wogeo, New Guinea." *Oceania*, XV, 324–352. 1945.

——. "Native Culture of Wogeo." *Oceania*, V, 308–337. 1935.

——. "Native Land Tenure in New Guinea." *Oceania*, X, 113–165. 1939.

——. "Puberty to Marriage: a Study of the Sexual Life of the Natives of Wogeo, New Guinea." *Oceania*, XVI, 185–209. 1946.

——. "Social Reaction to Crime: Law and Morals in the Schouten Islands, New Guinea." *Journal of the Royal Anthropological Institute*, LXVIII, 223–262. 1938.

Xosa (Bomvana group)

Cook, P. A. W. *Social Organization and Ceremonial Institutions of the Bomvana*. Cape Town, 1931.

Yaghan

Gusinde, M. *Die Feuerland-Indianer*, Vol. I: "Die Yamana." Mödling bei Wien, 1937.

Yako (Umor group)

Forde, C. D. "Fission and Accretion in the Patrilineal Clans of a Semi-Bantu Community in Southern Nigeria." *Journal of the Royal Anthropological Institute*, LXVIII, 311–338. 1938.

——. "Government in Umor." *Africa*. XII, 129–162. 1939.

——. "Kinship in Umor—Double Unilateral Organization in a Semi-Bantu Society." *American Anthropologist*, n.s., XLI, 523–553. 1939.

——. "Marriage and the Family among the Yakö in South-Eastern Nigeria." *London School of Economics and Political Science Monographs on Social Anthropology*, V, 1–121. 1941.

*Yakut

Jochelson, W. "The Yakut." *Anthropological Papers of the American Museum of Natural History*, XXXIII, 35–225. 1933.

Seroshevskii, V. L. *Iakuty*. St. Petersburg, 1896.

Yankee (Connecticut group)

Murdock, G. P. Unpublished observations in a Connecticut community.

Parsons, T. "The Kinship System of the Contemporary United States." *American Anthropologist*, n.s., XLV, 22–38. 1943.

Yao

Sanderson, M. "Relationships among the Wayao." *Journal of the Royal Anthropological Institute*, L, 369–376. 1920.

Stannus, H. S. "The Wayao of Nyasaland." *Harvard African Studies*, III, 229–272. 1922.

ᵉYaruro

Petrullo, V. "The Yaruros of the Capanaparo River, Venezuela." *Bulletin of the Bureau of American Ethnology*, CXXIII, 161–290. 1938.

Yuchi

Eggan, F. "Historical Changes in the Choctaw Kinship System." *American Anthropologist*, n.s., XXXIX, 34–52. 1937.

Speck, F. G. "Eggan's Yuchi Kinship Interpretations." *American Anthropologist*, n.s., XLI, 171–172. 1939.

——. "Ethnology of the Yuchi Indians." *Anthropological Publications of the University Museum*, University of Pennsylvania, I, 1–154. 1909.

Yuma

Forde, C. D. "Ethnography of the Yuma Indians." *University of California Publications in American Archaeology and Ethnology*, XXVIII, 83–278. 1931.

Gifford, E. W. "Californian Kinship Terminologies." *University of California Publications in American Archaeology and Ethnology*, XVIII, 62–65. 1922.

*Yurok

Gifford, E. W. "Californian Kinship Terminologies." *University of California Publications in American Archaeology and Ethnology*, XVIII, 27–29. 1922.

Kroeber, A. L. "California Kinship Systems." *University of California Publications in American Archaeology and Ethnology*, XII, 339–396. 1917.

Waterman, T. T., and Kroeber, A. L. "Yurok Marriages." *University of California Publications in American Archaeology and Ethnology*, XXXV, 1–14. 1934.

Zulu

Krige, E. J. *The Social System of the Zulus.* London, 1936.

*Zuñi

Kroeber, A. L. "Zuñi Kin and Clan." *Anthropological Papers of the American Museum of Natural History*, XVIII, 39–204. 1917.

Parsons, E. C. "The Kinship Nomenclature of the Pueblo Indians." *American Anthropologist*, n.s., XXXIV, 377–389. 1932.

INDEX

Address, terms of, 97–8, 107–8
Adultery, 261–2, 263, 265, 288, 317
Affinal relatives, 41–2, 95, 102, 310–11
Affinity, criterion of, 103, 122, 123, 133–4
Age. See Appropriate age, Division of labor, Relative age
Aggression, 83, 90, 282, 294
Aginsky, B. W., 91, 123
Alden, A., xii
Alternating generations, 53
Ambil-anak, 21, 45
Ambivalence, 275, 278, 291–2
Amita-clan, 71
Amitalocal residence, **71**
Amitate, 71, 168–9
Analogy, as a social equalizer, 136, 138–9, 169
Anthropology, xiii–xv, 128, 197, 283, 292, 298–9, 300. See also Culture and personality, Evolutionism, Functionalism, Historical anthropology
Appropriate age, gradient of, 318–19
Armstrong, J. M., xi
Assumptions, 131–8
Australian social organization. See Bilinear kin groups
Avoidance relationships, 272–5, 276–7, 279–80
Avuncu-clan, 70–1, 72, 155
Avunculate, 71, 168
Avunculocal extended family, 35
Avunculocal residence, 17, 35, 70–1, 147, 148–9, 202, 207–8, 211, 220, 242, 326–7

Bachofen, J. J., xiv, 58, 185, 264
Bakke, E. W., xiii
Band, 80, 81, 85, 88, 89, 204, 214
Barnett, H. G., xvi, 197

Bastian, A., 185
Behavior, principles of, 131–3. See also Discrimination, Generalization, Psychology
Bennett, W. C., xi
Bernard, L. L., 290
Bestiality, 315
Bifurcate collateral terminology, 141, 142, 145–7, 151, 182, 227, 237, 327
Bifurcate merging terminology, 118, 125, 141, 142–3, 149–51, 154–6, 164–6, 169, 176–7, 181, 182–3, 237, 243–4, 328
Bifurcation, criterion of, 104, 133–4, 152, 154, 163, 169
Bilateral descent, 15, 44, 56–8, 60–1, 157, 188–9, 209, 212, 217–18, 219, 227, 229, 231–2, 233. See also Deme, Kindred
Bilateral extension of incest taboos, 227, 229, 246, 302–3, 305–6, 308, 327. See also Kindred
Bilinear kin groups, 51–6, 170–1, 212
Bilocal extended family, 35, 228
Bilocal residence, 16, 147, 152, 202, 204, 209
Bingham, A. T., 289
Birge, J. S., 313
Boas, F., xiii–xv, 188, 190, 219
Bogardus, E. S., 265
Borrowing. See Diffusion
Bowers, R. V., xiii
Brant, C. S., 276, 281
Bride-price, 19–21, 207
Bride-service, 20–1, 207
Briffault, R., 185, 264
Burrows, M., 21

Capture, marriage by. See Wife-capture
Celibacy. See Status chastity
Ceremonial license, 262, 267

379

Chapple, E. D., 276
Child, I. L., x
Child care, 9–10
Clan, 18, 65–78, 89, 154–6, 203
Clan-barrio, 74
Clan-community, 74, 76, 214–15
Classes. See Marriage classes, Social classes
Classificatory kinship terms, 99–101, 108–9, 125–6, 132–5. See also Extension of kinship terms, Kinship terminology
Clique, 88
Coincidence, as a social equalizer, 136, 172–3
Collaterality, criterion of, 103, 133–4, 148
Community, 79–90, 318. See also Band, Clan-community, Deme, Marriage, Neighborhood, Village
Community studies, 83
Compromise kin groups. See Clan
Concubinage, 26
Conflict, prevention of, 90, 275, 295
Consanguineal kin groups. See Bilinear kin groups, Deme, Kin groups, Kindred, Lineage, Moiety, Phratry, Sib
Consanguineal relatives, 43, 95. See also Kinship, Relationship
Conscience, 273
Consciousness of kind, 83, 319
Consideration in marriage, 19–21. See also Bride-price, Bride-service, Sister exchange
Coon, C. S., 276
Cooper, J. M., 25
Criteria of kinship classification. See Affinity, Bifurcation, Collaterality, Decedence, Generation, Polarity, Relative age, Sex, Speaker's sex
Cross-cousin marriage, 52, 122, 172–4, 272, 283, 287, 321
Cross-cousins, 5. See also Kinship systems
Cross-Cultural Survey, vii–viii, xi
Crow terminology, 102, 123, 125, 166–9, 177, 224, 232, 244, 305, 309
Crow type of social organization, 244–8

Cultural lag, 118, 126, 137–8, 198, 304, 323
Culture, 82–3. See also Evolution
Culture and personality, xii, xv, 314. See also Psychoanalysis, Psychology, Relationships, Socialization
Culture areas, 194–5
Culture change. See Diffusion, Evolution, Transitions in social organization
Cultures, as statistical units, x
Dakota type of social organization, 235–8
Davie, M. R., xiii
Davis, K., xiii, 98, 99
Deacon, A. B., 51–2
Decedence, criterion of, 106
Deme, 62, 68, 75, 78, 89, 158–61
Denotative kinship terms, 99
Derivative kinship terms, 98
Descent, 14–15, 42–5, 59–60, 65–6, 180–1, 186, 194, 201, 327. See also Bilateral descent, Double descent, Kin groups, Matrilineal descent, Patrilineal descent, Unilinear descent
Descriptive kinship terms, 98–9, 100, 118, 237
Differentiation, of kinship terms, 133, 134, 138, 159
Diffusion, 198, 296, 299; of the forms of social organization, 58, 191–2, 196, 199–200, 248
Direction, of exogamous extensions, 302–4, 307–8, 309
Discrimination, 92, 132–3, 299
Distance, of exogamous extensions, 302–4, 308–9
Distant relatives, 95, 320
Division of labor, by age, 8–9; by sex, 7–8, 36, 203, 213–14
Dollard, C., xi
Dollard, J., xvi, xvii, 83, 131, 198
Doob, L. W., 83
Doshay, L. J., 289
Double descent, 15, 45, 50–6, 170, 212, 218–19, 241, 243, 244, 246–8. See also Bilinear kin groups
Dowry, 20

Drift, linguistic, 198-9
Dual organization. See Moiety
Durkheim, E., xiv
Dynastic incest, 13, 266, 320

Economic determinism, 137, 206. See also Property
Education, 10. See also Socialization
Eggan, F., xvi, 91, 248, 272, 275
Elementary kinship terms, 98
Ellis, H., 291
Elopement, 20
Emeneau, M. B., 218
Endo-deme, 64
Endogamy, 18, 62, 262, 265-6, 315
Eskimo terminology, 100, 223, 227, 235, 241, 328
Eskimo type of social organization, 226-8
Esprit de corps, 83, 84
Ethnocentrism, 84, 90, 265, 297, 315
Evans-Pritchard, E. E., 91, 92
Evolution, cultural, xii, 116, 131, 184, 197, 199-200, 219, 221-2, 250, 304. See also Evolutionism, Transitions in social organization
Evolutionism, xiii-xiv, 58, 116, 131, 184-91, 200, 218-19
Exogamy, 18, 47-9, 54, 64, 77-8, 162, 163-6, 211, 226, 262, 267-8, 288, 301, 304-5, 306-7, 309-10, 316. See also Extension of incest taboos, Hypergamy
Exploitation, 84
Extended family, 2, 18, 23-4, 32-7, 39-40, 41, 58-9, 66, 68, 75-6, 78, 89, 153-4. See also Avunculocal extended family, Bilocal extended family, Matrilocal extended family, Patrilocal extended family
Extension of incest taboos, 287-8, 297-8, 301-12, 316-17. See also Bilateral extension, Exogamy, Matrilineal extension, Patrilineal extension
Extension of kinship terms, 132, 138, 159-60. See also Classificatory kinship terms
Extension of sex privileges. See Privileged sex relationships

Factions, 90
Family, 1-2, 23-4, 36, 39-40, 41-2, 65, 79-80, 153-4, 193, 296. See also Extended family, Fraternal joint family, Nuclear family, Polygamous family
Family of orientation, 13, 33, 94
Family of procreation, 13, 33, 94
Family relationships, 3-4, 8-10, 39, 92-4, 159, 273-5, 284-5, 291, 293-4. See also Kinship
Ford, C. S., xi, xvi, 267
Fornication, 262-3, 288
Fortune, R., 45, 290
Fox type of social organization, 232-5
Fraternal joint family, 33
Fraternal polyandry, 26, 29
Frazer, J. G., xiv, 49, 264, 273
Freud, S., xvii, 12, 280, 291, 292, 293, 294. See also Psychoanalysis
Fromm, E., xvii
Functionalism, xii, xv-xvi, 58, 111, 126, 196-7, 249, 352. See also Integration

Galton, F., 51
Generalization, 92, 119, 132, 269, 298. See also Extension of incest taboos, of kinship terms, of sex privileges
Generation, criterion of, 102, 133-4, 166
Generation terminology, 118, 142, 152, 158, 160, 228, 328
Genetics, 95-6, 290
Gens, 67
Gifford, E. W., 91, 117, 123, 126
Gillin, J. P., xvi, 197
Giraud-Teulon, A., 185
Goldenweiser, A. A., 49, 189
Goodenough, W. H., xi, 81
Gorer, G., xi
Government, 84, 85-6, 205-6
Graebner, F., xiv
Grimm's Law, 198
Group marriage, 24-5
Group solidarity, 50, 83, 121, 297, 299
Guinea type of social organization, 235-6
Gumplowicz, L., 185

Half-marriage, 21, 77
Hallowell, A. I., xvi, 197
Harlow, F. C., xi
Harrington, J. P., 351
Hawaiian terminology, 223, 228, 235, 241, 328
Hawaiian type of social organization, 228-31
Hawthorn, H., xi
Henry, J., 24
Heredity. See Genetics
Hilgard, E. R., 132
Hindmarsh, A. E., xi
Historical anthropology, xiii–xv, 58, 111, 113–17, 131, 188–96, 200, 249, 251, 323, 352
Historical reconstruction, 118–19, 251, 258–9, 323–52
Hobhouse, L. T., 206
Hoebel, A. E., 16
Holmberg, A. R., xi, xvi
Homosexuality, 317–18
Horney, K., xvii
Horton, D., xi
Household, 23, 39. See also Family
Hovland, C. I., x, xvi
Howard, G. E., 185
Howard, L., xi
Hull, C. L., xvi, 119, 132, 269, 298, 299
Human relations, science of. See Social science
Huntington, E. V., 127
Hypergamy, 262, 266, 316

Immateriality, as a social equalizer, 136–7
Inbreeding, alleged dangers of, 289–90
Incest, 12–13, 261, 262, 288–9, 318, 319, 320. See also Dynastic incest
Incest taboos, 12–13, 16, 42, 262, 267–8, 273–5, 284–312. See also Exogamy, Extension of incest taboos
Incontinence, 262
Individualism, 203
Infantile sexuality, 291, 293
In-group, 83. See also Ethnocentrism, Group solidarity

Inherent distinctions, 133–5. See also Affinity, Bifurcation, Collaterality, Generation, Polarity, Sex
Inheritance, 37–9, 59, 328
Instinctivism, 135, 290
Integration, cultural, 197, 249, 258. See also Cultural lag, Functionalism, Group solidarity
Invention, independent. See Parallelism
Iroquois terminology, 125, 223, 231, 236, 243
Iroquois type of social organization, 243–5

Jealousy, 294
Joking relationships, 112, 272, 275–7, 278–9, 281–3
Jus primae noctis, 266

Kardiner, A., xvii
Keen, B., xi
Keller, A. G., xii–xiii, 137, 185, 197, 264, 267, 290, 297, 299
Kennedy, R., xi, xiii, 45, 210
Kin-community, 88–9
Kindred, 46, 56–7, 60–2, 157–8, 308, 328
Kin groups, 41–57, 59–64, 65–8, 72, 88, 89, 125, 157, 159, 161–2, 193, 201, 208–9, 304, 307–8, 309–10, 330. See also Bilinear kin groups, Clan, Deme, Descent, Family, Kindred, Lineage, Moiety, Phratry, Sib
Kinsey, A. C., 260, 269, 289
Kinship, 91–2, 96, 319–21. See also Affinal relatives, Consanguineal relatives, Distant relatives, Family relationships, Kinship behavior, Kinship systems, Kinship terminology, Primary relatives, Relationship, Secondary relatives, Tertiary relatives
Kinship behavior, 14, 92, 96–7, 107–12, 272–3, 274–5, 276–7, 280–1. See also Avoidance relationships, Family relationships, Joking relationships, Privileged sex relationships, Respect relationships
Kinship systems, 91–2, 94, 96, 100,

194, 222–4. *See also* Kinship terminology

Kinship terminology, 13–14, 97–126, 130–77, 179–83, 201, 222–4, 311–13, 329. *See also* Address, Classificatory kinship terms, Criteria of kinship classification, Crow terminology, Denotative kinship terms, Derivative kinship terms, Descriptive kinship terms, Differentiation, Elementary kinship terms, Eskimo terminology, Extension of kinship terms, Hawaiian terminology, Iroquois terminology, Kinship systems, Omaha terminology, Reference, Sudanese terminology

Kin-types, 96, 133–4

Kirchhoff, P., 34, 91, 118, 122, 141

Kluckhohn, C., xvi

Kohler, J., 123, 185, 264

Kroeber, A. L., xiv–xvi, 17, 91, 101, 104, 113–14, 119, 124, 125, 133, 135, 164, 189, 194, 197, 218

Land tenure, 81–2. *See also* Property

Lawrence, D. H., x

Lawrence, W. E., xi, xvi, 34, 51–3, 54, 69, 91, 138, 244, 259

Lesser, A., 91, 123, 125, 126, 187

Levirate, 29, 122–3, 124, 174–5, 176–7, 270, 281–2. *See also* Secondary marriages

Levi-Strauss, C., 91

Lewis, O., xi

Leyburn, J. G., xiii

License. *See* Ceremonial license, Joking relationships, Premarital sex freedom

Limited possibilities, principle of, 115–17, 200, 250

Lineage, 46, 74–5, 78, 162–5. *See also* Kin groups

Lineal terminology, 142, 152–3, 156–7, 179, 227, 230, 328

Linguistic change, 198–9. *See also* Evolution

Linguistic determinants of kinship terms, 117–18

Linguistic stocks, 195–6, 346–52

Linton, R., xv, 3, 10, 18, 39–40, 58–60, 73, 79, 81, 90, 197

Lippert, J., xiv, 6, 185, 204, 206

Love, parental, 9

Lowie, R. H., xiv, 3, 38, 46–7, 58, 59, 66, 67, 71, 77, 91, 97, 98, 101, 104, 107, 114, 118, 120, 122, 123, 124, 125, 137, 141, 164, 166, 189, 202, 206, 209, 219, 259, 268, 275, 276, 290, 322

Lubbock, J., xiv, 185, 264

Lundberg, G., xiii

Malinowski, B., xii, xv, 91, 104, 108, 111

Marett, R. R., xiv

Marital sexuality, 4–5, 261–2, 265, 269

Marquis, D. G., xvi, 132

Marriage, 1, 4–8, 22, 171–2, 265, 278. *See also* Consideration, Family, Residence

Marriage, change of community in, 18–21, 213–14

Marriage, forms of, 180–1, 193. *See also* Group marriage, Monogamy, Polyandry, Polygyny

Marriage, regulation of, 52, 161–2, 285–7, 301–2; rules of, 122, 201. *See also* Cross-cousin marriage, Endogamy, Exogamy, Preferential mating, Secondary marriages, Sex regulation, Sexual choice

Marriage classes, 53–5. *See also* Bilinear kin groups

Marx, K., 137

Mason, L., xi

Mathews, R. H., 52

Matri-clan, 70, 76, 154–5, 215, 243

Matri-deme, 64, 76

Matri-family. *See* Matrilocal extended family

Matrilineal descent, 15, 37–8, 44, 58, 70–1, 77, 164, 166, 167, 168, 184–7, 210–11, 241, 243, 244, 246

Matrilineal extension of incest taboos, 243, 303, 304, 306–8, 328–9

Matrilocal extended family, 34–5, 76, 243

Matrilocal residence, 16, 31, 37–8, 70,

147, 148–9, 150, 202, 204–6, 210, 213–14, 217–18
Matri-patrilocal residence, 17, 147, 149–51, 207, 330
May, M. A., xi, xvi, xvii
McLennan, J. F., xiv, 25, 58, 185
Mead, M., 7, 45
Menstrual taboos, 266–7, 288
Merging, 104, 141, 145, 149, 154, 162, 169, 176. See also Extension of kinship terms
Merton, R. K., xiii, 261
Métraux, A., xi
Miller, N. E., xvi, xvii, 83, 131
Miner, H. M., 90
Miscegenation. See Mismating
Mismating, 261, 262, 265–6, 318
Moiety, 47, 90, 124–5, 162–5, 169–70, 215, 241. See also Bilinear kin groups
Monogamy, 24, 26–8, 36, 140, 147, 227, 243
Morgan, L. H., 58, 91, 118, 124, 185
Mother-in-law. See Avoidance relationships
Mowrer, O. H., xvi, xvii, 83
Multiple factors, as social determinants, 113–14, 121–2, 126, 178–9, 200–1
Murdock, B. B., x
Murdock, G. P., viii, xii, 45, 111–12, 124, 165, 168, 186, 213

Nagler, A. M., xi
Names, personal, 97, 132; of kin groups, 49, 77–8
Nankanse type of social organization, 241–2
Neighborhood, 80
Neolocal residence, 16–17, 18, 34, 147, 152–3, 202, 203–4, 208–9
Nuclear family, 1–12, 32, 40, 41, 156–7, 227

Obligatory sex regulations. See Hypergamy, Marital sexuality, Preferential mating, Sexual hospitality
Ogburn, W. F., xiii, 81, 118, 138, 198

Olson, R. L., 191
Omaha terminology, 102, 123, 125, 166–8, 177, 224, 232–3, 239–40, 244, 246, 305, 309
Omaha type of social organization, 239–41
Opler, M. E., xvi, 91, 107, 126, 197
Opler, M. K., 26
Ore, O., x
Ostracism, 82

Parallel cousins, 5, 120, 159–60
Parallelism, 116, 192–6, 200, 259. See also Diffusion
Park, W. Z., xi, 25
Parsons, E. C., 266, 351
Parsons, T., xiii, 15
Participation, 136, 153, 154, 159, 161, 303
Parties, political, 90
Paternity, ignorance of, 15, 58, 185–6, 289
Patri-clan, 69, 77, 154–5, 180, 235, 236. See also Clan-community
Patri-deme, 64, 77, 161
Patri-family. See Patrilocal extended family
Patrilineal descent, 15, 44, 58, 69–70, 71, 77, 144, 145, 147, 165, 167–8, 210, 212–13, 216, 218, 233, 235, 237, 240–1
Patrilineal extension of incest taboos, 235, 236–7, 303, 304–5, 306–8, 329
Patrilocal extended family, 2, 34, 76, 235, 236
Patrilocal residence, 16, 18, 20–1, 69, 144, 145, 149–51, 182, 202, 206–7, 211–13, 216
Paul, B., xi
Pavlov, I. P., xvi
Peace, 85
Pence, H. L., xi
Permissive sex regulations. See Ceremonial license, Premarital sex freedom, Privileged sex relations, Promiscuity, Sex regulation
Perry, W. J., 191
Peter, Prince of Greece, 26
Phratry, 47, 162–5

Polarity, criterion of, 104–5, 133
Political organization. See Government
Polyandrous family, 26
Polyandry, 2, 24, 25–6, 36
Polygamous family, 2, 23–4, 32, 41. See also Polyandrous family, Polygynous family
Polygamy, 2, 24. See also Polyandry, Polygyny
Polygynous family, 28–32
Polygyny, 2, 24, 26–8, 30–2, 36–7, 140, 143–7, 151, 155, 182, 206, 217–18, 228, 235, 236. See also Sororal polygyny
Population of communities, 81
Postulates, 127–8, 130, 138
Postulational method, viii–ix, 127–8, 130, 177
Poznanski, G., xi
Preferential mating, 121, 122–4, 172–4, 222, 262, 268, 269–72. See also Cross-cousin marriage, Levirate, Secondary marriages, Sororate
Premarital sex freedom, 5–6, 262–3, 265
Primary marriages, 28–9, 301
Primary relatives, 94–5, 100, 320
Primogeniture, 204
Privileged sex relationships, 4–6, 25, 112, 262, 263, 268–72, 282, 310–11, 317
Prohibitory sex regulations. See Adultery, Endogamy, Exogamy, Fornication, Incest taboos, Incontinence, Sex regulation, Status chastity
Promiscuity, 262, 264
Property, 37–9, 82, 137, 205, 206–7. See also Inheritance
Propinquity, gradient of, 318
Propositions, 128, 160, 175, 176
Proximity, 136, 147–8, 153, 154
Psychoanalysis, xvii, 12, 275, 278, 292, 297, 300, 319
Psychological determinants of culture, 119–20, 131, 140
Psychology, 128, 283; behavioristic, xvi, 119–20, 131–3, 292, 298–9, 300, 313; social, 83. See also Instinctivism, Psychoanalysis

Radcliffe-Brown, A. R., xv, 14, 51–3, 60, 91, 107, 111, 119, 120–1, 134, 135, 171, 276
Raglan, Lord, 289
Reaction formation, 292
Reciprocity, 104
Reed, S. W., xiii
Reference, terms of, 97–8, 107
Relationships, biological, 95–6. See also Consanguineal relatives, Kinship, Paternity
Relationships, interpersonal, 82, 86, 90, 91, 260. See also Avoidance relationships, Family relationships, Joking relationships, Kinship, Respect relationships
Relative age, criterion of, 105, 110, 130
Relative efficacy, of kinship determinants, 134, 180–3
Repression, 292, 294
Reproduction, 9
Reproductive sex taboos, 262, 266–7
Residence, in marriage, 16–21, 33–6, 37–8, 59, 65–6, 68–9, 137, 147–8, 181–3, 194, 201–18, 329. See also Amitalocal residence, Avunculocal residence, Bilocal residence, Matrilocal residence, Matri-patrilocal residence, Neolocal residence, Patrilocal residence, Unilocal residence
Residential kin groups. See Family
Respect relationships, 272, 274, 276–7, 278
Riemer, S., 289
Ritual continence, 262, 267
Rivers, W. H. R., 15, 46, 91, 119, 120, 121, 122, 123, 124, 135, 169, 172, 185, 219, 264, 273
Roberts, J. M., xi, 296
Ross, J., 84
Rouse, M., xi

Sampling, statistical, viii–ix
Sanctions, social, 288, 295. See also Government, Social control, Socialization
Sapir, E., xv, 91, 120, 121, 122, 124, 176
Schmidt, K., 266

Schmidt, W., xiv, 192
Sears, R. R., xvi, 83
Secondary marriages, 29–30, 123–4, 174, 177, 271. *See also* Levirate, Sororate
Secondary relatives, 94–5, 302, 316, 320
Sections. *See* Bilinear kin groups
Seligman, B. Z., 91, 108, 162, 174, 268, 280, 295, 296, 299
Sex. *See* Division of labor by sex, Sex regulation, Sexual choice
Sex, criterion of, 102–3, 133. *See also* Speaker's sex
Sex behavior, channeling of, 90, 311, 313. *See also* Extension of incest taboos, Sex regulation
Sex regulation, 4, 6, 260–74, 301. *See also* Avoidance relationships, Endogamy, Exogamy, Hypergamy, Incest taboos, Marriage, Obligatory sex regulations, Permissive sex regulations, Preferential mating, Premarital sex freedom, Privileged sex relationships, Prohibitory sex regulations, Ritual continence, Sexual choice
Sexual choice, 314–21
Sexual communism. *See* Promiscuity
Sexual hospitality, 262, 264
Sexual indifference through habituation, 291, 297
Sheffield, F. D., x
Sib, 47, 67, 69, 72–3, 78, 162–5. *See also* Kin groups, Unilinear descent
Siblings, 9. *See also* Avoidance relationships, Family relationships, Respect relationships
Siblings-in-law. *See* Joking relationships, Levirate, Privileged sex relationships, Sororate
Siegel, B., xi
Simmons, L. W., xi, xiii
Sister-exchange, as a mode of marriage, 20–1, 122, 172
Slavery, 87, 207
Snedecor, G. W., 129
Social classes, 44, 87–8, 89, 265–6
Social control, 82, 84, 86, 295

Social differentials, 136–7, 140, 147, 153, 154, 157, 180
Social distance, 265–6, 319. *See also* Ethnocentrism
Social equalizers, 136–7, 138–9, 140, 147, 153, 154, 157, 171–2, 180, 303
Social laws, 120–1, 135, 275, 314. *See also* Social science
Social organization, types of, 187, 222, 224–5, 248–57, 259, 324–6. *See also* Crow type, Dakota type, Diffusion, Eskimo type, Evolution, Fox type, Guinea type, Hawaiian type, Iroquois type, Nankanse type, Omaha type, Sudanese type, Transitions in social organization, Yuman type
Social science, vii–viii, xvi, xvii, 183, 259, 283, 292, 300, 322, 352
Socialization, 10, 273–4, 293–4
Sociological determinants of kinship terms, 115–17, 120–2, 124–5, 135. *See also* Relative efficacy, Social differentials, Social equalizers
Sociology, xi–xiii, 79, 83, 128, 137, 197–8, 283, 292, 295–7, 299, 300, 321, 352
Sororal polygyny, 29, 30–2, 140–1, 143, 181, 243, 329–30
Sororate, 29, 122–4, 175–7, 270, 281–2. *See also* Secondary marriages
Speaker's sex, criterion of, 105–6
Speck, F. G., 81
Spencer, B., 52
Spencer, H., 185
Spier, L., xiv, 76, 78, 91, 105, 223, 224
Spoehr, A., xvi, 91, 199
Status chastity, 261–2, 266
Statistical methods, x–xi, 129
Steward, J. H., xvi, 25, 79, 81, 89
Strong, W. D., 246
Sublimation, 260, 261
Subsections, 54. *See also* Bilinear kin groups
Succession, 39, 328
Sudanese terminology, 224, 232–3, 237–9, 244, 246
Sudanese type of social organization, 237–9
Sumner, W. G., xii, xiv, 83, 84, 138, 197

Survivals, 118–19, 185, 186, 213, 241, 251, 258–9, 323, 330–1. *See also* Cultural lag

Swanton, J. R., 58, 73, 188

Syngenism, 83

Tax, S., 91, 107, 117, 119, 120, 140

Teknonymy, 97

Territory, of the community, 81–2

Tertiary relatives, 95, 320

Theorems, 127–8, 139, 141, 143, 144, 146, 148, 149, 150, 151, 152, 154, 157, 158, 162, 163, 164, 166, 167, 169, 170, 172, 173

Thurnwald, R. C., 91, 205

Time lag, in cultural integration. *See* Cultural lag, Integration

Titiev, M., 78, 202

Tomkins, J. B., 289

Totemism, 49–50

Transitions in social organization, 17, 74–7, 190–1, 202, 203, 208–22, 231, 232–3, 250–7, 324–6, 327. *See also* Evolution

Tylor, E. B., xiv, 17, 97, 120, 124, 185, 201, 299

Uniform descent, rule of, 119, 140

Unilinear descent, 46, 58–60, 68–9, 74–5, 154, 161–2, 163–6, 169, 181, 182–3, 188–90, 191–2, 209–10, 330. *See also* Clan, Lineage, Matrilineal descent, Moiety, Patrilineal descent, Phratry, Sib

Unilocal residence, 74–5, 125, 148, 182–3, 209–10. *See also* Avunculocal residence, Matrilocal residence, Matri-patrilocal residence, Patrilocal residence

Vanderbilt, M. L., xi

Vetter, G. B., 294

Village, 80–1. *See also* Community

Vinogradoff, P., 185, 201

War, 85, 207

Ward, L. F., 264

Warner, W. L., xvi, 13, 88, 91, 98, 99

Watson, J. B., xvi

Wealth distinctions, 87. *See also* Social classes

Webster, H., 265, 267

Westermarck, E., xiv, 185, 201, 291, 300

Weyer, E. M., 80

White, L. A., 91, 116, 125, 168, 187, 240, 246, 309

Whiting, J. W. M., xi, xvi–xvii

Wife-capture, 20

Wittenborn, J. R., x

Wissler, C., xv

Women, status of, 204, 205; uncleanness of, 267

Young, K., 30

Yule, G. U., x, 129

Yuman type of social organization, 231–2

Zinn, E. F., xvii